PRAISE FOR *THE MASTER OF DRUMS*

"Elizabeth J. Rosenthal has done an excellent job in taking the myth and making it into a man. Ringo Starr, Keith Moon, John Bonham, and Animal from the Muppets are all happily in Gene Krupa's debt. I know I am."

—SLIM JIM PHANTOM OF THE STRAY CATS

"Gene Krupa was the swing drummer who rocked. His flair, talent, and obvious joy behind those Slingerland kits became the template for multiple generations of players who followed. He exploded the music with showmanship and dazzling technique, and dragged the drums out of the shadows and right onto the lip of the stage. Elizabeth J. Rosenthal has produced an exhaustively researched account of the man and the times. It's the story of a famous drummer, but will surely appeal to everyone interested in the history of modern American jazz. Splendid!"

—ROB HIRST, DRUMMER/SONGWRITER, MIDNIGHT OIL

"The worldwide jazz community has long needed a thorough, meticulously researched book about the man who made the drums a solo instrument. *This is it!* It's been said that drums wouldn't be played the way they are today had it not been for Gene Krupa. Elizabeth J. Rosenthal's superb work tells us how . . . and why."

—DR. BRUCE KLAUBER, AUTHOR OF *WORLD OF GENE KRUPA* AND *GENE KRUPA: THE PICTORIAL LIFE OF A JAZZ LEGEND*

"Elizabeth J. Rosenthal brings Gene Krupa's story to life with a precision and mastery that match her subject's legendary playing—on-point, sharp, and, above all else, she makes it swing! Presenting Krupa's earliest roots from the streets of Chicago to the heart of jazz's golden age, this wonderful book makes it clear that modern music owes a great debt to Krupa—and music historians owe it to Rosenthal for her incredible modern take on his life and legacy. A must-read for jazz fans and drummers alike."

—C. M. KUSHINS, AUTHOR OF *BEAST: JOHN BONHAM AND THE RISE OF LED ZEPPELIN*

"No one played the drums like Gene Krupa, and no one has captured his life story as poignantly as Elizabeth J. Rosenthal does in *The Master of Drums*."

—JEFF APTER, AUTHOR OF *KEITH URBAN* AND *CARL PERKINS: THE KING OF ROCKABILLY*

"The first superstar percussionist, Gene Krupa was not only a pioneer who led the way in establishing the drums as a solo instrument, but also an innovator whose influence has reached far beyond the jazz world to help shape numerous genres of popular music. So, an in-depth reappraisal of the man and his artistry has been long overdue—and it's finally arrived with this definitive account of the Chicago Flash's personal and professional peaks, valleys, conquests, and controversies. Liz Rosenthal knows how to tell a story, and this one engaged me right from the start. A must-read."

—RICHARD BUSKIN, *NEW YORK TIMES* BESTSELLING AUTHOR

"With deep affection and astoundingly detailed research, Elizabeth J. Rosenthal paints a rich portrait of Gene Krupa as a musician and a man. Krupa's life in jazz gets the chronicle he deserves: powerful yet subtle as a player, restlessly inventive, tirelessly working, a true friend, and always looking to bridge racial divides through interracial music-making. Rosenthal assembles a cloud of witnesses to Krupa's greatness and makes you want to listen again and anew."

—TODD DECKER, AUTHOR OF *MUSIC MAKES ME: FRED ASTAIRE AND JAZZ*

"The gods gave Gene Krupa fame and fortune in the '30s, then terrorized him in the '40s with a selective drug war on pot, as the Bureau of Narcotics became to musicians what HUAC soon would become to liberals. Rosenthal's noirish narrative of stardom and scandal summons a time when the unseen was feared most."

—JOHN MCDONOUGH, SENIOR CONTRIBUTOR, *DOWN BEAT*, AND PROFESSOR OF JAZZ HISTORY, NORTHWESTERN UNIVERSITY

"One historian called drummer Gene Krupa 'the first Elvis in some ways,' by projecting sex and sensuousness. That statement might seem hyperbolic at first, but it is anything but. Indeed, Krupa was a gravitational pull in the development of jazz during the swing era, but as Elizabeth J. Rosenthal convincingly argues, he influenced generations of drummers in modern jazz, popular music, blues, rock, and even punk. For such a ferocious musical hurricane who was successful artistically and commercially, he was generous, modest, and approachable. As a member of the Benny Goodman Quartet in the 1930s, he was in the vanguard of racial integration in jazz. This well-researched and eminently readable biography also serves as a wonderful bookend to Stephanie Stein Crease's 2023 biography of drummer/bandleader Chick Webb."

—TAD HERSHORN, AUTHOR OF *NORMAN GRANZ: THE MAN WHO USED JAZZ FOR JUSTICE*

"Gene Krupa may not have been the greatest jazz drummer of the 20th century, but he was in the minds of millions and was certainly the most famous and influential. He was the consummate artist who first put the drums out front, where they remained for half a century, whenever he was onstage. In *The Master of Drums*, Elizabeth J. Rosenthal not only eloquently details the life lived by this legendary musician, but delves deeper, revealing the simple humanity that guided him beyond 'Sing, Sing, Sing,' 'Drum Boogie,' the movies, and concert halls. It is a wonderfully unique American story."

—HANK O'NEAL, AUTHOR, PHOTOGRAPHER, MUSIC
PRODUCER, AND CHAIRMAN OF THE JAZZ GALLERY

"There was far more to *The Gene Krupa Story* than Hollywood showed us in its flashy but superficial biopic of the legendary drummer. Elizabeth J. Rosenthal has meticulously documented Krupa's fabulous career with the kind of thoroughness—including more than seventy personal interviews—that he's long deserved. Krupa was revered by both the general public—he was a pop idol, the man who put drummers on the map and inspired countless youths to take up drums—and fellow musicians. One of the greatest concerts I've ever attended was the all-star tribute to Krupa after his passing, hosted by Ed Sullivan, in which seemingly every noted drummer—from Zutty Singleton to Louie Bellson and Buddy Rich—came together to honor him. Rosenthal details what Krupa contributed and why he mattered. The casual interactions onstage and on-disc of his featured stars—Anita O'Day, who was white, and Roy Eldridge, who was Black—helped break down racial barriers. And Krupa paid a heavy price for doing the right thing. It's all here."

—CHIP DEFFAA, AUTHOR OF *VOICES OF THE JAZZ AGE*,
JAZZ VETERANS, AND *SWING LEGACY*

THE MASTER
OF DRUMS

Gene Krupa and the
Music He Gave the World

ELIZABETH J. ROSENTHAL

CITADEL PRESS
Kensington Publishing Corp.
kensingtonbooks.com

In loving memory of Morris and Gloria Rosenthal

CITADEL PRESS BOOKS are published by

Kensington Publishing Corp.
900 Third Avenue
New York, NY 10022

All Kensington titles, imprints, and distributed lines are available at special quantity discounts for bulk purchases for sales promotions, premiums, fund-raising, educational, or institutional use. Special book excerpts or customized printings can also be created to fit specific needs. For details, write or phone the office of the Kensington sales manager: Kensington Publishing Corp., 900 Third Avenue, New York, NY 10022, attn Sales Department; phone 1-800-221-2647.

CITADEL PRESS and the Citadel logo are Reg. U.S. Pat. & TM Off.

10 9 8 7 6 5 4 3 2 1

First Citadel hardcover printing: May 2025

Printed in the United States of America

ISBN: 978-0-8065-4326-0

ISBN: 978-0-8065-4328-4 (e-book)

Library of Congress Control Number: 2024950915

The authorized representative in the EU for product safety and compliance
is eucomply OU, Parnu mnt 139b-14, Apt 123
Tallinn, Berlin 11317; hello@eucompliancepartner.com

Contents

Foreword

By Slim Jim Phantom of the Stray Cats

"**W**HO DO YOU THINK YOU are, Gene Krupa?"
This heated question came from my mother and was delivered in full voice. She had to yell to be heard over the great racket I was making.

I've always had a love affair with the drums. I don't even remember how or when it exactly started. The first time I saw a drummer on TV on a rock program or a talk show, I was taken over by the thought that I would someday be a drummer.

This time, I had taken all the pots and pans out of our kitchen and had rearranged them in size order on our living room floor and was banging away on them with wooden spoons. I was trying to play along to a record, cranking the volume on our hi-fi and definitely lost in my own world. I was startled and embarrassed.

"Who's that?" I asked.

"Gene Krupa—he's a famous drummer. Now, I need those pots and pans to cook dinner. Bring them back in here."

So, I sheepishly brought the pots and pans and wooden spoons back into the kitchen. I was ten years old and didn't know that this was to be the first of five thousand times I would break down a drum kit.

I went to the trusted family set of World Book Encyclopedias and looked up Gene Krupa. Amazingly, he was in there. I couldn't believe there was a drummer in the encyclopedia. The presidents and kings and queens whom I had looked up for book reports made sense, but a jazz musician was an unexpected and welcome find. There was a basic biography, but it was enough to get me hooked. I researched further at the public library and saw a picture of Gene, and it sealed the deal for me. With that shock of black hair, tuxedo with a slightly crooked bow tie, and look of wild abandon, he became, in my eyes, the coolest guy in history.

I discovered that one of the records he played on was in our house. My family was not a musical one, but it seemed everyone back then had a few albums and some type of stereo system. We had a Benny Goodman record among ours. I put it on, and there it was: side A, track one, "Sing, Sing, Sing." It was the first recorded drum solo, and that track catapulted Gene to becoming the first famous drummer. I also found a number called "Drumboogie," which further proved that a drummer could be the main cat in a band. Everything about him was perfect. I related to him completely. His setup, his threads, his energy and power—they all pulled me in further to the idea that I, too, could be a famous drummer.

Now, how do you go about that? Gene was a big help with my parents because they had heard of him and he was proof that it was possible. I eventually graduated from pots and pans and wooden spoons to a practice pad, real drumsticks, and a copy of the first twelve rudiments. I took lessons from a local cat named Mousey Alexander who had also played with Benny Goodman. Mousey lived not too far away, and I found him through his ad in the local newspaper. He was a real jazz cat who sported a goatee and beret and really called people "Daddy-O." He was a real-life American treasure living on Long Island, just a few train stops away from where I lived. He knew Gene and had some fantastic first-hand stories about this mythological being.

Around this time I saw The Gene Krupa Story starring Sal Mineo. His life seemed like it was filled with ups and downs, and even in the down times, this was a life that was continually exciting. This seemed to be the true embodiment of the man and further cemented my fascination with Gene.

I went on to become a professional drummer and realized another part of the story written between the lines: the making-a-living-out-of-it part. Gene was always trying to straddle the line of playing what he wanted in an artistic way and the hard, cold truth of being the drummer in a realistic environment where the drummer was not always the boss. I always continue to use Gene Krupa as a template for what a cool and technically proficient drummer should be.

Information is easier to come by now, and I know a few more facts and details about Gene's contributions to the world of drums. His influence on the instrument cannot be overstated. If you're a drummer in any genre, you are influenced by Gene every day. He became the first endorser of a drum company when he endorsed and worked with Slingerland Drum Company. My first real drum kit was, by no coincidence, a Slingerland. He developed the first tom-toms that were tunable on both top and bottom heads. The basic setup we all use was standardized by Gene. He coined the names for the ride, crash, and splash cymbals. What were they called before he reinvented hi-hat cymbals and was one of the first drummers to record with a bass drum?

He was ahead of the curve when he was the drummer for Thelma Todd & Her Playboys. This was the first well-known big band to be led by a swinging gal. Gene must've been less enthusiastic to be one of the first musicians to be busted. Gene went down for a little weed in 1943. The whole thing turned out to be a bad joke, but the damage was done. Gene overcame that one, too.

He was the first internationally famous drummer who brought a big personality and reputation with him wherever he played.

He reinforced the idea to me that you gotta *look* great and *play* great.

Gene Krupa was definitely the first and probably still is the best world ambassador the drums have ever had.

Elizabeth J. Rosenthal has done an excellent job in taking the myth and making it into a man.

Ringo Starr, Keith Moon, John Bonham, and Animal from the Muppets are all happily in Gene Krupa's debt.

I know I am.

"The Breaking Down of Old Traditions"

JAZZ DRUMMER AND KRUPA ADMIRER Cliff Leeman was looking back at the impact that Gene had had on jazz drumming, as well as on the drums themselves, when he said: "His part in the drumming world is a legend in itself—not only as a playing artist, but in the breaking down of old traditions and the drum's importance in bands. The huge growth of drum equipment and sales is an outgrowth.... All of us drummers in the jazz era were affected in some way or another by his predominance. A legend in his time, without peer."[1]

Never before had a jazz drummer *intentionally* brought drums to the forefront, where they would be regarded as a solo instrument, not just a timekeeping mechanism—an instrument like any other in a musical setting with something to say. Gene's influence on his contemporaries, students, fans, and subsequent generations of drummers has been immeasurable.

The use of drums in jazz as a solo instrument was extremely controversial at the outset among many of his fellow jazz musicians, as well as among most jazz critics. It's still controversial. And as much as some would like to think that Gene's success and influence were due largely to his handsome looks, these pages will show this to be

1

a false notion. He was sincerely committed to jazz and drumming—
in fact, to music in general.

A side effect of Gene's percussive assertiveness helped lead to
the development of early rock and roll music, including the ubiqui-
tous Bo Diddley beat, and rock and roll's graduation from small
clubs to stadiums. Drumming superstars emerged, like Krupa acolytes Ringo Starr, Keith Moon, and John Bonham.

A natural athlete, Gene participated in sports ranging from softball to surfing. Onlookers took note of his athletic physicality in
drumming. But in his profound inner life, Gene bore an innate love
for people and led an existence of kindness, generosity, friendship,
surrogate fatherhood, and growing intellectual interests. Yet his
story would have more than its share of soul-searing drama.

CHAPTER 1

"Yearning to Breathe Free"[1]

Eugene Bertram Krupa began life on January 15, 1909, in a South Chicago, Polish-immigrant neighborhood. Eight years had passed since the death of Britain's Queen Victoria, who took with her the royal's namesake era and its eroding mores. People and products of the period, vivid memories, and old habits remained. When Gene was four, hundreds of thousands of Civil War veterans across America observed the fiftieth anniversary of the Battle of Gettysburg.[2] Yet there was a widening gulf between the world that Gene was born into and the one that emerged and developed in his boyhood.

It was a long road to Chicago for Gene Krupa's forebears. Gene's mother, Anna Oslowski, was born on February 12, 1865, in Shamokin, Pennsylvania—"Coal Country," USA. She was the daughter of immigrant parents, Peter and Katharina Oslowski, whose roots were in Kujawsko-Pomorskie, northern Poland.[3] Prussia's control of the region since the late 1700s prompted the first great wave of Polish emigration to other countries, including the United States.[4] Anna's parents were among this first wave. Married in Poland in 1853, they emigrated to the United States that same year and settled in Shamokin.

Gene's father, Bartlomiej ("Bartley") Krupa, was born in Łęki Górne, a village situated in the Austria-governed Galicia region of southeastern Poland, on July 29, 1857.[5] Galicia, impoverished, over-populated, and largely illiterate, gave the United States its second wave of Polish immigrants.[6] Bartley's family emigrated to America as early as the late 1870s. While most of the Krupas settled in Mt. Carmel, Pennsylvania, Bartley appears to have bypassed Mt. Carmel and come to reside at 8845 Commercial Avenue in South Chicago,[7] where Gene Krupa would spend his early years.

Bartley's home sat amid Polish South Chicago's social, religious, economic, and commercial communities. Street cars clanged over cobblestone. Ugly utility poles were everywhere. Steps away were banking, restaurants, theaters, taverns, department stores, and mom-and-pop concerns. Behind the bustle was an earnest, working-class population.[8] Although South Chicago offered employment in various industries—the railroads, river dredging, brewing, shipbuilding, and others[9]—the steelworks dominated.[10] Bartley's place at Eighty-Eighth and Commercial sat within walking distance of several steelworks.[11] He was likely a steelworker from the start—an unskilled, daily laborer—and would be for at least twenty years. In 1882, he became one of the "pioneering" parishioners at the Immaculate Conception Roman Catholic Church on Eighty-Eighth Street.[12] Two years later, Bartley was naturalized as a U.S. citizen.[13]

As a day laborer, which is how Bartley was listed as late as the 1900 U.S. Census,[14] he would have been among those unskilled men who daily gathered at a steelworks' gate, angling for selection by a foreman for the day's work.[15] Laboring in a Chicago steel mill in the late nineteenth century was extremely dangerous, especially for unskilled workers, who, in the case of Poles, usually worked in the "blast furnace department." Regardless of a worker's specific duties, it was all grueling, with extreme heat reaching 150 degrees Fahrenheit. There were no workplace safety standards. Workers were always in danger of being badly burned or injured in explosions. Most fatal accidents at the steelworks occurred in or near the blast furnace. Some of the injuries and conditions men suffered were exhaustion, hearing loss, tuberculosis, and nervous disorders.

Twelve-hour shifts and six-day workweeks were the norm. Bartley was fortunate to have survived it.[16]

Steelworks sights and sounds impacted adjacent neighborhoods, including Bartley's. The blast furnaces colored the sky with magenta sparks; screeches and clanging attacked the ears. Next to the mills, trains transporting steel products made loud heaving noises and burped smoke circles into the air.[17]

Gene Krupa's mother, Anna Oslowski, moved in the 1880s from Shamokin to Chicago, joining sister Rosalia and her husband, who had resettled there.[18] Chicago is likely where Anna met Bartley. They were married on February 2, 1887.[19]

One might expect that, given Gene Krupa's musical ambition, outsized personality, and love of people, his home life would have been joyous and devoid of tragedy. While the household was a loving one and Gene's siblings close-knit, significant loss was a major part of the Krupa family experience.

Three siblings, including a first-born girl in 1888 and a brother and sister in the 1890s, did not survive infancy. Just over two years before Gene's January 15, 1909, birth, in mid-December 1906, his eleven-year-old brother Kazimierz—known as "Walter"—went to the butcher's a block away to buy meat for the Krupa family dinner and never came home.[20] In late January 1907, his body was found, frozen in mud and ice three miles away near the Calumet River in a "desolate swamp."[21] The coroner waited for Walter's remains to thaw before he could perform an autopsy.[22] The boy had been beaten and strangled to death, dragged to the distant swamp, and dumped. The murderer was never found.[23]

Bartley Krupa died of complications from an infected boil in 1916 when Gene was only seven years old.[24] The boy's twenty-nine-year-old eldest brother, Clemens, married and working at a print shop, perished almost exactly two years later of double pneumonia during the 1918 flu epidemic.[25] Anna Krupa was left with one daughter and four sons, including little Gene.

In the last decade of his life, Bartley had managed to escape the steelworks. In his forties, he was likely no longer able to toil at a job so demanding. To support his family, he would have to seek other opportunities. By 1907, he was a laborer for the City of Chicago[26]; by 1914, he had become a "City Water Inspector."[27] He also had a livery business,[28] which probably involved deliveries of wood, coal, and other societal staples. How did he do this? In a word: networking. According to Chicago historian Dominic Pacyga, Bartley had a major resource available to him and other Poles in South Chicago—the neighborhood saloon. There he could learn of jobs, read the newspaper, make phone calls, obtain loans, find a lawyer. He could also make political connections, a necessity if he wanted a job with the city in the days before civil service reforms.[29] These saloons weren't fancy, offering nothing more than spittoons (and no seats).

Children played in the streets, on street corners, and in the alleys between houses. Gene and his brother, Julius, three years his senior, would wait for their father "in the evening several blocks from the house so they could jump in the [livery] wagon and ride to the stable." Bartley spent time at the saloon nightly, to maintain established connections and possibly create new ones. His wife typically sent their children to the saloon, "one by one," to lure him home—even young Gene, who danced "on the bar for the entertainment of his father and his cronies."[30]

Gene and Julius were inseparable. When it was time for Julius to attend school, he refused to go without Gene.[31] School was Immaculate Conception on Eighty-Eighth Street, attached to the church of the same name. Gene had his first music lessons there, from Sister DeSalles.[32] The instrument was probably the saxophone, since he remembered playing the sax before discovering the drums.

At eight, Gene began smoking cigarettes.[33] It became a destructive, lifelong habit. One hopes that the habit wasn't facilitated by his brother, Peter, eight years Gene's senior. According to Gene's nephew, Peter was a sometime self-employed dabbler in rackets, including "an informal black market in cigarettes from Indiana."[34] Gene was wont to hide his pack of cigarettes in a shadowy space between two bricks of the family home. Once, he put his hand between the bricks to retrieve his cigarettes, pulled out the pack, and found horse dung where his smokes should have been. It was his mother, he thought. His suspicion was seemingly confirmed that night at supper. He noticed that she couldn't stop grinning.[35]

Anna Krupa and daughter Elenor converted the front of their home into a millinery enterprise to help support the family after Bartley's death.[36] Yet Anna seems to have mostly retreated from motherly duties after losing her husband and her eldest son, Clemens. She had had her fill of loss by then. Elenor, sixteen years Gene's senior, effectively became the "matriarch" of the family.[37] She assumed the duties of raising Julius and Gene and in 1919 married real estate agent Michael Bloch, which automatically bettered the lives of all of the Krupas—including Gene's brothers, Leo, twenty-three; and Peter, eighteen, who worked, respectively, as an electric company handyman and a repairer for a music store.[38] The Krupas moved to a better neighborhood just outside of South Chicago, at 7841 South Burnham Avenue, the residence of the extended Krupa family for decades to come.

CHAPTER 2

"I Could See This Little Face About Every Night"

CHICAGO WAS A PERILOUS PLACE in Gene's boyhood. He later told stories about a "swirling, turbulent world, violent, chaotic, but shot through with tough humor and energy."[1] Although Chicago was exciting with its "upward rush of buildings and the horizontal rush of traffic,"[2] it was "riven by labor conflict, racial and ethnic divisions, and crime." Rival newspapers hired people to assault or "intimidate" employees—even *readers*!—of rival papers. Over two dozen people were killed in these competitions when Gene was small.[3]

In 1920, Gene was eleven. His brother Pete, a repairer at Brown's Music Shop, got the boy a job as a "gofer." Gene's passion had been playing baseball, and it would continue to be.[4] But on a break one day, he decided that drumming was it. The attraction was a drum set shown in a sales catalog, the cheapest instrument pictured. When he was able to save up some money, and with help from Pete, Gene acquired the object of his interest—a Japanese drum set, which featured a "great, high wide bass drum, with a brass cymbal on it, a wood block and a snare drum."[5] Drumming became his focus.

It's not that Gene hadn't been tugged toward drums before. When he was small, Bartley had taken him to a carnival where

Gene saw his first live band, including a drummer.[6] Before Elenor married in 1919, one of her boyfriends was the pit drummer at the Calumet Theater on South Chicago Avenue.[7]

Gene noisily practiced at every opportunity. His brother-in-law Michael Bloch asked neighbors for old egg cartons, which, for soundproofing purposes, Bloch affixed to the walls of the room at 7841 South Burnham, where Gene pounded.[8]

At first, Gene couldn't find any boys to play music with. It was piano-playing girls or nothing. Boys seemed more interested in "having gang wars."[9] He joined the school band. By twelve, he was performing at days-long Polish weddings.[10] By thirteen, he was a professional drummer, his showbiz bow taken at the Wisconsin Beach summer resort where he had been working as a "soda jerk" opening soda bottles for customers. The drummer for a dance band called the Frivolians got sick. Gene subbed. When the original drummer recovered, he became the soda jerk and Gene had joined his first band.[11]

Because of this and some other engagements, he was eligible to join the American Musicians Union. They didn't necessarily get you *good* jobs, but they were *jobs*.[12] AMU "guys played the rougher, cheaper jobs," said Gene, "but they were more talented in jazz. You'd go down on Saturdays, try to pick up what gigs you could for the week, and chat with the guys."[13]

Gene remembered playing at Wagner's Hall in the tough "Bush" neighborhood of South Chicago. About the Bush, he said, "Boy, if you got caught around there just minding your own business, you were in danger." Inside Wagner's Hall, trouble brewed. Late in the evening, gang "factions" in attendance began brawling. At the end of the night, it was time for the band to pack up. Fortunately, since many of the combatants liked Gene, the sea of fisticuffs would part as he passed through with his drums.[14]

Besides the physical danger, Gene found a widespread bias within bands against the musical importance of the drummer. The drums were regarded solely as a timekeeping mechanism. Said Gene: "[The drummer] used to be the broom of the orchestra. In other words, if a trumpet player hit a clinker, why, the leader would glower at the drummer, and then the drummer would have to take care of the [music] library, his drums, and then sweep the stand after they finished."[15]

Krupa wasn't discouraged. He followed around other young drummers, absorbing pointers and sometimes assisting them in assembling their kits.[16] African-American drummer and New Orleans native "Zutty" Singleton was playing regularly with a band at a tavern in "deep South Chicago." Singleton later recalled seeing "this little face about every night" peering through an open window in the back where Zutty's kit was set up. Later, Zutty learned that the "little face" belonged to a boy named Gene Krupa.[17]

South Chicago was transitioning into an early jazz mecca. Black New Orleans musicians like Zutty Singleton had begun settling there by the early 1920s, joining many of their nonplaying African-American brethren who had been arriving in Chicago from the South for some years already. Among the migrants were future jazz greats like bassist Milt Hinton. Later a contemporary and friend of Gene's, Hinton witnessed a lynching as a small boy in Vicksburg, Mississippi. He and his aunt heard gunfire on their way home. "When we got up there they had a guy stretched up by a wire on a tree, and they had a big drum of gasoline under him and he was burning...And they were still shooting his body." The next day, frightened little Milt had no choice but to walk past the site en route to school. Within a year, the Hintons had moved to Chicago.[18]

Gene played drums in a band at Bowen High, where he would have enrolled in the fall of 1923. Bowen, built in 1910, was a five-story, modernistic South Chicago structure at East Eighty-Ninth Street equipped for 1,400 students. An 1,800-seat auditorium was perfect for rehearsals and performances. Former Mississippian Milt Hinton later recalled a band competition at Northwestern University in which twenty-three Chicago high schools were represented. Besides Hinton in his school band, there was a youngster named Benny Goodman in *his* school band, Nat "King" Cole's brother Eddie in *his*, plus Gene Krupa in Bowen's band. At the end, remembered Hinton, the bands played together under the direction of the aged John Philip Sousa.[19]

Overall, Gene wasn't doing well at Bowen. Captivated by jazz, he was lost to school. Like some of his eventual white friends who had plunged into black music with fervor, Gene became a "headache" to his family.[20]

Because of his nighttime gigs, if Gene showed at school at all, he fell asleep in class.[21] When awake, he was sent to the principal's office on multiple occasions for drumming on his desk.[22] Sometimes his jazz gigs yielded no earnings. "Chicago was a veritable gangland," Gene said later. "If a boss decided not to pay us, why, he just didn't pay us, and we didn't dare go to the union for fear of getting our heads beat in."[23]

Baby brother Gene not getting paid didn't agree with his family, nor did his career choice. "Most of my family hated jazz,"[24] said Gene. "They looked down on musicians and thought I was a bum."[25] Gene's brothers and sister staged what might now be called a career "intervention." He needed to make a choice—attend school, which seemed a lost cause, or make a real living working. Gene's mother, who affectionately called him "Yudge"[26] (short for "Eugene"), proposed a compromise: devote a year to studying for the priesthood. If, after the year, he still wanted to be a drummer, he would have her blessing.[27]

One more heartache intervened. Peter Krupa's early adulthood was marked by tragedy. He and his young wife, Polish-born Marjanna (Mary), had moved to the unofficial pulmonary tuberculosis capital of America, Phoenix, Arizona, around July 1923, where she received treatment for several months before dying on December 5, 1923. Peter returned to Chicago with Mary's remains. She was buried with the other Krupas six days later.[28]

In the fall of 1924, Gene left for the high school division of St. Joseph's College in Rensselaer, Indiana. Governed by the Catholic Society of the Precious Blood, the campus was spread over 900 acres, which included farmland, parks, orchards, gardens, and lawns. Students spent much of their time in the Main Building, a four-story Gothic structure housing the dormitory, personal lockers, classrooms, study hall, and bookstore. The Alumni Hall–Gymnasium offered a venue for sporting events, a theater, and the

Department of Music. The chapel housed the dining rooms. Outdoors, students found baseball diamonds, tennis courts, a swimming pool, and gymnastics equipment. The campus was self-sufficient, producing most of its food and generating its own energy via a brand-new coal-powered plant.[29]

St. Joseph's students lived a strict, regimented life. Cursing, smoking, cliquishness, vengeance, and lateness were all prohibited. Family visitation was limited. Students could not leave the campus without special permission. Incoming and outgoing mail were subject to inspection. Participation in scheduled activities was required. The student calendar was packed. The day began at 5:30 A.M. and ended at 8:45 P.M. Recesses were brief. Had Gene followed through with studies for the priesthood, he would have spent six years in a "classical course of study."[30]

For entertainment—besides sporting, theatrical, oratorical, choir, band, and orchestral events—students saw mostly year-old silent movies, such as *The Hunchback of Notre Dame* starring Lon Chaney and *The Thief of Bagdad* with Douglas Fairbanks.[31]

Gene failed algebra[32] and was ejected from the orchestra for "trying to make the *Blue Danube* flow faster."[33] His positivity and natural friendliness overcame what might otherwise have been a difficult experience at St. Joseph's. Years later, he would look back fondly at the one year he spent there, from the fall of 1924 through the spring of 1925.[34] Father Ildefonse Rapp, a "legit" trumpet player and the school band director, was a valuable mentor. According to Gene, Rapp was "marvelously relaxed and cool about all music including jazz," declaring that there are really only two kinds of music—"good" and "bad."[35] Gene kept in touch with fellow students for years, as well as one of the priests, and joined the alumni association, whose meetings he attended even as a famed bandleader. He welcomed any campus news.[36]

Returning to Chicago in the summer of 1925, it was all drums now for Gene. He was able to join the American Federation of Musicians by demonstrating his press roll and paying $50. Through the AFM he found better-paying jobs.

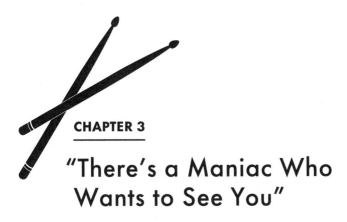

CHAPTER 3

"There's a Maniac Who Wants to See You"

Elenor took her baby brother to see Roy C. Knapp, a heavyset, thirty-four-year-old percussionist then playing at Chicago's Capitol Theatre on Halsted and West Seventy-Ninth who also taught drums. During a break between shows, Knapp was relaxing in the musicians' room when he heard the doorman calling down to him. "Hey! There's a maniac up here who wants to see you."

Knapp went upstairs to meet the "maniac" and found a hyperactive, sixteen-year-old boy and his older sister. Wielding tympani mallets, Gene drummed on any surface within reach—chairs, the wall, and his abdomen. In those days, said Knapp, Gene was "a little bit wild." (How did he get through a whole year at St. Joseph's without major incident?)

Gene thought he already knew everything about drumming and wanted to learn tympani. Knapp persuaded him to further study drums before pursuing anything else. Years later, Knapp said that Gene was "the greatest talent I ever had to work with."[1]

There was still the earning a living thing to worry about. To do this, Gene took jobs with whatever dance bands were hiring, "Mickey Mouse" bands, as white jazzers called them, or white dance orchestras that permitted, at most, a few bars of jazz to creep in. Such bands kept down the number of jazz or "hot" players for fear of "hot pollution" spoiling the music for the white clientele. Fairly non-jazzy jobs with Joe Kayser, the Benson Orchestra, the Hoosier Bell Hops, and others allowed Gene to contribute to his family's coffers, have money of his own, and make connections.[2]

Jazz was mainly played by black musicians, who, unlike whites, made a living at it. The white audience for jazz was negligible. Racially integrated ensembles performing onstage were forbidden by the unwritten rules of an American racial caste system. With rare exception, these prohibitions also applied to the recording studio. White jazz players settled for watching black musicians play at black South Chicago clubs and hopefully chatting with them and receiving between-set pointers.

Gene was far from the only white youngster who yearned to play jazz. Networking had helped his father Bartley find better employment. Networking did that for Gene, too. Whether he noticed the white Chicagoans first or they him is uncertain. Their sometime guru, frequent companion, and marijuana supplier Mezz Mezzrow once wrote about them: "As they roamed around town in their knee-britches, sniffing for signs of life like a scavenger snagging cigarette butts, they bumped into other defiant, music-starved kids like themselves. . . ."[3]

A drummer whom Gene admired, Al Silverman, referred him to Dave Tough.[4] To hear Dave, Gene caught two shows a night, with three more on Saturday, at the Commercial Theater on South Commercial Avenue. In this movie house pit band were some of the young white jazzers Mezzrow wrote of—besides Dave, Bud Freeman on tenor sax, and Eddie Condon on banjo. These youths somehow avoided disapprobation playing "hot" music to a somber newsreel depicting a wreath-laying ceremony at the Tomb of the Unknown Soldier.[5]

Krupa, their number one fan, was startled when Tough approached and complimented him on his own playing. Gene said likewise.[6] He also admired the drumming of George Wettling, another "Chicagoan." The Chicagoans were a loose assemblage of white jazz-loving youths who were still finding each other.

Dave invited Gene to hear black drummers he and Wettling had been enjoying at various African-American clubs. Number one on the agenda was New Orleans native "Baby" Dodds, then playing with his clarinetist brother Johnny at Kelly's Stables on the Near North Side.[7] For some years Dodds was the drummer Gene would point to as his number one influence.

Baby has been described as a holdover from the ragtime school of drumming. He relied on military-style rudiments, adding improvisation and "hokum," the latter imported from vaudeville, in which Dodds and other African-American jazz drummers had accumulated substantial experience. Another ragtime practice was the rim shot, executed with the butt of a drumstick.[8]

Dodds was fairly modest when it came to his drum accomplishments and philosophy. It was his job to keep time. He adjusted his playing depending on who was soloing. Negativity will get you nowhere. He used rim shots because they sounded so much prettier than the noise made by hitting a woodblock. He picked up the idea for the "shimmy beat" from a soldier during World War One who shook "all over" to Baby's press roll.[9]

To Gene, Dodds was much more than that. "I kept going back to hear Baby. . . . Not only was he a great showman, the man played with fantastic drive. Those press rolls! He could really get things moving."[10] Gene considered Dodds "THE rim shot man,"[11] and adopted Baby's drum tuning and "concept of tone."[12] He was so enthralled with Dodds that he intentionally copied him.[13]

There was Zutty Singleton, on whom Gene had impressed a memory of his face outside a club window sometime back. Zutty, playing with clarinetist Jimmie Noone, inspired Gene with his imagination and timekeeping ability—"watch that tempo [and] give notes their full value . . ."[14] At least as important were the basics Gene learned from Zutty and another drummer, "Tubby" Hall, who performed with Carroll Dickerson's band (featuring Louis Armstrong and Earl Hines!). Some of the basics included the purpose of cymbals; how to accompany horns; "what to do at the turn-arounds" or transitions from the end of a song back to the beginning; and how to choose between drumsticks versus wire brushes and rims versus woodblocks.[15]

A basic principle that Gene gleaned from Tubby Hall was that "sound effects" are fine, but it's the drums on which the drummer must focus.[16] Then there was Cuba Austin with McKinney's Cotton Pickers, whom Gene saw as essential to the ensemble's success when it came to "commercialism and musicianship."[17]

For an ambitious young jazzer in the 1920s, Chicago was the place to be. Gene lived and played in what amounted to a free music school. As jazz writer Otis Ferguson once wrote: "Chicago in the early and middle twenties was the place for a man to learn music, because to anybody who had an ear for it, the city streets were alive with it.... You would do very well to be a kid with an instrument, learning it and trotting around to hear other people playing it, in the streets of Chicago during the years between 1922 and 1928."[18]

The Krupa-Tough association didn't end with clubbing. Dave told Gene he was leaving a Chicagoan aggregation, the Blue Friars, for the Wolverines, a group that often featured young cornetist "Bix" Beiderbecke. Could Gene take Dave's place in the Blue Friars? *Why, yes!*[19] This served as Gene's initiation, however informal, into the world of the Chicagoan. It was the most important connection he had made in music thus far.

"I didn't know that they were picking me not because of any talent but because they knew I was not on a commercial kick and was young, and they could mold me," said Gene. He soon learned that the Blue Friars were "so noncommercial that they would pass up some dates and play others for no dough at all!"[20]

Remembered pianist Art Hodes, "To play jazz, to worship at the shrine[,] you must have been willing to make sacrifices, such as not eating regularly or too well, [or] not worrying about clothes (I still remember meeting Krupa for the first time with his long pants a bit too short)."[21]

But Gene needed to make money. Thus, he continued playing with bands he didn't like to earn a living. A consolation might be the presence of one or two Chicagoans in the lineup, such as clarinetist Frank Teschemacher, whom everyone called "Tesch." "We kept our connections with the righteous music," Gene declared.[22]

The clarinet- and sax-playing Mezz Mezzrow—Milton Mesirow to his parents—helped maintain this connection. Mezzrow, in his midtwenties, was white, Jewish, and middle-class, but so drawn to African-American culture and music that he identified as black and prided himself on speaking in a kind of black dialect.

To Mezzrow's surprise, an acquaintance asked him to assemble a real jazz band for an upscale place called The Rendezvous at Clark Street and Diversey Avenue. He gathered Tesch, Floyd O'Brien, Joe Sullivan, Eddie Condon, and others, but couldn't find a suitable drummer. Then he heard about Gene, whom, he was told, "had a gang of talent and it could be brought out easy." Gene, described by Mezzrow as a "neat, well-dressed, very good-looking youngster," was thrilled to have the opportunity to work with so many of the musicians he looked up to.[23] Mezzrow made the rounds of black establishments with his new charge and educated Gene about African-Americans.

According to Mezz, they'd talk for hours. "The subject that we kept coming back to, over and over, was this," he said. "How in hell could people be so stupid that they overlooked the wonderful things the Negro had to offer us? The same thing was happening inside Gene's head that happened inside mine years before.... You start out with just a technical interest in their music-making, but soon as you begin analyzing it you wind up trying to dig how they live and think and feel ... Gene's head kept nodding like he had the palsy—he agreed with everything I said about the music and the Negroes who made it up.... 'Don't think I'll ever forget what you taught me about the colored race, Milton,' he said later...."[24]

Perhaps less intense were the get-togethers at friends' houses. Some were Chicagoans, others passed in and out of the alliance. They talked, listened to records, and practiced for hours.[25] Attendees might include Gene, Bud Freeman, pianists Joe Sullivan and Art Hodes, and a much-admired, somewhat older trumpeter named

"Wingy" Manone, so called because he lacked a right arm.[26] (Manone did have a prosthetic limb.)

Paying jazz work surfaced. Wingy's band—including Art Hodes, Bud Freeman, trombonist Floyd O'Brien, and Gene—secured two well-paying engagements at the Aragon Ballroom in Uptown Chicago, playing opposite a "Mickey Mouse" orchestra. According to Hodes, the youngsters impressed people the first night but squandered their good will by not showing up the next. The boys had stayed up till sunrise talking and playing records. "The next afternoon we were a mess," said Hodes. "Nobody felt like playing."[27] Or they didn't feel like playing opposite a Mickey Mouse band at the Aragon. According to a different account, the second night found the group in a "second-rate ballroom."[28]

Another way the Chicagoans maintained their jazz connection was by dashing over to the Three Deuces after finishing their respective "Mickey Mouse" jobs for the night. The Three Deuces was the unofficial name of the basement below a speakeasy at 222 North State Street. There, the Chicagoans jammed till dawn. Besides Eddie Condon, Dave Tough, Floyd O'Brien, George Wettling, Tesch, Bud Freeman, and Joe Sullivan, there were the McPartland brothers, Jimmy and Dick, who played trumpet and guitar, respectively. "What a gang!" Gene said.[29]

The speakeasy sat across from the Chicago Theater, where successful bands like Paul Whiteman's came through. Bix Beiderbecke, then a Whiteman sideman, had practically the entire Whiteman band in tow, including a young trombonist named Tommy Dorsey. The jam session that resulted was so memorable that musicians who weren't there knew all the details.[30]

Beiderbecke also unveiled some of his piano compositions—"In a Mist," for one—to the awe-stricken Chicagoans. Drinkers from upstairs climbed downstairs to see what the hubbub was about.[31]

A clarinet-playing teenager named Benny Goodman often dropped by to sit in or watch. He was a member of Ben Pollack's band, regarded as way too commercial by many of the Chicagoans.[32] Goodman remembered the Three Deuces as awash with

THE MASTER OF DRUMS 19

gin. "Sometimes when you'd go in there sober, it almost knocked you off your feet," said Benny.

The "boys that hung out there," Goodman said, "were terrifically talented guys, but most of them didn't read, and we thought their playing was rough, although we liked to jam with them."[33] Gene Krupa, he thought, "was beginning to play good drums at that time."[34] From the beginning, Gene held Benny's musicianship in high esteem. Years later, he said, "I made it my ambition to do with drums what Benny does with a clarinet."[35]

Another young clarinetist, Artie Shaw, spent eight weeks in Chicago with Irving Aaronson's orchestra. Shaw noticed the Chicagoans "hanging around in these smoke-filled, dimly-lighted joints..." Gene Krupa stood out—a "black-haired, snap-eyed kid."[36]

The Chicagoans played Chicago-style jazz. For 1930s French jazz commentator Hugues Panassié, the Chicagoans were the "first of their race to play in Negro style and extend it."[37] Jazz historian William Howland Kenney later saw Chicago style as a "wilder, freer music... [arising] not from race but from the excitement of urban life."[38] Jazz writer Richard M. Sudhalter would praise the Chicagoans: "The combination of edginess and relaxation, aggressiveness and lyricism, a certain devil-take-the-hindmost ardor and cockiness, is brand-new and very attractive...."[39] Devices used in Chicago style demonstrate its aggressive approach: an "explosion" or two-bar "flare" at a chorus's end, "stop-and-go devices," and "double endings."[40] Regardless of how one heard it, Chicago style was a hugely influential development in jazz.

Toward the end of 1927, when Gene was eighteen, the Chicagoans stumbled upon a rare commodity—good luck. It came with "Red" McKenzie, who walked into the Three Deuces one night. McKenzie, the leader and vocalist of the Mound City Blue Blowers, specialized in "blue blowing" (blowing into a comb wrapped inside thin paper that made a kazoo-like sound). McKenzie was also a recording studio veteran with connections.[41]

Eddie Condon, in an early demonstration of his storied aptitude for drawing attention to his associates and to jazz, convinced

McKenzie to take a chance on some of his friends. McKenzie agreed, lining up two recording dates for them, on December 8 and 16, 1927, at Chicago's Okeh Records. They were to be billed as McKenzie and Condon's Chicagoans. The personnel were Jimmy McPartland on cornet, Bud Freeman on sax, Tesch on clarinet, Joe Sullivan on piano, Jim Lanigan on upright bass, Eddie Condon on banjo, and Gene Krupa on drums. Mezzrow was present on both dates.[42]

The first date began badly. Producer Tommy Rockwell objected to Gene using a bass drum because he feared the drum's "boom," as Mezzrow later put it, would "knock the needle right out of the groove..." McKenzie took responsibility for problems that might arise.[43] For good measure everyone placed their coats over the drum.[44] Mezz supplied the marijuana.[45]

The four sides were "Sugar," "China Boy," "Nobody's Sweetheart," and "Liza." Gene's bass drum isn't audible, but his lead-ins, transitions, backbeat, rim shots, and cymbal crashes are placed where they should be and are well represented. It's often thought his use of the bass drum was the first on a jazz record. This isn't true (Gene debunked this idea himself),[46] although it may have been the first on the Okeh record label.

When the two 78s were released, according to jazz historian Richard Hadlock, they "made a favorable impression on Eastern jazzmen...The biggest surprise was Krupa, an unknown, whose well-recorded drum work on these sessions rocked the New York jazz cliques...Krupa's intense study of Dodds, Singleton, and Tough, along with his vast natural energy and superb sense of time, placed him...in the front rank of jazz drummers."[47]

"Even in the late 20s stuff, you can hear where he's [Gene's] going," said English traditional jazz drummer Nick Ball. "The birth of what he was gonna do later. The mainstream of jazz ended up going that way...The styles that the other guys were doing just didn't last, or ended up not being the kind of prevailing culture in the end."[48]

"My idols, jazz-wise, were Davy Tough, George Wettling, Baby Dodds, Zutty Singleton," Gene said years later, "and I think maybe

I was a little better equipped technically than these guys[.] I would take one thing that they did and try to build around it."[49]

One of the Chicagoans' alternative sobriquets (such as the "Austin High Gang," for the high school that several boys had attended) was the "Condon Mob," named for Eddie Condon. He hailed from the Chicago suburbs and became the face of the group. Condon and Krupa were especially close.

Gene and Eddie would move in different directions musically. Eddie took what might be called a jazz vow of poverty; he refused to play or promote anything he perceived as commercial or not pure jazz. For him, pure jazz was improvised in a small ensemble with no arrangements or rehearsals.

Conversely, Gene bridged the divide between pure jazz and commercialism, giving audiences what they wanted while remaining dedicated to jazz, as jazz historian Gunther Schuller noted.[50] But nothing could keep Gene and Eddie from remaining the closest of lifelong friends.

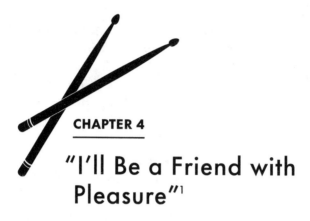

CHAPTER 4

"I'll Be a Friend with Pleasure"[1]

EARLY IN **1928,** GENE HAD an extended stint playing real jazz with "Milton Mezzrow and His Purple Grackle Orchestra" at a purple-colored Elgin, Illinois club called the Purple Grackle. Outside Mezz and the Chicagoans, Gene was also a sideman with Thelma Terry and Her Play Boys, for whom he gigged in Chicago ballrooms and recorded. Terry, with her petite facial features and wavy, bobbed hair in the fashion of the day, was one of the first female leaders of an all-male band. She offered a hybrid of dance and jazz music. The jazz pedigree of some of her "Play Boys" was real. Besides Gene were, among others, Floyd O'Brien, clarinetist Bud Jacobson, and alto saxist Mike Platt, the latter of whom would become one of Gene's lifelong friends. (The band's volunteer roadie, Frank Verniere, another Krupa friend, would play a management role in the drummer's early band-leading years.) Bud Freeman and guitarist Herman Foster, another Chicagoan, often sat in.

The Golden Pumpkin, a large Chinese restaurant on Madison Street in western Chicago, served as a reliable live venue for Terry and her boys. The nightly entertainment involved "an elaborate floor show, followed by hours of dancing." But also, to the consternation of the restaurant's owner, raucous jazz emanated from a "band within the band." "China Boy" especially got a workout, with endless choruses. Terry threatened to take her band elsewhere if the owner continued to object to their anarchic ways.[2]

They recorded four sides on March 29, 1928. Notable were "Mama's Gone, Goodbye," with Gene and Thelma trading licks, and two tracks that revealed Krupa's growing percussive versatility. He is heard with castanets on "Lady of Havana" and, apparently, chimes (or vibraphone) on "Starlight and Tulips."

Gene recorded six sides with some Chicagoans in early and late April 1928 under the names Chicago Rhythm Kings, Jungle Kings, Frank Teschemacher's Chicagoans, and Louisiana Rhythm Kings. Here, the Chicagoans, buttressed by excellent studio conditions, really coalesced, with everyone—Mezzrow, Tesch, Sullivan, Condon, Gene, and others—settling into a perfectly blended sound. Krupa's frequent bass drum fills, suggestive of the future Bo Diddley beat, and some clever stick-on-stick accompaniment, continued him on his percussive path.

Later that spring, a number of Chicagoans—Gene, Eddie Condon, Bud Freeman, Jimmy McPartland, Red McKenzie, Tesch, and Joe Sullivan—traveled to New York City for a big opportunity, or so they thought. Instead, they found an unwelcoming metropolis and no money for food.

Maybe the way they left Chicago portended ill. Mezzrow hadn't been invited. "They didn't want a monomaniac tagging along on this trip," said Mezz. Because of his strict views on what constituted real jazz, he admitted that he "wouldn't be very good company in New York."[3] He was upset, nevertheless. On the night before the Chicagoans were to catch their train, they and Mezz said their goodbyes on East Thirty-Fifth Street at the Nest, where Jimmie Noone and his band were playing. Eventually, every Chicagoan but Mezz and Gene had gone. Gene didn't want to abandon his mentor on what Mezz later called his "sorrowful night,"[4] and stayed with him until dawn.

Manhattan in those days was, as it is now, congested and overwhelming in its high-rise habitat. It could be said that, in the 1920s, New York was America's art deco capital, its eye-catching designs visible all over the new construction going up in this economic boom time. As the Chicagoans arrived in New York, ground was being broken on Lexington Avenue for what would become the Chrysler Building, one of the most iconic paeans to art deco and the tallest skyscraper in the world until completion of the Empire State Building in 1931.[5]

Besides brand-new apartment towers, one of the most imposing, just-completed structures was the Paramount Building on Broadway, boasting copious office space for the film company and a 3,600-seat movie "palace." It was a startling edifice. Ornate and geometric, the Paramount's tapered levels, flaunting floodlights, and four giant clocks represented the height of concrete beauty.[6] Come the 1930s, the Paramount's "palace" would make swing music history, and Gene would be at the center of it.

What the Chicagoans had hung their hopes on was an offer from Bee Palmer, a Chicago native and successful vaudeville singer, to play behind her at a new club opening in New York called the Chateau Madrid. She had discovered the Chicagoans at the Three Deuces and "helped us raise the train fare," as Gene recalled.[7] Unfortunately, the likelihood of the plan going forward was somewhat contingent on Palmer reconciling with her manager-husband, Al Siegel.[8] Worse, Lou Schwartz, the club's owner, disagreed with Palmer's taste in bands. The boys weren't apprised of this fact until after they had checked in at the Hotel Cumberland at Fifty-Fourth Street and Broadway, right across from the new club.[9]

The Cumberland's quarters were cramped. The boys were "stacked up," said Gene, in one small room. "One guy registered" and the others snuck in. Ultimately, a violin group opened at the Chateau Madrid in their stead. "Man," said Gene, "the panic was on."[10]

Palmer felt responsible for the boys' turn of fortune, as she should have. She sent them to agents and dragged them to parties. Nothing helped. The Chicagoans took to playing in their room, which had positive and negative consequences. "We played every night until the complaints began," said Condon. They did draw many admirers: Don Voorhees, a broadcast radio bandleader; cornetist-bandleader "Red" Nichols, one of the few whites making a go of playing jazz in New York; Nichols's drummer Vic Berton. "When we saw Vic Berton listening with admiration to Krupa," said Eddie Condon, "our faith in our future rose."[11]

One of New York's popular society bandleaders, Pancho, liked their style and offered them a job in Newport, Rhode Island, as an "alternate band" and "interesting novelty" at the societal debut of a foreign princess. The Chicagoans were such a "novelty" that the guests just stared and drank; one was overheard anthropologically likening the music to a "demonstration of the freed libido."[12]

Gene, Eddie, and the others did snag a couple of recording sessions in July 1928. The first was their inaugural outing with Red Nichols, though under trombonist Miff Mole's name, with "Windy City Stomp" and "Shim-Me-Sha-Wabble." Especially on the latter, Gene's bass drum and tom-tom accents already suggested his famous 1930s playing with Benny Goodman. But, overall, there was no work, no money, and no food for the hopefuls.

Said historian Robert W. Snyder, "Even in good times, a certain amount of want and insecurity were part of working in New York."[13] This the Chicagoans felt all too keenly.

"There were some guys there who wouldn't let us go hungry— not TOO hungry," said Gene, referring to Bix and Tommy and Jimmy Dorsey.[14] Mostly, it was olives and cherries from cocktails, the latter of which, though still illegal under Prohibition, were a lot easier to get than meals, plus canned tomatoes bought with pennies they scrounged.[15]

Occasional jobs weakly trickled in and presented a sartorial challenge for Krupa and Condon, who, between the two of them, owned just one brown pair of shoes and one black. Only black was acceptable on the bandstand, so if they had a job together, "Krupa would hide his one brown shoe behind the bass drum and Condon his brown one behind the guitar player's step."[16] They were lucky to share a shoe size.

To the rescue came Tommy Rockwell, who had produced McKenzie and Condon's Chicagoans just seven months earlier. He was in New York and Eddie persuaded him to give Gene, Sullivan, Tesch, and himself a record date, which coincided nicely with the boys' impending eviction from their hotel room due to unpaid bills.[17] Perhaps Gene was overcompensating for his hunger with overly loud punctuations on "Oh! Baby" during Joe Sullivan's two-fisted piano solo. Both that side and "Indiana" featured Gene's rocking backbeat, plus a couple of rare Condon vocals.

Just as Mezzrow decided to join the Chicagoans in New York, Gene received a telegram from his family: his mother had had a stroke. While her youngest son was on a train going home, she died at sixty-three. As much as he loved the compatriots he'd left behind, Gene didn't return to the metropolis until early 1929. It's not like there was much work in New York; in Chicago, his family provided a roof to live under and food to eat, and there were jobs.

While home, Gene participated in two recording sessions. The first was with a Wingy Manone aggregation in September that also included Chicagoan chum Bud Freeman, who had likewise returned from New York. The sides were the Manone-penned "Downright Disgusted" and "Fare Thee Well," two excellent blues numbers. Aside from Gene's pounding tom-toms, also evident in his drumming were more suggestions of what would become known as the Bo Diddley beat, something he would continue to develop in the next couple of decades.

Gene also joined Bud Freeman for another Chicago session in December. Other Chicagoans on hand were Floyd O'Brien, Bud Jacobson, Dave North, and Herman Foster. The side "Craze-O-Logy" is noteworthy for early examples of Gene's interesting stick-on-stick work and rim shots.

Finally back in New York, Gene joined his friends at the Riverside Towers on Riverside Drive at Seventy-Ninth Street. Condon called it the "Riverside Showers" because the building was "so tall and narrow."[18]

In the fall of 1929, Gene drummed on a couple of the first racially integrated recording sessions beginning on September 30. The group was Fats Waller and His Buddies, all black (including trumpeter Henry "Red" Allen and the vocal group, The Four Wanderers) except for Gene, Eddie Condon, and a relative newcomer, trombonist Jack Teagarden. The songs were "Lookin' Good But Feelin' Bad" and "I Need Someone Like You." Said Waller's son later, "For [white] musicians of such caliber to appear with a black artist was quite a blow to Jim Crow-ism. My father appreciated it, and I believe he was just as proud to work with these men as he was for having composed [the 1929 Broadway musical] *Hot Chocolates*."[19]

About two weeks after the stock market crash that ushered in the Great Depression, Gene recorded with Red McKenzie's Mound City Blue Blowers. This session, along with McKenzie's hopping, comb-paper tooting technique, boasted another racially integrated ensemble. The solos of then-unknown African-American tenor saxist Coleman Hawkins were at least as hopping as McKenzie's. New Orleans bassist "Pops" Foster was the other black musician on this date. Other guests included clarinetist "Pee Wee" Russell, soon to become a Condon stalwart, and trombonist-arranger Glenn Miller.

From 1929 through 1931, the Chicagoans joined forces with Red Nichols in groups large and small, under such names as the Wabash Dance Orchestra and the Midnight Airedales. By Nichols's "own admission [he] had trouble loosening up and swinging," but his biographer said the Chicagoans got him going.[20] When Nichols added "some of the best of the young, white Chicago musicians who had learned from [King] Oliver and Armstrong (including Eddie Condon and Gene Krupa)," they inserted the "vital ingredients of life and fire."[21] Dan Morgenstern, the retired head of the Rutgers University Institute of Jazz Studies, said that Gene introduced a "very strongly African-American influenced beat into white jazz."[22]

Noteworthy Krupa contributions in January 1930 come under the Nichols alternate appellation, the Louisiana Rhythm Kings. In "Swanee," Gene played what would become known as the ride cymbal beat behind Jack Russin's piano solo—but on the rim of the bass drum.[23] This is one of the earliest known recordings by anyone of the beat, and possibly the earliest for Gene Krupa. On this side and on "Squeeze Me," Gene also displayed his fondness for random, one-note accents, something he would be known for throughout his career, which has been noted as a prime practice of bop drummers later on.[24]

Gene and Joe Sullivan conspired to specially insert some of that aforementioned "life and fire" on at least one Nichols side. In the July 1930 recording of "China Boy," Sullivan remembered, he and Krupa "quietly decided" during his piano solo to accelerate the tempo and get the band playing just as fast.[25] Sullivan's revelation suggests that any perceived rushing of Gene's later as a Benny Goodman sideman was probably intentional rather than a defect in his timekeeping.

This version of "China Boy" also showcases another early recorded use by Gene of the ride cymbal beat, this time likely on the suspended cymbal. He employed this beat on the suspended cymbal in a couple of Bix Beiderbecke sides two months later, and on many a 1930s recording, long before it became a staple of jazz drumming.

The Nichols side "After You've Gone," according to British writer Harry Francis, thrilled British jazz drummers toward the end of 1930 and changed their playing "almost overnight." Explained Francis: Gene's "use of accents gave the whole thing an atmosphere of real grass-roots jazz and his phrasing and general ensemble work were a delight..."[26] Gene's "four-bar break... [was] one of the most exciting ever."[27]

Some of Gene's Nichols sides contained vocals by Harold Arlen, a few years away from composing the beloved songs of *The Wizard of Oz*. Around this time, Gene recorded with "Hoagy" Carmichael and played on some of Bix Beiderbecke's last recordings before he died of alcoholism at only twenty-eight in 1931. (The following year, the Chicagoans' Frank Teschemacher, who had returned home to Chicago from New York and whose promise the Chicagoans and other jazz fans thought still unfulfilled, was killed in an automobile accident.)

Mezzrow was dismayed that the Chicagoans had joined Nichols and made what he considered "corny white" music that shouldn't be played by musicians like Krupa and Condon, who were "schooled in the same idiom as me." And although he thought that Harlem was the "greatest Negro community in the world," he was disappointed that they didn't play New Orleans–style jazz. Mezz thus "laid aside his horns" for a time,[28] concentrating on making African-American friends in Harlem and developing a booming marijuana business.

Before laying aside his horns, Mezz assembled a memorable all-white band for a performance before an all-black audience at Harlem's Renaissance Ballroom during the fall of 1929. The band featured some Chicagoans—Gene, Joe Sullivan, Bud Freeman, and a Bostonian newcomer, a trumpeter named Max Kaminsky. Also on hand were the Dorseys and Bix Beiderbecke. Said Kaminsky later, "It was quite an unusual thing to have white musicians play for a colored dance...."[29]

Although some members of the Condon Mob came to despise working for Red Nichols because they thought his methods too stilted—quitting, firing, and rehiring became a common occurrence—Gene remembered the "Red Nichols days very, very fondly, because I gained so much musical experience."[30] Nichols provided steady employment as the Depression deepened and offered some historic opportunities.

By 1930, the Depression had exacted a major toll on New York. Seventy percent of Broadway hotel rooms were vacant, and a thousand vaudeville performers quit the profession for lack of work. Twenty percent of dance halls had closed since 1929. The number of empty stores mounted, and commercial and residential rentals in the area were down by as much as thirty percent from the previous year's figures.[31]

Besides taking his band to play colleges and clubs, in December 1929 Nichols secured a job at the Hollywood Restaurant on Broadway and Forty-Eighth Street supporting the Nils T. Granlund Revue, featuring several dozen female dancers. Nichols brought along a thirteen-piece band: Gene, Condon, Pee Wee Russell, Joe Sullivan, and Glenn Miller, among others. A Samoan number foreshadowed future Krupa success; it prompted Gene to compose a "hot tom-tom routine"[32] that he said, less modestly than usual, made the chorus line "girls go crazy. And talk started going around town."[33]

The Hollywood Restaurant engagement segued into two of the most eventful stints for Gene (just turning twenty-one) in the

Nichols pit band for the 1930 Gershwin musicals, *Strike Up the Band* and *Girl Crazy*. The orchestra may have been the most illustrious in Broadway history, given the stardom that sidemen would enjoy just a few years later—besides Gene, there were Benny Goodman, Glenn Miller, Jimmy Dorsey, and Jack Teagarden. The Nichols-Gershwin opportunity probably evidenced a trend, that "in some contrast to the more delicate sonorities of the 1920s," the use of jazz musicians meant an evolution in Broadway's music, as well as the direction that Gershwin's own compositions were taking.[34]

It was a golden age for Broadway. Some of the day's performers just starting out, on their way to stardom, or already huge stars, included Fred and Adele Astaire, Fred Allen, Jack Benny, Bob Hope, Jack Haley, Eleanor Powell, Jimmy Durante, Bill "Bojangles" Robinson, W. C. Fields, Patsy Kelly, Ethel Waters, Ray Bolger, and Ed Wynn.[35]

Strike Up the Band, a reboot from a failed out-of-town run three years earlier, opened on January 14, 1930, at the Times Square Theater. It was the *first* Broadway musical of the 1930s, running for 191 performances—a hit for the time. George Gershwin himself conducted on opening night. He used not only a baton, but a cigar, his shoulders, his hips—indeed, his whole body.[36] The title song and "I've Got a Crush on You," the latter originating in a rare Gershwin Broadway flop, 1928's *Treasure Girl*, would become jazz standards, with hundreds of versions between them recorded through the decades.

Girl Crazy, a new musical, opened on October 14, 1930, at the Alvin Theater, and, with 272 performances, was more successful than *Strike Up the Band*. During intermission, wrote one Gershwin biographer, Nichols's "men took off on jam sessions, thrilling audiences."[37] Gene was the *first* drummer for Ethel Merman, the star of *Girl Crazy* and a newcomer to any stage. The musical was the second vehicle for Ginger Rogers, who had a supporting role. It proffered several soon-to-be jazz standards—"Embraceable You," "But Not for Me," and "I Got Rhythm." Together, they represent thousands of recordings. Gene Krupa was the *first* drummer to play on these American classics.

Krupa friend Max Kaminsky recalled that "Gershwin was crazy about...[Gene's] playing...because Gene was the first white drummer in a Broadway pit band who could swing the beat so that the chorus girls could kick in time."[38] Gene remembered alerting Gershwin to the "freeze beat" after seeing it used in a Duke Ellington show; it probably wasn't that different from the "stop-and-go" Chicagoan device. Krupa persuaded Gershwin to employ it as a replacement for a four-bar temple block solo in *Strike Up the Band*, the corniness of which made him "sick to my stomach."[39] (Philosophically, he was already on his way to removing what he considered extraneous items from the drum set.)

During the Gershwin period, when Gene was "flush" with cash, as Kaminsky put it, he would treat Max, Condon, Freeman, and Dave Tough to a night in Harlem. A favorite hangout was the Saratoga Ballroom, where Luis Russell and his band performed.[40] Another was Smalls Paradise, featuring Charlie Johnson's band and a drummer named George Stafford. Gene remembered Stafford "frightening drummers by the dozen."[41] When Krupa returned to Chicago in 1928 because of his dying mother, he missed a recording session organized by Condon that included a tune called "I'm Gonna Stomp, Mr. Henry Lee" on which Stafford guested.

Gene heard "Henry Lee" afterward and urged jazz fans to obtain this recording by any means necessary. To him, Stafford's drumming was "out of this world, figuratively, literally, and physically."[42] In "Henry Lee," aspects of Krupa's drumming are audible in Stafford's aggressiveness and use of sticks like castanets.

Harlem bandleader-drummer Chick Webb was Gene's choice discovery. Krupa saw him at the Dunbar Palace sometime after first arriving in New York. Gene was amazed and inspired. He cited Chick's use of sticks on the high-hat as pioneering, praised the Harlemite's speed and clean technique, and observed how Webb "had that bass drum going all the time...Before I got to know Chick, I was more on a small-band kick, the Chicago style offshoot of Dixieland. Chick brought out a more modern band kick."[43]

Gene's adoration of Chick Webb aside, he may have been selling himself short. "Chick affirmed him in the direction he had already taken," said English-American jazz drummer and historian Geoffrey Smith, "which was much more driving, much more open, much more incisive and present."[44]

Krupa sat in with every Harlem ensemble that he could—Chick's and Russell's included—and had the thrill of his life jamming with Louis Armstrong at Connie's Inn. "My personal experience is that sitting in with Louis makes a drummer feel like somebody turned on the current," said Gene.[45] He noticed an increased intermingling of ideas between black and white musicians, uptown and downtown, from one to the other and back.[46]

ETHEL FAWCETT, BORN a New Yorker in 1909 to Dexter and Rosetta Fawcett, lived in Brooklyn and Queens for the first two decades of her life. By 1930, she was a telephone operator,[47] which also happened to coincide with Gene's stint in the *Girl Crazy* orchestra pit. She performed her duties at the switchboard of the twenty-four-story Hotel Dixie at 241 West Forty-Second Street in Manhattan.[48] Gene, staying at the Dixie, asked for afternoon wakeup calls. Ethel obliged. Their chats soon moved beyond the simple business of getting the drummer up and into more personal territory.

"He just loved her voice," said Michael Bellino, a Krupa family friend.[49] Gene asked someone to point her out to him.[50] He saw that she had light brown hair, a cute little nose, and a Hollywood smile. It took about a month for him to get a first date with her. He proposed marriage in a drugstore.[51] Ethel said she would marry him on one condition: that he give up marijuana.[52] Apparently, he agreed. They were married on June 22, 1933. At first, they thought they'd settle down in New York, or Ethel did. This was impractical, so she accepted a life on the road with her young husband.[53]

Even when traveling, Gene was preoccupied with something else. "The man practiced all day long," said bandmate "Pee Wee" Erwin. "No exaggeration."[54] Gene would arrive at the theater where they had an engagement and, apart from playing the gigs, he practiced, with no breaks. Ethel brought him his meals.[55]

CHAPTER 5

"Ask Any of the Boys Around New York"

D**URING REHEARSALS FOR** S**TRIKE** *Up the Band*, Gene saw that, because he couldn't read music, he didn't know when to come in on the drums. Glenn Miller rescued him, humming the melodies and giving him the cues he needed. His great skills as a mostly self-taught drummer were not enough. Said Gene: "I realized how hopelessly incompetent I was as far as legitimate music was concerned." Learning to read was a must, which he did while other musicians slept.[1] For drum lessons, he went to the top—to the king of rudiments, Sanford "Gus" Moeller. Gene's idea was to start at the "bottom stair," as if he knew nothing about drums. This meant keeping his real name from Moeller "because I think he would have known about me" and taught him differently.

Gene couldn't hide his identity forever. Nine months into his lessons, probably around the time he was playing in the *Girl Crazy* pit band, who should be sitting in the front row but Gus Moeller? "You son of a gun," he said to Gene. "I thought there was something wrong." When Krupa explained his strategic anonymity, Moeller agreed it was probably better that he didn't know whom he was really teaching.[2]

As a student of Moeller, Gene was heir to the historical lineage of traditional military drumming: English-American drummer Charles Stewart Ashworth outlined his methods in an 1812 instructional book; George Bruce built on it in an 1862 manual; and Moeller on Bruce's in 1925.[3]

Movies helped in studying the "form of our great athletes and dancers," said Moeller, and applying it to drumming.[4] A Moeller trademark, the "up-and-down stroke method, which incorporates movement of the arms in concert with wrist and finger action," allowed Gene to "move easily around the set . . . and extract a better sound from the instrument."[5] Gene would become much admired for the smooth athleticism of his drumming. It was a visual as well as aural delight.

Gene didn't stop there. He was a lifelong student of drumming, seeking out masters across the U.S. during the height of his fame and for decades thereafter.[6] He took lessons from drummers of successive generations who were awed by him. He took lessons from former students. He was always seeking pointers formally and informally. He loved sharing his ideas and learning the ideas of others. This quest for drumming knowledge carried on to the end of his life. Jazz commentator Whitney Balliett, not a Krupa fan, thought him the "first book-learned drummer."[7]

As the Depression descended to absolute bottom, New York "became a city of unemployment, breadlines, and evictions." A Central Park "settlement of shanties" was dubbed "Hoover Valley,"[8] named for President Herbert Hoover, who was wedded to the laissez-faire economic philosophy of doing nothing. A shocking scene in Chicago circa 1932 saw fifty men "fighting over a barrel of garbage which had been set outside the backdoor of a restaurant." Chicago was in a panic. In June 1932, when the Democratic National Convention opened there, expecting that they would nominate New York's Governor Franklin D. Roosevelt for president, almost forty banks in that city alone had just failed. Nationally in 1932, many men resting on park benches or standing in breadlines had been jobless since 1929. By early 1933, after a steady increase yearly since the stock market crash, over a million "transients," those without a job or a home, were riding the rails. Some estimated that two hundred thousand of these aimless travelers were children without a parent or guardian.[9]

With a city-wide reputation on the drums, Gene didn't have to worry for long about working. After finishing with *Girl Crazy*, he joined Irving Aaronson and His Commanders, which concentrated on the hotel and theater circuit.[10] One of his biggest opportunities, though not particularly jazzy, came in 1932 with his recruitment into the Russ Columbo Orchestra, a newly formed assemblage for the violinist and popular crooner of the romantic liquid voice. Columbo was in direct competition with Bing Crosby, whose voice was smokier and less liquid. Russ's handsome face suggested tragic melancholy. Just a year older than Krupa, Columbo had led various house orchestras; this one he would control and mold to his liking.

Who did the recruiting for Columbo? Benny Goodman. Columbo's manager, Con Conrad, had asked Goodman to assemble a band with an eye toward something "jazzier than those 'sweet' bands of Rudy Vallée or Guy Lombardo."[11] Goodman admitted that, as Columbo's contractor, he "drove a pretty hard bargain with some of the boys, which they resented,"[12] although, as Columbo biographer Lou Miano noted, "Conrad had given him a limited budget to work with."[13]

Gene was a Columbo sideman for its entire existence in 1932 through the first quarter of 1933. Joe Sullivan served as one of two pianists (in a "dueling pianos" concept). Also recruited were Benny's brother Harry on bass, Jimmy McPartland on cornet, and "Babe" Russin—within a couple of years a key player for Goodman—on tenor sax. Benny himself played alto sax and clarinet, conducting while Russ sang.

A sticking point for Gene from the beginning was Benny's insistence that he use wire brushes instead of drumsticks. This came up, perennially, whenever Benny was boss. Despite the disagreement, playing for Columbo "was a very happy association," said Gene, "because most people know, and knew, Russ Columbo was a great singer. He was quite a violinist, too."[14] Besides drums, Gene played vibraphone, chimes, and tympani for Russ.

The orchestra was contracted to play for ten weeks at the idyllically set Woodmansten Inn in Westchester County, New York, just north of the Bronx. Performances were broadcast six times a week at 11 P.M. over NBC's Red Network. They were also heard twice a week at dinnertime on local radio station WOR and a few times on NBC's *Lucky Strike Dance Hour.* Woodmansten Inn's opening night brought out the celebrities, as did a special engagement at the *New York Graphic*'s Seventh Annual All Sports Dinner, which took place at the Hotel Astor in Manhattan. Among those attending was Babe Ruth, which likely brought out the baseball fanboy in Gene.[15]

Krupa remembered being on all Russ Columbo recordings during the New York sessions coinciding with the Woodmansten Inn run. Toward the end, the venue's owner cut Columbo's salary (and thus the sidemen's salaries) by $500. The inn was also behind one week in paying Russ.[16] These were side effects of the Depression, although they didn't absolve the inn's management of its responsibility to pay what was owed contractually.

Gene wasn't alone in having issues with Benny Goodman. So did Con Conrad, Columbo's manager, who blamed Goodman for the band's sudden transition to improvised jazz as soon as Columbo left the stage to schmooze the guests. Audiences loved it, but Conrad didn't think anyone but Russ should be receiving applause.[17]

NBC had further work for the Columbo men—a two-month theater tour that brought the band through Brooklyn, Reading, Cleveland, Chicago, Atlantic City, and Boston—before concluding in New York City. There, the band played three weeks at theaters in Manhattan and Brooklyn. They backed Columbo as well as vaudeville acts.[18] Gene thought he "gained good experience" having to musically shift gears so often.[19]

The press noticed Gene's contributions to the show. The Cleveland *Plain Dealer* called him a "clever drummer."[20] *Variety*'s reviewer was struck by Krupa's physicality: "The lighting cues [are] deserving of special note. The latter also goes for Columbo's gyrating drummer. Judging from the unspotlighted act he puts on, the lad must be an Albertina Rasch alumnus,"[21] Rasch being a famed dancer-choreographer.

After the New Year, Russ and orchestra went on another Midwestern tour, stopping in Detroit, Omaha, Minneapolis, Chicago (again), and Cincinnati. According to Columbo's biographer, Lou Miano, when Columbo's pay was halved (as was pay for many touring acts), he decided to cancel the remaining five weeks of the tour.[22] Gene remembered it differently. Columbo "found ... [a girl-friend] problem so pressing he had to set us adrift."[23]

———————

EDDIE CONDON AND Max Kaminsky, rooming together at a hotel on West Seventy-Third Street, intruded on the Krupas' marital bliss, once. Having taken the jazz vow of poverty, Condon especially refused to take just any job. In the winter of 1934, Condon and Kaminsky were unemployed again. One unusually frigid night, they spent hours at a bar where a friend treated them to drinks. Returning at 4 A.M. to their hotel, they found their room locked because they owed $55. They only had money enough for breakfast.

Out in the cold again, they looked for a phone. Calls to friends and acquaintances yielded no floor space. Then Eddie remembered Gene and Ethel's apartment nearby, but that they were celebrating something. He took a chance. On the phone, he began explaining his and Max's predicament. Gene unhesitatingly said to come right over. He would ready the daybed for them and leave the front door open. He also "waited up for us, gave us a drink, and tucked us in," said Eddie.[24]

The next day, somehow, Max and Eddie found work. Unable to return to their room to retrieve their things, they needed suits. It just so happened that Gene and Eddie shared not just a shoe size but clothing sizes, too.[25] That was one problem solved.

———————

WHEN RUSS COLUMBO dissolved the band, bandleader Horace Heidt acquired all the sidemen. Gene couldn't stand Heidt's emphasis on "gimmicks and tricks" at the expense of music, let alone jazz.[26] Mal Hallett, a 1920s bandleader of prodigious height, was interested in rejoining the fray and hired arranger "Spud" Murphy to find sidemen. The timing couldn't have been better for Gene. Murphy also selected, among others, alto saxophonist "Toots" Mondello, and trombonists Jack Teagarden and Jack Jenney.[27] "Gene came up, and played," said Mondello, "and boy, they went wild!"[28]

Around this time, Gene and recent Harvard graduate turned Boston-based jazz writer George Frazier became friendly. Frazier later remembered that, during a Hallett band intermission, Krupa introduced him to marijuana. (One hopes this occurred before Gene's pledge to Ethel to forsake it for their marriage.) Krupa also introduced Frazier to some of the best jazz around and shared his thoughts on what made jazz special. "No one ever gave me so deep an insight as Krupa into the nature of Jazz," said Frazier.[29]

Hallett's band impressed people. Bassist Milt Hinton recalled Chick Webb, Cab Calloway, and Coleman Hawkins raving about the Hallett group. "Man, if you go up to New England," they would say, "look out for that Mal Hallett band, because they had some bad cats in there."[30] But Hallett enjoyed few months of true glory. "Mr. Hallett, an old-fashioned showman type of leader, simply did not know what he had," wrote a commentator, "[which was] the nucleus of the greatest white jazz band of his time."[31]

Clueless Hallett couldn't keep his biggest stars long. Gene moved on to Joe Haymes for a potentially good experience. The band featured, among others, Pee Wee Erwin on trumpet, Toots Mondello on alto sax, old Chicago friend Remo "Ray" Biondi on guitar, Dick Clark on tenor sax, and Johnny Mince on clarinet. Some of them would join Gene in Benny Goodman's first major band by the end of 1934. "We had a pretty good band," said Gene. "We rehearsed very diligently for two weeks, and we were very happy with what was happening musically. So then Buddy Rogers came on the scene and we played the same old stale things he used to play before."[32]

Rogers was a movie-actor-turned-self-styled-multi-instrumentalist. His band was a hit, but Rogers didn't treat his sidemen like the excellent musicians they were. He added corny stunts. During the show, the band would play a medley of patriotic songs, which, it being early in the first administration of Franklin D.

Roosevelt, led into each sideman raising a lit black box showing a letter of the alphabet. Together, the letters spelled "Roosevelt-NRA."[33] It didn't end there. As an American flag fluttered wildly, someone sang "Home on the Range."[34]

Worse, Buddy Rogers's showstopper involved his walking from musician to musician and playing their instruments—very badly. Gene's drums were not immune to the spectacle. He was so bothered by Rogers's pitiful drumming that he almost got himself fired following the first night's performance. He entered the bandleader's dressing room, overflowing with women, photographers, and interviewers, and interjected: "Look, Mr. Rogers, if you're going to do that drum solo, let me teach you a decent sixteen bars." Rogers ordered him out. A manager kept him from firing Gene, labeling Krupa a "drum mad" kid.[35]

Given how disappointing Gene's time with dance bands had been since drumming for Irving Aaronson in 1931—bands holding promise but ignoring or neglecting their jazz potential—Gene was fortunate to find outlets for his urge to play real jazz. As he later reflected, he earned "enough money to go out at night and jam someplace with the bands and guys you wanted to play with."[36] Also, he was invited to play on some significant recording sessions in late 1933 and early 1934, which caught the ears of many.

New Yorker and Vanderbilt heir John Hammond, a recent Yale dropout, organized the sessions. Hammond had begun inserting himself into the jazz scene, trying to make things happen. His special mission was to assemble racially integrated groups. Over time, he delighted some while offending others. Jazz writer Otis Ferguson saw him as a privileged, tunnel-visioned egomaniac with good intentions but an insensitive, impolitic way of communicating with others.[37]

Hammond contracted with a couple of English record labels to provide them sides recorded by an integrated group of musicians. He approached several African-American bands, including Fletcher Henderson's, for players. Benny Goodman was to be leader of the group. Benny, under whose name the sides would be made, nixed the integration idea as likely damaging to his career, even in New York. "He was right," Hammond later remarked. Ultimately, the band consisted of, among others, Jack Teagarden and his trumpet-ing brother Charlie, Joe Sullivan on piano (on later sides, Frank Froeba), guitarist Dick McDonough, and Gene Krupa. Hammond borrowed Jack and Gene from Mal Hallett's band, then playing in Boston. Initially, Gene refused; Krupa didn't want to work with Goodman again after his negative experience in the Columbo days. But he relented when Hammond guaranteed a smooth experience.[38]

The sides, some of which were released in America after all, in-cluded Jack Teagarden vocals, like the Fats Waller ditty, "Aintcha Glad?" and a bluesy ode to marijuana called "Texas Tea Party," co-written by Teagarden and Benny Goodman. Especially notable were two sides featuring vocals by an African-American teenager named Billie Holiday who was making her first-ever recordings— "Your Mother's Son-in-Law" and "Riffin' the Scotch." Gene Krupa was Holiday's *first* drummer in a recording studio.

Because of England's enthusiasm for these offerings, Hammond scheduled more dates early in 1934. The racial barrier crumbled when Coleman Hawkins joined Benny, Gene, and several of the same musicians from previous dates for some beautiful reed work. Mildred Bailey, one of the first white vocalists to sing in a jazz vein, was there, too. These records "have long been favorites with the jazz connoisseurs," said British jazz writer Brian Rust.[39]

HAMMOND, WHO TENDED in the early days to promise people things before doing preliminary work, before contracts had been signed, before talking to affected parties, orchestrated a fiasco that made the music papers for months on end from mid-1934 to mid-1935. He had promised British bandleader Jack Hylton a racially in-tegrated, all-star band whose European tour Hylton would manage. Besides Goodman, Krupa, and Jack Teagarden, the names being thrown around included alto saxophonist Benny Carter, pianist Teddy Wilson, tenor saxophonist "Chu" Berry, xylophonist "Red" Norvo, and flautist Wayman Carver. When the plans fell through in November 1934, Hammond blamed Hylton, while Hylton blamed Hammond for producing a mere "hypothetical" band.[40]

Gene Krupa remembered arriving in New York for the promised European tour and finding it canceled.[41] To Hammond's credit, as if to make up for the mess he had created, he wrote in *Melody News* that Gene was the "best white drummer anywhere."[42]

Before reaching prominence with Count Basie, African-American drummer Jo Jones played in various bands, including Grant Moore and His New Orleans Black Devils. "Gene, really the first time that he took my notice was when he was with Buddy Rogers [in Minneapolis]," Jones said later. "I was late on my job, the first time in my life I was ever late on my job with Grant Moore, watching Gene."[43]

In discussing Buddy Rogers's engagement in Chicago, *Down Beat* magazine reported: "Back of the drums is Gene Krupa, a boy that really beats those pig skins, one of the very few good drummers. Ask any of the boys around N.Y. about this boy's reputation."[44]

Dawn of Duende

Gene's penchant for what many have called "showmanship" was his way of performing beats, experiencing them one drum or cymbal strike at a time. Beats generated body movements—bouncing, swaying, head shaking, grimacing, or all of them simultaneously. To a rather flippant writer for *Down Beat* in August 1934, Gene's bodily and facial expressions unconsciously executed as Buddy Rogers's drummer made him the "comedian of the band..."[45] His mode of performance was better described by another reviewer: "He burns—though it may better be said that he bobs—with the divine fire."[46]

Krupa's expressive performing style eventually galvanized some jazz devotees and repulsed others. Acclaimed country music drummer Kenny Malone said that what set Gene's drumming apart was the "joy he had in it. He was happy when he was playing. He was dancing with his own rhythms."[47] Loren Schoenberg, jazz scholar and founder of the National Jazz Museum in Harlem, thought Gene the "first Elvis in some ways," projecting sex and sensuousness.[48]

Jazz critic Gunther Schuller complained that Gene exuded "exuberant vulgarity."[49] An audience member of a 1955 jazz round table protested: "It looked at times with this tremendous play-acting as though the man himself was not serious about it. How can you take him seriously if he doesn't take himself seriously?"[50] Such reactions were countered by jazz scholar Dan Morgenstern's belief that Gene's manner of playing the drums "came naturally with him. He wasn't showing off, so to speak. He got so involved in what he was doing."[51]

George Frazier finally figured it out, linking Gene's dramatic physicality to "duende."[52] It was, someone else said, a "quality that few people have and most people desire."[53] But Frazier had noticed only the surface indications of duende.

Duende was most memorably explicated by Spanish poet-playwright Federico García Lorca, who had reached the height of his fame in the 1930s just as Krupa's fame was rising and not long before Lorca's murder by Franco's Fascist forces in Spain. For Lorca, duende was a "force," an internal struggle that "surges up, inside, from the soles of the feet" of an artist, generating "an almost religious enthusiasm" that consumes him and brings him to the precipice of pure emotion.[54]

Gene's duende, his genuine, deep-seated emotionalism, spurred bandmates on and electrified audiences. He couldn't help his other-worldliness, his body propelled by a frightening energy that burst spontaneously from within. A tween named Gloria, watching Gene at a Brooklyn theater with her teenage sisters Rozzie and Betty, "didn't know how he could have survived it."[55]

CHAPTER 6

"In the Palm of His Hand"

O N DECEMBER 5, 1933, PROHIBITION ended with the repeal of the Eighteenth Amendment to the U.S. Constitution. Liquor, wine, and beer were no longer illegal under federal law.

This was great news for tax revenue, hotels and other nightspots, music, and musicians—great news, perhaps, for jazz, which had been struggling to bust out of the confines of speakeasies and the strictures of white jazz-shy bandleaders. Reported in music magazine *Melody News* in October 1934: "Countless bars, clubs, cafés and restaurants have been opened since repeal, and most of them are giving their customers music with their food and refreshment." The "average musician" could expect better job prospects now than in the previous two or three years.[1]

Up until December 1934, Benny Goodman had recorded dozens of sides under his own name and others. Earlier that year, he came upon what he had hoped would be a big break for a band he was putting together with John Hammond's assistance. Billy Rose hired Benny's new orchestra for the newly named Billy Rose Music Hall (formerly the Hammerstein Theater) on Broadway and Fifty-Third Street in Manhattan. The engagement lasted about six weeks before the Goodman aggregation was ousted.

Word came that NBC radio was inviting bands to audition for a new nationally broadcast program sponsored by the National Biscuit Company (better known later as "Nabisco") called *Let's Dance*. The debut date? December 1, 1934. It was to be continuously broadcast from New York for three hours, beginning at 10:30 P.M. Saturday night and ending at 1:30 A.M. the following morning. Each hour represented a live, repeat performance; 11:30 P.M. served Mountain Time; 12:30 A.M., Pacific.

Goodman was to share airtime with Xavier Cugat and Kel Murray. Murray represented "sweet" music (think Guy Lombardo), Cugat Latin, and Goodman "hot"—meaning jazz; or, as it was becoming known in a larger band context, "swing," of which there were few white exponents.

After the first air date, Benny still aimed to improve his lineup. Stan King, whom Gene had supplanted as Red Nichols's favored drummer by 1930, was now Benny's, and about to be supplanted by Gene—again. "We were getting along with what we had," said Goodman, but his band needed more. "A good drummer can do more in the way of giving swing to a band...than almost any other man in the outfit. There was only one drummer at that time who would fill the bill.... That was Gene Krupa."[2]

John Hammond went to fetch Gene, still with Buddy Rogers, for a second time. Hammond caught up with the band in Chicago and found Gene during intermission. Said Benny later: "Probably Gene had some not too favorable recollections of our previous jobs together."[3] This was true.

"Again, John?" Gene was to have testily responded to Hammond's invitation. "You must be kidding."[4] It wasn't just Benny whom Gene was annoyed with, but Hammond. Two months had passed since Hammond's proposed tour of Europe with an integrated band had fallen through; Gene still remembered rushing down to New York from Boston for nothing. Then there was the issue of economics. "I was in hock up to my neck at that time," Gene said.[5]

Hammond told Gene that the new Goodman band was "really swinging," unlike the Rogers aggregation. Gene acquiesced, despite the pay cut to $87.50 a week and his indebtedness. An attractive selling point was Hammond's guarantee that Gene's drums would be "featured."[6]

Goodman greatly admired Gene's musicianship: "He always had tremendous instinct for music, even back in the Chicago days at the 'Three Deuces,' and the amount of work and study he had put in since then had given him brilliant technic [sic] on drums... From the time he joined us... Gene gave the band a solidity and firmness, as far as rhythm was concerned, that it never had before."[7]

Said Loren Schoenberg: "I think Benny knew that he never would have become the King of Swing... without Gene."[8] D. Russell Connor, Goodman's biodiscographer, remarked that the "importance of Krupa's union with Goodman cannot be overstated. Benny got in Gene, in addition to Gene's technical proficiency, rock-solid beat, feeling for jazz and showmanship, a loyal coworker who gave everything he had to make the new band a success."[9] According to British jazz drummer-historian John Petters, "The Goodman band of that period sounded unlike any other band because of Gene's drums."[10]

BEFORE GENE'S ARRIVAL in December 1934, eighteen-year-old Goodman vocalist Helen Ward, to make her own impact on 1930s female jazz singing, wondered why they needed a new drummer. "We already have one," she said. "You'll see!" Benny told her. She later admitted, "Boy, did I ever!"[11]

Initially, Gene thought that work with Benny would be light, with just one rehearsal on Wednesdays and the three-hour radio program on Saturday nights. This meant that he could devote that much more time to "study."[12] If this was the arrangement, it didn't last long.

There are three similar stories about a band trip from hell that happened during these early days. Only one of them reads credibly—this one:

Benny's management had hired a glass-topped Coney Island tour bus to get to Johnson City, Pennsylvania, from New York City.

The snow was falling so fiercely that band members "crawled" out of the vehicle every half hour to remove the heavy accumulation from the glass top's sides. They arrived in Johnson City two and a half hours late. The audience was so angry at the delay that they were "practically snarling." They also had no taste for the band's brand of music. The men returned to New York the next day in the same glass-topped vehicle, quite dejected.[13]

The Goodman crew played other scattered engagements across the twenty-six weeks of *Let's Dance*, in Boston; White Plains, New York; Scranton, Pennsylvania; even Rocky Mount, North Carolina. Helen Ward said that these one-nighters helped them learn new arrangements to be played on the Saturday night radio program. Some of the time, she said, Gene and his wife, Ethel, became "road buddies," using each other's cars for various trips. If Ethel stayed home, Gene rode with Helen and Benny.[14] At the time, Gene and Ethel were residents of a "stout beige building," the Whitby Hotel on Forty-Fifth Street, just west of Eighth Avenue. Then, as now, the Whitby attracted musicians, actors, and artists.[15] Many Goodman sidemen and musicians from other bands lived there. Their wives became friends.[16]

The band also performed one-nighters opposite Chick Webb's band in Harlem's Savoy Ballroom,[17] likely a real treat for Gene especially.

Two of the soon-to-be most-acclaimed talents in jazz moved in, out, in, and out of the Goodman group during the first half of 1935—namely, Jack Teagarden and trumpeter "Bunny" Berigan. Arrangers—many were needed for the *Let's Dance* program's half-year existence—included, most notably, Dean Kincaide, Spud Murphy, African-American musician Benny Carter, and the most prolific—another African-American—Fletcher Henderson, also a struggling bandleader.[18] Fletcher's brother Horace also supplied arrangements.

Let's Dance broadcast its last program on May 25, 1935. Although the show boasted a large fan base, and Goodman's sets were favorites with listeners, all of this popularity didn't mean the general music-loving public stood ready to welcome the band with open arms wherever they went. Benny secured what should have been a lengthy engagement with the Roosevelt Grill at the Hotel Roosevelt at Madison Avenue and Forty-Fifth Street. The band's time there was short-lived. Guy Lombardo's music was more to the taste of hotel management, staff, and dancers, and Goodman received notice on the first night that their services wouldn't be welcome much longer.[19]

On June 6, the band, under the name The Rhythm Makers, recorded fifty songs in eight hours for NBC radio's Thesaurus transcription service. These were intended for radio play but not public sale. Each sideman received a total of $51,[20] or a dollar a song. That may not sound like much now, but consider that the $51 of 1935 was worth over $1,000 in 2023.

In the wake of, at best, sputtering success, John Hammond was not shy about touting the band he had been instrumental in forming. Any good publicity, even from an interested party, could help. The three most valuable assets of a band that had yet to find real commercial success, he said, were Goodman, Krupa, and Henderson. Added Hammond: "Until Gene, who drums as well as any mortal, joined the orchestra it was a ragged, scuffling group."[21] Hammond had finally convinced Helen Oakley, a wealthy young Chicago-area jazz promoter, that he was right about Gene. She said: "If not undisputed king, then certainly he [Krupa] is the next thing to it . . . He holds it [the band] in the palm of his hand . . . He is a veritable source of inspiration."[22]

What could be better now than returning to the recording studio under the Goodman band's own name and continuing where they left off after their marvelous April dates? Those had yielded such great sides as "Hunkadola," "The Dixieland Band," and "Japanese Sandman." (Krupa's performance on "Hunkadola" may have featured the most exciting, varied, and imaginative Krupa rim shots on any recording up to that time.)

Thus, the band followed the Thesaurus sessions with some of their best-loved recordings—"Blue Skies," "Sometimes I'm Happy," and that dancer's delight, "King Porter Stomp," all Henderson arrangements.

Gene Krupa demonstrated on "King Porter" how a drummer could create something from nothing. As was typical of band arrangements in those days, Henderson's offered no real drumming guidance. Gene had come up with his own drum part from start to finish.[23] Loren Schoenberg, an expert on jazz recordings of the era, couldn't think of any other drummer who was doing what Gene was doing at that time. Not Chick Webb, not "Big Sid" Catlett. "If we go by the recorded evidence," said Schoenberg, "he had a way of accenting the figures that they [the band] played, designing fills and things in between what they played ... Gene was composing a part. It was tremendously influential and tremendously dynamic." Only Jo Jones, "slightly after Gene," can be considered to have done something similar.[24]

Schoenberg also observed that, on the basis of recorded evidence, such as on "Sometimes I'm Happy," Krupa was "dropping bombs" using the bass drum at least a couple of years before Teddy Hill's drummer Kenny Clarke, who was credited with innovating this practice and paving the way for bop drumming. This isn't to say that Gene was absolutely the first to drop a bomb, but it may be said that he was the first recorded doing so.[25]

In May 1935, with the future of the Goodman band still uncertain, *Metronome* nominated Gene for its "Musicians Hall of Fame." He was "recognized as the leader in his field." *Metronome* said Gene was "trying to improve his already amazing technique by practicing and by analyzing it via giving lessons to others." He was also taking lessons in xylophone and tympani. Gene and Ethel—plus their Scottie—often gave parties in their Whitby Hotel apartment, but he reportedly couldn't stay away from his drum pad or xylophone for long.[26]

IN JUNE 1935, something happened that no one saw coming. Benny Goodman attended a party at Mildred Bailey's place in Queens after one of the ill-fated Roosevelt Grill shows. One guest was African-American pianist Teddy Wilson, then performing with Willie Bryant's band at the Savoy, which alternated with Chick

Webb's. Wilson started playing the piano, Goodman took out his clarinet, an amateur drummer and cousin of Bailey's sat in on drums, and they had the makings of something special. Wilson's type of playing was different from the usual jazz piano; it was fleet, fluid, and fast.

Benny quickly arranged studio time.[27] A new trio was born— Goodman on clarinet, Wilson on piano, and Krupa on drums. They recorded four memorable sides, the most up-tempo of which was "Who?" Here, Gene played the longest of any solo he had recorded until then—thirty-two bars—and possibly the longest recorded drum solo by anyone up to that time.[28] And he did it all with wire brushes.

One wonders whether, given Benny's strong preference for brushes over sticks, Gene circumvented this limitation by playing brushes in a way one couldn't ignore. He could play them ("The Glory of Love") with the metal tips, one of which he used for a cymbal crash. "He had the physical ability to easily spin a brush in his hands," said Hal Smith, a jazz drummer and historian.[29] Smith also mentioned Gene playing brush rolls the "hard way" on "In a Sentimental Mood." "Let your wrists go limp and just drop the brushes and make them flutter," said Smith. "That's what he was doing . . . for almost a whole chorus. And it's very difficult to do unless you have extremely loose wrists."[30]

Benny and Gene would have their differences, but Gene always loved playing with Goodman: "He gives you a springboard. You feed him, and in turn, he feeds you; he gives you a whole chain of ideas to go by."[31]

Decades later, prominent jazz clarinetist Ken Peplowski remarked that Gene "was at the service of the music, and responding to what Benny and Teddy were playing, and also giving them stuff to play off of. And the same you could say about Teddy Wilson."[32] Thinking of how the Trio's individual solos varied in different takes of the song, Peplowski said that it was "amazing how much confidence they had as players at those young ages of theirs. All three of them."[33] (Goodman and Krupa were twenty-six, Wilson twenty-two.)

The reasons to make a fuss about the beginnings of the Benny Goodman Trio are twofold: they commenced a trend toward jazz "chamber" groups,[34] and, once they performed in public during the first quarter of 1936, they broke racial taboos. A few months later they added a fourth member, black vibraphonist Lionel Hampton, and played publicly as a Quartet, thus broadening the breaking of racial taboos.

As jazz writer John McDonough put it, "Here were four men who came together and created a whirling ferment of sounds which was vastly larger than the considerable sum of its parts."[35]

LOS ANGELES'S PALOMAR Ballroom at Vermont Avenue and Second Street symbolized the manufactured glamour of the movie industry, and beckoned those seeking moderate weather, palm trees, neo-Spanish architecture, and a place to enjoy food and dance in a glitzy atmosphere. Patrons could order a full dinner for as little as seventy-five cents—one might ask for the soup du jour, a main course of spaghetti with chicken livers and mushrooms, and coffee or tea with ice cream for dessert. Bigger spenders could order appetizers, too, like canapé of caviar for a dollar or crabmeat cocktail for fifty cents. If they chose to dance in a space built for thousands, they could stretch out their dinner for an entire night. Liquor was plentiful.[36]

The Palomar was the destination of Benny Goodman and his orchestra in the summer of 1935—a make or break engagement—but first they had to travel across America, stopping in towns along the way, and hoping they would be received reasonably well. They had their dreams, hoping to discover a jazz-swing Elysium that would lead to, at least, remunerative success.

The band's trip west was overwhelmingly discouraging. A decent two nights in Milwaukee—which brought out many of their Chicago friends—was followed by disastrous dates in Colorado. First was Elitch's Gardens in Denver; then the Mile-Away Dance Pavilion in Grand Junction. At Elitch's Gardens, the manager almost immediately objected to the band's brand of music—but especially its penchant for allowing time for its soloists. Songs were supposed to last about three minutes, not five or ten, because the business model involved men paying a dime for three dances with a "hostess." Management found the "music . . . too loud, the beat . . . too deep, [and] it was all too disturbing."[37] The group was urged to play nice waltz selections and other bland numbers. This they did, to keep the job, but business was poor.[38]

Grand Junction was scary. "A net had been set up in front of the bandstand to catch the empty bottles that the audience might launch," said one of the band's newest members, pianist Jess Stacy.[39] The handful of other stops en route to Los Angeles prompted signs of appreciation, but not much more. "By the time we reached Los Angeles," remembered Gene, "it was agreed that the Palomar date would be the end of the tour, the end of the band and the end of a dream."

Their Palomar reception on August 21, 1935, wasn't what they had expected. "Man, I'll never forget that sight!" said Gene. "The entrance was jammed and we had a terrible time even getting in the place. For a while, I thought we had the wrong address."[40]

The band started out gingerly. They had been spooked by all the objections and rejections they'd weathered that summer. But here, the crowd was waiting for something different. Goodman figured they might as well go all out and see what happened. He had the band reach for their Henderson arrangements. "To our complete amazement, half of the crowd stopped dancing and came surging around the stand. It was the first experience we had with that kind of attention, and it certainly was a kick . . . That first big roar of the crowd was one of the sweetest sounds I ever heard in my life."[41]

Wrote a *Los Angeles Times* reporter: "Benny Goodman's band is creating more of a stir among local dance enthusiasts than any orchestra that has come to these parts in many a year. I've never heard dancers give a rousing cheer after a number has been played by another band as they do at the Palomar."[42] The band's reception was so great that the engagement was extended through October 1. Every night, it seemed, the band's reception got better and better.

How was this possible? What made Los Angeles different from many of the other cities the band had limped through on the way over? The twenty-six weeks of the *Let's Dance* program were heard during primetime—for Southern California's young people, who were enjoying their Saturday night parties, Goodman's Henderson arrangements gave them a large charge. Local radio stations were playing the band's music.[43] Significantly, Los Angeles was enjoying substantial growth in its "music and jazz community" because of an ever-greater use of music in movies. And hearing the Goodman band live in all of its bright, unfettered glory, in contrast to what they sounded like with poor radio reception and the recording fidelity of those days,[44] plus seeing Krupa in person in all of his intense duende, made the Palomar engagement a milestone in American music history.

This Palomar triumph is recognized as having kicked off the "Swing Era." It makes sense that the Goodman band, probably the greatest white swing band at the time and for some years to come, and certainly among the greatest swing bands of all time regardless of race, had led the white public to finally accept, even adore, a form of jazz called swing. The American musical landscape would never be the same.

A Los Angeles music store ad in *Tempo* highlighted the enormous impact that Gene Krupa was making on audiences. There he stood, smiling, a snare drum in his hands, an old-fashioned bass drum's front cornily depicting an image of a sailing ship. The ad's tagline read: "Boys Take a Bow . . . Here He Is . . ."[45] Something else besides the band's success was happening, and right on time.

CHAPTER 7

"When Mr. Krupa Beats Those Riffs, He Don't Let You Down"[1]

WHAT WAS THIS "SWING" ON which a musical era was built? It was jazz, but more than that. Rather than embrace the pure improvisation of traditional jazz, it involved mainly "big bands," but also small bands and smaller groups, that played music written in "jazz terms" but allowed soloists to show their stuff while still advancing the musical piece as a whole. It was a *"freshness and spontaneity that could not be indicated by accents, note-values or other written symbols."*[2] African-American bands like Ellington's, Webb's, and Henderson's had been playing swing for some years, but there was no market for white jazz and thus no familiarity with or commercial potential for swing among the white public. With Goodman's explosive debut at the Palomar, this state of affairs rapidly changed.

From the Palomar, and an uproarious stint at the Paramount movie theater, also in Los Angeles, the band played other California dates before going eastward. While still in California, Gene had a minor brush with the law. The band had been "making the jumps" between gigs in a collection of motor vehicles. Gene and Benny's bass-playing brother Harry traveled in what became known as the "death car," possibly because they had been hit by a truck that left the back of the vehicle "pretty well crushed." Rushing to a one-nighter, they were stopped by police who cited Gene for speeding. Because Harry naïvely offered the cop five dollars if he would drop the ticket, the bassist went to jail for a few days. Unlike Harry, Gene had only to pay for the ticket. He somehow made the date that they'd been rushing to.[3]

Traveling eastward, the band made several successful stops in Texas. Then came an opportunity to play the Joseph C. Urban Room at the Congress Hotel on South Michigan Avenue and Congress Street in Chicago. Goodman accepted the offer, despite a rash of dysentery cases among hotel clientele,[4] which had considerably dampened business. Although the hotel announced that they had replaced their plumbing, business still lagged, which may be why the Urban Room was known as a place where bands went to die.[5] The band stayed seven months.

Gene had just signed with the Chicago-based Slingerland Drum Company to promote their products; a natural result was the company's promotion of Gene. As a new signee, Krupa was featured in what apparently was his first Slingerland ad, in the November 1935 issue of *Down Beat*. He grinned from behind a drum set lacking extraneous gadgets beyond a cowbell. The bass drum's face evidenced small Krupa initials inside a heraldic shield; outside it loomed Benny's larger ones, no corny artwork in sight. Trumpeted the ad: "Says Gene Krupa 'The King of Swing,' 'when I take off, my Slingerland drums ride with me—they never slow me down.'"[6] Gene was crowned the "King of Swing" before Benny! Goodman himself thought the media hadn't regally dubbed him until at least December 1935, after the first Urban Room jazz concert.[7]

The December 8 event, sponsored by the Chicago Rhythm Club of which young heiress Helen Oakley was president, was billed as a "tea-dance." It attracted over 700 people in a room purportedly built for 550. Few danced. They were so enthralled that "all they could do was listen and watch," said *Down Beat*.[8] Observed *Orchestra World*, "About the most talked-of man in the band is Gene Krupa, the drummer. People stop dancing just to watch this young fellow go to town."[9] Helen Oakley remembered Gene saying that this concert was the "biggest thrill he'd had so far, for the people just to *listen* to them."[10]

It remained obvious that Benny owed much to Gene for his band's success; it can't be said often enough that the Swing Era wouldn't have been what it became without Gene. As jazz historian Grover Sales stated: "The premier showman of the band was the demonic drummer Gene Krupa, no less responsible for the Swing craze than his boss... Krupa's tribal beat formed the hypnotic pulse that radically changed the way white America danced, listened, and responded to music."[11]

Other things steered twentysomething Gene toward grizzled old jazz veteran status. These were special studio sessions. In November 1935, he and other Goodmanites each recorded with their own one-off ensembles, John Hammond producing. These were intended for English—not domestic—release on the Parlophone label purportedly because of Americans' lack of sophistication, jazz-wise.[12]

Gene's assemblage featured, besides himself, Benny, Jess Stacy on piano, Allan Reuss on guitar, Nate Kazebier on trumpet, Joe Harris on trombone, and a Hammond find, sixteen-year-old African-American bassist Israel Crosby, then playing for Albert Ammons. The drummer called this group Gene Krupa and His Chicagoans; naturally, its flavor was distinctly retro Chicago style. Yet it also sounded contemporary, enmeshing boogie-woogie with Gene's plentiful, varied rim shots; Dixieland with blues; Crosby's melodic bass lines with delicate press rolls behind; quietude with crescendo. The sides were "The Last Round Up," "Jazz Me Blues," "Three Little Words," and "Blues of Israel." Over eighty years later, Schoenberg deemed this recording date "one of the great sessions of all time."[13]

The sides wouldn't see American light until 1941 on Decca's *Gems of Jazz No. 2* compilation. "Blues of Israel," woefully New Orleans-ish and a Krupa composition beginning and ending with Israel Crosby's bass, captured most of the critical praise and enjoyed legendary status before being sold in America.[14] As Yale student and jazz aficionado George M. Avakian had complained in *Tempo* four years earlier, "It should be worth somebody's while to release some of them here."[15]

Better known are the four sides recorded in February 1936 by Gene, other Goodman regulars, Israel Crosby, and a couple of guests from Fletcher Henderson's latest aggregation then playing in town: trumpeter Roy Eldridge and tenor saxophonist Chu Berry.

Gene and Roy's lifelong friendship thus began. Said Roy: "Me and Gene were just like brothers."[16] Their "bromance" was light-heartedly described in *Music and Rhythm*—in a way that might raise twenty-first-century eyebrows—a few years later when Roy joined Gene's band. They frequently jammed and ate ribs together, noted the magazine, but race kept them from regularly playing shoulder to shoulder in the same orchestra. Said the magazine: "It was like two lovers meeting at a secret rendezvous, content and happy while together, but prevented by circumstances from being together where others could see."[17]

The February 1936 Krupa ensemble was called Gene Krupa's Swing Band. Upon release, the group's four sides got more press stateside than had the previous songs, due to their release in America and Britain. The songs were "I Hope Gabriel Likes My Music," "Mutiny in the Parlor," "I'm Gonna Clap My Hands," and a tune with co-songwriting credits going to Krupa, Eldridge, and Berry called, "Swing is Here." It certainly was. The middle two sides featured the trademark swinging vocals of Goodman's singer, Helen Ward.

Most significant, besides the joining of Henderson bandmates Eldridge and Berry—one hot and high-noted, the other warm and flowing—is the Eldridge-Krupa chemistry: They loved fast tempos and strong musical statements. "I'm Gonna Clap My Hands" was a bestseller—Gene's first—on the American Victor label.[18] The four sides introduced Roy and Chu to the broadest of jazz-fan audiences.[19] Before his untimely death in a 1941 car crash, Chu had mentioned this recording session as the "greatest record date that I ever played."[20]

———————————

THE BAND STILL at the Congress Hotel in spring 1936, Benny debuted the Trio, with Teddy Wilson on piano and Gene on drums, at the band's second Chicago Rhythm Club concert. It would be the first of innumerable Trio performances to play during band breaks. Integrated public performance was groundbreaking and daring.

"I soon got to know Gene Krupa for the great jazz drummer he was: his perfect control of his drums, his sense of rhythm, and his touch especially, which was beautiful," said Teddy Wilson.[21] The Wilson-Krupa artistic union, beyond Benny's formidable musicianship, was the subject of admiration. The "lack of a bass [in the Trio] pegged the sound of the group," read one evaluation. The perfect partnership of Wilson and Krupa made up for the absence of a bass, supplying "the group's rhythmic backbone."[22] Krupa's ability to contribute just what was needed must be acknowledged. "At the time, he must have been one of the most flexible and accomplished drummers in jazz," said another. "He could scale down his normal attack" and reach a level of sublime intimacy with his Trio mates.[23]

Within months, African-American vibraphonist Lionel Hampton made the Trio a Quartet and expanded the ensemble's groundbreaking nature. They learned of Lionel while Benny and the band were in Los Angeles playing their second go-round at the Palomar and filming their first movie, *The Big Broadcast of 1937*. John Hammond recommended him to Benny, who attended one of Hamp's performances at the Paradise Nightclub before retrieving Teddy and Gene. "The four of us got on the bandstand together, and man, we started wailing out," said Lionel. "We played for two hours straight."[24]

Lionel was also an accomplished drummer; his third specialty was playing two-fingered piano. Gene Krupa harbored a "great respect for his [drumming] speed and the uniqueness of his ideas."[25] They engaged in hours-long practice sessions, each trying to outdo the other.[26]

Most important was Lionel's virtuosity on the vibraphone; he could be exciting, touching, or witty, as Gene could be on the drums. The first number the Quartet recorded, in August 1936, was the softly twinkling "Moonglow." Gene's light bass drum patter, underscoring—emotionally supporting—Benny's penultimate four-beat statement, is among the most moving moments of the Trio's or Quartet's recordings.

Personality- and appearance-wise, the Quartet was an odd combination of individuals. Benny resembled a mild-mannered math teacher; Teddy, a no-nonsense professor of dead languages. Gene's and Lionel's faces usually glowed with joy. "Hooray!" might have been their motto.

The backgrounds of each Quartet member were further divided. Benny and Gene, the white offspring of immigrants, were high school dropouts whose parents had had limited, if any, schooling. Lionel, of African-American parentage, grew up in Alabama before moving to Chicago. All of his aunts and uncles had finished high school and attended at least some college.[27] Lionel himself worked toward finishing high school through an extension course at the University of Southern California, California being where he played with Les Hite. Teddy Wilson was also an Alabamian. His parents were faculty members of Tuskegee College; he majored in music theory at Talladega College before playing with Louis Armstrong and Benny Carter.[28]

ISSUES AROSE ABOUT the Goodman band's volume. Although there were later complaints about the loudness of Gene's drumming, the high decibel levels had other sources. When Goodman acquired Alex Bartha's trumpeter "Ziggy" Elman in Atlantic City, Elman brought with him a really powerful diaphragm. His trumpet section mates, Chris Griffin and Zeke Zarchey, were having trouble matching Ziggy's power. Griffin complained to Benny. Benny talked to Ziggy. Ziggy reminded Benny who had recruited whom, and he (Ziggy) could rejoin Bartha if Benny would like. That settled that.[29]

Benny Goodman had a "100-decibel brass section," said one commentator.[30] Another thought Goodman "might well balance his mikes and not blast the customers into the drugstores," but admitted that corrective measures weren't likely given the band's box office dominance—"and how!"[31]

The Elman episode brings us to a Benny Goodman personality digression. In handling Benny, self-confident band members did better than meeker types. Ziggy was a self-confident sideman. Gene was another. He persisted in calling Goodman "Ben" although Benny hated that; his gum chewing was tolerated although Goodman hated that, too.[32] And Goodman gave Gene leeway in his playing (brushes versus sticks notwithstanding). It didn't hurt that Gene was probably as important to the success of the band as Benny was himself.

It shouldn't be assumed that Gene was an obnoxious guy who had Benny cowed because the drummer was a celebrity in his own right. In fact, Gene was the opposite of obnoxious. Testaments to his kind and caring nature are legion; everyone liked him.

Gently speaking, Benny's personality was impersonal; his handling of affairs with the Columbo band is but one example of his poor people skills. Tenor sax player Art Rollini's autobiography, *Thirty Years with the Big Bands*, described myriad instances of Benny's behavior, which appalled Rollini. Depending on the situation, Benny was "fickle," "inconsiderate," "thoughtless," or "tactless," but always the "best clarinet player in the world," which he most probably was.[33]

Benny was known for a look he gave on the bandstand called "The Ray." The Ray surfaced if he was disappointed with a sideman's performance. It terrified band members. Goodman's leadership was characterized, in part, by his callous firings.

Benny's biographer James Lincoln Collier described him as a "leader with an almost pathological insensitivity to the feelings of the men who worked for him." Collier quickly added that Benny could also be great company and very funny.[34] We will see a caring side of him later on, when Gene Krupa was experiencing the worst crisis of his life. And Benny had the highest opinion of Gene as a person and a musician.[35]

IN LOS ANGELES for the second time in less than a year, the band was ridiculously busy, playing the Palomar again; their other big job was filming *The Big Broadcast of 1937*, which starred, among others, Jack Benny, Burns and Allen, Martha Raye, and Ray

Milland. The band performed at the Palomar from 9 P.M. to 2 A.M. every day but Sunday. On Sundays, they played single dates around southern California. On weekdays, after a long night at the Palomar, they awoke early enough to be at Paramount Pictures in time for morning makeup and filming's start. "We were all pretty tired," said trumpeter Pee Wee Erwin, "and I could fall asleep sitting upright in a chair."

Classical conductor Leopold Stokowski, also in the film, "was fascinated by Gene Krupa" and in "seventh heaven" watching him perform, remembered Erwin. "I think he would have stolen Gene for his symphonic orchestra if he had any kind of an opportunity."[36]

Upon finishing the movie, the band recorded nearly a dozen sides, including the famed "Down South Camp Meetin'" and the Quartet's first waxing, "Moonglow." They also continued their Palomar engagement, where they commanded a fee three times greater than their fee of 1935. Excitement at the Palomar was at least as great. When the second floor show ended (which could be Muriel Gardner & Marvin Kane, "Dancers Extraordinary"; Joe Mole, "a loose nut on wheels"; or the Hudson-Metzger Girls, a dance troupe), Palomar patrons rushed the stage, jostling for the best position, in what looked like a "football riot." The ballroom was a main attraction for musicians, who had also flocked to the Congress Hotel in Chicago.

Tempo said Gene was "better than ever, if it is possible . . . bringing every number to a climax that brings cheers from the regular customers, [and] shrieks of sheer delight from the real Goodmaniacs." Rumors Gene would be forming his own band were unfounded, but would beset him and Goodman for the foreseeable future, a major indicator of how popular Krupa was by the middle of 1936—indeed, how popular he had been for some time.

The Big Broadcast of 1937, released that fall, featured the band's flaming-hot performance of "Bugle Call Rag." Gene's drumming and sheer presence captured the most footage—more than Goodman himself. Gene, white-suited behind his drums, banging out a ruckus of rim shots for the main refrain; mouthing along with the music; his face, emotional—near tears, perhaps; his eyes, seeing but not seeing, liquid, swimming from side to side. All of this was natural: Gene's duende in all of its glory.

Setting the Tone With Slingerland and Zildjian

The Slingerland Drum Company made Gene Krupa their first celebrity endorser in 1935. Gene became invaluable to Slingerland, dramatically escalating the company's sales. In recognition of his fame and usefulness they placed his picture on the cover of every Slingerland catalog from 1936 through 1967. Except for one unidentified individual in 1930, no one else's image had appeared on the catalog cover before or since. "Krupa almost single-handedly popularized the drum set as a solo instrument, and in the process brought recognition (and sales) to Slingerland,"[37] said Slingerland expert Rob Cook, adding, "It would be hard to overstate Krupa's importance not only to Slingerland, but to the development of Swing music, the drummer as a solo instrumentalist, and even the development of the drum set as we know it today."[38]

Gene's interest in simplifying while improving the drum set changed its standard components and certain aspects of those components for all time to come. He eschewed wood and temple blocks, bells, whistles, devices that imitated the calls of various animals and the noises emitted from trains, steamboats, and anvils, and other doodads he considered corny and unnecessary. He kept only the resonant cowbell, stripping the drum set's components down to less than a handful of drums. These were one snare, one bass drum, one rack tom-tom, and one floor tom-tom. For the Goodman Trio and Quartet recordings and performances, his drum set included one snare, one bass drum, two rack toms, and the cowbell. Gene chose the beautiful white marine pearl color for his drums, which made them stand out.

The biggest innovation to the drum set came with Gene's request to Slingerland's Sam Rowland for dual-tensioned, or fully tunable, tom-toms that could be tuned on the top and the bottom of the drum. Gene explained that fully tunable toms would "help him make the drum set into a solo instrument." Before Krupa, toms "had tacked heads and were considered more of a special effects-drum or novelty," said Rob Cook.[39] The drummer didn't have much control over the sounds they made. Gene began using his new drum set, with fully tunable toms, around September 1936.[40] Now he could experiment with the new toms' potentialities. The drum feature, "Sing, Sing, Sing (With a Swing)," would be one result.

Sam Rowland absconded to Ludwig, a Slingerland competitor, with his tunable tom knowledge, enabling Ludwig to use the innovation.[41] The tunable toms and all other aspects of Gene's drum set became the industry standard.

Over the years, Gene acted as a Slingerland consultant, "constantly" experimenting and advising Slingerland of the results. "I find out different things about the drums," said Gene. "Possibly a holder that would keep the bass drum from sliding, or . . . a tone control that would get a better sound from the drums . . . If it works out with me, then I give it to the factory."[42]

The look of the bass drum improved. As we've seen, Gene disliked the fanciful scenes dressing the front of the typical 1930s bass drum. The plain white front with Gene's initials inside a shield is the look that virtually all drummers used from then on.[43]

Gene's cymbals, from the Avedis Zildjian Company, tended to be a high-hat, a ride, and a large crash, with the addition later of a little splash. He became a Zildjian celebrity endorser. "Gene worked with my grandfather [Avedis] during the early years," said Craigie Zildjian, Executive Chair/President of the Avedis Zildjian Company. "Based on Gene's advice, Zildjian made our whole line of cymbals much thinner. Gene worked on the Splash, Crashes, Ride and Hi-Hats—basically every line we developed. Gene had a close personal relationship with both my grandfather Avedis and my father Armand."[44] A line of thinner cymbals, in particular, expanded the range of sounds one could extract from them. Gene's ideas ultimately benefited all drummers.

Gene's impact on the drums isn't an academic or theoretical notion, nor is it limited to one music genre. One only need look to the sets of Jackie Cooper (movie star and jazz drummer wannabe), Buddy Rich, Mel Lewis, Jake Hanna, Les DeMerle, Ed Thigpen

(Oscar Peterson Trio), Frankie Dunlop (Maynard Ferguson), Norm Jeffries (Les Brown), Elvin Jones, Ringo Starr (The Beatles), Joe Morello (Dave Brubeck), Mitch Mitchell (Jimi Hendrix), Charlie Watts (The Rolling Stones), John Densmore (The Doors), and Clyde Stubblefield (James Brown).[45]

Despite Sam Rowland's defection to Ludwig, that company struggled for years to compete with Slingerland, simply because Gene Krupa dominated the drum field. Everywhere William F. Ludwig II went, he was faced by life-sized Krupa standees. Drum dealers would ask Ludwig if he had any Krupa drums or sticks or brushes to sell. No matter how hard he tried, he couldn't draw Krupa away from Slingerland. "How I suffered," Ludwig lamented. He recalled that Slingerland spent the "bulk of their advertising budget on Krupa." Other Slingerland drummers were left with the crumbs.[46]

CHAPTER 8

"A Guy Named Krupa Plays the Drums Like Thunder"[1]

G ENE'S HORIZONS EXPANDED DURING THE rise of the Goodman band. Besides Moeller, Krupa studied under Billy Gladstone, percussionist for the Radio City Music Hall Symphony Orchestra; Harry Augustus Bower, classical percussionist and drum inventor; and Carlton Edward Gardner, one-time percussionist with the Boston Symphony Orchestra and writer of drum method books.[2]

Krupa gave lessons to less experienced jazz drummers like nineteen-year-old Maurice Purtill. Young Purtill had played with Charlie Barnet and Red Norvo but only made a favorable impression on writers like George Frazier and George T. Simon in mid-1936, after studying with Gene.[3]

Freely sharing tips on drumming well, Gene believed the drummer's mental state was key. He told Sam Rowland in 1936: "The truly great drummer must be emotional, so first, he must break down self-consciousness and eliminate top-hatted dignity." As self-consciousness shrinks, "self-control must be built up." It's also the drummer's job to "prevent listlessness" or "moodiness" in sidemen. Gene certainly adhered to these principles. He was never staid or afraid to show his true self. If necessary—and he must have thought it often necessary—he boosted the band's spirits.[4]

This advice presaged things he wrote in his drumming column, initially called "Drummers' Dope," which debuted in *Metronome* at the end of 1936, beginning the era of columns by star swingsters. Gene's writing evidenced a young man having the time of his life and offered insight into his outgoing personality. It was friendly and informal, filled with youthful enthusiasm and swingy phraseology. He offered tips on cymbal selection, maintaining the tempo on the bass drum, bass drum tuning, playing rim shots, ambidexterity in playing rolls, how (if you're right-handed) to make your left hand playing skills on par with your right. He advised discarding warped cymbals: "Unless it [the cymbal] contains a plethora of tonal quality within its innermost recesses (you cats didn't know I could write, did you!), it ain't just no good no moh', my frans!"[5]

Gene preferred his snare with lots of "ring": "It certainly sounds better to your audience out front." Rarely one to use derogatory language, he wrote, "Deadening the drum via some foreign application seems to be a sissy's way out of it, and I don't want to encourage any of you to be sissy drummers."[6] He observed that bandleaders tended to be "pro-brushes." They're "scared stiff that you'll make too much noise." Addressing this hang-up is something Gene faced with Benny Goodman. He wrote, mischievously, "You'll notice that they'll never tell you to pipe down when you have a pair of brushes in your hands . . . You can probably play twice as loud with brushes as you can with sticks before your leader will even begin to suspect."[7]

He announced that he was studying the piano, which he did to "learn more about music in general." He and his wife, Ethel, were "going at the keyboards zealously and jealously!"[8] Thus began a lifelong interest in the piano, which motivated him to learn classical piano pieces, just for fun, and afforded him insight into the vast world of classical music, of which he became a passionate proponent.

Praise for other drummers Krupa dished out liberally—for Ray Bauduc, Ray McKinley, Chick Webb, Jo Jones, Dave Tough, Zutty Singleton, his one-time student Maurice Purtill, and Lionel Hampton, the latter having subbed for Gene when Krupa reportedly had the flu in late 1936 and early 1937. (The likelier reason for Gene's absence was the death of his forty-year-old brother Leo from kidney disease on January 1, 1937.)

———————

HONORS FOR THE Goodman ensembles filled up a good portion of a *Metronome* evaluation of the year's "best" swing sides. "Swingtime in the Rockies," arranged by the inestimable Jimmy Mundy, was the "most sensational Goodman record and clarineting of the year, featuring astounding ensemble attack and Krupa drums."[9] Next to the forthcoming "Sing, Sing, Sing," it was probably the most ferociously swinging Goodman recording yet, giving Gene some of his best opportunities to show how he could rouse record listeners. "Benny and Gene propel each other rhythmically," said Loren Schoenberg, adding that the "little cymbal Krupa plays on the coda always delighted Benny when listening to this record."[10] This was a light, airy sound Gene produced by tapping the cymbal's dome. Hal Smith likened it to "a chime or a bell effect."[11] It was a clever way to bring the proceedings to a surprisingly gentle halt and as good an example as any of the originality and humor of Gene's drumming.

For a while, the Goodman band had chiefly been attracting college-age youth. One such youth was Jim Chapin, a freshman at Bard College in upstate New York. A friend had piqued his interest in the Goodman band. Over the 1936–1937 winter break, Chapin went to see the band at the Madhattan Room of the Hotel Pennsylvania, across the street from Pennsylvania Station.

"This marvelous, charismatic character was behind the drums. Gene Krupa," said Chapin. "Well, I used to go up behind the bandstand, and I would stand behind him and watch him." Chapin spent three or four nights a week admiring Krupa through January and February 1937. "That experience of hearing Gene Krupa playing in this band ruined me for any other kind of life but music," Chapin said. Finally, he asked Gene for drum lessons. By then, apparently, Gene was too busy to teach. "Kid," Gene said, "I don't teach." Krupa recommended Gus Moeller to Chapin, who took the advice. Eventually, Chapin became a well-known drummer[12] and authored several books touting the school of drumming known as "independence," which meant playing with all four limbs working independently of each other.[13]

———————

SOMETHING EXPLODED IN March 1937 with the Goodman band's run at New York's Paramount Theatre, where, from morning till night, Benny and the boys performed in between feature film screenings. Future drumming star and Krupa protégé "Sonny" Igoe was twelve years old in 1937 when he persuaded his parents to take him on a Sunday to see the band at the Paramount. "We were on line for three blocks," remembered Igoe. "It took hours and we finally made it into the theatre and we were probably in the last row and the last balcony up. I almost came out of my seat when I saw and heard the band and saw Gene Krupa."[14]

Tens of thousands of high school kids arrived long before the first showing of the movie, *Maid of Salem*, starring Claudette Colbert. They streamed out of subway stations, snaked around the block, impeded traffic. Inside, when the band, rising from a platform below, began its theme song, "Let's Dance," the pandemonium was deafening. All day every day, teenagers skipped school, packed the seats, screamed and cheered, jitterbugged in the aisles, and occasionally danced on the stage. They also bought a record-breaking amount of candy at the concession.

John Hammond noticed that the number of Goodman's African-American fans in any given Paramount audience had increased from the typical three percent elsewhere to fifteen percent—a growth of over 500 percent![15]

The Paramount, at 1501 Broadway in Times Square, wasn't a place one would have associated with hordes of noisy kids. It was among a number of movie theaters in New York "designed as treasure palaces, their interiors heaped high with exotic plaster riches."[16] What had drawn these acne-faced New York kids to the Paramount? What had caused such hysteria? Suggested Russ Connor: "The children of the Depression were full up with the monotony austerity had imposed upon them; they were desperate for something daring and different." Goodman at the Paramount also meant an affordable day for them—with not just movies and vaudeville acts, but the hottest swing band around.[17] Their truancy was something for school administrators to worry about and the Paramount management to be thankful for.

There was no coasting for this Goodman band. After playing all day and into the evening at the Paramount, they finished the night at the Madhattan Room. One night a week, they ran over to CBS studios for their weekly installment of the *Camel Caravan* radio program. Rehearsals abounded. It was nonstop playing for everyone in the band.

Now that swing was the province of college *and* high school students, it really broke open as a major phenomenon nationally. Benny and the boys were still at the top, and the top was getting higher. They faced hysterical fans everywhere. "High school boys and girls, with books and lunchboxes, stormed the theatre early," reported the *Boston Post* of the band's debut at the Metropolitan. "Their applause was simply titanic … [and] made the applause accorded to bands in the past sound like a baby's 'pattycake.'"[18]

Gene Krupa drew special attention. Art Rollini said Gene was the "idol" of girls waiting at the stage door, and he "signed many autographs. I never saw him with a girl. He loved Ethel, his wife."[19]

The Krupa fan frenzy portended frenzies to come, for Elvis, The Beatles. "Gene could hardly come out of a theater without a large escort," said Teddy Wilson, "because the fans would tear the clothing off his body, rip them apart for souvenirs, grasp at a button or whatever, and he was often literally in danger of being physically hurt by the adoration of his fans."[20]

Teddy Wilson wasn't just waxing strangely. *Caesar's Hour* remembered the Krupa mania of the late 1930s some seventeen years later in a brief sketch leading into a performance of a reconstituted Goodman band that included Gene. As band members "arrived," walking through Caesar's onstage crowd, Caesar stalwart Howard Morris yelled hysterically, "Hey! Hey, there's Gene Krupa!" As Gene appeared, he was thronged by "fans," who emerged from the fray, one by one, to share their Krupa loot with the audience. "Oh, boy! I got Gene Krupa's autograph!" "I got Gene Krupa's handkerchief!" "I got

Gene Krupa's tie!" Huge Sid Caesar surfaced, his arm around the much-shorter Gene's neck. "I've got Gene Krupa!" he exclaimed.[21]

Backstage privacy wasn't always possible. Gene, his clothing "stuck to him" from the extreme perspiration he generated during a performance, was undressing when several female fans walked in. "Go on, you," said Krupa. "Can't a man change his clothes around here?"[22] They left, supposedly "embarrassed," but it may have been just the encounter they'd wanted.

———————

GENE BECAME KNOWN for motivating untold numbers of boys to take up the drums. "It happened over and over and over again with little kids who wanted to be like Krupa," remarked Marshall Stearns, "they 'want to be a drummer when they grow up.'"[23] There were ads like Wurlitzer's in the *New York Daily News*. Boys were told that Wurlitzer would make it "surprisingly easy for embryo Gene Krupas" to learn the drums.[24] As Goodman sideman Jess Stacy remembered, "Youngsters wanting to be drummers hung around before and after sets and Gene was always nice to them, letting them sit at his drums and beat a little. They loved him."[25]

From mid-1936 onward, there had been talk of Gene Krupa leaving to form his own band. He denied the rumors and signed a new contract with Benny in the spring of 1937, becoming the highest-paid sideman in the business.[26] Frank Verniere, Gene's longtime Chicago friend, became his personal manager.[27]

By the summer of 1937, Gene was receiving almost as much media attention as Benny, if not more. Still only a sideman, his face adorned the cover of the August issues of *Tempo* and *Metronome*. He had claimed top honors as a drummer in the 1936 and 1937 *Metronome* and *Down Beat*[28] polls, and in early 1938 was named Musician of the Year by *Orchestra World*. His boss, Benny, reached number four in that category (although Goodman did win as best orchestra leader).[29]

As usual, the November 1, 1937, issue of *Life* magazine covered national and world events. A United Airlines "Mainliner" had crashed in Utah's Uinta Mountains, killing all nineteen passengers, including newsreel men making a movie called *The Safety of Trans-continental Flying*.[30] New York's Hayden Planetarium debuted its spectacular new exhibit, "What Will the End of the World Be Like?"[31] Photographic proof existed of the involvement of Fascist Italy's military in Spain's civil war.[32] Manhattan's Museum of Modern Art held its first-ever exhibition of the works of an African-American sculptor, William Edmondson.[33] In "The Yellow Race Looks at its Dead in War," Japan continued its advances in China.[34] Alfred Lunt and Lynn Fontanne, "the theatre's greatest married team," began off-Broadway tryouts for their new production, *Amphitryon 38*.[35] In *Life*'s regular photographic feature, "Life Goes to a Party," the subject this time was "Benny Goodman and His Swing Band" at the Hotel Pennsylvania's Madhattan Room. There were three pictures of Benny, one each of trumpeter Harry James (the band's newest star), Lionel Hampton, Teddy Wilson, and Harry Goodman, and *six* of Gene Krupa demonstrating various aspects of his duende.[36] Benny Goodman couldn't have been pleased.

During the summer of 1937, Benny and the band, plus the Quartet, contributed a couple of sensational performances in the Busby Berkeley–directed movie musical *Hollywood Hotel* (1938), starring Dick Powell. The Quartet number, "I've Got a Heartful of Music," showed all four members in the same white outfits accented by dark cravats, playing fiercely, swiftly, joyously, as equals. The African-American newspaper *The Pittsburgh Courier* reported that the Board of Censors of Memphis, Tennessee, had ordered the Quartet portion deleted from the film's local showings. The reason was that "there shall be no scenes portraying 'social equality' among the races..." It would disturb white people too much.[37]

Disturbing, perhaps, for Benny Goodman was Gene Krupa's screen time in the movie's band number, a short version of "Sing, Sing, Sing." Benny dominated, but the viewer's attention was centered on Gene (and Harry James) in mid-song, and only on Gene in latter moments, his hair flopping, sticks flying, arms seemingly commanding the drums from the air.

Gene's acclaim and the ear-piercing cheers for him got to Benny. "The harder Madman Gene Krupa banged with those drumsticks," declared the *Tribune* of Watertown, Massachusetts, "the harder that sea of humanity tapped and swayed and applauded."[38] Said Goodman, "There was always Gene and his 'showmanship' for the writers to talk about, even if they didn't have any idea of what a great drummer he was."[39]

According to John Hammond, Benny felt increasingly uncomfortable with the bestial nature of the crowds that the band's ferocity was feeding.[40] (Hammond may have been projecting on Benny his own feelings. In early 1937, he had moaned that Jimmy Mundy's "killer-diller" arrangements dampened the band's musicianship.[41]) Besides the frustrating amount of attention Gene had been attracting, his drumming was a central element in the band's aggressiveness. Yet Benny knew how important the drummer had been to his band's success. He gave tacit if not overt approval to Gene's drumming. Krupa brought other things to the organization. He approached Benny with concerns about how the band sounded, or what it was doing right or wrong. "You would've thought my band was *his* band the way he fussed over it," said Benny.[42] Goodman treated Krupa like his "number two" man, and not just salary-wise. The bandleader left Gene to rehearse the band when he was away.[43]

"The Little Giant of the Big Noise"[44]

African-American Baltimore native Chick Webb was born in 1905[45] and, as a young child, developed tuberculosis of the spine from a bacterial infection. This affliction led to a serious malformation of his spine and a noticeable hump on his back. He stopped growing at four feet tall. He lived with serious pain all his life, enduring surgeries and hospitalizations. Yet at some point, he discovered drums and, like Gene Krupa, got his first set at age eleven.[46]

In the early 1920s, Chick drummed for the Jazzeola Orchestra on excursion boats in Chesapeake Bay.[47] He went to New York City around age twenty with his good friend, guitarist John Trueheart. Amid periods of unemployment, they played at various Harlem venues, including Small's Paradise. An ally, Duke Ellington, secured Webb possibly his first major band job, one that Ellington had intended to book into the Black Bottom, another Harlem club. The band didn't have a leader; the other band members urged Chick to be that leader, although he was more interested then in just playing drums and participating in "cutting contests," or competitions between jazz musicians.[48]

As we've seen, soon after arriving in New York, Gene was smitten with Chick: galvanized, thrilled, inspired. He loved catching performances and sat in with Chick's band. He spent plenty of time in Harlem listening to other bands and drummers.

Another iteration of Webb's band became a fixture at the Savoy Ballroom. The Savoy opened in March 1926, stamping an enormous footprint in Harlem, occupying a whole city block between 140th and 141st Streets on Lenox Avenue. Advertising itself as the "World's Finest Ballroom," it pioneered racial integration in a public setting. The dance floor inside the two-story building measured over ten thousand square feet. There were two bandstands, which came in handy for the band battles that took place there.[49]

The relative lack of press interest in Chick Webb changed somewhat when Benny Goodman's band was booked into the Savoy opposite Chick's orchestra on May 11, 1937. It was billed as a "battle of the bands" and attracted a massive overflow crowd. Chick ought to have had the home court advantage; it appears that he did. An informal voice vote of dancers was taken that night and Webb's band received the greater ovation. But the acoustics at the ballroom were poor, which especially hurt the crowd's appreciation of Benny's Trio and Quartet.[50] Regardless of who "won," however, it would be a mistake to view the contest as a showdown between Gene Krupa and Chick Webb. It wasn't characterized that way at the time, and press coverage of the event carried no real comparisons of the drumming of each man. The contest was between the bands.[51]

Krupa himself may have been responsible for affording that night its legendary status as well as adding a new perspective: his own. He did this after Chick had died an untimely death at Johns Hopkins University Hospital in Baltimore from kidney and bladder disease on June 16, 1939. Chick's death came just as his band and his amazing singer, Ella Fitzgerald, were finally gaining traction not only outside of Harlem but outside of black venues outside of Harlem.

In homage to Chick and referring to the May 1937 Goodman-Webb battle, Gene wrote in his August 1939 *Metronome* column: "I know that it's a rather unoriginal thing to eulogize a man after he's gone, but, honest, I've never been cut by a better drummer than Chick Webb! I'll never forget that night—he just cut me to ribbons—made me feel awfully small . . ."

Gene said, "When he felt like it, he could cut down any of us, and he sure did a thorough job on me that night!"[52] A survey of Webb obituaries reveals no mention of the 1937 event, suggesting it was not on the music press's radar as it would be later, thanks to Gene.

Adding to the legend, in a 1941 column about his favorite drummers, Gene again referred to the Savoy contest, remarking, "I've never been cut by a better man."[53] In a 1943 *Down Beat* article about the best drummers of past and present, writer John Lucas praised Chick Webb but never mentioned the 1937 Savoy battle.[54] Gene did, though, a few months later in a *Metronome* piece about drummers. "Chick gassed me but good, on one occasion at the Savoy, in a battle with Benny's band," he said, "and I repeat now what I said then, I was never cut by a better man."[55] But Gene didn't say anything of the sort "then." His mistaken memory of the event in this 1943 piece further enlarges the legend. In a way, Gene helped keep the memory of Chick Webb alive.

Since then, in books and articles, that night at the Savoy is recounted as a milestone in jazz history, reframed as a tête-à-tête between the two drummers, Gene being soundly defeated in the contest. Details of the event are duly embellished. Interviews with some of the Savoy Ballroom dancers were included in an extensive look at the Savoy match by Ken Burns in his 2001 *Jazz* PBS series.

Looking again at Chick's tragic death, we'll see something else of what he meant to Gene. Early on the day before Webb's Baltimore funeral, Gene sat for hours next to Webb's casket, sobbing. The casket was on view at Webb's grandparents' home. Webb band member and multi-instrumentalist Garvin Bushell, who had earlier noted Gene's grieving presence by the casket, returned to see Gene still sitting there. "He stayed all day," said Bushell.[56]

Krupa was an honorary pallbearer at the funeral, along with Jimmie Lunceford, Cab Calloway, and Duke Ellington.[57] He was also one of only two white bandleaders to attend. (The other was Van Alexander, Chick's arranger prior to becoming a bandleader himself.)[58]

In the decades following Chick's death, just about every interview that Gene gave included an homage to him.

Small Ensembles Send Swing

Benny Goodman's biographer, James Lincoln Collier, said that "these first small groups were the model . . . for a great deal of jazz that followed, for they showed that there was a large audience in America for small band jazz."[59]

"Just listen to Armstrong and Ellington on down," Loren Schoenberg said. "All of them. You'll find nothing like this. And [today] it's become such a well-known idiom, this kind of thing . . . But who else is playing this in 1935? . . . Or '36, I should say."[60]

Leonard Feather said there had been small groups before, particularly in the 1920s. But the original Goodman Trio and Quartet were qualitatively different, and "brought new life" to the genre. The band-within-a-band concept had not been a phenomenon in the 1930s before Goodman. Following on Benny's heels were such groups as Tommy Dorsey's Clambake Seven, Bob Crosby's Bob Cats, Count Basie's Kansas City 6 and 7, Artie Shaw's Gramercy Five, Cab Calloway's The Cab Jivers, Woody Herman's Woodchoppers, Chick Webb's Little Chicks, and various Duke Ellington offshoots.[61]

Jazz writers of the time were aware of the specialness of Goodman's small groups. *Variety* pronounced the Trio's "After You've Gone" and "Body and Soul" "ultra-modern" works.[62] *Down Beat* observed that the Trio recordings of "Who?" and "Someday Sweetheart" contained "more original things . . . than can be described here."[63] At the end of 1936, Otis Ferguson said of a live performance of the Quartet: "This is really composition on the spot, with the spirit of jazz strongly over all of them but the iron laws of harmony and rhythm never lost sight of; and it is a collective thing, the most beautiful example of men working together to be seen in public today."[64]

In the twenty-first century, the original Goodman Trio's and Quartet's works are viewed as quintessential 1930s music. Ken Burns, in 2014, used their recordings to tell the story of America's most significant political family, the Roosevelts. The Quartet's "Runnin' Wild," which Gene thought showcased his best Quartet drumming, was used prominently in discussions about Eleanor Roosevelt.[65] The Trio's "Body and Soul" served as a backdrop to President Roosevelt's last year of life.[66]

Consider the effect of Goodman's original small groups on modern-day ears and music. In 2016, a Jazz at Lincoln Center event called "The Legacy of the Benny Goodman Quartet" celebrated an inimitable group in observance of its eightieth anniversary as a musical entity. Before the musical performances began at Lincoln Center, actor Wendell Pierce took the stage to recognize the "great impact" that the music of the Quartet had made on America. "Benny Goodman. Gene Krupa. Teddy Wilson. Lionel Hampton," he said. "No one could replicate their distinctive sound. You will have to hear that on your records, each one an intricate, miniature masterpiece of swing."[67]

The Quartet was unique—yes. But it and the Trio led to the formation of innumerable small groups, their influence still heard long after the decade of the 1930s. It changed how we hear jazz today.

Did Gene Krupa's Drumming Go Past the Speed Limit? Was the Drive Smooth and Even, or Bumpy? Also, Was the Drive Too Loud?

"It damn near paralyzed my left arm trying to hold his tempo down," said pianist Jess Stacy of keeping up with Gene.[68] Jazz drummer-historian John Petters asserted that, by the mid-1930s, "his speed [was] second to none."[69]

The live Goodman band version of "I Know That You Know" from early 1938 is frighteningly fast and much faster than the original. "That is a difficult tempo for anybody to keep up with," said drummer Hal Smith, "but he [Gene] did it and made it sound easy."[70] Was Gene forcing the band to play at such a rapid pace? It doesn't sound like it. "Get Happy" (1936) is a good example of a really rapid Goodman band studio recording, as is "Bugle Call Rag"—especially the version from the movie, *The Big Broadcast of 1937*. Numerous Trio and Quartet recordings run at quick tempos. Great examples are "I've Got a Heartful of Music," from *Hollywood Hotel*; and 1937's "Handful of Keys" and "I'm a Ding Dong Daddy (From Dumas)."

Still, Gene Krupa is often accused of "rushing" the tempo. One such accuser was John Hammond. Said D. Russell Connor, "Gene Krupa, stung by John Hammond's criticism that he varied the tempo on "Roll 'Em" [1937], timed the 78 [rpm record] with a metronome, [and] found John's tempo was awry, not his."[71]

Gene was not a sloppy drummer. He was an educated drummer who always strove to learn more from every possible teacher, and devoted himself to hours of daily practice. As we've seen, he *intentionally* (not inadvertently) sped up the tempo as far back as the early 1930s, in a conspiracy with pianist Joe Sullivan.

Loren Schoenberg made interesting observations on "rushing" in the context of the Goodman band and small groups, and not just concerning Gene Krupa. Schoenberg cited a *rubato*-like effect that the band achieved on "I Would Do Most Anything for You" (1936). This meant that "they're going a little ahead, they're going a little behind . . . and sometimes the rhythm section is involved in a shuffle . . . [but] the shuffle is between the precision of their quarter notes and the anticipations of the horn section."[72]

Schoenberg described the Quartet's performance of "Runnin' Wild" (1937) as Chaplin-esque. Like Charlie Chaplin, known in his movies for comically rounding a corner on one foot, thus momentarily accelerating his speed, the Quartet did likewise—musically. "They rush a little bit as they're going, but on purpose," he said.[73] On one take of the band's jumping "House Hop" (1936)

Gene is heard "in front of the band, just a hair, and he's pulling them along," said Schoenberg, "and it seems like Harry Goodman and [guitarist Allan] Reuss were kind of keeping up with him."[74] Maybe this is where Jess Stacy's left arm went numb. But these occurrences seem like intentional tempo speedups—in which Gene and some bandmates are in on the conspiracy. These tempo techniques may not always have worked perfectly, but the musicians, including Gene, were thinking and feeling as they played to get where they wanted to go.

"I know there are people who say that Krupa's time wasn't that great," said Dan Morgenstern. "I think that's a lot of bull ... It was his great time that got all the dancers out and that made him so popular during the Swing Era."[75]

GENE'S INSISTENCE ON making a drum set as important an instrument as any other in the band was his drumming philosophy. He once told *Orchestra World* that drums should be played to be heard. "If the drummer in the band has to be hushed, it's better not to have one," he declared. "Drums will always arouse most anyone, dancers or non-dancers."[76] John Hammond and Leonard Feather, as much as they admired Gene's talent, disagreed with the notion that drums were a solo instrument.[77]

Central to the idea of drums as a solo instrument, or an instrument treated equally to all other band instruments, was volume—that is, the volume of Gene's playing. It's generally agreed that Gene played louder—on the up-tempo numbers, at least—than did other big band drummers, with the possible exception of Chick Webb. Krupa's friend and Goodman bandmate Pee Wee Erwin knew of Gene's prodigious practicing schedule, especially in the Buddy Rogers days. "By this time all his practicing had developed so much strength that he was getting awfully heavy. But at the same time I must admit that he tempered this with very good taste ..."[78]

As we've seen, the Goodman band was a loud one. Saxist Babe Russin joined Benny in fall 1937. On his first night, he was so overwhelmed by the powerful attack of the trumpet section behind him that he thought he'd have to quit the band. Fortunately, he gave it a little more time and adjusted to the mighty trumpeting of James, Elman, and Griffin.[79]

Although he did have positive things to say about Gene Krupa, jazz critic Gunther Schuller's snobbishness emerged when it came to the taste of the masses. Krupa's "show-biz genius lay in the discovery that rhythm, reduced to its unsubtlest common denominator, has for a mass public a universal, primitive, irresistible gut-appeal," said Schuller. "There are always far too many people who are impressed by mere energy; and Krupa had plenty of that."[80]

Gene's volume differed in the studio versus live performance. Hearing his interactive—subtle, even—mode of playing with the band or small groups is delightful and instructive. Teddy Wilson, who played as closely with Krupa as anyone, said, "He played with a beautiful touch even when he was playing with plenty of volume. His drumming sounded equally well on recordings and in person, and I always found him a very inspiring musician."[81]

A drummer who relies on volume couldn't be nearly as interactive a player as was Gene. Jazz drummer Kevin Dorn said that, if someone else is soloing, Gene "is really changing things up so much, it's almost like he's playing a counter-line..." Gene could be "driving and aggressive" in the small groups, but then do the "opposite." "There are so many aspects to his playing," remarked Dorn. "That really interactive, constantly changing thing—I love hearing him do that."[82]

University of Massachusetts jazz and drumming Professor Theodore Dennis Brown noticed a Krupa solo during the Quartet version of "Liza" (1937) involving a "superimposition" of one kind of pulse over another, with accents switching between tom-toms and rim shots. Gene's playing tended to become "more complicated and energetic" near a song's close to "build a climax." This approach would become a "standard part of the drum solo," without which future audiences would be disappointed.[83] More important than an audience's expectations was Gene's ability to build things up, to insert stimulating changes to modify his approach as time passed. The volume might start low and rise over time. The playing might begin simply and become increasingly complicated, and, in all likelihood, louder.

Gene Krupa may have played loudly, which served his belief in the drums as a solo instrument. But he also was a dynamic, flexible, interactive, and imaginative drummer, one who should not be pegged as doing too much or too little of any particular thing.

CHAPTER 9

"Hey!"

Gene Krupa celebrated his twenty-ninth birthday on January 15, 1938. The band played "Happy Birthday" in his honor.[1] Benny Goodman wouldn't be twenty-nine for another five months. They were among the "old geezers," like fellow 1909-er Hymie Schertzer (lead alto sax player). Lionel Hampton turned thirty in April; the early thirties contingent included Benny's brother Harry, Jess Stacy, and Vernon Brown (trombone). Otherwise, for most of the remaining Goodmanites, including Harry James, Ziggy Elman, and Teddy Wilson, thirty was years off. This was a young aggregation.

"We had such a lively spirit, a brashness, a force, and determination," Benny Goodman said in 1978 about the band he presented at Carnegie Hall on January 16, 1938. "There's nothing like youth and brashness in a good player, you know. I've studied music a lot since then, and I'm sure I know more about it today. But that was a very special band and a remarkable group of musicians."[2]

Then, as always, Gene Krupa was a special asset to the band. "The thing about that concert is that, if it had been any drummer other than Gene I don't think it [the eventually-released recording] would have had the popularity that it had," said John Petters. "Because there is something about his playing, with the Goodman band in general, that in particular on that concert elevated it above the ordinary."[3]

The august structure called Carnegie Hall hosted its first live performance in 1891 with Tchaikovsky conducting. Its seven stories and imposing façade, of an "Italian Renaissance Revival Style" in reddish-brown brick, appear daunting now as it must have then.[4] The five-story Main Hall, where the Goodman Orchestra was to perform, offered numerous sections from which to enjoy a show, from the parquet up to the highest balconies.

History was being made in this historic structure on more than one count. It was not a stranger to jazz, but this would be the first *swing* concert at Carnegie Hall. Nevertheless, it traditionally served as a home to classical music and musicians. Audiences were not typically infiltrated by screaming teenagers.

Also historic were the racially integrated proceedings. There were the black and white Goodman Trio and Quartet, which had been featured with the orchestra for some time. Almost all of the special guests were African-Americans drawn from Duke Ellington's and Count Basie's groups, including Count Basie himself. From Ellington's orchestra were Johnny Hodges (soprano sax), Harry Carney (baritone sax), and "Cootie" Williams (trumpet). From Basie's, besides the bandleader, were Lester Young (tenor sax), Buck Clayton (trumpet), Walter Page (bass), and Freddie Green (guitar). The white guest was young cornetist Bobby Hackett. These invitees filled out smaller ensembles that also featured a few Goodman sidemen, including the most essential one, Gene Krupa. He drummed on every song that night.

The interracial nature of the night, much more substantial than the Goodman Trio and Quartet could claim, was, perhaps, a thumb in the eye of America's racial caste system. It was especially strong in the South, with its Jim Crow laws, to which the South still clung as tenaciously as ever. Congress remained unable or unwilling to address the lynching of black people in the South. A half-dozen Southern U.S. senators—representing Texas, Mississippi, Louisiana, Alabama, South Carolina, and Georgia—walked off the Senate floor when a colleague made a speech about the "gruesome . . . blow

torch lynchings" of African-Americans in Mississippi and the torture death of a black man in Florida.[5]

EVERYBODY WAS NERVOUS before the big show. Gene acknowledged, "Sure, I'm nervous! But gee! I always get nervous[;] every
time we change hotels I get nervous!"[6] He snuck onstage to retune
his tom-toms but couldn't escape watchful eyes. He received a huge
ovation before he could disappear backstage.[7] He, Teddy Wilson,
and Ellington's vocalist, Ivie Anderson, were treated to a tour of an
exclusive club usually reserved for "members of the Philharmonic
Symphony Society only," and were particularly impressed with the
portraits of Toscanini.[8]

There were several rows of *onstage* seats—late additions to accommodate the gigantic demand for tickets—plus a multitude of
standees at the back of the hall who paid to be uncomfortable. The
fashionable Dress Circle saw society women wearing white gloves,
holding lorgnettes to their eyes, and men in formal penguin gear.[9]
Musicians in radio were "out in force."[10] Radio "announcers and
production men" enjoyed the concert at CBS studios. This exclusive experience came courtesy of one stage microphone that, on
other nights, broadcast the New York Philharmonic.[11]

During the concert, if ovations "that whirlwinded through the
house—often in the middle of a selection—could be called applause,
then the Mississippi River is a rippling rill," said one witness.[12] During "Sing, Sing, Sing," "one kid after another commenced to create
a new dance trucking and shagging while sitting down," said
another.[13] "Near maniacs," said yet another, had a "stupid habit of
whistling and clapping vociferously" for every soloist. One killjoy
arose whenever the "near maniacs" began their vociferousness and
admonished, "Shut up, you punks!" "Shushing" was heard whenever audience noise picked up.[14]

REVIEWS OF THE event were plentiful. "Goodman's Vipers Slay the
Cats," trumpeted *Variety*.[15] "Goodman Jam Session Jams Carnegie

Hall," observed the *New York Daily News*.[16] "Benny and Cats Make Carnegie Debut Real Howling Success," said *Metronome*.[17]

Gene was singled out for a mention, whether good, bad, or snarky. "The drummer...did everything but skate on the ceiling," said the *New York World-Telegram*.[18] "Mr. Gene Krupa, the group's super-expert percussionist, whose gestures and facial expressions proved unusually engrossing for those near enough to note them in detail...suggested that he has talents as an actor as well as an instrumentalist," reported the *New York Herald Tribune*.[19] "Most notable was Gene Krupa's consistent performance throughout the evening, commanding a pivotal position around which the entire cast clung closely for rhythmic inspiration," said *Down Beat*.[20]

John Hammond, a Krupa ally except when he wasn't, protested that Gene "fell down badly" during the jam session (based on "Honeysuckle Rose"), which featured almost all of the guests, because, as Hammond saw it, Gene was trying to "dominate" his fellows, which ruined their solos. Hammond said it "pained" him to criticize Gene this way, because he thought Gene was the "most accomplished white drummer." There was "no one in the business with better technique or a more sincere love of music." But drums were not a solo instrument. Drummers should provide "an integrating force and a stimulus to soloists," he said, and no more.[21]

———————————

GENE'S THRILLING PERFORMANCE deserves illumination. The inaugural number, "Don't Be That Way," was the show's pacesetter. During live numbers, he often yelled things to buoy others. So it was with "Don't Be That Way." In its opening refrain, Gene, who may have been the most relaxed of anyone, spontaneously blurted, "Hey!" Several more of these happy blurts peppered the song. At his first opportunity, he let loose with an accented single-stroke roll—many of the accents ringing rim shots—earning the evening's first cheers, unwinding the band, and presaging drum breaks in a still-to-come genre known as rock and roll.

"You could play that today in a rock drum break," said jazz drummer Kevin Dorn. "It would work." Crescendo press rolls behind some of the soloists began quietly and ended as distant mortar fire. Another drum fill, which Dorn considered a "classic" Krupa expression heard throughout his career, he described as "playing the bass drum on one and three, and the snare drum and crashing a cymbal on two and four." Dorn called it "very primal" and portended a punk rock approach. If any Goodman sidemen needed more loosening up at song's end, Gene unleashed another drum break that, as Dorn noted, "kind of explodes," because Krupa started it "two beats earlier from where it should normally start," surprising everyone.[22]

Concert highlights abounded. The "Twenty Years of Jazz" segment paid tribute to the Original Dixieland Jazz Band, Bix Beiderbecke, Ted Lewis, and Louis Armstrong. For Gene, this was not an academic exercise, as it would be for drummers even slightly younger than he was. It was the music of his youth, much of which served him well in his Chicago jazz internship. He played convincingly all the way through, sometimes mixing in modern touches.

The jam session allowed Count Basie, some of his sidemen, and a few Ellingtonians to demonstrate their engaging, accomplished musicianship before new listeners. John Hammond's protestations to the contrary, Gene played supportively and deferentially and did not overwhelm the soloists.[23]

The remainder of the show's first half was also notable for some flaming Trio and Quartet work, but it was the second half that really raised the temperature, giving certain audience members excellent reasons for their reviled noisemaking. Benny's trumpet section blared plenty, beginning with "Blue Skies." Screaming the essence of the evening was "Swingtime in the Rockies," with Ziggy Elman's terrifying trumpet solo and Gene's fire-breathing drumming.

"Swingtime" was born as "Take It Easy." Jimmy Mundy had arranged it for Earl Hines several years earlier before Mundy brought it to Benny. There was nothing "easy" about the tune; it was renamed with a more apropos appellation. Its explosive ending at Carnegie Hall, Gene's drumming at peak energy, differed from the almost powder-puff finish of the Goodman studio version.

The Quartet returned for a trio of songs, the most exciting of which were "China Boy" and the new "Dizzy Spells," both run like races to an invisible finish line. Jon Hancock, Goodman Carnegie Hall concert historian, described Gene's playing toward the end of "China Boy": "He laid down a wonderful sizzling beat with his brushes and then suddenly, with what would appear to be an extra pair of arms, he added another layer and started picking out rhythms on the tom-toms too. On the recording, it sounds increasingly impossible with each listening."[24]

Typical of the Trio and Quartet numbers that night were Gene's calls to Benny or the others to "take one more!" During what Jon Hancock called Gene's "increasingly impossible" drumming toward the end of "China Boy," he emitted a long bellow that seemed to complement his playing: "Take one more, Benny-y-y-y-y-y-y-y!" Hancock observed that, purposely or inadvertently, Gene was taking charge of the small band performances,[25] a no-no with the leader standing right there. Gene's actions probably partly fueled the conflicts between Krupa and Goodman to come.

ALONG WITH "DON'T Be That Way," "Swingtime in the Rockies," and the climactic "Sing, Sing, Sing," "Bei Mir Bist Du Schön" stands out as one of the concert's major band highlights. The Goodman-Carnegie version is two-parted—the swing band first half, arranged by Jimmy Mundy with a vocal by Martha Tilton, and the klezmer second half, which belied its Jewish theatrical origins. The first half beckoned to jitterbuggers; the second to hora dancers. Gene introduced the second half with fiercely executed, genuine klezmer rhythmic patterns. These led into and supported Ziggy Elman's powerful trumpet showcase of nimble, "mordent-like"[26] up-down-up-down notes typical of Jewish music. Elman and Goodman's exciting interplay later, backed by Gene's crashing and thrashing and the band's buckled-floor underpinning, invoked the celebrations of Eastern European Jewry, the sounds of which Jews had brought with them when they emigrated to America over the decades.

The concert's highlight among highlights, the most famous Goodman song, and the one most associated with Gene Krupa long after he'd left Goodman, has been recognized as the first drum feature. The song was "Sing, Sing, Sing (With a Swing)." It was written by Louis Prima and recorded by his "New Orleans Gang" several years earlier. Prima's original recording may be described as "corny." It fluctuated between Dixieland, a limp approximation of swing, and pure pop, bearing little resemblance to the Goodman band's rendition.

Jimmy Mundy arranged Goodman's edition, which became the song's defining expression. In 1936, when the band first started performing it in public, Helen Ward sang Prima's lyrics. It continued this way for a while, although the words, despite the parenthetical in the song's title ("With a Swing"), harbored perhaps the least swing potential of any lyrics ever to find themselves in the Goodman band book.

How did things change? Gene Krupa provided the impetus for making much, much more out of it. It's arguable that he couldn't have done what he did without the fully tunable tom-toms, which Slingerland had introduced at his urging.

As Ward remembered, the scene was the summer of 1936 at Los Angeles's Palomar. The song ended at its usual three-minute mark, but Gene kept drumming. Benny started "noodling" along on his clarinet.[27] Goodman recalled something similar. "One night at the end of the number," Goodman said, "Gene Krupa started monkeying around on the drums and the spirit caught and the others came in on a minor key."[28]

Gene said his tom-tom introduction began as a four-bar solo. "I heard something in these first four bars, as well as in what the band did every time we played it," Gene remarked. "I'd say, 'Let me take eight instead of four,' and then sixteen instead of four."[29]

The band's live performances of "Sing, Sing, Sing" were receiving attention. An *Orchestra World* columnist awarded "pats on the back" "to the arranger of 'Sing, Sing, Sing' which the Goodman gang interprets with inimitable swing finesse; and to Krupa's tom-tom[m]ing on the skins."[30]

Helen Ward's vocal was dropped. As Gene thundered along, the saxophone, trombone, and trumpet players came up with different riffs, with new passage after new passage "tacked on" to the end of the tune.[31] There was a major insertion in the middle, a sped-up interpretation of a rather dark, march-like swing tune, "Christopher Columbus" (written by Chu Berry and arranged by Henderson), which the band had originally recorded—separately—in 1936. It's often erroneously assumed since then that this part was just another section of the song, although it was convincingly sucked into the "Sing, Sing, Sing" creative vortex.

Gene's primal tom-tom rhythm, which suggested Bo Diddley, opened the song and continued in varying ways throughout the 1937 studio version as well as the live Carnegie interpretation. "Gene Krupa, without a doubt, has a great sound with that kind of groove. That Gene Krupa tom-tom groove," said Kevin Dorn. "He had something special going on with that beat, and . . . if you hear later Benny Goodman bands—when they play 'Sing, Sing, Sing' . . . to me, it never sounds totally right without Gene Krupa."

Despite what may seem like a simple drum groove, Dorn said, it requires much more skill and inventiveness than one would think. "There's a lot of subtlety within that beat," said Dorn. "He's playing [some] pretty crazy sticking. Not very intuitive sticking . . .[32] It really works. It really just gets the sound." Dorn added, "He's not necessarily playing every single eighth note. He's leaving a couple out here and there . . . There's a lot of subtlety and things going on that are actually really, really hard to do . . ." Dorn pointed to the "depth" of what Gene played and the substantial "technique" necessary to carry off the number.[33]

At Carnegie Hall, the band and such soloists as Benny, Harry James, and Babe Russin wound through the different phases of the musical epic. One of the great high points of "Sing, Sing, Sing" came in the form of Jess Stacy's surprise piano solo. He incorporated classical and jazz passages, solemnity and merriment. Gene was heard to say that it was "like a symphony, man!"[34]

Krupa's ending of "Sing, Sing, Sing," at Carnegie, is one of the most thrilling endings in all of jazz. He signaled the conclusion with four pairs of simultaneous stick strikes on snare and rack-tom. These evoked the resonant crunch of mechanized modernity. Without pausing, three mighty rim shots segued into a shining four-beat cowbell phrase announcing the end. His hair-raising single-stroke roll in triplets,[35] uncaged as the band joined in for a last, raucous statement, suggested world turmoil to come.

People congratulated Ethel Krupa, who was in the audience, on her husband's performance.[36] Also there was Saul Goodman, tympanist with the New York Philharmonic. "There isn't a drummer I know that has the feeling for rhythm that Gene has," Goodman, who was no relation to Benny, said. "Even when he sets into a chorus cold, he seems to have some subconscious idea of a pattern that is perfect for what he's playing."[37]

Another compliment came from Indian percussionist Vishnudas Shirali. Gene had been eagerly watching Shirali play a conglomeration of twelve drums in rehearsals at Carnegie Hall for the Uday Shankar Ballet Troupe. Krupa also sat in. Shirali and the Shankar aggregation were set to play at Carnegie the night following the Goodman event.[38]

Shirali attended the Goodman concert. "The man has a genius for rhythm," he said of Gene. "I am amazed to find that he makes almost a melodic instrument out of the drums. His variations are so intricate that they seem to have an absolute melodic line."[39]

In his *Metronome* column following the show, Gene gushed, "Benny and the boys sent me more than they did anybody in the whole room. I've never heard them cut loose the way they did. I've never heard them play everything so perfectly."[40]

The Cultural Impact of "Sing, Sing, Sing"

New Yorker Ed Bonoff started jazz drumming as a boy because of "Sing, Sing, Sing," a new record at the time. "That pushed me off," said Bonoff. "There's so many like me that were affected by that." Bonoff so loved Gene's tom-toms on the song that when he took drum lessons, he only wanted to play the toms; it took some persuading for him to try the snare first. Bonoff and his friends were so bitten by the Krupa bug they all tried to make their drum kits look like Gene's, with initials on the bass drum the crowning touch.[41]

At the end of 1937, *Down Beat* conducted a poll showing that musicians' favorite arrangement of the year was Mundy's "Sing, Sing, Sing."[42] The song was also number six on *Metronome*'s "best records of 1937."[43] That was just the beginning. It was inducted into the Grammy Hall of Fame in 1982. That, too, was just the tip of the iceberg.

Glenn Miller's "In the Mood" notwithstanding, Goodman's "Sing, Sing, Sing" is the recording most associated with the Swing Era. As I write this, "Sing, Sing, Sing" is everywhere.

"The music is so inbred in us that we can't escape it," remarked rockabilly-swing guitarist Brian Setzer, who gained fame as the leader of the Stray Cats in the early 1980s. "Sometimes it goes under the surface but it never disappears." Setzer cited Gene Krupa, Count Basie, and Bobby Darin as his chief influences.[44]

Given the number of movies, TV shows, and commercials that have featured "Sing, Sing, Sing" or a reasonable facsimile thereof, said jazz writer Mike Zirpolo, the song "has become a part of the fabric of American culture."[45] Gene's drumming is the linchpin of "Sing, Sing, Sing" and its continued popularity, regardless of changes in American popular music.

Its hold on American culture began before "Sing, Sing, Sing" was released as a single. See the Fred Astaire movie, *A Damsel in Distress*, which opened theatrically in November 1937. It features a "Drum Dance" as part of Gershwin's "Nice Work if You Can Get It." Astaire's routine incorporates a collection of drums, including tom-toms, which he plays with his feet. This film sequence is recognized as an homage to Gene Krupa's drumming in "Sing, Sing, Sing."[46]

How was this tribute possible with the movie released in November, which probably meant filming over the summer, or earlier? The "Sing, Sing, Sing" two-sided, twelve-inch single wasn't released until early fall as part of a four-record set called *A Symposium of Swing*. Fats Waller, Tommy Dorsey, and Bunny Berigan shared space with Benny.[47] The single wasn't released by itself until the end of 1937 as an edited, two-sided ten-inch.

Fred Astaire was a Krupa fan. He had likely heard some of the Goodman broadcasts that included "Sing, Sing, Sing" prior to its studio recording. He may have visited the set of *Hollywood Hotel* in Los Angeles over the summer to see Goodman's group filming a truncated version of the song. More than certain are the noticeably Krupa-esque features of Astaire's "Drum Dance" in *A Damsel in Distress*.

Since "Sing, Sing, Sing" made its mark on the listening public, bandleaders were "looking around for something good for a drummer to do as a solo in a band," said Johnny Blowers, then drumming for Bunny Berigan.[48]

In response to "Sing, Sing, Sing," Chick Webb was inspired to record a couple of drum features, something he was not known for doing in the studio: "Harlem Conga," recorded in November 1937, and "Liza," recorded in May 1938.[49]

Cliff Leeman, then drumming for Artie Shaw, said the tom-toms in "Sing, Sing, Sing" motivated Shaw to use them during the choruses of at least a few band recordings. Leeman's job was to make this happen, although he used one Chinese tom instead of the modern, fully tunable toms Gene had innovated. Some of the famous Shaw records incorporating this approach include "Begin the Beguine," "Back Bay Shuffle," and "Indian Love Call."[50]

In June 1938, Chauncey Morehouse, one of the late 1920s New York drummers whom Gene Krupa had skipped over during his early '30s rise, introduced a percussion instrument he called N'Goma drums. Their use recalling African rhythms, N'Goma drums were a large battery of variously sized tympani. Morehouse played them on his 78-rpm single, "Plastered in Paris,"[51] reminiscent of Krupa's playing in general, and "Koo-Lai-Ay," which Morehouse debuted in a film short that was more than redolent of "Sing, Sing, Sing." The arrangement for Leith Stevens's band, which backed Morehouse in this performance, recalled the Goodman recording.

As Mike Zirpolo said, with Gene Krupa's tom-toms prominent in the mix, "Sing, Sing, Sing" has been featured or evoked in numerous TV commercials. A few are: Chips Ahoy! (1993); General Electric (2011); Knorr stocks (UK, 2018); the Toyota Corolla hybrid (UK, 2019); the City of Wilmington, Delaware (2020); Turner Classic Movies Wine Club (2020–2021); the Nissan Altima (2021); Boar's Head (2023); Ancestry.com (2023); and Yuengling beer (2023).

One commercial for a line of Spalding golf clubs caused litigation because the ad agency used music evoking "Sing, Sing, Sing," while flashing the phrase "swing, swing, swing" as golfers swung Spalding clubs.[52]

"Sing, Sing, Sing" is heard in at least two video games (*Mafia II* [2010] and *L.A. Noire* [2011]) and appeared in three Broadway productions (*Dancin'* [1978], *Fosse* [1999], and *Contact* [2000]).

It's been used, covered, or mimicked in many TV series, drumming almost always leading the way. The first show to employ or evoke it was probably *M*A*S*H* in 1973. Krupa fan Gary Burghoff (Radar on the show) played marvelously Krupa-esque drums in tribute to Gene on season one's last episode, "Showtime." (Later, Burghoff recorded "Sing, Sing, Sing" with his Mardi Gras Celebration Jazz Band on the album *Just for Fun*.)

Other TV shows somehow showcasing the song include *Golden Girls* (1987, "One for the Money"), *Ken Burns: Baseball* (1994, "Sixth Inning"), *The X-Files* (1998, "The Triangle"), *Everybody Loves Raymond* (1999, "Dancing with Debra"), *The Simpsons* (1994, "Lady Bouvier's Lover"; 1999, "Make Room for Lisa"; and 2009, "Coming to Homerica"), *Third Rock from the Sun* (2000, "Shall We Dick"), *The Sopranos* (2007, "Remember When"), *Ken Burns: The Roosevelts—An Intimate History* (2014, "A Strong and Active Faith"), *NCIS* (2019, "Musical Chairs"), *Power Trip: The Story of Energy* (2020, "War"), *Penny Dreadful: City of Angels* (2020, "Sing Sing Sing"), *A League of Their Own* (2022, "Batter Up"), and *Murdoch Mysteries* (2023, "The Long Goodbye Part 1").

It's been a favorite recording to include, cover, or imitate in movies. Besides Astaire's *Damsel in Distress*, in *Strike Up the Band* (1940) the indomitable Mickey Rooney plays a drummer evoking Gene in style and mannerisms. A movie highlight is "Drummer Boy," a Krupa band hit, in which Rooney is accompanied by film studio orchestration suggestive of "Sing, Sing, Sing."

An unusual use of "Sing, Sing, Sing" transpired in the making of George Lucas's *Star Wars* (1977). The cantina scene, in which actors in alien costumes perform a swing-like tune for intergalactic bar patrons, wouldn't have worked out well without Lucas's insistence on playing the original Goodman recording of "Sing, Sing, Sing" during filming "to get the tempo and movements right for the actors." Composer John Williams remembered that "Sing, Sing, Sing" "gave [the director] rhythmic continuity shot to shot, cut to cut."[53] The song was not heard in the movie, however.

Other movies employing or evoking the song are *Big Business* (1988), *Manhattan Murder Mystery* (1993), *Swing Kids* (1993), *Deconstructing Harry* (1997), *Pollock* (2000), *The Wedding Ringer* (2015), *Florence Foster Jenkins* (2016), and *Finch* (2021). *The Artist* (2011) paid homage to "Sing, Sing, Sing" in a trailer, "Peppy & George," with Krupa-style toms, clarinet, and blaring trumpets.

There was the Richard Linklater–directed, *Me and Orson Welles* (2009). Based on a 2003 novel, the film recounts the experiences of a Brooklyn high school boy, Richard Samuels (Zac Efron), auditioning for and securing a bit part in Welles's 1937 Broadway production of *Julius Caesar*. In his audition, Samuels had to demonstrate his drumming chops. Standing among the actors who waited outside the theater for Welles, Samuels played on a snare and declared to anyone listening, "I'm Gene Krupa!" In 1937, it wouldn't have been at all strange for a young drummer to do that. All the young drummers wanted to be Gene Krupa.

More important was the Goodman-and-Krupa-heavy score. Besides the original Goodman recordings of "This Year's Kisses" and "In a Sentimental Mood," plus "Sing, Sing, Sing," there was a new composition, "Ode to Krupa," written by Michael J. McEvoy, composer and musician on the soundtrack.

The scene in which "Ode to Krupa" is heard sees Samuels late for rehearsal; he and his girlfriend run through a museum; then he races through the theater's lower recesses before belatedly arriving. "I was imagining Gene Krupa playing drums on the track," said McEvoy. "And the drummer who I used . . . [from UK band James Langston and His Solid Senders] had an authentic Slingerland kit, the drums, worn skins, everything." "Ode to Krupa" is almost all drums—and quite toms-heavy—except for some big band flavor that is quite suggestive of that elephant in the room, "Sing, Sing, Sing."

Gene is present in the movie in a way that musicians in soundtracks usually aren't. "Gene Krupa as a drummer, and his work as a personality, as a figure," said McEvoy, "summed up the kind of positive, 'let's go get it, make it happen,' kind of energy, which really felt good in the film."[54]

The Long Reach of Krupa's Drumsticks

"It should be remembered that the popularity of Gene Krupa pervaded jazz drumming in the thirties and, as a result, few drummers were left uninfluenced by his playing," said drumming historian Theodore Dennis Brown.[55]

Being a drummer in the Krupa era wasn't easy if you were of a different drumming mindset. Cab Calloway's drummer Leroy Maxey was one such individual. His forte was show drumming. As bassist Milt Hinton, in Calloway's band at the time, explained, "Every time a chorus girl kicked her legs up he had that cymbal right there. He emphasized every anticipation that a dancer could do . . . But before Gene Krupa there were no drum solos. There was just play for the band."

"Then came along Gene Krupa with the drum solos, and Cab . . . said, 'Maxey, play drum solos.' Well, he . . . hadn't played any, so when he gave him sixteen bars he really didn't know what to do with it. And, naturally, Cab, I believe, wanted to go along with the times."[56]

Late fall 1938 saw the end of Maxey's career with Calloway. He was replaced by "Cozy" Cole, a veteran of Jelly Roll Morton, Blanche Calloway, Benny Carter, Willie Bryant, and, most recently, "Stuff" Smith. Hinton considered Cole a "great soloist," and Cab must have agreed. An entertaining performer who played in a crisply articulated manner, Cole was an admirer of Gene Krupa's and played within the Krupa mold. Some of Cozy's most notable

Calloway recordings, like "Ratamacue" and "Paradiddle," were based on drum rudiments. Gene and Cozy were two close friends devoted to continued drum study, which would come in handy when they opened a Manhattan drum school in 1954, as we will see.

CHAPTER 10

"I'm Givin' You Air"[1]

THE KRUPAS HAD TOURED TOGETHER—been together continuously—through the uncertain pre-Goodman years and the explosive swing-mania years.[2] The drummer, reported *Tempo* in October 1937, would likely leave Benny Goodman when his contract expired and settle in California with Ethel: "Mrs. K. is tired of traveling and would like to homestead here."[3] Settling down may have been on Ethel's mind, but definitely not on Gene's. This was likely an increasing source of friction between them as time passed.

Gene couldn't ignore the "sales talks all the various agencies gave me," he said of their aggressive drive to make him a bandleader. "They showed me big fat contracts and everything."[4] Going out on his own was overdue given his fame and achievements as a mere sideman. He'd always wanted his own band. Serving as Benny's "concertmaster" confirmed his ambition to seek more—more money, more drumming, more artistic freedom in general.[5]

The last weeks of Gene's tenure with Goodman weren't fun. The unpleasantness, for Benny, may have been kicked off by Gene's untempered duende at Carnegie Hall. That wasn't all. Benny might think that he'd just played an amazing solo while Gene got all of the plaudits—although this was nothing new. According to Helen

Ward, Gene detested Benny's practice, which he considered ineffec-
tual, of "waving around his bent index finger" to start a tempo. She
said Benny and Gene also had differences over tempo; to Gene,
Benny's kickoff might be too slow or too fast, while Krupa "would
try to settle into whatever the time was actually supposed to be."[6]
As we have seen, tempo differences within the band could be intentional or unplanned, natural or conspiratorial.

Goodman may have had a change of heart concerning the direction of the band, according to John Hammond. The bandleader's
preference for a softer, subtler swing that would invite attentiveness
from an audience rather than hysteria, Hammond said, got in the
way of Gene's desire to fulfill the desires of the audience.

"Benny didn't like all the crazy antics and the sensationalism that
he felt were overshadowing the real music," said Lionel Hampton.
"Gene thought the craziness was just basic showmanship. Although
I tended to agree with Gene, I stayed out of it."[7]

The clarinetist's aim, unpropitiously timed given the theatrical
tour that lay ahead, was to, in effect, tamp down Gene's duende.
Hammond said that trying to comply with Benny's wishes led to
some "harrowing experiences" for Gene; his boss wanted one thing
and the crowds wanted another.[8]

Art Rollini recalled that Benny began giving Gene's bass drum,
which could be overpowering, "The Ray."[9] While at Philadelphia's
Earle Theatre in February 1938, Krupa was a "very subdued
drummer boy," reported *Billboard*. "Despite the cries from the hip-
cats of 'we want Krupa,' he refused to get to his usual hot self,"[10]
quietly pointing in Benny's direction as if to say, *He won't let me,
kids.*[11] "The feud between them really got hot and heavy," remembered Hamp. "They were going at it right on stage."[12] It took a lot
to anger even-tempered Gene.

One night that week, "Gene couldn't stand it any longer," said
Art Rollini. "Finally, on stage, in full hearing range of all of us, Gene
(who rarely swore) flared up and blurted, 'Eat some shit, Pops!'"
Rollini remembered Gene in his dressing room tearing up his
Goodman contract.[13] Krupa's last day with Goodman was March
3, 1938. Benny didn't try to enforce the contract against him.

On an emergent basis, Hamp moved from his Quartet vibraphone to the drumming chair. Eventually, Benny settled on Dave
Tough, Gene's old Chicagoan friend. Dave, observed *Radio Mirror*,
was "an excellent musician, but hardly known as the Dizzy Dean
of the drums."[14] Tough didn't suit Benny, who kept him for only
a few months. The Goodman drum chair was never stable after
Gene left. Even the hugely admired African-American drummer
"Big Sid" Catlett didn't last long under Benny's judgmental glare.

———————

IN HAMMOND'S ENCOMIUM to Gene upon his departure, the
commentator-impresario wrote admiringly of Krupa's drumming
ability and his dedication to practice, teaching, and learning. Hammond also cited Gene's importance in the Goodman band's
success.[15] But Hammond was no innocent bystander in the Krupa-
Goodman controversy. Irving Kolodin, best known as a historian
of the Metropolitan Opera, was also a jazz fan and coauthor of
Goodman's 1939 autobiography, accused Hammond of causing the
Goodman-Krupa breakup in a piece responding to a 1942 Hammond lamentation over the quality of Goodman's then band. "John
himself was a monumental factor in Benny's alteration of attitude
toward Gene," said Kolodin. Although the "break would have come
eventually . . . fuel was added to the fire by the line that John took
in making Benny super-conscious" of what Hammond considered
Gene's faults.[16]

However Gene and Benny felt about each other personally, publicly they were cordial. Just over two months following Gene's
angry resignation from Benny's band, and after Gene's eventful
band debut, he invited the Goodmanites to attend his new orchestra's appearance at Philadelphia's Arcadia Ballroom. Gene
"warmly welcomed" Goodman, who took the microphone to wish
his former drummer the best, after which the two "retired . . . to
the bar" for a private chat. Two days later, the bands squared off
to play softball; Benny's boys defeated Gene's embarrassingly by
a score of nineteen to seven. Despite the loss, all was now well in
swingdom.[17]

FOR GENE TO go out on his own required quite a bit of preplanning, which he couldn't have done in the six weeks that elapsed between leaving Goodman and debuting his new band. You have to sense when the time is "ripe" for the public to accept your band, said Gene a couple of years later, although you may jump in too early or too late.

"It's a lot of work and a prolonged headache both in forming a new band and keeping it in operation," Gene acknowledged. "The main requisite of a new band, just like any other business, is money." His financial backers were manager Arthur Michaud and Michaud's attorney. They loaned him $7,000—average, he thought, for a band start-up. He paid off the loan in a short time. Initially, he needed money for "arrangements, rehearsal halls, rehearsal salaries, uniforms, music stands, [and] the expense of traveling around auditioning and gathering men." But "the expenses keep mounting," Gene said, which will be a problem if you can't secure "lucrative dates right off." He was fortunate that "there was a demand for the band immediately."[18] Now all he had to do was please fans and keep the band at a musically high level.

Gunther Schuller, usually critical of Krupa, decades later favorably described his new band: "Performance standards were high . . . [its] musicianship was generally excellent, and . . . [it] maintained a fine roster of jazz soloists."[19]

"All of Gene's bands, from day one, were extremely well-rehearsed," said jazz drummer and Krupa biographer Bruce Klauber. "Beautiful section work, solos, attention to dynamics, etc. As a precision crew, it rivaled Goodman's. To Gene's credit, he got what he wanted out of his men in a manner entirely different from Benny's."[20] Jazz drummer Les DeMerle's sentiments were similar. "His bands were always tight," he said, "with a lot of detail to every arrangement, and dynamics and little stop-time things . . . Gene Krupa was a genius."[21]

After quitting Benny's band on March 3, the rest of March saw Gene finish hiring musicians for *his* band, which he had begun before leaving Benny. Among the new sidemen were two friends from Gene's Chicago days, Ray Biondi on guitar and Floyd O'Brien on trombone. Tenor saxman Vido Musso, once with Goodman, signed on; upon his departure after a few months, he was replaced by Sam Donahue, whose solos and arrangements were welcome. The sound of new clarinetist Sam Musiker was reliably flexible but lighter than Goodman's. Also coming aboard was pianist Milt Raskin. His style recalled Teddy Wilson and Jess Stacy. Gene signed several musicians from Ben Young's group, including "hot" trumpeter Dave Schultze. Nate Kazebier, a swingingly laid-back trumpeter and Gene's friend from the early Goodman days, eventually joined the roster.

Gene chose several African-American arrangers to help shape his sound, including, especially early on, "Chappie" Willet and Jimmy Mundy, the latter of whom had given Benny Goodman some of his band's most exciting charts. Other black arrangers for Krupa in the late '30s and early '40s included Fred Norman, Benny Carter, and Elton Hill, the latter especially providing some of Gene's richest arrangements.

As we have seen, among Gene's biggest influences, in Chicago and New York, were black drummers. "My first major success in New York had *everything* to do with the Chicago drum style," said Gene. "Unlike the New Yorkers, we Chicagoans were raw . . . on the black side."[22] Given the African-American influence on Gene's drumming, he naturally wanted a "black" orchestra sound to distinguish his from other white orchestras and give him a recognizable cachet. "Arrangements by Mundy and Chappie Willet . . . helped us achieve identity," said Gene. "People said they could tell it was the Krupa band on the radio."[23]

As musicologist John Wriggle said, "For Krupa, commissions from black arrangers like Mundy and Willet (and later Fred Norman and Elton Hill) and performance of repertoire associated with black orchestras . . . may have offered a competitive identity." This identity would have been consistent with Gene's progressive racial beliefs and actions, which would become even more apparent in the 1940s and served as an "indicator of personal integrity but also of musical authenticity."[24]

Chappie Willet, a native south Philadelphian, studied piano and composition in college. He eventually moved to Harlem, founding what would become a humming business, the Broadway Music Clinic. Over time, the Clinic offered services in not just arranging, but recording, talent management, and music publishing.[25] Gene was Willet's first white client.[26]

Atlantic City's Steel Pier was the setting for the Krupa band's inaugural performance on Easter Sunday, April 16, 1938, before a youthful, shrieking crowd of five thousand. *Metronome* writer George T. Simon lauded almost everything about the new band and noticed the displays of youthful exuberance in the audience: "Throughout the evening the kids and kittens shagged, trucked, jumped up and down and down and up, and often yelled and screamed at the series of solid killer-dillers that burst forth from the instruments of the Men of Krupa."[27] A *Tempo* reviewer marveled that the Krupa opening was "probably the wildest ovation ever accorded the initial appearance of a new band."[28]

Gene's choice of a long-term female vocalist was initially uncertain. Although Jerry Kruger sang at the Steel Pier and on gigs that followed, and recorded one ballad with Gene's band the following month, her stay was otherwise abbreviated. In the couple of days leading up to the Steel Pier, the band's female vocalist on its first recording date was none other than Helen Ward, the great Goodman singer who had left at the end of 1936 to start a family. But here she was, singing on the Krupa sides "One More Dream" and "Feelin' High and Happy." Since this session was all that Helen did with Gene's new band, it's a mystery why she was there to begin with. Had Gene been hoping to coax her into joining? Since 1936, Helen had done only sporadic work. Maybe she wasn't ready to be someone's full-time singer again.

It's surprising that Gene's band was as productive on the session as it was, with superb instrumentals in addition to the two Ward sides, since Krupa and Ward "spent a good deal of the studio time recalling what happened to us on this, that, and the other calamity which took place regularly in the early days."[29] Irene Daye, seemingly influenced by Ward, soon filled the female singer void.

Besides Jerry Kruger, the other Krupa vocalist unveiled at the Steel Pier was African-American singer, multi-instrumentalist, and highly eccentric personality Leo Watson. Like white comic actor and movie star Joe E. Brown, Watson had one of the largest mouths ever seen onstage, but may have only revealed this fact as the spirit moved him, unlike Brown, whose gigantic mouth was his stock-in-trade.

The spirit moving him may have begun with his membership in the Spirits of Rhythm, a popular act on Manhattan's Fifty-Second Street. Gene first saw Leo pre-Spirits in Ben Bernie's Sepia Nephews at the Hotel Sherman in Chicago. Krupa sat in with the Spirits or the Nephews, as applicable, whenever their paths crossed.[30]

"It was unusual, at that time, to have people like that," said Dan Morgenstern of a white bandleader taking on a black singer of such strange stripes.[31]

Gene considered Watson the "first of the modern scat singers, and ... one of the best, too."[32] Watson's approach was called "stream of consciousness"[33] or a spontaneous spewing forth of a "combination of words and meaningless syllables fitted to intensely rhythmic phrases."[34] However he came across, Watson was a novel force in jazz history who contributed to the Krupa oeuvre by vocally splattering his way through such Krupa sides as "Tutti Frutti" and "Nagasaki." Onstage with the band, Leo was known to do the same with, of all things, "The Midnight Ride of Paul Revere." "What a wild cat!" said Gene.[35] After eight months, Leo returned to New York and the Spirits of Rhythm.

Chappie Willet handed arrangements for the same songs to Gene, Louis Armstrong, and the Mills Blue Rhythm Band, with some variations. These were a compelling blend of European classical music and jazz. Frequent traits in these arrangements were ragtime effects like a "syncopated 'walking' bass line scored for brass or low saxes," a "sax section trill," and the piano "chime."[36] Some or all of them appeared in Willet's charts.

Each band—Armstrong's, Mills Blue Rhythm, and Krupa's—interpreted the same songs differently, despite the nearly identical charts they used. One distinguishing quality for Gene was his use of drums. Also unique to his band was the assignment to each sideman of a small tom-tom attached to his music stand. Whether they knew drums or not, Gene taught his sidemen enough fundamentals to pound the toms as instructed on certain songs,[37] which often were the Willet-arranged numbers.

The Willet-arranged "Blue Rhythm Fantasy" was played live by the Krupa crew for almost two years before they recorded it on two sides, unlike versions by other bands. Two parts were needed to give voice to extensive drum passages. The band's toms were used to dramatic effect, with Gene's drums, accented by cymbal crashes as the beat edged toward a crescendo, moving as a cross-current of turbulent energy over his sidemen's beats in this near-symphonic recording. Gene's rendition relied much more on his study of African tribal drumming for the overall sound than on Willet's arrangement. His obsession with the percussion of the Belgian Congo,[38] memorialized in recordings made during the 1935 Denis-Roosevelt expedition, had paid off. "Jungle Madness" (1939) is another Willet chart to which Gene added Congo-flavored drums. Where the Mills Blue Rhythm Band featured piano, Gene's tom-toms dominated in the extra-hot Krupa band version.

Another example of Willet's work was the almost Disney-esque interpretation of "Grandfather's Clock," Gene's first single. This recording was made as big bands dipped into the well of children's nursery rhymes for fun, light pieces.[39] "Clock" showcased Gene's clever use of every part of the drum kit to evoke sounds of clock machinery.

The side's commercialism, which demonstrates his "playful side," said Kevin Dorn, also shows musicianly "depth." One solo involves just cymbals. "His breaks," said Kevin, "work beautifully and the subtlety is what makes those breaks so great."[40] Gene showed restraint for those who thought he was just a grandstander.

———————

GENE WAS ASKING a $600 minimum for one-nighters[41] and $5,000 on a weekly basis. The latter was "plenty for an established ork," reported *Billboard*, "but for a new and practically untried outfit it's phenomenal."[42] Months later, Gene's asking price leveled out.

Money was rolling in. Gene Krupa bought a new "cream-colored" Packard. On tour, he traveled with Ethel and their mischievous Scottish terrier Napoleon, who enjoyed chewing mutes.[43]

It wasn't all polished drumsticks and shiny snares for Gene's new band. Arthur Michaud, Gene's manager, instituted a policy applied also to Bunny Berigan and Tommy Dorsey, wherein a promoter or theater was guaranteed a refund if a date wasn't "profitable." Michaud said his bands could "maintain top prices" and operators would be shielded from a "licking" because of "adverse local conditions."[44] Berigan believed this policy encouraged venue owners to underreport attendance numbers[45]; it may have adversely affected Gene, too.

Cries of "We want Krupa!" filled New York City's windswept Randall's Island Stadium on May 29, 1938, toward the end of a history-making event—the Carnival of Swing and the first jazz festival. Gene closed the program to "thunderous applause" as Eddie Condon bravely stood next to him, taking the brunt of drum beats and persistent blasts of air. The concert lasted anywhere from five to seven hours, depending on whom you asked. Emceed by WNEW's Martin Block, host of the radio program *Make Believe Ballroom*, almost everybody who was anybody (and their bands) played at this benefit for hospitalized union musicians. This meant, for a start, Chick Webb, Duke Ellington, Count Basie, Charlie Barnet, Woody Herman, John Kirby, and Joe Marsala, but not Benny Goodman. Given the electricity generated by the roughly 25,000 black and white jazz devotees, it may also have been a Woodstock precursor, although fans' attempts at dancing in the aisles were mostly squelched by authorities.[46]

When Gene played Philadelphia's Earle Theatre in June, the city suffered a "scarcity of drums" due to, as *Metronome* called it, the "Krupa menace." Philly's Wurlitzer store had reportedly sold 250 kits since Gene first played the city in May.[47]

Krupa didn't just cause an excessive demand for drum sets. Something that had been simmering for a while and was boiling now that Gene was a famous and successful drummer-bandleader may be called an anti-drum-solo bias.

Variety's reviewers, in particular, were disturbed by Gene's drumming in his band's movie theater appearances. He was accused in a *Variety* review of a Pittsburgh show of overemphasizing his drums to the detriment of the full band: "a solid hour of drum-beating, no matter how spectacular, can grow pretty monotonous." He was just speaking for himself, though, admitting that the "jive hounds are going stark, staring nuts over his tom-tomming, and yelling for more."[48] A Detroit review by *Variety* likewise called Gene's drumming "monotonous."[49] A performance of "Blue Rhythm Fantasy" in Indianapolis verged on "sending non-swing customers to a psychopathic ward."[50]

John Hammond panned several bands, including a new one led by great African-American trumpeter "Hot Lips" Page. As for Gene, Hammond complained that the band's worst part—none of it was any good—was the rhythm section, which he called the "least secure musically." Then he acknowledged it may have been his problem rather than Gene's: "I just don't like drum solos no matter who does them."[51]

This anti-drum-solo bias found its way into reviews of Gene's records, too. In his innovative composition "Wire Brush Stomp," he made his delicate brushes sound like sticks beating a mid-tempo journey building upon itself repeatedly and supported by light but engaging band work. *Billboard* missed the subtleties, calling "Stomp" the "usual Krupa skin-beatings, with the effect minimized by sustaining the same rhythm too long."[52] A *Metronome* review of six not especially drummy Krupa sides scolded him for being "often guilty of breaking up the general rhythmic effect by too much drumming—he should watch that on records."[53]

Reviewers criticized the overall volume of Gene's band. One sensitive-eared writer in Washington, DC, suggested that Gene relocate his brass section to "some faraway island."[54] A critic in Pittsburgh moaned that "Gene Krupa and his fellow assassins of swing tore my ears off."[55]

Then again, there was lots of appreciation for—surprise!—the delicate balance between loud and soft that Gene's band, and his own drumming, achieved, not to mention that the band played and recorded many slow numbers.[56]

Gene was becoming known for his skills as a bandleader, rehearser, and emcee, as well as how much he sweated during a performance. One writer expressed surprise over Gene's "soft-spoken" manner despite his tremendous energy and stage presence. In Indianapolis, Gene and band were to support some vaudeville acts. Gene exhibited a good-natured "complete willingness" to spend the necessary time—two and a half hours—rehearsing for the vaudevillians. He "firmly but quietly pointed out mistakes" to his sidemen and rehearsed them in this pleasant manner until they were "letter-perfect." Gene was unperturbed by a bandage on the edge of his hand; he'd cut it on a metal part of a drum while performing. As an emcee, he modestly made announcements from the nearest microphone and wasn't self-conscious reading aloud from a clearly visible sheet of paper.[57]

His sweat was to become a thing of legend. Coming off a performance at New York's Paramount Theatre, Gene was "soaking wet with perspiration. His trainer helped him peel off his shirt, trousers, and underwear. Then wrung them out and tossed them over a chair. Gene completely stripped, stretched out on the studio couch while his trainer gave him an alcohol rub-down." To the reporter witnessing these proceedings, Gene was as upbeat as if he'd just won a boxing match.[58]

Zealous "Zonks"

Gene Krupa had already been giving private lessons to aspiring swing drummers. In April 1938, Robbins Music Corporation published his first drum instruction book, *Gene Krupa Drum Method*. Said Gene in the Introduction: "Artistic Drumming comes only with years of varied musical and emotional experiences, and the attainment of success depends largely upon the development of an individual musical personality."[59]

Drummer-educator Dom Famularo said that *Drum Method* was the "first book about drum sets that really kind of hit the ground running." It was the "most modern book of its day," said Daniel Glass, another drummer-educator. "This really was treating the drum set the way we would treat it [today]."[60] *Drum Method* contained advice and information about the different parts of the drum kit, note values, practicing and practice pads, rudiments, and playing the high-hat and cymbals, enhanced by a plethora of examples, exercises, and photos of Gene showing arm, hand, and stick positioning.

Much has been said about drummers who pioneered drumming using four-limb "independence." In early 1938, this technique was so new and perhaps little discussed that it didn't have a name, so Gene called it being "quadridextrous." He explained: "You have to use both feet and both hands, each playing different rhythms on different instruments [parts of the drum set] at the same time."[61] Gene offered numerous ways of doing this. Professor Theodore Dennis Brown said Gene was utilizing this technique in 1937 while still with Benny Goodman.[62]

Gene is regarded as a stick and rim shot master, "something he developed to a very high degree," said Dorn. "It's also one of his trademarks."[63] Drummer-historian John Petters said, "He anticipates the beat with it. He doesn't play them right on the beat. You'll hear it cropping up all right the way through [the 1930s]. That I don't hear anyone else doing in the '30s."[64] Said drummer-historian Hal Smith, "It's hard to make that connection all the time between the metal rim and the snare drum head. It's easier to miss it than to hit it. You've gotta have confidence to make that connection" before trying to do it.[65]

In *Drum Method*, Gene described getting "masculine, pile driving 'zonks,'"[66] one of his favorite techniques. Jazz writer Whitney Balliett credits him with "instituting the crackling rim shot,"[67] which was probably a "zonk," as Gene put it.

Krupa's Karma

A nonmusical theme throughout Gene's life was how beloved he was. Bassist Milt Hinton called him a "beautiful man."[68] Trumpeter Max Kaminsky, who knew Gene as far back as the early '30s, said in the '60s, "Gene was as good inside as he looked outside in those days, and he has never changed."[69]

"I got to meet him at a very early age, and I fell in love with the guy," recalled Mel Tormé. "He's one of the nicest human beings God ever put on earth."[70] "Beautiful cat, great man," said bebop saxophonist Sonny Stitt. "I loved him."[71] Modern jazz drummer Max Roach called Gene "a gentle and wonderful human being."[72]

Acclaimed musician-songwriter Bobby Scott, who, as a teenager in the mid-1950s, played piano with Gene's Quartet, remembered that the "old man's ease created the right kind of atmosphere."[73] ("Old man" was something jazzers called their leaders, even if the leader was younger!)

"He was a sweetheart, man," said modern drummer and Krupa mentee Mel Lewis. "The guys loved him. He was fun to work with and treated everybody nice."[74] Another mentee, drummer Les De-Merle, founder and artistic director of the annual Amelia Island Jazz Festival in Florida, said, "He was an incredible man, and he was so generous to every musician I've ever seen work with him ... Every one of those guys had nothing but praise and great things to say about Gene Krupa. He was just so incredibly warm."[75]

"He was such a wonderful person," said bebop drummer Roy Haynes, who gained prominence playing with, among others, Charlie Parker. "He was so different from some other drummers I had known." Haynes recounted how his bassist told him Gene had been complimenting his drumming on the radio. "That was very inspiring," said Haynes.[76]

Gene Krupa, despite the prosperity and achievements of his life, was not impressed with "opulence." "I'd rather have a ketchup sandwich in my kitchen," he declared, "than the finest steak in the world."[77]

"Red" Rodney was a bebop trumpeter who joined Gene's band as a teenager in the mid-1940s. Later, he played with Charlie Parker. Gene "was the greatest leader of men I've ever met," said Rodney. "He was sensational. He was a beautiful man. He was a real intellectual. Artie Shaw was supposed to be the intellectual, and maybe he was. But I know Gene was. Gene was well versed on any subject you wanted to speak about. He was a teacher. He would come back in the bus and speak with us. He was a mensch."[78]

When Dan Morgenstern was editor of *Down Beat* magazine some decades ago, he once watched Gene interact with people at a convention of the National Association of Music Merchants (NAMM). Gene, still Slingerland's main endorser, was dutifully representing them. "So he was sitting there . . . as a target for all kinds of people who came by, asking for autographs, or wanting to know things about drums," said Morgenstern, "and he was the most friendly, and the most pleasant guy I'd ever seen in that role . . . I remember to this day what a sweet guy he was. And I think that was fairly typical of Gene. He was very much liked by all the musicians who ever worked with him."[79]

Gene loved people—meeting them, befriending them, learning about them. If there was a good deed he could do, he did it. This was true whether the favor was giving friends turned out on the street a place to sleep, or sticking up for a fellow musician being treated disrespectfully by a club manager, or standing in as a father or a brother for his sidemen, or displaying high tolerance for low behavior, or quietly setting aside money for a young, talented band member with no financial bearings. He loved encouraging up-and-coming musicians, child novices, and people experimenting with music differently. His warmth as a person was always evident. If he said he cared, he really did.

CHAPTER 11

"Some Like It Hot"

Within nine months of the Krupa band's establishment, they were featured in a fair-to-middling Paramount musical-comedy with Bob Hope and Shirley Ross, *Some Like It Hot*. (This movie must be distinguished from Billy Wilder's 1959 movie starring Tony Curtis and Jack Lemmon.) One of the film's intertwined plots was the conflict between sweet versus hot music, and this conflict is what the title refers to. The title song, cowritten by Gene and his right-hand man, guitarist Ray Biondi (with lyrics by Frank Loesser), illustrated the issue. Gene's band represented the hot-swing contingent in the controversy; predictably, for over half the movie, his band was out of favor with the owner of the pavilion-on-the-pier, who preferred sedate, corny fare, and refused to hire Gene's band.

The Motion Picture Producers & Distributors of America, Inc., commonly referred to as the "Hays Office" after its head, Will H. Hays, could censor movies based on a sweeping decency code they had adopted. They thought the film's proposed title, *Some Like It Hot*, sounded sexually suggestive. Eventually, Paramount Pictures wore down the Hays Office and obtained approval for the title's use.[1]

The movie's best parts saw Gene and band swinging it with "Wire Brush Stomp" and "Jungle Madness" as zany-looking movie extras wildly danced to the rhythm. Gene recorded his drums apart from the rest of the band. "First of all, they recorded all the band members without me at all and a few days later photographed us playing to playback," he said. "After that I had to record solo on drums, listening to the playback through earphones and watching my actions on the screen. Finally, they dubbed the two tracks."[2] He didn't mention that, while they recorded his drumming, his mouth was stuffed with a cloth napkin to prevent him from spontaneously vocalizing ("ehhhhh"), as he often did.[3]

A Paramount press release boasted that *Some Like It Hot*, released on May 26, 1939, featured the first-ever drum solo in a movie. It also announced that it was the first movie in Hollywood history to be prescored—that is, readying all of the music before filming had begun. Gene worked with musical supervisor Arthur Franklin to arrange and score variations on the movie's main songs, to which the movie action would be adapted.[4]

Gene's first attempt at acting is mediocre at best, although, to be fair, his lines were badly written. "The lines I was given were not natural to me," he said, "nor to any other musician that I know."[5]

THE FAME OF the drummer man helped get the band the attention it deserved. It was on an ever-upward trajectory. Krupa was accorded that respect that comes with being a leader of a top band. When Tommy Dorsey went on vacation, he asked Gene to sub for him on a radio broadcast.[6]

Gene and his band were so busy that, as of October 1939, they had had no days off since March 11, and only an aggregate of two weeks off since their start on April 16, 1938![7]

Polling showed that "Gene Krupa has come up almost sensationally as his records have grown more and more popular."[8] Songs were original in interpretation and frequently electrifying. The Krupa-penned "Apurksody" (1938), the band's theme song ("Apurk" being "Krupa" spelled backwards), suggests Aaron Copland with a

THE MASTER OF DRUMS   111

melancholy tinge. The day before Gene debuted his band in April 1938 at Atlantic City's Steel Pier, they recorded "I Know That You Know," a mid-1920s Broadway tune and favorite in jazz circles. Here, it starts with a sweet elegance in this Willett-arranged number. The intensity builds until Gene and others cheer—"Yeah! Yeah!"—over turbulent sonic waves punctuated by one brief drum break.

Another Krupa-penned tune is "On the Beam" (1939). Arranged by Fred Norman, it emphasizes riffs and gives jitterbugs plenty to work with. "Don't Be Surprised" (1939) has a humorously choppy, stair-step melody, slyly peaking as Gene executes a climactic drum roll. His "Siren Serenade" (1941) is cleverly structured, with forward-looking brass and reed solos. It's also distinguished by a crescendo-decrescendo siren-trumpet passage marked by a drum roll and a percussive wink—that is, an abruptly executed rim shot and cymbal crash.

Most of the Irene Daye sides are pretty without being corny, witty without being stale, or sufficiently beat-laden without overwhelming her vocals: "Never Felt Better, Never Had Less" (1938), "You and Your Love" (1939), "You're a Lucky Guy" (1939), and a Cab Calloway ditty, "Boog It" (1940).

Gene made headlines when he opened up new ballrooms and clubs. The Panther Room opening was especially newsworthy. It had been carved out of the College Inn at Chicago's Hotel Sherman and was still being decorated (in a jungle-panther theme), when the Krupa band arrived on March 11, 1939. Night after night, the room was stuffed with swing fans and jitterbuggers; hundreds were turned away. Jitterbug contests were broadcast nationally on NBC radio. Business was so good that management extended Gene's stay well into May.[9]

On the Panther Room's opening night, Gene's brother Peter brought the basketball team he managed in his spare time. He had outfitted the boys in gear matching Gene's bass drum head, the "GK" heraldic shield prominent.[10]

The Krupa band broke box office records, but his success at New York's Paramount Theatre on April 24, 1940, was especially sweet. The record he broke was Benny Goodman's, when Gene was still

Benny's sideman. "The largest matinee crowd in the history of the Paramount Theatre," reported *The New York Times*, showed up for Gene and—oh, yes, the Jack Benny movie, *Buck Benny Rides Again.* Young people lined up "four and five abreast [and] circled the block bounded by Forty-third and Forty-fourth Streets."[11] Weeks later, Gene achieved another milestone, this one at Frank Dailey's Meadowbrook in New Jersey. No other band but Krupa's had had the box office power to play at the popular venue three times in the previous six months.[12] *Orchestra World* reported that Gene's "records started going like the proverbial hot cakes."[13]

It was always evident that Gene was good to work for, although working conditions for all touring bands could be unpleasant. After finishing a job at 1 A.M., the band might leave immediately for the next gig, with no time to stop at a hotel. "Sometimes we'd go straight through to the next town and we'd barely have time to wash . . . in the rest-room of a gas-station before going to work at 9 P.M. the next day," said trumpeter Graham Young, then nineteen. Things improved when the American Federation of Musicians negotiated a 400-mile limit between one-nighters, so that a band had time to sleep in a hotel.[14]

Social conditions on the bus could be a bit coarse. Graham Young first joined Krupa in early 1941. His parents were saying goodbye at the bus station when it was announced that the bus couldn't leave until someone found Norman Murphy, another trumpeter, "who had a penchant for whatever he drank," said Young. "Half an hour later the band-boy arrived with Murphy over his shoulder. He puts him on the bus on the back seat, lays the drums on him and off we go, with my folks standing there wringing their hands."[15]

Young said Gene conversed with people on the bus while using his practice pad, which Krupa did "constantly." "He had a dime imbedded in the pad," said Young, "and he could carry on a conversation and keep those single strokes going with an even, metallic tap."[16]

Alto saxist Clint Neagley joined Krupa just before a national radio broadcast scheduled at the last minute. "I had just come from a smaller band, where broadcasts were rather nervous affairs," he said.

"But this was a relaxed band. Gene was still calling out numbers while the broadcast was going on. He made it easy to do."[17]

Disaster seemed guaranteed when Gene arrived ahead of the band in Hershey, Pennsylvania, for a one-nighter and learned that the band bus had broken down and probably wouldn't show up for another two hours. Everything was on that bus—the sidemen, the instruments, Gene's and everyone else's luggage. Two thousand Hershey-ites were waiting for a show. "So there I was," recalled Gene, "unshaven, in a slacks suit, without even a drumstick." The ballroom manager asked him to explain to the audience what had happened. He did more than that, entertaining them with "gags and stories about the band and the boys." Gene played some of his records on a jukebox and related anecdotes about recording sessions. "After that, I answered questions they shot at me," he said. Once the bus pulled in, audience members were in a sympathetic mood and helped the band bring in and set up their instruments. "The boys played just as they were dressed," said Gene, "and we had a very happy, relaxed groove and never did have a more successful engagement." When Gene told this story on the radio in 1941, in his self-effacing way he cited it not as an example of how he saved the evening but of the "sportsmanship of the American public."[18]

———

IN 1940, GENE introduced one of his earliest visual spectacles that went beyond his natural duende; it was preplanned. The month was April, the place New York's Paramount, and the number "Blue Rhythm Fantasy, Parts 1 and 2." Performing the song now involved phosphorescent-treated drumsticks and gloves for all sidemen. With lights off, Gene's drumming especially emitted "streaks of blue light" as he played at a rapid pace.[19]

Gene employed phosphorescence similarly at the Paramount in his percussive treatment of Nacio Herb Brown's "American Bolero" in 5/4 time. Trumpeter "Shorty" Sherock recalled rehearsing it at 6 A.M. because they had about seven shows to play at the Paramount that day and into the night. "We all played our drums—and Gene had a bunch of kettle drums—and even had the theater organist in on it. We put it in the act the same day."[20] *Orchestra World*'s Charles Colin enjoyed the performance's glow-in-the-dark aspect but mostly heaped his praise on the musicianship of Gene and the band for playing what was essentially "long-haired," or classical, music. "The band shadings and tonal qualities are tops," raved Colin.[21]

THE HISTORIC NEW York World's Fair of 1939–1940, held in Queens—Flushing Meadows, to be precise—seemed to offer the public access to almost anything and everything one would desire in the world, for a small fee. Its theme was "Building the World of Tomorrow." It envisioned future peace and prosperity with assistance from modern architecture and technology. Two large expanses on the grounds were called the Lagoon of Nations and the Court of Peace. The fair opened on April 30, 1939, just a few months before Nazi Germany invaded Poland, thus commencing World War Two.

There were many ways people could be entertained, informed, dazzled, and fed. The Theme Plaza, from whence all exhibits, features, pavilions, and amusement areas radiated outward, consisted of two colossal, seemingly space-aged structures, a 200-foot "steel-framed" Perisphere or globe, and the Trylon, a 700-foot high "tapered pillar." The two were connected by a ramp dubbed the "Helicline." At night, prismatic, colored lights shone over the fair's radiating avenues; the Perisphere lit up with moving marble-like patterns.[22]

Gene's band was a major attraction at the World's Fair, which, it should be understood, was open only in the warm months of 1939 and 1940. In September 1939, he and the band played seven days at the "band shell." He was seen one day interacting with a Native American percussionist.[23] But the Zulu drummers at the Victoria Falls exhibit (the Falls being situated in the British colony of Rhodesia) made a bigger impression on him. Through interpreters, he communicated to the Zulus his fascination with their drumming and interest in learning their methods. They all jammed together. He later exclaimed, "They're real cats!" The Zulus inspired him to acquire a conga drum—tall and narrow—and use his hands to "be closer, more intimate, with the drums."[24]

In 1940, filmmaker and Broadway producer Mike Todd's World's Fair Dancing Campus floundered financially until he signed Gene's band. Krupa, who performed stretches in July and September, was "pulling the jitterbugs at twenty-five cents a head." A "gawker's terrace" cost more for those who preferred watching to dancing.[25] Gene broke attendance records on several occasions that season. He also hosted at least a couple of amateur drumming contests while there.[26]

With all this talk of Gene sincerely loving drums and nearly salivating at the *thought* of learning more about them, and *in fact* learning more about them, one would have thought that the anti-drum solo bias in jazz might have a rest. But it did not.

Gene sometimes tried to head off criticism by explaining himself. "Of course I think drums are a solo instrument," he said, "as much as any other instrument in a jazz orchestra. It's natural for me to play drums; it's what I like to do better than anything else, so I just try to be myself. Maybe this results in too much drums, but I always try to keep myself from hogging the show."[27] Gene's records were balanced, even during "killer-dillers." His soloists had many opportunities to show off without being trod upon by drums. The band was a rousing crew of young men eager to please dancers, themselves, and Gene. They loved being Krupa sidemen.

Krupa's expressed intentions, and the reality of the music he produced, made no impression on the anti-drum contingent. This was clear in a clueless review of "Blue Rhythm Fantasy, Parts 1 and 2." "Sixteen drums pounding away for two ten-inch sides," grumbled a *Down Beat* critic. "Noise. And more noise. What Gene was trying to do probably won't ever be revealed, but it's safe to say he failed."[28] Gene could explain his methods until he shed his last drop of sweat, but it wouldn't have mattered.

The two-part "Blue Rhythm Fantasy" came under scrutiny again, this time in *Swing* magazine. The reviewer said the recording had "several quiet melodic movements and some impressive jungle-brass effects, but degenerates into a drum solo in

Part II."[29] A peeved critic said that Gene "covers up bad rhythm production with fast pounding noise."[30] An equally annoyed commentator protested that a "drummer . . . should not be heard . . . He should be *felt*."[31]

Krupa's effect on jazz drumming was profound—drummers everywhere wanted to be the next Krupa. Critic George T. Simon, a one-time drummer himself, cautioned a young Buddy Rich, then playing with Artie Shaw: "Like so many drummers who have grown up in the Krupa era, he's cursed with the misconception that a drummer's supposed to do much more than supply a good background."[32] In *Music and Rhythm*, a writer with an apparently throbbing head griped: "My own nerves are so ragged from the constant beating of a thousand drums that I would like to have every Gene Krupa in the country committed to a padded cell for life."[33]

For John Petters, the more drums, the better. If, indeed, Gene had played "too much drums," that was fine. "Gene was never unobtrusive, and rightly so," said Petters. "He laid down the beat, you had no mistake where the beat was, and he drove whatever band he was playing with."[34]

While Gene was regularly deprecated for playing drums his way, critics couldn't decide whether his band was too sweet, too hot, or sweet *and* hot. "The Krupa crew has changed from raucous to sweet swing," declared *Variety*. "Net result, a big adult following."[35] A different reviewer for *Variety* had a different view months later. The band, said the reviewer, was "chiefly a hot outfit."[36]

As we have seen, Gene's drums caused consternation in many, and their consternation disconcerted him. Krupa wanted it understood that he was engaging in a balancing act to keep dancers dancing and fans of pop songs and soft music happy. "Try to meet a $2,500 a week payroll by not playing a goodly share of commercial stuff!" he challenged his decriers.[37]

A major commercial concession that nevertheless didn't dampen the excitement his band generated onstage was the February 1940 hiring of Howard Dulaney, a white male vocalist, White bands were expected to feature a male purveyor of romance to sing ballads for ballroom slow dancing. The white public may have only embraced swing to a point, reserving a place in their harmonic hearts for a milder sound.

Gene gave the deep-voiced Dulaney ample—perhaps overly ample—opportunities to balladeer in the studio. One of the Krupa band's biggest records was the two-sided 1941 hit, "High on a Windy Hill / It All Comes Back to Me Now," romantic ballads sung by Dulaney that misled listeners about the band's nature. To some, perhaps, Gene's group had become the kind of thing he had loathed back in the late '20s and early '30s, a "Mickey Mouse" concern. Yet people kept protesting against his drum solos and the detectability of his drumming.

One could ponder this dichotomy, but Gene was again *Down Beat*'s drumming winner in January 1940 (based on voting from late in 1939). He was also voted the number four favorite musical soloist; the only other drummer on the list was Ray Bauduc, at number twenty-five.[38]

Down Beat's polling policy changed with the January 1941 poll results (based on late 1940 polling). Bandleaders were no longer eligible to be voted the best on their instruments. Thus, Gene's name was absent from the drummer list issued in January 1941.[39]

Metronome's policy remained unchanged. Gene won their drumming title in January 1940[40] and January 1941.[41] The magazine hosted an annual recording session featuring the winning musicians to benefit a musicians' charity. Although Gene won the drumming title in 1939 and 1941, as well as 1940, he participated only in the 1940 *Metronome* session, presumably because of scheduling conflicts. Thus, *Metronome*'s 1939 All-Star Band included runner-up Ray Bauduc on drums, while its 1941 band substituted runner-up Buddy Rich.[42]

Gene Krupa: A Grizzled Old Jazz Vet

Gene Krupa was a guest on *The Tonight Show* with Johnny Carson in 1962 when Carson asked something that revealed what a lot of people assumed about Gene's career—that he got his start with Benny Goodman. "You've been playing, what, twenty-five—I'm takin' a guess now," said Johnny. Gene responded, "A lot longer than that, Johnny," and proceeded to reminisce about the 1920s and his old Chicago stomping grounds.

Reminders continue to surface of how long it had taken Gene to achieve fame and the entwining of his career with jazz's development. *Down Beat's Yearbook of Swing*, by Paul Eduard Miller, was published in 1939. The volume's fourth chapter, "A Representative Record Library," laid out Miller's selections of important records from jazz's beginning to time of publication. Many were definitive or especially compelling versions of classic tunes, such as "Black & Tan Fantasy" and "Caravan" by Ellington, "King Porter Stomp" by Jelly Roll Morton, "Sugar Foot Stomp" by King Oliver (with Goodman's recording also listed), "In a Mist" by Bix Beiderbecke, "Numb Fumblin'" by Fats Waller, and "St. Louis Blues" by Louis Armstrong. Goodman's "Sing, Sing, Sing" was there, as was "Someday Sweetheart" by the original Goodman Trio.

If one were to tally up the number of recordings on which each drummer appeared, Gene Krupa, with eighteen, was second only to Duke Ellington's drummer, Sonny Greer, with twenty-three. Gene's presence on the list represented sessions with Goodman, Red Norvo and His Swing Octet, Reginald Foresythe and His Orchestra, Eddie Condon and His Orchestra, Fats Waller and His Buddies, the Mound City Blue Blowers, Jess Stacy, McKenzie and Condon's Chicagoans, and Billy Banks and His Orchestra.[43] (The book credits Zutty Singleton's drums on the latter, the song being "Oh, Peter," but at least one Krupa expert has determined that the drummer was Gene.[44])

Collectible early jazz records were a favorite topic of the jazz columns; Gene had had a hand in a lot of them. "Hello Lola" and "One Hour" (both 1929) by the Mound City Blue Blowers (including Gene) were pegged in 1941 as tracks that "turn up on every serious list as a great jazz record."[45] A rerelease of Red Nichols sides featuring Gene, Benny Goodman, Glenn Miller, and others was recognized in 1943 as "heralding the advent of swing."[46]

An illuminating 1934 article published in *Esquire*, before Krupa was known except in limited circles, discussed jazz connections between groups of musicians. The pre-1920s white New Orleans group The Original Dixieland Jazz Band had "perforce, to assimilate the Negro's music," whose influence was detectable among several 1920s ensembles of whom Gene was variously a member: the Mound City Blue Blowers, the Chicago Rhythm Kings, the Louisiana Rhythm Kings, Red Nichols, and Bix Beiderbecke. Gene is also listed separately, along with Joe Sullivan, Jack Teagarden, Benny Goodman, and Duke Ellington, as "jazz-conscious individuals" influenced by this trend.[47] That all of the musicians listed were also profoundly inspired by African-American jazzers and that Duke Ellington was one himself should not minimize the importance of the connections recognized in this 1934 article.

Esquire's Jazz Book (1944) republished the 1934 piece alongside a companion chart illustrating the flow of influence among white and black groups that directly led to the development of the Swing Era bands. The white artists—McKenzie and Condon's Chicagoans, the Chicago Rhythm Kings, Red Nichols, Miff Mole, and Bix Beiderbecke—were listed in connected boxes that themselves connected to the Swing Era bands. Gene had been a member of all these ensembles, and, as we know, established his swing band in 1938, as also indicated in the flow chart.[48]

Gene was a grizzled old jazz vet—and a formative influence on jazz itself.

Fans and a New Drumming Point of Reference

Gene's popularity grew and Krupa fan clubs sprang up across the United States. A group of self-professed "swing addicts" at the University of Alabama elected Gene their "honorary president."[49] Young Charlotte of Downingtown, Pennsylvania, announced a fan drive for her Krupa club.[50] A consortium of New England fan clubs greeted Gene when he arrived in Boston for an engagement.[51] Fan clubs were organized in New Jersey, Illinois, California, New York, North Carolina, Minnesota, Pennsylvania, Nebraska, Michigan, and Florida. Gene could be among several jazz stars honored by the same club, like The Solid Set out of

Minneapolis, whose other objects of admiration were Ellington, Basie, Goodman, and Eldridge. Rochester, New York, was home to the Sinatra-Krupa Society.

Fans boasted of their Krupa-related achievements. John in Larchmont, New York, claimed he had seen Gene live sixty-five times in thirteen days and owned three drum sets just like his. Bob in Columbus, Ohio, bragged that he owned a collection of Krupa photos, a drum autographed by Krupa, a wire from one of Krupa's wire brushes, a broken Krupa drumstick, and a Krupa record collection. Scotty from the Bronx announced that he had traveled up and down the East Coast to see Gene. Charles of Claremont, California, crowed that he had traveled one thousand miles per month to see the drummer man.[52]

Gene was everywhere, even when he wasn't. The drummer for the Casa Loma Band swung "like Gene Krupa."[53] Ben Bernie's drummer was a "virtuoso on those traps who's in the Krupa class…"[54] Errol Flynn, beating drums on the set of *The Private Lives of Elizabeth and Essex* (1939), was "just a Gene Krupa at heart."[55]

Krupa was a member of every band imaginable throughout America and the world. How? He changed his name, ethnicity, gender, age, or size, as necessary. There were the "Swiss Gene Krupa" Berry Perritz, leader of the Berries, a Zurich band[56]; the "female Gene Krupa," Viola Smith, with the "all-girl" band The Coquettes[57]; the "Gene Krupa of Girl Drummers," Des Thompson, with Phil Spitalny[58]; Henry Van Leer, the "Gene Krupa of the Netherlands"[59]; a World War Two refugee, Stanley Fraszczynski, duplicatively dubbed the "Polish Krupa"[60]; Joseph Hancock, drummer for Sherdina Walker and Her Swing Band and Detroit's "Sepia Gene Krupa"[61]; in San Francisco, a "12-year-old Gene Krupa," Walter Lund, Jr., who won a radio station drum contest[62]; Victor Feldman, an English drumming prodigy called "Kid Krupa" by the British press during World War Two[63]; Alex Sheftell, the "Gene Krupa of Roosevelt High School" in Philadelphia[64]; and Pete Dutka, the "Gene Krupa of Fort Taylor," a Key West military base.[65]

Gene Krupa enjoyed various hobbies. Charley Chaney was the "Krupa of the keyboard."[66] Washington, DC's Walter Long was a "Gene Krupa with his feet."[67] Bandleader Charlie Spivack's secretary was a "Krupa on the typewriter."[68] Gene changed species, alighting on a tree trunk: The downy woodpecker pounding with the best of them, but not a songster, was named the "Gene Krupa of the bird world."[69]

CHAPTER 12

Enter "Little Jazz"

O NE OF GENE KRUPA'S MOST spectacular drum performances happened in mid-1940, when he and the band recorded the old favorite "Who?" He didn't do anything *new*, exactly, but what he did, he did awfully well. A big section of the song was given over to Gene. He sounded like an accelerating phalanx of drums in a marching band punctuated by increasingly frequent rim shot claps—concluding, somewhat anticlimactically, with a simple "period," as he often did, expressed here as a little "thump" on the bass drum. What Gene did not do was get in the way of his sidemen. He turned "Who?" into a drum feature—a valid way of approaching jazz, even if it dismayed the jazz intelligentsia.

Krupa's drums on "Who?" raised dim or no praise. Said one critic: "Krupa does a very swell job of drumming on this side and if you like drum solos this is a good record to dig."[1] Another critic said: "Krupa's solo for the kids to admire is on *Who*. It's fine drumming, but makes for poor listening."[2] The anti-drum solo bias was as strong as ever.

———————

FROM TIME TO time, aspiring barely teenage drummer Melvin Sokoloff of Buffalo, New York, who later gained fame as Mel Lewis, was Gene Krupa's sidekick while Gene toured. Krupa was the boy's mentor, affording him insight into his drumming that few could ever hope for, and a taste of what road life was like. Lest Mel's mother worry, Gene reassured her that "the kid will be alright. I'll take care of him." And he did.[3]

"The chicks went nuts for him, you know," said Mel, "and he had a class about him . . . I knew that since I was a kid, when I first met him, when I became his little pal."

Mel's memories reveal Gene's warmth and love for drumming, music, and performing. "I'd be sitting up there; sometimes I'd be standing on the side of the bandstand watching him work," said Mel, "and he'd be talking to the guys in the band while he's playing along. You know, he's smiling. And remembering something funny. He'd look over at me and he'd nod to me to look out at the audience 'cause there was somethin' funny going on out in the audience. Or he'd nod to me to dig so-and-so who was gonna play a solo . . . 'Listen to this new guy I got.' And so on. He was like that."[4]

"ONE DAY, NO one knew my name and the next day everyone did. He got me out of Chicago," said Anita O'Day of Gene.[5]

Born Anita Colton in Chicago, Anita O'Day (her chosen surname being pig latin for "dough") was mostly on her own by her early teens due to boredom and an indifferent mother. One of her first professional jobs, if one could call it that, was as a contestant in a "walkathon."[6] This meant being half of a couple walking on a stage or in a tent for hours, days, or weeks in front of spectators. Breaks were minimal. Occasionally, walkers became "sprinters" for a couple of hours. Couples were allowed to hold each other up, but sometimes walkathon promoters prohibited this, chaining couples together five feet apart. This was a horrific way to earn a living, but Anita survived. Her biggest payday yielded $95, a huge sum in those days. The organizers were simply perverse, inhumane seekers of riches. Audiences salivated over the beastly drama.[7]

Eventually, Anita turned to singing; she played drums, too. Around 1939, Gene Krupa discovered her in a Chicago club, the

Off Beat. He sent Ray Biondi to bring her over to his table, told her he liked her improvisational style, and offered her a job—which would start whenever his then-current singer, Irene Daye, quit. "I don't fire people," he explained.[8]

The day finally came in February 1941 when Irene Daye left the band to marry one of Gene's trumpeters, "Corky" Cornelius. Anita was hired. As she was a "girl" singer, she went through some rituals, with assistance from Gene and his personal manager, Frank Verniere, that the sidemen weren't troubled with—choosing an easy-to-maintain hairdo, finding attractive clothing to wear onstage, and posing for publicity photos with and without Gene.[9]

In a first for female band singers, Anita told Gene she would prefer to wear gowns only in hotels or ballrooms. For one-nighters, she wanted a jacket-shirt-skirt combination matching the look of the sidemen. Suits would be easier to wear and maintain under the difficult conditions of traveling by bus from place to place.[10]

This "girl" singer proved one of Gene's best talent acquisitions. She developed a mode of melodic experimentation wherein she used her voice like a musical instrument. It had little vibrato, but that was unimportant. Anita left a unique stamp on many a Krupa recording. She cited two major influences: Billie Holiday and Martha Raye, oddly enough, the latter a comic actress and vocalist. "I always got a boot out of Anita," said Gene Krupa. "She started a style for girl vocalists which is still going on today [1955]. I would say that it grew out of Billie Holiday's way of singing, but is still mostly Anita."[11]

Two particularly avant-garde Krupa records on which O'Day sang were "Slow Down" (1941) and "That's What You Think" (1942). On the former, she demonstrated her ability to use her voice as an instrument—in this case, something that would have sounded perfect as a sax solo.

"That's What You Think" leaned forward with a sensual, futuristic jazz feel. O'Day's scat voice presaged bop vocalese, which Gene's band would pioneer within a couple of years. Another appealing feature of the recording, which Gene seemed to favor on many an O'Day side, was rhythmic, unison shouting by the sidemen when

Anita paused; this raised the temperature of the proceedings considerably. In "That's What You Think," it was an uncomplicated "Hey! Hey!" Other tunes getting the rhythmic unison-shouting treatment were the exceedingly fun "Alreet" and "Kick It."

The way that Gene's good friend Roy Eldridge joined Krupa was more complicated. Gene, Ethel, Frank Verniere, and some Krupa band members often went to hear Roy and his five-piece ensemble in Chicago when the Krupa band was in town.[12] According to Roy, who was often called "Little Jazz" largely due to his diminutiveness, he and Gene had previously tried to negotiate an arrangement for him to join the band. "Man, those plans never worked out," said Roy. "There were too many contracts in the way."[13] Then Eldridge sat in with Krupa's band in October 1940 when Gene's then-lead trumpeter, Shorty Sherock, was ill.[14] It worked so well that Gene raised the issue again of Roy joining permanently.

The problem was Eldridge's five-year contract with manager Joe Glaser, who opposed a Krupa-Eldridge deal. Consequently, Roy could play with Gene only as a special feature rather than a full-fledged member of the band. Roy finally extricated himself from Glaser by buying back his contract.[15]

Now "Little Jazz" sat and played shoulder to shoulder with Gene's white musicians (and earned more than he had as a bandleader himself), while also being featured out front on special numbers. Roy's employment with Gene is cited as among the very first times, if not the first, that a white bandleader hired a black musician as a full-fledged band member, and not just a special-features performer.

"There are all these trumpet players," said Dan Morgenstern. "Cootie Williams with Benny Goodman, Hot Lips Page with Artie Shaw, but Roy with Gene is the one that stood out, because Gene featured him so well."[16] Cootie Williams himself said that he had a one-year contract only with Benny Goodman's sextet, not the full band.[17]

Eldridge now had the national platform he needed to show off his talent. Gene "made Roy Eldridge a star," said Newport Jazz Festival founder George Wein. "That helped him for the rest of his life."[18] Roy said about Gene: "With him drumming for me, I've got an inspiration like I've never had before."[19]

Later on, "Little Jazz" said he'd "made" the Krupa band. Gene's orchestra certainly had more hits, although part of this success is attributable to Anita O'Day. There were also Elton Hill's arrangements; Hill and his aggressive trumpet trills and pretty sax flutters added thrills that matched Gene's vision for the band more than the work of any other arranger at the time. It might best be said that the Krupa band reached a new level of success with Roy and Anita. Still, the band offered much from the beginning and had been monumentally popular—beset by screaming fans, breaking box office records—long before Roy and Anita came aboard.

But Roy deserves his due. He contributed a zest, a beauty, an indescribable magic to many of Krupa's best band numbers. Two classics include "After You've Gone" and "Rockin' Chair." Showing how comfortable Gene was with his status as a major bandleader and a star, he generously handed over those two sides to Roy to do with what he would, although the band provided tasteful support and occasional solos to complement Eldridge's playing. "After You've Gone" was the speedy number; Roy excelled at playing extremely fast and high. It was an exhilarating record. Gene and Roy were perfectly matched as they played, linked in the utter speedy joy audible in every note. "Rockin' Chair," a slow, pensive ballad, as its author, Hoagy Carmichael, had envisioned it, gave Roy a chance to demonstrate his ample lyrical side. The master trumpeter also sang in a light bluesy style; the Louis Jordan–penned "Knock Me A Kiss" is a perfect example of "Little Jazz" seeming to presage Smokey Robinson.

Although Roy supplied superb trumpet solos to most sides on which he appeared, several Eldridge showcases included duets or interactions with Anita O'Day. Among them: "Thanks for the Boogie Ride," "The Walls Keep Talking," "Stop! The Red Light's On," and, most notably, "Let Me Off Uptown."

"It became a big hit," said Dan Morgenstern of "Let Me Off Uptown," "but there you had a white girl and a black man doing this thing together and people resented that."[20] Gene brought the song and the Roy-Anita performance to theaters and ballrooms across the country. "Uptown" was the number three bestselling Okeh Records single in 1941.[21]

EARLY THAT YEAR, before Anita and Roy joined, the Krupa crew had starred in its first short film—eleven minutes long—called *Gene Krupa and His Orchestra*. The Paramount mini-movie, nationally released to show with other short subjects leading into feature films, also starred Irene Daye and Howard Dulaney. They performed four songs that showed the band to flattering effect. Opening with an instrumental number, "Hamtramck," a lively, riff-laden tune, the highlight was probably "Tonight," a variation on the hit song "Perfidia." "Tonight" was Dulaney's vehicle for exhibiting his beautiful, if completely unjazzy, voice. Better was the song's closing portion in which the band fell into a Latin groove with Gene's huge conga drum— slung over his shoulder, it covered nearly his entire body—leading the way. His rhythmic pattern, a cadence he had been using and enriching over time in varied settings, still didn't have a name. Eventually, it would be called the Bo Diddley beat.

THE SAMUEL GOLDWYN comedy *Ball of Fire*, starring Gary Cooper and Barbara Stanwyck, and released on January 9, 1942, afforded Gene's band the broadest exposure yet. They performed only one number, but the "popularity of Gene Krupa and his band," observed one trade magazine, "is strong enough among adolescents to warrant billing the aggregation prominently."[22] This they got.

Ball of Fire presented Gene's most memorable film performance up till then. It involved a new song, "Drumboogie," and a little coda, sometimes referred to as "Match Boogie." "Drumboogie" is one of several songs on which Gene and Roy Eldridge collaborated as songwriters. It was a hot number. Barbara Stanwyck lip-synced to the vocals of Martha Tilton as the band scorched its way through. (It's unknown why Anita O'Day didn't sing here.) Roy Eldridge stood up for a sizzling solo.

The next scene consisted of the so-called "Match Boogie" number, noteworthy for a display of Gene's extraordinary technique. Stanwyck sat at Gene's side and Gary Cooper, among others, stood in the background "la-da"-ing the "Drumboogie" melody. Delicately yet perfectly, Gene shuffle-drummed the matchsticks, lightly held in his thick fingers, across the side of a little matchbox. Suddenly, the matchsticks were aflame. Gene and Barbara together blew out the tiny flares, sprang up, and left the scene arm in arm.

The *Ball of Fire* set almost erupted into controversy during filming in October 1941. "Here's what Roy told me," said Dan Morgenstern. "When the band was setting up for the scene...and they spotted Roy, somebody said to Gene that they did not want him in the shoot, whereupon Gene said, *Ok, then we'll pack up.* That caused some alarm and the person immediately went upstairs if you know what I mean and the end result was that Roy stayed in the picture. Roy often said Gene was 100 percent when it came to race issues."[23]

Roy did make the studio's November 11, 1941, "analysis chart" for the just-completed movie. The chart itemized the film's characters and addressed whether crimes, violence, or drinking were depicted. Under "races or nationals," a "colored musician" was referenced as having a "minor, straight" role with an "indifferent characterization." A couple of weeks later, an internal communication by Goldwyn employee Marvin Ezzell discussed a potential problem with Roy's presence: "There is one negro in the [Krupa] orchestra who in most of the orchestra scenes is relatively inconspicuous but in two places he rises, once alone and again with other members of the band, during the playing of the number. In these instances he is conspicuous. The question has arisen here as to whether or not any objection might be registered by Southern audiences based on racial prejudice due to the inclusion of a negro in a white orchestra." Ezzell asked whether the scene should be cut and a replacement inserted for Southern theaters. No answer to this question appears extant.[24] But the scene remains in the film to enjoy for all time to come.

BY SUMMER 1940, Nazi Germany had overrun most of central and western Europe, while imperial Japanese forces continued their rampage through East Asia and the South Pacific. To build up U.S. armed forces before America was drawn into the war, President Roosevelt in September signed the Selective Training and Service Act, instituting the first peacetime draft in U.S. history.[25]

The draft impacted the big bands by littles. Most noticeable at first was a surge of patriotic entertainment in movies and songs. Big bandleaders were not impervious to the trend, and Gene Krupa jumped on it pretty quickly.

Even before the commencement of selective service, Gene had begun recording patriotic tunes. There was the duet between Irene Daye and Howard Dulaney on the blatantly titled, "(Shout Wherever You May Be) I Am an American," recorded in July 1940. In October, Dulaney sang "Oh! They're Making Me All Over in the Army." In January 1941, Irene Daye had a very up-tempo, light-hearted vehicle in "Boogie Woogie Bugle Boy." In April, it was Dulaney with "Don't Cry, Cherie," which harbored a touch of "La Marseillaise." More Dulaney: "'Til Reveille" and "Got a Letter From My Kid Today" in mid-1941.

When the U.S. entered the war, Gene was on a roll, with "The Caissons Go Rolling Along," "Harlem on Parade," "The Marines' Hymn," and "Fightin' Doug McArthur." Fortunately, these records swung, fiercely. Howard Dulaney had been inducted by this time; Johnny Desmond, late of the Bob Crosby band and who could occasionally swing a tune, replaced him and alternated with Anita O'Day on the wartime ditties.

In October 1941, the War Department pitched a brand-new song to Gene, which he gladly recorded with the band—"Keep 'Em Flying"—intended as a recruiting tool for the Army Air Corps. This recording received perhaps the biggest promotion ever seen for a mere piece of shellac. The War Department reportedly sent a copy of the record to every radio station in the United States, with extra copies going to radio stations close to military bases. A push was also afoot to get the record into as many jukeboxes and on as many record store shelves as possible.[26] Gene and band performed the song on an installment of the NBC radio program, the *Fitch Bandwagon Show*.[27] And the drummer man had a "Let's Go! U.S.A. Keep 'Em Flying" slogan—plus war plane art—emblazoned on his bass drum head, where it remained for the duration of the war.

BIG BANDS WERE losing musicians to every branch of the armed services. "That personnel changed so fast during the war years that I couldn't keep up with it," said Gene. "By the time you learned a guy's name, he was gone."[28]

The turmoil enabled Krupa's acquisition of some of the best young talent. Charlie Ventura (then "Venturo," before he changed his surname), a great player of all saxophone types, in mid-1942 was working at the Philadelphia Navy Yard. Roy Eldridge jammed with him and others in the evenings and mentioned Ventura to Gene, who hired him.[29] Ventura was a tall, swarthy man with a pencil-thin mustache. Aside from his sax aptitude, his solos were affecting and emotional. He was, perhaps, a product of the Coleman Hawkins school, but he had a unique, desperate-sounding style. Gene and Charlie enjoyed one of the longest-lasting musical associations of either man, playing together over extended periods in the 1940s, '50s, and '60s. "Gene was instrumental in getting my dad's career going," said Ventura's daughter, Rita Ventura Lenderman. "They respected one another."[30]

Later, Gene was losing so many men to the draft that he took the rare (for him) step of "raiding" another band to fill his vacancies. This entailed identifying the musicians he needed and offering them more money than they were earning. In this case, the unlucky bandleader was Johnny "Scat" Davis. Among the lucky sidemen were pianist "Dodo" Marmarosa, trumpeters Joe Triscari and Jimmy Pupa, trombonist Tommy Pederson, and the biggest prize of all, clarinetist "Buddy" DeFranco, who replaced the just-drafted Krupa stalwart Sam Musiker.[31] After his stint with Krupa, DeFranco would go on to become a celebrated bebop clarinetist.

"He was the nicest person I think I ever worked with," said Buddy DeFranco of Gene Krupa. DeFranco cited Charlie Ventura, Roy Eldridge, and Gene as influences.[32]

Because of the recording ban instituted at the beginning of August 1942, essentially a labor dispute between the American Federation of Musicians and the big record labels, bands were not making new recordings. This is a shame, especially when Gene's new crew was so ripe for memorialization. Numerous songs Gene and band performed live weren't saved for posterity: "Blues in the Night," "Embraceable You," and "Jersey Bounce."

It was probably just as well. As the war progressed, the federal government enacted myriad changes to everyday living in support of the war effort that would eventually deflate the big bands' balloon. These changes led to stringent "curtailment" of the manufacture of some musical instruments or their components[33]; the banning of shellac, the material used for making records[34]; tire shortages[35]; the unavailability of buses for bands to charter[36]; gas rationing and the prohibition of "pleasure driving"[37]; limitations on "inter-city" bus lines[38]; and train service essentially closed off to bands, although standing room was sometimes allowed.[39] In a humane move, the federal government approved limited exemptions for African-American bands traveling in the South from the ban on chartered bus use; these bands needed the buses because, due to "Jim Crow," public transportation was not available to them.[40]

Otherwise, the restrictions and injunctions not only hurt the bands—members of which sometimes took different modes of transportation to the same venue, at the risk of a late arrival or no arrival at all—but devastated club and ballroom revenues. The legendary Glen Island Casino in New Rochelle, New York, and the Meadowbrook in Cedar Grove, New Jersey, closed their doors.[41]

WITH EVERYTHING IN flux, that Anita and Roy hadn't been getting along was all the more disconcerting. A mutual jealousy developed from their live performances of "Let Me Off Uptown." Out in front, while Roy played his big solo, Anita danced a few steps. He believed that Anita's dancing deflected attention from his playing. Anita wanted something to do while he played.[42] Gene found mediating a challenge. He eventually persuaded them to leave their differences backstage.[43]

When Anita left the band on December 29, 1942, after Krupa's engagement at the Hollywood Palladium, she said: "I'm just tired and want to take a rest."[44] Her differences with Roy did not affect her decision. Touring life with Gene was "grueling," she said. To her, it was endless one-nighters.[45] Gene's public statement, despite the suddenness of her departure and the boost she had given the band, betrayed no ill feelings, if he had any: "I'm sorry to see Anita go. We've been together a long time and I know she has been a big asset to the band."[46] Anita returned three weeks later[47]—temporarily—after marrying Carl Hoff, golf-pro-turned-Army-pilot. She felt guilty about "deserting Gene because my replacement [Penny Piper] wasn't working out."[48] Following her second departure, she would not rejoin Krupa until 1945.

———

PEOPLE DIVORCE FOR all sorts of reasons.

Trumpeter Pee Wee Erwin, Gene's friend and a Goodman bandmate, once observed: "A musician's married life is understandably different from the average guy's. For one thing, he's almost always working on holidays and weekends and other times when most people are looking for entertainment, and this makes it pretty rough for the musician's wife, who enjoys social activity and wants to be with her husband. Unless she can adapt herself to these conditions, she has little chance to succeed as a musician's wife."[49]

This is probably why Gene and Ethel split. For years, they were together—she traveling with him and whatever band he was playing for at the time, including his own.[50] He lavished her with gifts. He was seen with her "swathed in silver fox."[51] She had hoped to settle down in California with Gene once he was finished with Goodman. As we've seen, that didn't happen.

As the years passed, Gene's fame grew and his responsibilities increased. A normal home life seemed increasingly impossible. Yet, in 1941, Gene purchased property in the Park Hill section of Yonkers, New York, intending to build a home.[52] Maybe he and Ethel would settle down after all. She demanded a soundproofed room for his drum practice.[53]

Building a home could have been related to their desire to have children. They were unable to, but probably kept trying and hoping. The odds were against them. Only one of Gene's many siblings had had any children—his brother, Julius, and just one: a boy. "Evidently, something inherent prevented them from having children," observed friend D. Russell Connor, adding, "Ethel and Gene loved children."[54]

Gene still referred to Ethel affectionately not long before while discussing his showbiz-related superstitions with a reporter. He revealed that he would go onstage only if his dog were back in his dressing room. He refused to shave before a performance. Neither could he play without the identification bracelet his wife had given him.[55]

It appears that Ethel spent little to no time in the new home once it was built. Rumors surfaced early in 1942 that she was in Florida filing for divorce.[56] She confirmed the rumors in Miami with an April submission of divorce papers.[57] A judge granted the split on May 1.[58]

Gene Krupa confirmed the news with equanimity. "You can't blame a woman for not wanting to stay married to a musician," he said. "She told me she was leaving so I could stay married to my drums."[59]

According to Anita O'Day, Gene "wasn't handling the temptations that go with success too well." He had "developed a roving eye." There were "girls on the road" like vocalist Dinah Shore. He had an affair with young Hollywood actress Lana Turner, whom he called "Dreamface." Gossip columnists cited this relationship as the cause of the Krupa split-up.[60] Anita remembered that, before a show, Turner would walk past O'Day's dressing room on the way to Gene's. Later, a "disheveled" Lana would knock on Anita's door and request a makeup mirror, comb, and brush.[61] Eventually, news came that Lana had dumped Gene for someone else.

Once Gene asked Anita if she would like to sleep with him, as follows: "Would you like to have breakfast with me?" O'Day, unafraid of bluntness, responded: "Sorry. I never mix business with pleasure." Krupa, in his usual good-natured way, responded, "Good girl." And that was it.[62]

The divorce didn't mean Gene and Ethel were permanently apart. Suddenly, they were seeing each other again. The gossip columns reported numerous sightings of them together. "Gene Krupa [is] making the early-morning hot spots with a very lovely young lady—the ex-Mrs. Ethel Krupa," said *Down Beat*.[63] "Gene and the former Mrs. Gene Krupa spent plenty of time together out in Hollywood, and no one will be surprised if they actually get together again," said *The Orchestra World*.[64] Was reconciliation in the air?

Drums, Boogie-Woogie, "Drumboogie," and Rock and Roll

Gene, a drumming man, developed drum features like "Blue Rhythm Fantasy, Parts 1 and 2." Other Krupa recordings also referenced drumming. "Drummin' Man" (1939) was an adaptation of the Earl Hines Band's "Piano Man" (Hines was a pianist). "Drummer Boy," (1940) with his as-yet-unnamed Bo Diddley licks, declared, "When he plays 'em, he just slays 'em." There was "That Drummer's Band" (1942), a Krupa-Eldridge cowrite.

As for boogie-woogie, possibly his earliest side to pay homage to a genre then embraced mainly by aficionados was "The Last Round Up," one of his 1935 sides under the moniker Gene Krupa and His Chicagoans. There were also "Boog It" (1940), "Boogie Woogie Bugle Boy" (1941), and later, "Boogie Blues" (1945), "Gene's Boogie" (1947), and "Bop Boogie" (1949).

One never-recorded gem that in 1942 Gene and band often played with Anita O'Day on vocals was the sizzling "Cow Cow Boogie." The slow-moving tempo and the chugging beat generated notable heat. "Often handled very vulgarly and primitively by white bands," said jazz scholar Gunther Schuller, "boogie-woogie was for some reason always approached by Krupa with a certain sensitivity, extrapolating the best out of this limited style."[65]

"Drumboogie" (1941) encompassed drums *and* boogie-woogie. It was based on a trumpet riff by Eldridge. Gene and arranger Elton Hill added the rest. Originally recorded in January 1941, it was sung by Irene Daye just before she left and Anita O'Day came in. "Drumboogie" was an important record, the kind of drum feature that excited one of his most visceral listener responses, and one associated with him almost as much as "Sing, Sing, Sing."

More important than the visceral response "Drumboogie" attracted was its rock and roll quality, and rock didn't even exist yet. "I've played that for people, just that drum part, and would say, 'What year do you think this is from?'" said jazz drummer Kevin Dorn. "And nobody thinks it's from the early '40s . . .

"That particular pattern which Gene Krupa would go into near the end of the arrangement—he would usually play that pretty straight, which actually makes it sound like a rock beat . . .

"Not only does it sound like something that drummers would be playing 25 years later in a completely different style of music— but also the way he played it . . . open-handed, riding the high-hat with his left hand instead of crossing over. That kind of open-handed playing . . . would become more popular many, many decades later. Very few people were doing that in 1941 . . ."[66]

Speaking of rock, let's look at "Stop! The Red Light's On." Toward song's end, when Roy Eldridge tears into his last solo, Gene is heard playing a slow but assertive series of bouncing tom-tom thumps reminiscent of the "bring it on home" attitude so often found in rock drumming.

"No Name Jive" (1940) evokes rock without using any rock and roll devices. Invoking his early idol, Baby Dodds, Gene's drumming on this number is, as *Modern Drummer* once said, a "slowly building five-chorus-long press roll."[67]

"This has that great continuous press roll, and he's playing some accents within the roll," said Kevin Dorn. "The tension really builds up."[68]

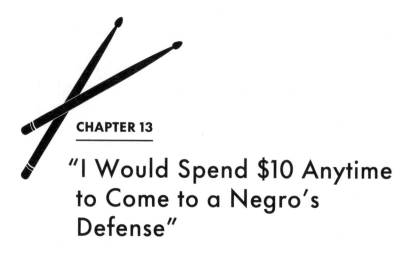

CHAPTER 13

"I Would Spend $10 Anytime to Come to a Negro's Defense"

AN ENDORSEMENT OF GENE KRUPA came from an unlikely corner—the hip-hop corner—decades after Gene's death. Fab 5 Freddy, a pioneer rapper, graffiti artist, and hip-hop mover and shaker, heard jazz growing up. In 2011, he talked about white people playing black music; there is a controversy in some jazz circles about whether whites could or should play jazz, since it originated among black musicians.

"There's Gene Krupa," Freddy said. "There are a whole lotta white dudes that you could just feel by how they articulate what they do on their instrument—you're like, 'Ok, dude gets a pass.'" He said his father usually dismissed white artists as unable to play authentic jazz. "They weren't dissin' white people," said Freddy. "But it really meant most of the time that they weren't as up to snuff as most of the official cats. I know that Gene Krupa got some love, and there were some white musicians that my father and them would okay, but not that many."[1]

Modern jazz drummer Max Roach, who collaborated with Fab 5 Freddy in his later years, once said, similarly: "He was more than just another *student* of Black music like most of the folks are," he remarked. "He was also a *contributor*."[2]

"Contributor" that Gene was, Fab 5 Freddy's statement that Gene "got some love" among African-Americans could more generally refer to the drummer's color-blind outlook. He embraced African-Americans and African-American culture and causes in a way rarely seen among white jazzers, let alone the general white public.

In January 1937, a few white musicians—Gene, Mezz Mezzrow, and Benny Goodman's cornet-paying brother Irving—attended a send-off in Harlem for black bandleader Jimmie Lunceford, who would soon be touring Europe.[3] In February 1939, a funeral overwhelmingly attended by African-Americans was held in Los Angeles for Count Basie's tenor man, Herschel Evans. Krupa couldn't be there, but may have been the only white person connected with jazz, other than disc jockey Al Jarvis, to send a floral wreath and a message of condolence read at the service.[4]

Gene was among three white musicians listed by black newspaper the *Phoenix Index*—the others being Benny Goodman and Ben Bernie—who played in August 1940 at the Polo Grounds in Manhattan at a benefit for an African-American college, Florida's Bethune-Cookman.[5]

In late 1940, the African-American newspaper *Evansville* (Indiana) *Argus* reported that, unlike when black opera singer Marian Anderson performed in town, the Krupa band's clientele were not racially segregated: "You sat at anyplace you so pleased...up high or down low." The paper noted that Krupa and the ticket-sellers were white: "They didn't pin any colored tickets on us, only tickets... ORCHIDS TO THE SPONSORS OF THE DANCE."[6]

A curious question came to the *Pittsburgh Courier*. "I wish to know of what nationality is Gene Krupa," wrote James H. Williams of Canonsburg, Pennsylvania. "I think he is white but I must have proof." The answer, in part, read: "We are told that he is white but as paradoxical as this question of color is, a person can be white and yet be black and one can be black and yet white. We in America waste a great deal of valuable time in differentiating and classifying the human race on the basis of color or other arbitrary methods."[7]

Gene's band appears to have been among the few to appear at black swing venues. This demonstrated his pull with black audiences, as well as his feeling for the African-American community. In November 1941, his band followed the Lionel Hampton aggregation into the Castle Ballroom in St. Louis, Missouri.[8] The showcase of African-American talent in Detroit, the Paradise Theater, announced in June 1942 that it expected many name bands in the fall, all of them black (Duke Ellington, Erskine Hawkins, Fats Waller) except for Charlie Barnet and Gene Krupa.[9]

Evidence of the regard Gene held for the black community continued from the 1940s through the 1960s, and, certainly, beyond that time. In fall 1947, Gene; the mixed-race tin pan alley songwriting team, Bennie Benjamin and George David Weiss; and Harlem-based jazz columnist Dan Burley together judged a songwriting contest sponsored by Louis Jordan's manager. Requested were lyrics best capturing the "spirit" of Christmas and the New Year, which could be applied to the music of Jordan's "Let the Good Times Roll." (A Baltimore housewife won first prize.)[10]

It wasn't surprising to see an advertisement in the *Pittsburgh Courier* that same year for the Harlem Records Supply Company in which, among the 8 × 10s for sale of celebrities, only Gene Krupa and the late President Franklin D. Roosevelt were white. (Others included Ella Fitzgerald, Lena Horne, Hazel Scott, and Count Basie.)[11]

In 1947, the Dayton, Ohio–area African-American newspaper *The Ohio Daily-Express* praised several celebrities for their civil rights activism—actor Canada Lee, Lena Horne, singer-songwriter Josh White, and two Caucasians: Frank Sinatra and Gene Krupa. These entertainers, said the *Daily-Express*, were activists in the spirit of the "new militant fervor that is gripping more and more people in America." The newspaper continued: "These artists have transcended the limits of lesser performers who, tho their slickness may have netted them a greater measure of pecuniary gain and popularity cannot be said to be doing any more than just sloughing along thru life... These latter are not true artists at all."[12]

In 1949, Gene Krupa, African-American jazz tenor man Illinois Jacquet, boxer "Sugar Ray" Robinson, and stage actress Juanita Hall appeared at the Jackie Robinson Ball fundraiser for the Sister Kenny Foundation.[13] Some years later, The *Pittsburgh Courier* reported that Gene Krupa and Fred Astaire attended the opening of a new show, *Too Poor To Die*, performed by black stand-up comedian Timmie Rogers at the Ebony Showcase in Los Angeles.[14]

THESE SEPARATE EVENTS and editorial mentions were great, but what did they mean? Bringing all of the foregoing into focus was a New York–based company that in 1946 Gene Krupa cofounded, Herald Pictures, with some film industry veterans. Its aim was to bring a regular nationwide supply of decently budgeted African-American movies to African-American theaters, which were often starved for content. Herald Pictures hoped for the broad distribution of films into as many "white" movie houses as possible. Gene was a vice president of the new company, his job listed as "musical director and talent supervisor."[15]

Besides musicals, Herald Pictures was to produce movie shorts and full-length documentaries focusing on black life around the United States. It was not an easy task for Herald Pictures to get its films distributed efficiently and regularly to black theaters; an agreement with Screen Guild Productions to distribute Herald Picture's products wasn't signed until nearly a year after Herald's founding. With Screen Guild on board, Herald expected that its movies would be shown in both black and white "locations." These combined efforts had never before been tried.[16]

The first high-profile Herald Pictures film, made in 1946 and released in 1947, was the musical *Boy! What a Girl!* Starring were veteran vaudeville acts Tim Moore and Patterson and Jackson; young actresses Sheila Guyse, Betti Mays, and Basil Spears; eccentric jazz humming-bassist Slam Stewart and his trio; pre-rock purveyors of doo-wop, Deek Watson and the Brown Dots; and esteemed drummer Big Sid Catlett and his band.[17]

Herald Pictures vice president Gene Krupa made a cameo. After Catlett and band played a number, there Gene was, having emerged from staged "woodwork." Dialogue ensued. Catlett: "What do *you* want?" Krupa: "Sticks!" Catlett: "What *for*?" Krupa: "I wanna get *kicks* with the sticks!" Catlett: "With *these* sticks?" Krupa: "Sure!"

The sticks were transferred from Sid to Gene. Krupa was full of duende and memories of his student days with Moeller as he performed with Catlett's band playing behind him. Afterward, Gene returned the sticks to Sid, who said, feigning surprise, "Hey—I know who *you* are. You're *Gene Krupa!*" Gene responded, "That's right, Sid, and I hope you'll do the same for me in one of *my* pictures!" Sid: "Will do." Gene: "Solid!" Krupa returned to the staged woodwork from whence he came.

Sid never appeared in one of Gene's films, although Gene only had a supporting role or two left in his limited celluloid career. Catlett died in 1951 at age forty-one.

Other full-length films released by Herald were *Sepia Cinderella* and *Miracle in Harlem*, but Gene didn't appear in either. It's unclear whether Herald Pictures released more full-length films after that. As we've seen, Herald had made a distribution agreement with Screen Guild Productions in 1947. In 1948, Herald signed another such agreement with National Film Distributors.[18] Possibly something had gone wrong with the Screen Guild contract.

Even if not much transpired with Herald Pictures afterward, it was an ambitious, much-needed initiative made at a time after World War Two when civil rights should have been making advances, but, for political and other reasons, were not. Gene Krupa's involvement with Herald Pictures was at least right-minded and laudable.

———————

AROUND 1941, A new kind of entertainment technology premiered— the "soundie" jukebox, the main difference from a regular jukebox being that you could hear only the music on a regular, whereas on a soundie you got a mini-movie. The small screen may have not been ideal for enjoying the soundie; still, you got your favorite band or singer for a dime. By 1944, at least 450 soundies had been made. There must have been something attractive in this new device given the number of soundies being churned out.[19]

Each recording artist typically made a total of four soundies for Minoco Productions. First, the band recorded the music. On

another date, they practiced miming to the recording. Their miming would then be filmed. The Krupa band recorded three songs,
not four. Only two Krupa soundies came out of these sessions. The
third recording was used for a soundie by separate artists.

The two Krupa soundies were *Let Me Off Uptown* and *Thanks
for the Boogie Ride*. Both featured the famed musical and verbal interactions between Anita O'Day and Roy Eldridge. For his soundies,
instead of placing his talent at center stage, Gene chose two songs
from the band book in which he took a backseat to the talents of
white Anita and black Roy. The O'Day-Eldridge collaboration was
probably more groundbreaking than the sides. Their interracial camaraderie gave the soundies their magic. *Let Me Off Uptown* went
further than *Boogie Ride*; in "Uptown," the camera cuts away to reveal two black dancers, "Jazzlips" Richardson and Jeanne Bayer, for
their ballroom interpretation of the song.

Uptown was released the week of January 12, 1942, and *Boogie
Ride* the week of February 9. The third song recorded during the
Minoco session was "After You've Gone," an Eldridge trumpet specialty on which, again, Gene Krupa took a back seat. This recording
was never used for a Krupa soundie. Instead, it was used in September as the music for a soundie called *Sugar Hill Masquerade
(After You've Gone)*, featuring African-American trumpeter and
former Earl Hines sideman Walter "Hot Lips" Fuller and his ensemble, plus black dancers—Whitey's Lindy Hoppers. This soundie
was released the week of November 23, 1942.[20]

It's unknown why the Krupa band didn't make a soundie with
their recording, but it's noteworthy that it was ultimately used by
black artists and that Walter Fuller, featured in the *After You've
Gone* soundie, was later featured in the second Herald Pictures film,
Sepia Cinderella. Maybe giving the Krupa band's recording of
"After You've Gone" to Fuller was Gene's idea.

The soundies were a short-lived phenomenon, although varied
uses were made of them in ensuing years. In 1943, Gene's *Uptown*
soundie was featured in movie theaters; the soundies' promoter,
Walter O. Gutlohn, said that *Uptown* was a "showstopper" in
every one.[21] In 1945, the soundies were marketed to organizations

searching for films to show at their events.[22] In 1946, Gutlohn pushed soundies to homeowners with sound projectors.[23] By 1950, television had taken over. A Los Angeles TV station purchased about one thousand soundies to broadcast in a "visual disc jockey program."[24] Subsequently, soundies sank from sight.

―――――――――

TEDDY WILSON WAS asked in 1977 whether he and Lionel Hampton, as black musicians, had had "any problem hotel-wise or restaurant-wise" when they played with Benny Goodman in the 1930s. "Yes," said Wilson, "but it's hard to call that a problem because it was the norm of that day. We didn't challenge the norm, which was that Lionel and I couldn't stay in the white hotels. If we'd had to make a battle of that thing in every town on one-night stands, you couldn't ever get to work..."[25]

Variety reported on December 3, 1941, that Gene had canceled all Southern one-nighters after learning that some Southern venues might prohibit Roy Eldridge from performing.[26] But the North also subscribed to a racial caste system. It just wasn't as blatant. Roy Eldridge once said that "you never know how colored you can be until you make the rounds with the ruling classes and you don't have to go south of the Mason-Dixon Line to find head-breaking prejudice if you forget the lines of demarcation." Gene's band contracts guaranteed Roy "access to all facilities available to the rest of the band."[27] Yet there was only so much Gene could do, night after night, hotel after hotel, restaurant after restaurant.

On Thanksgiving night 1941, after Gene and the band had played a one-nighter at York, Pennsylvania's Valencia Ballroom, Gene, Roy Eldridge, and a black employee of Gene's stopped to eat at a local restaurant, the Bury. A waiter refused to seat the two black men. Gene took umbrage and had words with a manager. A police officer eating in the restaurant said to Gene's party, "You heard what the man said. He didn't want to serve you, so get out." Gene gave the officer a "verbal lashing," which led to his arrest and jailing on disorderly conduct charges. He was released upon paying a ten-dollar fine. Roy Eldridge was not involved in the confrontation, nor was he jailed.

Afterward, Gene told the local newspaper, "I didn't want to cause any trouble, but I would spend $10 anytime to come to a Negro's defense..."[28] (Ten 1941 dollars is the equivalent in 2023 of over $200.)

The incident made him such a hero among African-Americans that he nearly won the *Pittsburgh Courier*'s third annual band contest trophy. Ultimately, he lost to Count Basie.[29] Better than this was Gene receiving the first annual Chu Berry Memorial Award, established by Pabst Blue Ribbon in memory of the Cab Calloway tenor saxophonist recently killed in a car crash. The award was to honor an individual "whose contribution to music can be judged the most unprejudiced and valuable to the advancement of the race in this great profession." Gene accepted the award in person from Chu Berry's mother while his band was working in Chicago.[30]

A *Pittsburgh Courier* columnist wrote: "Gene Krupa won the 'Chu' Berry Memorial Award because he believed in the principles of democracy and the way that he sponged and pressed those tank town, soap-headed, municipal officials on this 'color jive' makes him 'hep-hep' on the solid side."[31]

CHAPTER 14

Giving Careers a Lift

I T WASN'T ONLY ROY ELDRIDGE, Anita O'Day, and Charlie Ventura whom Krupa promoted to national fame, or Buddy DeFranco and Johnny Desmond whose careers Gene jump-started. He was instrumental in Glenn Miller's fame and fortune, too.

Maybe it was Gene's thank-you gift to Glenn for helping him drum the orchestra score during Gershwin's *Strike Up the Band* in 1930. As we've seen, one of Gene's early drum students was the youngster Moe Purtill, among the first in a long stream of Krupa-like drummers. Purtill joined Miller in 1939, in time for many of the most famous Miller tunes: "Pennsylvania 6-5000"; "In the Mood," in which Purtill rings the cowbell in Krupa-esque fashion toward the end; and "American Patrol," which features an especially good Purtill drum break.

Probably more important to Miller was tenor sax man and vocalist "Tex" Beneke. When Gene was assembling his first band in 1938, he was scouting for sidemen and attended a Cleveland performance of the Ben Young band from Texas, for whom Beneke was playing. Decades later, Tex still could barely utter the reverence with which he and his bandmates regarded Gene and describe their fright over knowing that Krupa was watching and would probably hire some of them. "The great Krupa showed up," said Beneke. "Man, we couldn't, uh—he was a big name and everything. We were all doing our best. Playing for him was like…" Tex just stopped there.

Gene selected three of Ben Young's "boys," but not Beneke. "I was so disappointed that he didn't take me," Tex said. He later learned that Gene already had a full sax section by the time he observed the Young band, and that Gene had recommended Tex to Glenn Miller. As Beneke remembered, Glenn said in his introductory phone call, "My name is Glenn Miller. I'm a trombone player and I'm startin' my own orchestra. And you come pretty highly recommended by a good buddy o' mine. Would you be interested?"[1]

Glenn Miller's band became the land's most popular. Gene's recommendation did Beneke no small favor. Tex's tenor solos were heard on many a Miller track, and his voice on some of the most well-known Miller hits, including "Chattanooga Choo Choo," "(I've Got a Gal in) Kalamazoo," and "Blues in the Night."

Krupa elevated many to success through his drumming contests. Initially, these were small-scale affairs in which Bill West, a friend, drummer, and drum shop owner, helped Gene select contestants and judge drummers. The contests commenced while Krupa was playing at the Dancing Campus of the New York World's Fair in the summer and fall of 1940.[2] These competitions were broadcast on the radio.[3]

In 1941, Slingerland Drums decided to sponsor what would become a regular event—"Gene Krupa's National Amateur Swing Drummers' Contest." First, there would be regional contests held in music stores around the country; then semifinals in a few key locations; then the finals, to be held in New York City.[4]

The first winner of the Slingerland-Krupa contest was 17-year-old Louie Bellson of Rock Falls, Illinois. "That kid… is one helluva fine drummer," reported *Metronome*. "Almost any big band could hire him as an improvement—he's that good."[5] Louie came from a very musical family. His father was a multi-instrumentalist who owned a music store. Bellson grew up on opera and classical music.

Bellson was probably the best drummer to come out of the contests and has been recognized as a Krupa disciple. After winning the competition, Bellson debuted with Ted Fio Rito's band—said Louie's sister Sarah, "Winning that contest...really started Louie's career off"[6]—and later secured a coveted spot with Benny Goodman. Later, he played with Harry James, Tommy Dorsey, Count Basie, and Duke Ellington. He also composed music and eventually became the musical director for his wife, singer Pearl Bailey.[7]

Other successful drummers to emerge from the contests, by winning or placing high in regionals or semifinals, included Karl Kiffe, who played with Jimmy Dorsey; Bobby Rickey, who drummed for Vaughn Monroe and Charlie Spivack; and Dave Black, who earned a place in Duke Ellington's band. Black could attribute his success not only to having won a Krupa contest but also to seeing Krupa—his idol—in person, at age thirteen; that experience set him on the pathway to professional drumming.[8]

Among Krupa victors, Sonny Igoe may have been second only to Louie Bellson in drumming stature. Gene had been Igoe's idol since boyhood. Sonny practiced to Goodman-Krupa records, and was lucky to have grown up in a musical household that hosted jam sessions in which he sat in. At sixteen, he entered a Krupa contest held at the Meadowbrook in Cedar Grove. Igoe was among forty hopefuls.

Igoe was third among roughly half a dozen finalists. To crown the winner, Gene assigned each boy to play a number with some Krupa sidemen. Igoe's experience jamming with others helped him greatly, and he won. Gene sent him to study under Bill West in New York City. "Gene kind of adopted me as his protégé," said Igoe, introducing him thusly whenever other people were around.[9] World War Two intervened, but afterward, he played with Les Elgart, Ina Ray Hutton, Benny Goodman, Woody Herman, and Charlie Ventura, and in the NBC and CBS television orchestras.[10]

Gene as a Cultural Reference Point

Gene Krupa's importance was about music and drumming, but he also impacted society and, to some, served as evidence of soci-

ety's downfall. As early as March 1937, he could be found in popular fiction. His duende, interpreted by the older generation as
borderline malignant, provided fodder for cautionary tales like
"Wild Boy" in the (Washington, DC) *Evening Star*. Well-behaved
teenager Isabelle is infatuated with Stanley, expelled from school
and already a drunk-driving convict. They love swing music and
Gene's unrestrained performances. Only after she tires of Krupa
and his "savage excitement" are she and Stanley cured of the
dangers he presents. The teens return to the arms of her conservative parents.[11]

There was Gene the Good. In October 1938, he was among several bandleaders named to the Non-Partisan Committee to Suppress Musical Bigotry. This was in response to complaints made to
the Federal Communications Commission by the Bach Society of
Newark. They objected to the trend among bands of recording
swing versions of classical pieces.[12]

Gene's credibility in jazz advocacy was recognized when, in November 1938, he was invited to join the new National Advisory
Board of the United Hot Clubs of America.[13]

A cartoon titled "Crackpot College" appeared in a 1939 issue of
Washington, DC's *Sunday Star*. In it, an elderly professor of languages frustratedly eavesdrops on two students speaking nearby
about popular music. Says one to the other: "Goodman savvies jive
but a Gene Krupa platter drives the rug cutters whacky when that
skin-beater gets in the groove."[14]

Ira Wolfert, writing for the *Evening Star* in July 1940, said that,
because of Krupa, the "drummer boys are in command." When
they are at their best, they sound like a "truck falling down hill." He
added: "When Gene Krupa ... plays a solo his hair falls over his
eyes and his eyes glitter and his mouth hangs open. He raps the
[drum] skin and the skin grunts ... The audience's eyes glitter and
their mouths hang open."[15]

More insightful was Frederick Lewis Allen, author of a history
of the 1930s, *Since Yesterday* (1939), the bestselling sequel to his previous bestseller, *Only Yesterday* (1931), which reviewed the 1920s.
As Allen recounted in *Since Yesterday*, Gene was at the scene of the

March 1937 series of Goodman Paramount shows where high school kids went crazy. "Feed it to me, Gene!" these youngsters were to have yelled. "Send me down!"

"A good swing band," wrote Allen, offered "furious improvisations" from the reeds and brass, with the "drummers going into long-drawnout rhythmical frenzies." Thus Allen called up images of Gene Krupa in all of his sweaty glamour. Allen cautioned that what might seem a "blare of discordant noise" was really "an extremely complex and subtle pattern, a full appreciation of which demanded far more musical sophistication than the simpler popular airs of a preceding period." Ergo, discerning listeners received a true musical education; Gene Krupa was explicitly and implicitly helping to improve the quality of American popular music.[16]

Other writers inserted Gene's name into nonmusical settings. He was mentioned in a newspaper report on an overworked racehorse named Alsab competing at Belmont Park raceway on New York's Long Island. The writer figured Krupa would have "been slightly green with envy" at how the jockey cracked the whip on the unfortunate Alsab to move him along.[17]

In early 1943, the Leroy Brothers went national with their idea of a "Krupa performance at the drums" using marionettes on a Minneapolis stage.[18] This show made the rounds of America's theaters into the 1950s.

Jokes circulated about the decibel level of Gene's drumming. One columnist complained that cocktail parties were so loud you went "home with eardrums that feel as though Gene Krupa had been practicing on them."[19] A funny column by Jay Carmody said a friend returning from military service had had quite the jungle experience. "When we pushed open the bushes," his friend said, "we found ourselves with ringside hiding places at the wildest jungle jam session any one ever saw. The drummers were going crazier than Gene Krupa..."[20]

The noise of World War Two's artillery fire caused everything from headaches to post-traumatic stress disorder. Antiaircraft gunfire in London had one reporter declaring it was so loud even "Gene Krupa is a piker by comparison."[21]

Gene's mother, Anna Oslowski,
daughter of immigrants
from northern Poland, 1880s.
Courtesy of Gene H. Krupa.

Gene's father, Bartley Krupa,
immigrant from Galicia in Poland, 1880s.
Courtesy of Gene H. Krupa.

Little "Yudge" and his
next older brother, Julius.
Courtesy of Gene H. Krupa.

Ready for Hollywood
Gene Krupa's first wife Ethel
circa late '30s, early '40s
Courtesy of the Michael A. Bellino Family

Ethel Krupa, circa early 1950s.
Courtesy of the Michael A. Bellino Family.

The original Benny Goodman
Quartet, 1930s.
Left to right: Teddy Wilson,
Lionel Hampton,
Benny Goodman, Gene.
*Benny Goodman Archives
at Yale University.*

Boys in men's clothing: Goodman band,
mid-1930s. Benny, center. Gene, left of Benny.
Jess Stacy, last row, second from left.
Art Rollini, middle row, far right.
Benny Goodman Archives at Yale University.

Goodman, Krupa, et al., while filming
Hollywood Hotel in summer 1937.
*Photograph by Schuyler Crail.
Benny Goodman Archives at Yale University.*

Goodman and Krupa while filming
Hollywood Hotel in summer 1937.
*Photograph by Schuyler Crail.
Benny Goodman Archives at Yale University.*

Benny Goodman and His Orchestra while filming *Hollywood Hotel* in summer 1937. Possibly the loudest trumpet section in swing is sitting at back. Left to right: Harry James, Ziggy Elman, Chris Griffin. *Photograph by Schuyler Crail. Benny Goodman Archives at Yale University.*

Benny Goodman's historic Carnegie Hall jazz concert, 1/16/1938. Notice Gene's alternate "Quartette" kit with two rack-toms. Left to right: Harry Goodman (bass), Gene, Babe Russin (tenor sax), Allan Reuss (guitar), George Koenig and Hymie Schertzer (both alto sax). *Gift of Lawrence Marx, in memory of Albert Marx. Courtesy of Carnegie Hall Rose Archives.*

Gene rehearsing with
his new rhythm section, 1938.
Left to right: Milton Raskin (piano), Horace
Rollins (bass), Ray Biondi (guitar), Gene.
Photograph by Otto F. Hess.

Eccentric extrovert Leo Watson, 1938.
At right are Ray Biondi, Horace Rollins, Gene.
Photograph by Otto F. Hess.

Gene Krupa with arrangers
and music industry men, 1940.
Left to right: Joe Glaser, Jimmy Mundy,
Morty Palitz, Elton Hill, Gene.
Photograph by Otto F. Hess.

"Like brothers": Gene and Roy Eldridge, 1942.
Courtesy of the Sherman Jazz Museum.

Gene enjoying Roy's solo, early 1940s.
Courtesy of the Sherman Jazz Museum.

Roy Eldridge loving Gene's playing, early 1940s.
Courtesy of PoPsiePhotos.com.

"Intermission" group of mostly Chicagoans at Carnegie Hall, 1/14/1942, in support of Fats Waller. Left to right: Eddie Condon, Bud Freeman, John Kirby, Gene, Max Kaminsky, Pee Wee Russell. *Courtesy of Maggie Condon.*

Happy to see each other: Anita and Gene gossip about times old and new backstage at New York's Capitol Theatre. This photo appeared on the cover of the 11/3/1948 issue of *Down Beat* magazine. *Photograph from Down Beat Archives.*

Gene's innovative singer Anita O'Day, 1940s. *Photograph by Maurice Seymour. Courtesy of Ronald Seymour.*

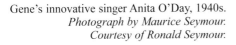

"Krupa, get up here": Gene and Eddie shoot the breeze at radio microphone, Town Hall concert, 1944. *Courtesy of Maggie Condon.*

Best friends forever: Gene and Eddie Condon, Town Hall concert, 1944. *Courtesy of Maggie Condon.*

Gene with his beloved sister Elenor, the Krupa family "matriarch," circa 1940s. *Courtesy of Gene H. Krupa.*

Gene and band, 1941, in photographer Gjon Mili's New York studio. Roy Eldridge and Ray Biondi are visible behind Gene. *Shutterstock.*

Gene's spectacular up and down strokes as seen through Gjon Mili's stroboscopic photography, 1941. *Shutterstock.*

mming at Condon's Club, New York, 7/17/1951.
eft to right: Condon, Lou McGarity, Gene,
Wild Bill" Davison.
ourtesy of Maggie Condon.*

Gene with Charlie Ventura (extreme left), Club Hato on the Ginza, Tokyo, Japan, April 1952.
Shutterstock.

Gene signing autograph for Japanese fans, Club Hato on the Ginza, Tokyo, Japan, April 1952.
Shutterstock.

Gene and Roy Eldridge with fans during 1953 Jazz at the Philharmonic tour of Japan.
Courtesy of the Sherman Jazz Museum.

Billboard marquee, 1949.
Courtesy of the Sherman Jazz Museum.

Gene wearing mentee Mel Lewis's glasses, 1940s.
LaBudde Special Collections, UMKC University Libraries. Courtesy of the Mel Lewis Family.

he "bromance" continues:
oy Eldridge and Gene Krupa, 1950s.
ourtesy of the Sherman Jazz Museum.

Gene with good friend Cozy Cole as they prepare to open the Krupa-Cole drumming school, 1954.
Courtesy of James Kriegsmann.

Goodman, Krupa, Hamp, and Teddy Wilson
recording LP *Together Again*.
Photograph by George Avakian.
Courtesy of the Avakian Trust.

Rare breaktime sighting:
Krupa playing piano during
1963 recording sessions of *Together Again*.
Photograph by George Avakian.
Courtesy of the Avakian Trust.

Jamming on 1/16/1968
at Benny Goodman's
New York penthouse to
celebrate the 30th
anniversary of the
Carnegie Hall concert.
Visible are Lionel Hampton
(left), Benny Goodman
(right), with Gene in back.
*Photograph by
John McDonough.*

Gene performing with
the Condon/McPartland
Chicagoans on 12/5/1969
at the Holiday Inn
in Meriden, CT.
Two young fans look on.
*Photograph by and courtesy
of Hank O'Neal.*

Celebrating the 30th
anniversary of the historic
1938 Carnegie Hall concert.
Left to right: Gene Krupa,
Benny Goodman, Ziggy Elman.
Photograph by John McDonough.

Gene and young drummer-admirer
Bobby Tribuzio at the Metropole Café,
early 1960s.
Courtesy of Bobby Tribuzio.

Joe Vetrano meeting Gene Krupa at t‍
Metropole Café, Times Square, July 196‍
Courtesy of Joe Vetran‍

Joe Vetrano with his surrogate dad,
Gene Krupa, at Your Father's Mustache,
Greenwich Village, 10/30/1971.
Courtesy of Joe Vetrano.

Coming out of retirement:
Gene performing at Plaza 9 jazz club,
Plaza Hotel, New York, 6/3/1970.
Courtesy of Joe Vetrano.

Jazz writer John McDonough
and Gene Krupa at
NAMM conference, June 1971.
Photograph by John McDonough.

Krupa at June 1971 NAMM conference,
pleasing everybody.
Photograph by John McDonough.

Wilson, Krupa, Hamp, and Goodman
at Timex All-Star Swing Festival,
Lincoln Center, Manhattan, October 1972.
Benny Goodman Archives at Yale University.

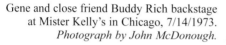

Gene and close friend Buddy Rich backstage
at Mister Kelly's in Chicago, 7/14/1973.
Photograph by John McDonough.

"I'll be joining you soon":
Gene offering emotional eulogy
at Eddie Condon's funeral, August 1973.
Courtesy of Maggie Condon.

Old and ill at 64, Gene contemplates
Eddie Condon's guitar and casket
at Condon's funeral, August 1973.
Courtesy of Maggie Condon.

Krupa earned a biographical profile in a 1991 book, *Chicago Portraits*. The author "chose individuals who, either negatively or positively, made a substantial impact on this city." The "individuals portrayed in these pages," she said, "capture the many faces of Chicago's past."[22]

In discussing jazz, *The Companion to Southern Literature* cited Gene "for his percussion improvisation, emulating the manner of the improvised solos by his associates in the wind section."[23] In other words, Krupa made the drums a solo instrument.

He pops up occasionally in fiction—for example, young adult novel *The Loud Silence of Francine Green* (2006)[24]; and a 2013 short story, "Welcome Jean Krupa, World's Greatest Girl Drummer!"[25]

He is a background figure in Nelson Algren's *The Man with the Golden Arm* (1949), for which the author won the first-ever National Book Award. Its protagonist, Chicago resident Francis Majcinek, or "Frankie Machine," is a morphine-addicted backroom card dealer and aspiring jazz drummer. Frankie gets his chance one evening in a club when an ensemble's drummer proclaims himself "Gene Krupa," says he wants a pack of cigarettes, and collapses. Machine plays substitute drums, thinking himself sometimes Gene Krupa, sometimes Dave Tough. Later in a stupor after a morphine shot, Machine mumbles fantastically that "Krupa been askin' around at the Musician's Club where he can get in touch with me, I guess some guys told him about that night... when I got everybody goin' like fools the way I was in the groove..."[26] Whether or not Frankie Machine accepted Gene Krupa's make-believe offer, Gene's impact on cultural America was too huge to ignore.

CHAPTER 15

Famous Fans and
Drumming Descendants

TEENAGE MOVIE STAR JACKIE COOPER—who, as a child, had co-starred in the *Our Gang* comedies and played in films opposite Wallace Beery—loved drums and was a big Krupa fan going back as far as 1938.[1] When Gene was playing in Los Angeles, Cooper "was there every night, watching, waiting for the chances Gene would give me to sit in with the band. I'd usually end up backstage, talking, listening, absorbing that atmosphere..."[2]

We know that Fred Astaire incorporated Krupa drumming concepts in some of his filmed dance routines. In a May 1939 *Photoplay* "Q & A," Astaire listed Gene as one of his idols, along with some golfers, a baseball player, various movie stars, and one other musician—Benny Goodman.[3] Gene's drumming made Astaire, who was subbing for columnist Ed Sullivan one day, think of railyard sounds: "The Streamlined Trains that skim along with a steady sustaining purr, as the wheels on the tracks beat out some terrific Gene Krupa riffs."[4]

Ten-year-old Bob Crane saw Gene perform in April 1939 at the New York World's Fair and knew that being a drummer was the career for him.[5] It didn't quite happen the way he imagined it would, although he did host a radio show on which Gene guested, resulting in a "drum battle" between the two men.[6] Crane married his acting with his drumming skills during the sixth season of *Hogan's Heroes*, when Crane performed a Krupa-esque drum solo.

In Britain, as World War Two ended, young Peter Sellers was trying to make it as a comedian, or a drummer, or whatever would work. At one point, Sellers billed himself as "Britain's Answer to Gene Krupa," but instead of answering Gene with his drumming, his playing was marred, in Clouseau-like fashion, by lighting malfunctions and a "drastically off-tempo" band.[7]

JAZZ WRITERS GENERALLY agree that Gene Krupa spawned innumerable drumming imitators, including some who adopted his stick twirling and other stick tricks. This was not lost on music paper cartoonists. *Orchestra World* featured Al Atkins's "Sharps and Flats"; in October 1937, Atkins presented four humorous scenarios. One was set in Times Square outside the Paramount Theatre. Drumsticks are flying through the air and clattering as they hit the sidewalk. People in the street, struck by sticks, develop welts on their heads. An officer on walking patrol explains the disturbance to a superior in a police car: "There's a new flash drummer up at Roseland[,] Sarge!"[8]

We've seen that many elements typifying Gene's drumming were ahead of their time and how they have become a part of what every drummer does or aspires to do: crafting a universe of rim shots and stick-on-stick work; playing the ride cymbal; "dropping bombs"; inventing a drum part in a band using accents, fashioning fills, and generally "playing the arrangement"; demonstrating his penchant for speed; applying his tremendous technique to play cleanly and precisely; and casting a gigantic shadow with his tom-toms.

Jazz drummer "Duffy" Jackson stated that Krupa "influenced every drummer who ever sat behind a drum set."[9] Dan Morgenstern said Gene established the drum solo as a "prominent element in jazz. He gets full credit."[10] Besides that, Krupa transformed drums themselves "into a solo instrument," as jazz critic John Lucas observed. The "idea was chiefly Gene's," Lucas asserted, "and its realization wholly."[11] Gene, being ever the student and the teacher, offered, as a student of Jim Chapin posited, the "first taste of a scientific, technical school of drumming."[12] Like Goodman, he caused his contemporaries to pause and consider their own technical equipment," wrote jazz historian Richard Hadlock. "Krupa was fast, accurate, and . . . a master of dynamics and tonal shading."[13]

Just *considering* the broad sweep of jazz drummers—regardless of nationality, era, race, or genre—who have been influenced by Gene Krupa is daunting.

Bebop drummer Frankie Dunlop, who played with bassist Charles Mingus and tenor sax men Sonny Rollins and Sonny Stitt, was probably best known for his work with Thelonious Monk. Notwithstanding the modern turn of Frankie Dunlop's career, Gene Krupa was his earliest influence. As a boy, Frankie played hooky to hear Gene's band all day long at his local Buffalo, New York, movie theater.[14] Years later, when Dunlop was drumming for Maynard Ferguson "on these little rattletraps that I'd brought from Buffalo," said the drummer, he met Krupa, who was on the same bill. Krupa commended Dunlop on his playing. "I never would have expected that," said Frankie.

Gene was still Slingerland's main endorser and had been searching on their behalf for young drummers "who can play and be exciting." Gene asked if Frankie would be interested in a Slingerland endorsement deal. Dunlop would receive a new Slingerland set annually and have promotional pictures taken. Naturally, the young drummer said yes. Gene's flattering comment about Dunlop's playing, and that "he wanted me to advertise for Slingerland," said Dunlop, "I think that was the biggest turning point for me."[15]

Tito Puente, of Puerto Rican origin, grew up in Spanish Harlem. As a teenager in 1937, his percussive ambitions were electrified by seeing Benny Goodman with Gene Krupa at the Paramount Theatre. With all of the other high schoolers, he "waited in line for hours," but it was worth it. "The band was great, and I couldn't take my eyes off what Gene Krupa was playing," said Puente. "I followed him as the band came up. He was at the back. My idol! I thought I died and went to heaven."

"I knew right there what I wanted," Puente remembered. "To be Gene Krupa. To play just like him." He added, "Gene Krupa kicked off 'Sing, Sing, Sing,' and it just blew my mind... All I could think about was learning that arrangement and getting it right. I had the record, and I practiced day and night, note for note." Puente's biographer cited certain characteristics of Gene's drumming—military style with a booming bass drum, the use of call-and-response between himself and other band members, and a "relentless" energy—that "Tito would use to his advantage when he formed his first Latin band." Puente became a Latin jazz pioneer and probably the most famous of its proponents. His music spilled over into rock when, in 1970, Santana covered Puentes's "Oye Como Va."[16]

Mel Lewis's daughter Lori Sokoloff Lowell, who recalled that Gene was her father's "idol," said Gene "created the philosophy my father had of filling up the music." Lewis learned from Gene to fashion his playing "as he was listening to all the other musicians." Gene set an example for her father to "stitch together all the pieces whether or not it was written down."[17]

Tony Allen, the Nigerian drummer considered an originator of "Afrobeat," began as a Gene Krupa admirer. Allen said he "tried to copy" Gene's solos. "Before I started club crawling," he said, "it was Gene Krupa. When I started, I tried to play like Gene Krupa."[18]

Steve Little, who drummed for Duke Ellington in the 1960s, grew up in Hartford, Connecticut. As a young teen, he saw Gene Krupa perform whenever Gene passed through Hartford. Krupa was "so popular," Little said, that "every kid in my school knew who Gene Krupa was." In those days, Little said, "my ambition for myself was to go and be another Gene Krupa."[19]

We've seen how boys the world over were inspired by Gene Krupa to take up drums. There were, as jazz writer Martin Williams once asserted, "literally thousands of amateur drummers who hounded their parents for a drum set of their own."[20] Cuban native Ignacio Berroa decided to take up drumming when, in 1964, his father brought home a record of big band music that included a Krupa solo.[21] Berroa, who has played with Dizzy Gillespie, McCoy Tyner, Freddie Hubbard, and Chick Corea, is cited for merging Afro-Cuban music with jazz.

Bruce Klauber, who leads small ensembles in Philadelphia and Atlantic City, became enamored of jazz drumming through Gene. "I was taken to night clubs from the time I was a kid," said Klauber. "I liked the lights and the flash and the drums seemed to embody lights and flash. Then I started listening carefully to jazz as a young-ster. I heard and saw Krupa, a man who played jazz, no less, and ended up in 26 movies, on television and had his life story made into a movie . . . I wanted some of what Gene had for myself. What young jazz drumming fan didn't?"[22]

Klauber believes, as did jazz writer Whitney Balliett, that Gene strongly influenced the playing of Jo Jones and Sid Catlett. We've seen Jones so impressed with Gene's playing during his Buddy Rogers days that Jones couldn't tear himself away and risked being late for his own job. Klauber said of Jo and Sid, "Listen to their solos and their conceptions of solos. The riffs, licks, the syncopated place-ment of rim shots and the actual use of ringing rim shots themselves, the tom work, and their methods of reaching crescendos with press rolls, single strokes, and cymbal crashes, were all rooted in the drum solo style of Gene Krupa."[23] John Hammond remarked that, when Jo Jones first arrived in New York with Count Basie, Gene often vis-ited him and they practiced together. "You have to remember how influential and busy Gene was in those days," Hammond said. "That he took the time indicated how much he thought of Jo."[24]

Much younger than Gene Krupa, Sid Catlett, or Jo Jones was Al-phonse Mouzon, whose varied drumming career began in jazz with Weather Report and subsequently weaved in and out of jazz and other contemporary music. Mouzon said that Gene "influenced me so much," and proudly referred to his drum introduction in the "Blue Spot" scene of the 1996 movie, *That Thing You Do!*, as "similar to the style of Gene Krupa."[25]

One might think it impossible for alto sax legend Charlie Parker to have been influenced by Gene Krupa. But he was. How? By being a fan of the original Benny Goodman Trio and Quartet and playing along with the groups' 1930s recordings of "China Boy" and "Ava-lon."[26] Concerning "China Boy," clarinetist Ken Peplowski said that the "way he [Parker] plays off the record—first of all, he must have listened to it a lot, because he knows the changes really well. And it has unusual chord changes, that song."[27] Benny Goodman, Lionel Hampton, Teddy Wilson, and Gene Krupa always heeded one another, from start to finish reacting to what each man played. The idea that Charlie Parker might only have been responding to Benny or Teddy or Lionel and not to Gene beggars belief.

At least as big a surprise is that, while Baby Dodds was one of Gene's earliest and greatest influences, Gene Krupa also influenced Baby Dodds. Dodds said he got the idea of using three tom-toms from a Krupa ad he saw sometime between 1940 and 1944 (presumably showing one rack tom and two floors). "Then I found they were very tunable so I tuned them to get the tone I wanted," Dodds said. Before that, Dodds had only used "one little Chinese tom-tom." In 1946, the tunable toms came in handy when he made his famous solo drum recordings at Frederick Ramsey's invitation. Without the tunable toms, a Krupa initiative, Dodds would have been unable to do what he did on the Ramsey sessions.[28]

Gene's most famous acolytes in jazz drumming were Louie Bellson and Buddy Rich. Whitney Balliett wrote that "what Gene started has been carried forward, in different ways, by Buddy Rich and Louie Bellson."[29] Percussionist Rupert Kettle said that, without Gene, "there never would, never *could* have been a Buddy, or a Louie, or a Sonny Payne, or a host of others."[30] "Stemming directly from Krupa" were Louie Bellson and Buddy Rich, declared *Down Beat* in 1960.[31]

Buddy Rich has been called the greatest jazz drummer ever. It's said he could do anything anybody else did, only much faster, and using more notes. Gene Krupa was always quick to praise Buddy. "As far as I'm concerned there's only one drummer: Buddy Rich," said Gene in the 1960s. "Oh, sure, Max Roach, Shelly Manne, Art Blakey are great. They are wonderful technicians . . . With Buddy it's a different thing. He's on a plateau all by himself."[32]

There's another way to view this. Chico Hamilton, who emerged from the younger crop of jazz drummers rising to prominence in the '50s and '60s, considered Gene among the drumming "innovators": "These people contributed something to the extent that they raised the level for others." There have been other great players, including Buddy Rich, but "none of them invented the way they play." Drummers like Gene were "style-setters... I don't care about how fast anybody can play, or how many left-hand strokes you can do... Credit must be given where it's due... Buddy Rich out-played Krupa all the way. But it was Gene Krupa who set that particular style of playing." Said Chico, "When you have that much influence on everyone who tries to play your particular instrument, you've got to be a genius. This is the difference between the innovators and the players."[33]

Ed Soph, a jazz professor at the University of North Texas who teaches jazz drumming, asserted that Gene's playing was "accessible." "What Rich did musically with 100 notes," said Soph, "Gene could do with 25!"[34]

In 1940, *Swing* magazine said Buddy Rich, then playing with Tommy Dorsey, emanated from the "Krupa school of hidebeaters."[35] George T. Simon noted in *Metronome*: "There have been a lot of drummers imitating Krupa. However, the one who plays most and best of all in the style Gene set is Buddy Rich..."[36] In 1961, *Down Beat* categorized Buddy as the "best of those who followed in the path Krupa had blazed."[37]

As we've seen, Ziggy Elman, Harry James, and Gene Krupa were bandmates during the Goodman days. In 1942, Ziggy played for Tommy Dorsey. Buddy Rich drummed. "Dorsey kids everything and anything for a laugh," reported *Variety*, "such as when trumpeter Ziggy Elman and trapster Buddy Rich finish a hot stanza of improvisation and he introduces them as Harry James and Gene Krupa."[38]

Rich's friend Mel Tormé recalled Buddy complaining about jazzers imitating other players. Tormé reminded Buddy about a "bass drum and cymbal break" that Rich had played with Artie Shaw on a tune called "At Sundown." "Right out of Krupa's repertoire, Kong. Heard him play it with Benny a hundred times before you came along." Buddy, annoyed, retorted, "I was young and impressionable at that time... If I copied a Krupa break it was unintentional." Tormé replied, "Sure."[39]

Buddy's interest in Gene's playing continued after he was no longer "young and impressionable." Said Klauber, a fan of Rich *and* Krupa, "If you want to hear one facet of Gene Krupa's direct influence on Buddy Rich, dig how Buddy copped Gene's use of the bass drum in small groups where Buddy played with no [string] bass." Klauber pointed to trios with which Rich recorded in the late 1940s and '50s.[40]

Usually, Rich acknowledged his debt to Gene. Vibraphonist Terry Gibbs, a friend of Buddy's, said, "He told me that Gene was a big influence on him. And Buddy wasn't the type of guy to give anybody credit."[41]

By the early '50s, Gene and Buddy were friends. As Gene's latter-years chum and mentee Joe Vetrano put it, Gene thought of Buddy as his "frisky" younger brother.[42] Buddy reminisced about how exciting it was to see Gene drumming with Goodman. "Gene covered all the bases," said Rich. "He could come down front and play with the trio and quartet or blow the band out, without having to make radical adjustments. He knew what to do. With the small groups, he used brushes and kept things soft and swinging . . . Yet when it was time to go back there with the band and get into 'Sing, Sing, Sing,' he just shifted gears, opened up and played like a monster. That's a great drummer!"[43]

Said Buddy: "Gene is absolutely the first man when it comes to drums . . . The inspiration for every big-name drummer in the band business today . . . I think at one time every drummer . . . wanted to play like Krupa or wanted to win a Gene Krupa drum contest. This is the big inspiration for drummers and naturally it has to be the same way with me . . . This is my man; and you can't say any more. This is the President. And that's it."[44]

The Krupa Intellect

Gene Krupa wasn't just a wild man on the drums, baring his duende to the shock, pleasure, amusement, or revulsion of the crowds. He was more than a spectacular drumming technician and influencer. He was more than the most important drummer in American music history. At heart—he had a great heart, as so many have attested—he remained the son and grandson of poor, uneducated Polish immigrants who grew up in a working-class Chicago home. The Krupas bore innate scars from the untimely losses of father Bartley in 1916 and twenty-nine-year-old brother Clemens in 1918. Gene inherited invisible wounds caused by the deaths of brothers and sisters who perished as children long before his birth, including one who was murdered, a story Gene shared with people close to him in his later years. Young Gene lived with these scars, imperceptible though they were; his adult mind kept them in deep storage.

The Krupa family's drumming son, a high school dropout who, as an older man, regretted his lack of college education, was self-taught in a broad array of subjects, expanding his vocabulary and interests with each passing year.

From the time Gene was a young man, he was devoted to drumming. He was a teacher and a student of drumming, but, as generous as he was with his knowledge, he was always more excited to learn—"study"—than to teach. He was passionate in his acquisition of knowledge through all stages of his life, knowledge about anything and everything. He read widely, starting with detective novels and branching out from there. He may not have thought of himself as an intellectual, but that's what he was.

In the early years of his superstardom, observers found him different from many of his fellow musicians. He was humble—"unaffected"—yes, but "intelligent, more of an analyst than most musicians."[45]

Drums were Gene's vocation and avocation. Other interests were composing, playing the piano, and astronomy.[46] People on the set of *Some Like It Hot* learned that Gene was a devoted amateur astronomer. He kept a small telescope that he used after hours—2 A.M.—to gaze at the infinite beyond. It was a distraction from his earthly worries. How puny the home planet was in the scheme of things!

In his best swing lingo, he schooled Bob Hope on constellations and stars he enjoyed studying. There was the Cosik-Peltier comet, in the news at the time. "Last night I spotted . . . [it], the one with the tail a million miles long, and don't tell me that's a tall-tale," said Gene.

"There are a lot of big-shot stars in the Orion constellation," Gene continued. "The so-called dog star, Cirius, is the top man in the whole industry—he's Mr. It, and very solid."

"You can tell the Pleiades [star system] because," Gene said, "they are all together in a little bunch like the keys of a licorice stick [clarinet]."[47]

After completing the Hope musical comedy, Krupa received notice from Columbia University astronomy professor Clement S. Brainin of his acceptance into the Amateur Astronomers Association.[48] Gene was to give a lecture before the association at the American Museum of Natural History in June 1939.[49]

That museum hosted another Krupa exposition two years later when he lectured on "The Origins of Primitive Rhythms." The Museum had asked him to address a group of one thousand young people, thus rebutting Robert Moses's plaint that Manhattan museums were "stuffy" and repelled youthful New Yorkers. The "scholarly thumper," as Time magazine called him, told attendees jazz began with black people in the South translating African rhythms into something uniquely American. "Crouching like a witch doctor over a clattery battery of traps," said Time, "perspiring, floppy-haired Gene Krupa beat out African war dances and eight-to-the-bar boogie-woogie bumps," and revealed "which was which." He did this on some of the museum's own percussive instruments—"signal drums, war drums, dance drums."[50]

In print, Gene said more about drumming's origins. "Through the ages," Gene said in 1945, "the beat of the drum has been as closely allied with man, in many ways, as the beat of his heart." He theorized that ancient man discovered rhythm by listening to his own heartbeat. Rhythm, Gene said, was found in the sway of elephants' trunks, the cries of monkeys, the chatter of birds, drops of rainwater. Africans may have incorporated sounds of modernity in their drumming—machinery, a motor boat.

"What I want to emphasize is," Gene said, "how much rhythm is a part of our lives. So important, in fact, that scientists have studied the drum and its beat, and its effect on human behavior."[51]

Fifteen years later in *Music Journal*, Gene mentioned what "ancient philosophers... called 'the music of the spheres,'" a basis for a "theory of the rhythmic and perpetual motion of the planets." On Earth, this theory was evidenced in the "obvious rhythm of the tides, the waves of the sea, the fall of rain, the gait of animals... and the most important functions of the human body." Gene referred to a German scholar who posited that rhythm was a "logical accompaniment to manual labor, making the work easier for all concerned." Rhythm laid the foundation for early man's communications, but the most basic of rhythms had crept into classical works like Beethoven's Fifth Symphony, Chopin's Funeral March, and Wagner's Wedding March.[52]

The American Museum of Art hosted a Krupa lecture in July 1942 on the "Lexicon of Swing" to demonstrate how much of the lingo had already infiltrated common usage. He drew an overflow crowd of about 700, young people as well as maturer individuals, and spoke without benefit of a microphone while standing at a lectern, his twenty-five-page presentation in front of him. Gene sprinkled references to Walt Whitman, Shakespeare, and Victor Hugo into his talk.

"'Out of this world,'" Gene said, meant "something so good or so original that to create it its author would seemingly have to reach out beyond the world and find it on some other celestial body." "From hunger," said Gene, meant "stagnant, unoriginal, repetitious and boring." Gene explained, "The connotation in this case, was that the musician seemed 'starved' for ideas..." Among the other swing sayings Gene discussed—sometimes with a sociological bent—were "solid," "what's cooking," "hello, what do you know," and "corny."

Some older adults seemed more interested in this sort of discussion than the young jitterbugging types; after all, Gene hadn't brought his drums. Girls were heard to comment, "Isn't he cute?"[53] Upon finishing, he left so hurriedly (to catch a flight from La-Guardia to Hershey, Pennsylvania, for a band date) that he left his lecture pages behind. "In no time," reported *The New York Times*, "an ardent disciple swiped them."[54]

Down Beat wrote approvingly that Gene had "demonstrated that it's possible for a swing musician to crawl out on a long intellectual limb without hanging himself."[55]

Sports-Loving Gene

Gene was an athletic man. "You'll know it's Gene Krupa when you run into a short guy with an athletic build who looks like a handsome prizefighter," revealed *Swing* magazine in August 1940.[56] While Krupa was still with Goodman, someone, probably Benny, commented in the context of the loud volume the band was increasingly known for that "Krupa banged the hide out of his drums, [and] got arms like the village blacksmith from the exercise."[57]

But Krupa, however well equipped he was for vigorous activity, had little time for the sports he loved because of constant band travel. His two health rules—avoiding alcohol and getting enough sleep[58]—were nearly impossible to abide by. Stress and personal disappointment led to drinking. He was subject to plenty of both. Excessive alcohol use was rampant in jazz anyway. There was Gene's chain-smoking, which hadn't taken a toll yet. Besides being a bandleader and a musician with more than his share of cares, intense hobbies, outside commitments, and voracious reading weren't conducive to getting enough rest.

The energy he expended when drumming was a hot topic. While Gene was filming *Some Like It Hot*, James Davies, the "health and exercise authority at the Paramount gymnasium," claimed to have measured the amount of energy Gene expended while jamming. Davies said Krupa used more energy than a "mile runner, a fleet halfback or the fastest tap dancer." Davies reported that the drummer had to "eat like a farmhand" to keep his weight up, and the perspiration he expelled ruined numerous tuxedos.[59]

All this information was disseminated in a single Paramount press release, upon which press reports in succeeding years seem to have relied. But Gene's management issued a press package around the same time that went into more detail about Gene's athleticism—especially his talent for expelling from his body copious amounts of sweat while performing.

One needn't look far to learn of his propensity for perspiration. Writings and reminiscences abound on this point. "Krupa was the first, and more importantly, the best sweater on the bandstand," said drumming blogger Michael Aubrecht, "meaning that he performed at a level that eclipsed the efforts of his peers, as indicated by his sweat. In fact, Krupa sweated so much that it literally became his calling card."

Aubrecht added, "Gene Krupa was absolutely an athlete in terms of physical exertion, and he obviously excelled in his field." Gene's "physical flair," as Aubrecht called it, "did not overshadow, but ultimately accented his brilliant musicianship."[60]

Gene had favorite sports for playing and sports for watching. An avid swimmer,[61] he surfed when his travels took him to Hawaii and Australia in the 1950s.[62] He also played golf and tennis and loved watching baseball. Wrestling as a spectator sport came in second.

Gene had loved baseball from childhood. As a boy he played shortstop (he remembered being regarded as a "hot ballplayer"[63]), but was forced to choose between baseball and drumming when he hurt his hand in a game.[64] In the big band days, no self-respecting orchestra could be caught without its team. The band teams played each other whenever possible. Baseball—and by extension softball—was the national pastime, after all. In the '50s and '60s, Gene pitched for his own Krupa's All-Stars. Regardless of his drumming accolades, the two newspaper clippings he kept in his wallet were local stories about shutouts he'd pitched.[65]

Krupa's interest in tanning seems to have started in the early 1940s. It may not have been related to his athleticism or love of playing sports. He may have just wanted to maintain a healthy aspect. Early on, he applied makeup to his face before band performances. As bassist Bill Crow later observed, Gene "used a pair of baby spotlights to light himself up during his drum solos, and they made him look pale as a ghost if he didn't have a tan. He hated having to wear makeup."[66]

Eventually, Gene decided to do something about it, although he may have gone a little overboard at first. In September 1944, *Down Beat* reported that he had "burned his eyes badly with a sun lamp," thus hampering a live performance or two at the Capitol Theatre in New York.[67] Said Crow: "He spent as much time in the sun as he could, and always had a nice tan when he played."[68] Crow's recollections are borne out by his bronzed features of the 1950s, '60s, and '70s. In 1962, Gene gave an interview to a *New York Daily News* reporter as he played on his drum practice set in the backyard. The reporter noticed that Gene was "face up to the sun to get an early start on a tan."[69]

Jealous of Gene

Some of Gene's drumming colleagues disliked being in his shadow, even if they probably wouldn't have come to the public's attention were it not for Krupa bringing drums out from the shadows.

"There was a lot of jealousy on the bandstand," said jazz drummer Duffy Jackson. "A lot of drummers, a lot of horn players who were bandleaders . . . were envious of the response that Gene got from the audience, because they couldn't get it." Explained Jackson of Gene's approach: "The thing is, don't shoot your best shot first, but just give 'em what you know they need to gain your trust. Then you take them on that magic carpet ride."[70]

"The overwhelming concomitant of overwhelming success with the masses is the overwhelming contempt of those who resent this success," Leonard Feather once observed.[71]

An unfortunate example of drummer jealousy in the public comments of one of the better swing drummers whom Gene praised more than once in his drumming column was Ray McKinley. Early on, McKinley played for the Dorsey Brothers and then Jimmy Dorsey. Gene commended McKinley on his drum breaks in Jimmy's "Parade of the Milk Bottle Caps" (1936).[72] He also congratulated

McKinley for his 1937 induction into the Metronome Hall of Fame (into which Gene had been inducted in 1935): "To me, Ray is one of the very greatest drummers in the land today."[73] In another column, he said, "He sure has been giving me some solid sends...Mac not only possesses the most remarkable rudiments...but uses beautiful taste as he swings very politely underneath Jimmy's band."[74]

By 1940, McKinley was coleading a band with Will Bradley. McKinley was usually silent on Krupa. But if he did comment on Gene, it was a confused swipe, such as declaring in *Metronome* that drummers are incapable of leading a band by themselves.[75] Gene said the opposite—after all, he *was* one of those solo drummer-leaders![76]

When McKinley got his own *Metronome* drumming column in 1940 (succeeding Krupa), he wrote, "[M]ost [drumming] veterans are habit-ridden fellows who read drum columns mainly with the hope of seeing their own names mentioned...Gene satisfies everyone."[77]

Gene also greatly admired Jo Jones. Immediately after the Goodman band's history-making Carnegie Hall concert on January 16, 1938, a large proportion of Goodman band members, including Benny himself and Gene (with his wife), attended the Chick Webb–Count Basie band battle at the Savoy. Afterward, while Gene and Ethel were walking home, he took to "singing the praises of Jo Jones at the top of my lungs." His youthful exuberance, which was probably disturbing the peace of the neighborhood, was cut short by an inquisitive cop. Krupa reported all of this in his drumming column the following month.[78]

To Gene, Jo got "an exceptional tone and beat from his high-hat cymbals and has done a lot towards making that fine Count Basie rhythm section."[79] Over the following years and decades, Krupa continued to publicly praise Jo Jones.

An affecting indication of how much Gene liked Jo as a person is illustrated in pictures snapped for a photo feature to appear in *Esquire*'s January 1959 spread, "The Golden Age of Jazz." *Esquire* meant to gather as many jazzers as possible for a group portrait on the steps of a Harlem brownstone. Gene is seen in various pictures talking and laughing with Jo as they wait for the final snaps; Sonny Greer joins in as well. When it's time for the final pose, Gene's arm is around Jones's shoulder.[80]

Later in life, Jones seems to have forgotten their friendship and how impressed he had been with Gene's drumming in the early 1930s, and to have ignored everything that had happened since. Unlike numerous other drummers Jones expostulated on in his LP *The Drums* (1973), he said little about Gene.

"There was a fella that came around that studied for the priesthood," Jones said. "He only played one beat. And it was a very simple beat. You know him as Gene Krupa. Now all he did was this." Jones is heard to play an overly streamlined version of the tom-toms from "Sing, Sing, Sing," as if all Gene ever played in his career was that one tom-tom beat.[81]

Seventeen-year-old Louie Bellson, a Krupa protégé in whom Gene took great pride, quickly rose to prominence in the swing world. A direct correlation existed between Bellson's success and his victory in the first national Gene Krupa–Slingerland drum contest. Subsequently, Bellson bestowed limited praise for his mentor's musical importance. He said Gene brought drums to the "forefront," was a great "showman," and little else. If Louie spoke further, he usually related an anecdote about how he and Buddy Rich would play complicated passages at a live event and receive respectful applause, whereas Gene would hit the snare and toms a couple of times and crash a cymbal and the audience went wild.

Drummer Max Roach shed light on what really happened on these occasions: In the 1950s, Krupa, Roach, Buddy Rich, and Louie Bellson fought a "drum battle" in which they took turns showing the audience what they could do. "We all got applause," said Roach, "but the people stood up for Krupa because he got the crowd moving with him ... before going into triplets and 16th notes and razzle-dazzle." Thus, Roach understood a drummer should do more than play for himself, more than show off his speed or strength. "You may have the fastest left hand and the fastest feet in the world," said Roach, "but it doesn't mean anything unless you can communicate and make people feel something, which is what Krupa could do."[82]

In later years, an interviewer found it very difficult to get Louie Bellson to talk about Gene. Finally, Louie said that, as a young teen, he often met Gene in Chicago prior to winning the drumming contest. He downplayed their interactions. "I first met Gene on one of my trips to go study with Roy Knapp," he recalled. "I used to go to the Panther Room in the Hotel Sherman, when Gene had his band there. I always found him to be very congenial. Whatever you wanted to do, great. He took time in between sets to come over and chat with me. I was just a kid. He'd buy me a drink. Of course it was soda then. No liquor . . . But he took time to show me things."[83]

In the same interview, Louie talked extensively about what he had learned from a range of other drummers, but didn't mention Gene, despite the time he admitted Gene had given him in between sets at the Panther Room, and the fact that Bellson, like Buddy Rich, was generally regarded as a drummer of the Krupa school. He also said that he was disappointed that his moment of glory—winning the Krupa drumming contest—happened at Wurlitzer's Music Store in Manhattan instead of at the Paramount where Gene was performing. "People [at the Paramount] paid to come in to hear him play. They didn't want a bunch of high-school kids playing drums. So we had it at Wurlitzer for the finale." He was also underwhelmed that Gene chose the victor based on how well the finalists played along to a recording of "Drumboogie."

"I gained a lot of publicity from that," Louie acknowledged. "*Down Beat* gave me a lot of coverage. *Metronome* magazine . . . gave me a lot of coverage. That gave me a lot of publicity, so the name was starting to bounce around." Bandleader Ted Fio Rito snapped Louie up.[84]

Buddy Rich was noticeably envious of Gene's success despite their close friendship. To his disappointment, he couldn't become Slingerland's top endorser with Gene still around.[85] Buddy was quite vocal in declaring himself the greatest of all drummers (an opinion Krupa shared), though Rich was an alumnus of the Krupa school, like Louie Bellson.

Despite Buddy Rich's massive ego, he spoke generously, as we've seen, about Gene's versatility and the impact that Gene had made on Rich's own playing and on the drumming world. Gene and Buddy "loved each other like brothers," said Les DeMerle, who was friends with both men. DeMerle emphasized that "they all came out of Gene. Number one, Gene Krupa, and then probably Buddy and Louie. If it wasn't for Gene and what he did, putting the drums in front, there wouldn't be a Buddy or a Louie."[86]

CHAPTER 16

"I'm Out Here All Alone on a Shelf"[1]

N 1943, GENE KRUPA'S PRIVATE life wasn't going too well, although he and Ethel sometimes went out as a couple, despite their finalized divorce. But he didn't have a steady relationship or satisfying love life to keep him emotionally balanced.

There were signs that jazz musicians were coming under increasing scrutiny on drug use by federal and local law enforcement agencies. Arrests were in the news. As Gene himself put it, the feds "were always hanging around the bands waiting for one of us to cough."[2]

In 1930, the drumbeat of anti-marijuana propaganda could be felt via the just-formed Federal Bureau of Narcotics within the U.S. Department of the Treasury and its head, Harry J. Anslinger. Prompted at least in part by anti-Mexican immigrant animus—hence the use by Anslinger and his allies of the Spanish word for the substance—the anti-marijuana drumbeat also reflected Anslinger's contempt for people of color. "The insanity of the racism is a thing to behold when you go into his archives," author-researcher Johann Hari recounted to CBS News. "He claims that *cannabis* promotes . . . interracial relationships."[3]

Anslinger loathed jazz musicians. He wrote: "Among those who first spread its [marijuana's] use were musicians. They brought the habit northward with the surge of 'hot' music..." Smoking cannabis, he claimed, had an "exhilarating effect upon the musical sensibilities," enabling the jazz musician to play with a "furious speed impossible for one in a normal state."[4]

The anti-marijuana drumbeat crescendoed with the ridiculous 1936 film *Reefer Madness*. The movie's perspective was pure Anslinger—that marijuana users are driven to loose morals resulting in premarital sex; acts of violence, even murder; and incurable insanity. Innocent white youth—the future of America—are being corrupted, even ruined, by exposure to marijuana.

In 1937, with Anslinger's support, The Marihuana [sic] Tax Act became U.S. law. While it didn't criminalize what had previously been known exclusively as *Cannabis sativa* in medical circles, it did impose taxes on almost everyone who might have had anything to do with it. Any such individuals were required to "register" with the federal government. A labyrinthine schedule of paperwork made compliance difficult, if not impossible. Penalties for noncompliance led to hefty fines and jail time. By the time of enactment, almost all states (with Anslinger's help) had outlawed the sale and use of cannabis.[5] Between the new federal law, the anti-marijuana state legislation, and scare tactics employed by government and private concerns, a generally benign drug with mild effects became to Americans perhaps the most frightening drug in history.

Marijuana was most commonly known to jazz musicians as "tea." It's unlikely that any surveys were conducted to measure its use by jazzers during the key years of the '20s through the '40s, but it seems to have been popular with them. As we've seen, Gene Krupa smoked it, as did friends and colleagues.

In August 1941, unwelcome notoriety came to Charlie Barnet's band following a reportedly wild party in Los Angeles thrown by members of several orchestras, including his. Two Barnet sidemen were briefly stopped for speeding. Minutes later, they crashed into a truck and were killed. Police found cannabis in the car. They searched the men's residence and found more cannabis.

Orchestra World accused Barnet's people of trying to suppress the story: "[We believe] ... that the problem of marijuana can't be discarded by hushing it up. That's appeasement—and everyone knows where appeasement leads to."[6] The jazz press and others in the business were worried about the widespread perception of jazzers as reprobates, and sometimes recommended ostracism of "tea" offenders.

Aside from his personal life and the general pressures of being a bandleader in challenging times, Gene had much to be glad about. He led one of the hottest bands in the country. His box office take was almost invariably colossal. He had signed a contract with America's top movie studio—MGM—to appear in one of several possible musicals in the works, like *Anchors Aweigh*.[7] He was scheduled to appear on Edgar Bergen's hugely popular radio show on Sunday, January 17, 1943, two days after he celebrated his thirty-fourth birthday and four days after he was to debut at the Golden Gate Theatre in San Francisco.

A reviewer wrote of one Golden Gate show that Gene "sits like an affable spider in his web of drums, making his two arms work like six ... [and is] "an authentic jazz artist, a rare thing for a white musician."[8] Ominously, the movie being shown at the theater was *Seven Miles from Alcatraz*.

———————

NEXT ON THE itinerary was neighboring Oakland, as the *Oakland Tribune* trumpeted in advance. Two days later, the newspaper had changed its focus from eager anticipation to this: "Krupa Pleads Not Guilty in S.F. 'Dope' Case."[9] His reputation had mutated from "versatile technician" and "master" to the sinister-sounding "famed 'jive man.'"[10]

On Monday night, Gene was questioned by two Federal Bureau of Narcotics agents backstage at the Golden Gate after one of his forty-five-minute between-movie performances. The agents had brought with them city and state narcotics officers. As usual, when Gene came off the stage, he was "perspiring quite a bit," as one of the agents remembered. The agents had gotten a "tip" that he possessed marijuana, which Gene denied. As he pleaded to be allowed to shower, they searched his dressing room and found nothing. Later, the agents stopped Gene's recently employed band-boy, John Pateakos, at the St. Francis Hotel, where the Krupa band was staying. Twenty-year-old Pateakos, a Gene-idolizing drummer, allegedly had on his person dozens of "reefers." Searching Gene's own room, the agents claimed to have discovered cannabis "fragments." Gene and Pateakos were separately interrogated at the hotel.[11]

The next night, after the Krupa band's last performance in San Francisco and in the presence of newly hired celebrity criminal defense attorney Jacob W. Ehrlich, police arrested Gene on a misdemeanor charge of contributing to the delinquency of a minor under California's Welfare and Institutions Code. (Technically, at twenty, Pateakos was a minor, but law enforcement and members of the press thought he was seventeen.[12])

"Krupa was still dripping perspiration from the exertion of playing his finale number, 'The Boogie Drag,'" reported the *San Francisco Examiner*.[13] The paper probably meant "Drumboogie." This small factual error must have rankled Gene. "Drag" is a smoking term when it doesn't relate to early jazz, or the act of pulling an object along the ground, or men dressing in women's clothing. "He dressed under eyes of the officers," continued the *Examiner*. From there they went to the city jail where Gene was officially booked, which meant having mug shots and fingerprints taken. He was released on $1,000 bail.[14]

Jake Ehrlich remembered: "Gene, who had never been in this kind of mess and who was actually a quiet, decent boy, was pretty well shaken up by the raid at the theatre."[15]

Prosecution was turned over by the feds to local authorities. On January 20, 1943, the day after Gene's arrest, he appeared in court with Ehrlich and pled not guilty to the misdemeanor. On Ehrlich's motion, Judge Thomas J. Foley continued the matter to the 26th so that Gene and his band could fulfill several engagements in the region. In the interim, twenty-year-old Pateakos was to be held in "juvenile detention."[16]

Roy Eldridge told Gene: "Lay some bread on me and I'll take the rap." Apparently, Roy wasn't joking. He thought if he could take Gene's place as the defendant, prosecutor Brady would be deprived of the "big cat" he needed to clinch his reelection. The proceedings against Roy would have been shorter and less expensive. Most important, Gene "would have been out scot-free." Krupa didn't take Roy up on his offer.[17]

Following the first hearing, Gene's appearance on a January 21 Coca-Cola–sponsored radio program was canceled.[18] He worried how his sister, Elenor, would take the news of his arrest, telling Ehrlich, "She brought me up."[19] Elenor and her husband, Michael, were house-sitting for Gene in Yonkers.

The signed statement that Pateakos gave after intense pressure by police alleged that he had "seen Krupa smoke brown cigarets [sic] . . . and that when he smoked them 'he went wild.'"[20]

Pateakos's statement also claimed that Gene had asked the band-boy to go to his hotel room, retrieve his marijuana cigarettes, and dispose of them.[21] At the preliminary hearing on January 26, Pateakos gave testimony corroborating his statement. Accordingly, Gene was further charged with using a minor to transport narcotics, a felony and a violation of the state's Health and Safety Code. While the misdemeanor could lead to a fine and probation and maybe county jail time, a felony conviction meant one to six years in San Quentin. Gene pled not guilty to both the misdemeanor and felony charges.[22]

Krupa was released on another $1,000 bail and was thus able to continue his tour until at least the next court date.[23] Newspaper columnist Danton Walker, without basis, suggested that Gene's legal difficulties were related to a "huge marijuana ring."[24] A few days later, Walker's bias was unmistakable when he wrote: "If radio doesn't act on Gene Krupa, the churches will."[25]

It helped Gene's public standing that he hadn't been convicted of anything. He enjoyed the "good will of the crowd" in Omaha, the night proving lucrative for the "appreciative management."[26] As *Orchestra World* reported, Gene's gigs at the Hotel Sherman's Panther Room in Chicago "did terrific business."[27] The only downside of his hometown stay was a fire in his hotel room caused, ironically, by a "smoldering" cigarette. He battled the fire with a hose that he had obtained by kicking open the hose's glass pane housing in the hallway. For his display of athleticism, he sustained a cut foot. The fire also consumed a portion of his wardrobe. On the plus side, neither the incident nor the injury prevented Gene from performing that night.[28]

In Columbus, Ohio, Gene's shows led to thousands of teenagers cutting school en masse to see him at his movie theater appearances. Demand was so great that the venue had to add shows.[29] *Variety* reported that Krupa had "standees . . . five deep in the back of the house" at Philadelphia's Earle Theatre.[30]

In February, a two-hour ballroom gig at the University of Wisconsin at Madison Field House for a "student war chest drive" attracted a crowd of 3,500—students, other civilians, and loads of soldiers and sailors—who "screamed and stamped time on bleacher seats." Later, still in Madison, the band moved over to the University of Wisconsin Memorial Union to play for the junior prom.[31]

Things wouldn't be this way forever. Frank Dailey, owner of the Terrace Room in Newark, New Jersey (which had succeeded Dailey's Meadowbrook, a suburban war casualty), was making noises in early March about wriggling out of his contract with Gene. Performances were to begin on April 18, 1943.[32] The following day, a widely circulated false report that Gene had just entered a guilty plea to one or both of the charges[33] made Dailey's request more pressing. The incorrect news led to cries from New York's Paramount Theatre that it, too, should be released from its Krupa contract.

The American Federation of Musicians ruled in favor of Krupa in the Dailey matter once it learned that reports of the guilty plea were untrue, although the practical impact of the controversy led to Gene losing one of the nights at the Terrace Room anyway.[34] Gene, attorney Jake Ehrlich, Gene's booking agent (MCA), and Paramount agreed behind the scenes to indefinitely postpone the Paramount dates. The engagement would have started around the time of trial on May 18. It would have been nearly impossible for the Paramount to secure a replacement for Gene at the last minute. Religious groups also threatened to picket outside the Paramount were Gene allowed to play there.[35]

Worse than the false report of a Krupa guilty plea was the rising number of press reports equating Gene's case with other drug cases, no matter how dissimilar or tawdry. The *New York Daily News*, for example, revealed that $7,000 worth of opium was found in the midtown apartment of a Broadway dancer and her dealer husband. The husband's criminal record dated back a decade. The same article likened Gene's predicament to the Broadway couple's and featured a large photo of him![36]

The big day came—May 18, 1943. Jake Ehrlich advised Gene to plead guilty to the misdemeanor, but not to the felony. The attorney expected the penalty to be a fine with no jail sentence.

Ehrlich thought that the long-time San Francisco District Attorney, Matthew Brady, who was running for reelection, ought to be thrilled to obtain a conviction at little cost or effort, and thus not bother with the felony charge. On the other hand, Ehrlich knew that Brady loathed him. The defense lawyer assumed that Brady's hostility dated back to a 1930s corruption case in which Ehrlich recalled having handily defeated the prosecutor.[37] Brady might do whatever it took to avenge his earlier courtroom loss.

A valid reason to think Brady might not prosecute the felony charge was the impact on it of double jeopardy, which means that a defendant cannot be tried on the same offense twice. As Ehrlich explained in his autobiography, *A Life in My Hands*, because the misdemeanor and the felony were based on the same event and conduct, "the misdemeanor was included and was part of the felony and the felony thus contained the misdemeanor. This was and is known as the doctrine of included offenses."[38]

Gene pled guilty to the misdemeanor and not guilty to the felony. To Krupa's and Ehrlich's astonishment, Judge Foley not only fined Gene $500, but sentenced him to ninety days in the county jail, which would start immediately. Gene calmly told Ehrlich, "Something went wrong. I'll make it—somehow."[39] In public, and in private with his attorney, his demeanor was stoic. A trial on the felony would commence at a later time.

A photo captioned "'hot' drummer" depicting an impeccably dressed Krupa averting his eyes from cameras as he hopped into the back of a "patrol wagon" on its way to jail was printed in newspapers nationally. The *New York Daily News* featured it on the front page's lower right-hand corner. Most of the page was occupied by war news: "Yanks Close on Attu Japs; Bomb Wake." There was a photo slightly larger than Gene's, labeled "Pathos," concerning the tragic death in Queens of a child run over by a streetcar. Those were the three top stories in America's largest city: the war, a fatal accident, and a very famous man convicted on a drug charge going behind bars.[40]

Before Gene pled guilty to the misdemeanor and was jailed, gossip columnist Walter Winchell had optimistically reported: "His network bosses will stand by Krupa."[41] After the plea, Winchell's scuttlebutt was that the "major networks will no longer air his band, so necessary to success . . . [Therefore,] Gene Krupa's big-time career is over."[42]

Following the guilty plea, Gene gave the band a ten-day paid layoff, after which they would return to the road under Roy Eldridge's baton, with mild-mannered Harry Jaeger on drums. For a while, the arrangement worked. They played Atlantic City and Philadelphia. When Jaeger couldn't make it, Roy played the drums; fortunately, he was a good drummer in addition to being a great trumpeter.[43]

Back in San Francisco, behind-bars Gene suffered from "shame, guilt, and depression of serious proportions."[44]

Benny Goodman visited. They had long since resumed their friendship, even if it was mostly professional. Gene often sat in with Benny's band or small groups during radio performances and other events. Benny publicly declared: "You know, he's a wonderful guy, and a wonderful drummer. Anytime, anyplace, anywhere he wants his old job back, it's his!"[45]

Gene's ex-wife visited. "Ethel had never stopped loving Gene," remembered Anita O'Day. Ethel returned to Gene their entire $100,000 divorce settlement, saying that he needed the money more than she did. She'd gone back to work. He had mounting legal bills and little money coming in. They cried together.[46]

The felony trial was set for June 8, 1943. Gene was found that day in his cell "in a semi-stupor" and rushed to the emergency room. He reportedly told doctors that he had "taken a fairly large dose—three half grain tablets—of a sedative." Upon returning to jail he felt a "slight intestinal disturbance.[47]

Not so much because of Gene's health but because the prosecution couldn't find their star witness, former band-boy John Pateakos, the trial date was postponed.[48] It finally commenced on June 29. District Attorney Matthew Brady assigned Assistant District Attorney Leslie Gillen to handle the case. Gillen had previously faced Gene's attorney, Jake Ehrlich.

The matter was going ahead despite the fact that the prosecution still hadn't found Pateakos[49] and that Gene had already pled guilty to a lesser included offense. Ehrlich moved for dismissal on grounds of double jeopardy. Judge Foley denied the motion, ruling that the question was one for the jury to decide. Although Ehrlich was upset by the decision, Gene retained his composure, "trying to reassure Ehrlich" as jury selection began.[50] The twelve jurors selected were nine men and three women.

The prosecution's sole witness was federal agent Giubbini, since John Pateakos remained missing.[51] (The latter was now wanted by the FBI for draft evasion.[52]) Assistant District Attorney Gillen tried to make the prosecution about irrelevant matters: whether Gene used cannabis and what effect it had on him. Then Gillen sought to sully Gene's character by sullying the character of all jazz musicians. This he did while trying to make Giubbini some kind of expert witness, which he was not.[53]

"Is it common knowledge that marijuana is frequently used because of its definite propensity for distorting time by so-called hot musicians?" Judge Foley overruled Ehrlich's objection that the question was irrelevant, immaterial, and unjust. Giubbini was free to answer yes.

"And that is so they can beat the drums or play a cornet or trombone without feeling the effect of doing it?" Giubbini said yes. Despite Ehrlich's objections, this line of questioning proceeded for several more minutes. In cross-examining Giubbini, Ehrlich asked whether he had stated previously that cannabis has "no effect on some people." Giubbini answered yes.

Ehrlich put Gene on the stand. Gene denied being "addicted" to marijuana, but said he had smoked it. He denied having used Pateakos to transport marijuana cigarettes.[54]

Under cross-examination, Gillen repeatedly questioned Krupa on whether jazz musicians found marijuana a "necessary prop." Gene said no, explaining: "If you have a half-hour radio program, and have to make a tune last just thirty seconds . . . and there is a difference of tempo—I am afraid the marijuana would be apt to hurt you rather than do you good."

But wasn't Gene known for "being able to attain a faster tempo and faster rhythm with his trap drums than any other trap drummer in the world?" Gene responded: "A man's ability to beat his drums faster than someone else is because he has developed his technique to a higher point and it is easier for him to play fast . . . If I am able to play faster than someone else it is because I have studied it, and developed my technique."

Cross-examination continued. *Isn't it true that when an orchestra plays "hot," that means "fast"?* No. *If an orchestra plays "hot or cold," isn't it assumed that they must have smoked cannabis beforehand?* No. *Gene admitted to having used marijuana recently. Why was that?* I was feeling low . . . I was sort of grabbing at a straw, like a drowning man.

On further cross-examination, Gene testified that the envelope of marijuana federal agents found must have been the envelope that a fan shoved into his hands at the stage door in Los Angeles. Gene explained that there were always people waiting around the stage door to give you something. The drummer put the envelope in his coat pocket and forgot about it until arriving in San Francisco and discovering the contents.[55]

After Gene finished testifying, Gillen requested a recess so that he could find a rebuttal witness. Judge Foley denied the request, since the prosecution had had several months to line up witnesses. Gillen said, in that case, he couldn't continue prosecuting the matter, and the judge threatened him with contempt. The *San Francisco Examiner* noted this exchange and *editorialized in its reporting* that the judge had given the defense every advantage, including sustaining all defense objections and overruling all prosecution objections.[56] This wasn't the way Jake Ehrlich remembered it.

Ultimately, the jury found Gene guilty. Judge Foley denied Ehrlich's motions for a new trial and an "arrest of judgment" (a stay). The judge sentenced Gene to the mandatory prison time of one to six years, the exact duration to be set by the prison board.[57] Ehrlich immediately filed a petition with the California Court of Appeal on the issue of double jeopardy. Gene was still required to finish serving his ninety-day sentence on the misdemeanor.

In apparently congratulating the jury on its verdict, Judge Foley issued a statement showing that he was convinced of marijuana's "vicious effects," adding: "I certainly trust that this case will bring to everyone's attention, especially to the attention of those who might use it for purposes of exhilaration, the consequences of its use."[58]

The *San Francisco Examiner* gloated that with the felony conviction Gene "must abandon his pedestal." The newspaper concluded its Krupa article of the day with an account of "killers" in "ancient Persia" who used "hashish," a concentrated form of cannabis, to "whip themselves into a frenzy before going out to commit murder."[59] In relating what was, at best, a questionable tale about hashish use a millennium ago, the *Examiner* was doing Harry J. Anslinger's bidding—using what in the twenty-first century one might call "talking points." Anslinger had made an almost identical assertion in his 1937 article, "Marijuana: Assassin of Youth" in *The American Magazine*.

Matthew Brady issued a statement celebrating the verdict. Calling marijuana "an unpredictable, excitive drug," he declared that Gene's conviction "will have a deterrent effect upon those who are careless regarding the welfare and morals of children and growing youth."[60] He got what he wanted—a victory in a notorious drug case that he believed would help him win reelection.

Brady and his deputy, Gillen, were publicly praised by Anslinger, who believed Gene's conviction had helped save America's youth: "Owing to the position which he occupied, I believe that Krupa was likely to do a vast amount of harm among young people because of the example he set in the use of the dangerous drug, marihuana [sic]."[61]

Gene's Eldridge-helmed band could no longer stay afloat. Band members sought other work. Eldridge explored whether to start up his own ensemble.[62] *Variety* estimated that Gene had lost $120,000 in band grosses because of future engagements that could no longer be kept, although this figure may have included the agreed-upon cancellation of the engagement at New York's Paramount Theatre, which had been scheduled to commence prior to the trial.[63] But this figure did not take into account future engagements yet to be booked. Although MGM kept silent about its contract with Gene, it was widely assumed he had been quietly dropped, an impression borne out by the fact that he hadn't been mentioned in any MGM ads in months and never did appear in an MGM movie.[64]

Mildly amusing gossip surfaced. The Leroy Brothers, now with the USO, kept the Krupa drumming puppet in their marionette act but sans his name, describing it as an "impression of a well-known drummer."[65] But the news that Gene's Manhattan business office was forced onto the street was embarrassing. "His office furniture was moved on to the sidewalk because rent for the space hadn't been paid," reported *Variety*. Rent had been the responsibility of Gene's then manager, Frank Verniere.[66]

Was there anything else that prosecutors and San Francisco's pro-prosecution press could do to Gene Krupa as he sat in jail, approaching the end of his misdemeanor sentence? Yes. Matthew Brady announced a grand jury to investigate the disappearance of John Pateakos during the pendency of proceedings against Gene. The FBI had found and arrested Pateakos for draft evasion (which charge would be dropped once he entered the service later that summer). The feds temporarily transferred Pateakos to Brady so that the former could testify that he was paid by a Jake Ehrlich associate to absent himself from California during the relevant period.[67]

The headlines were awful: "Krupa Valet's Pay-Off Probed." "Grand Jury Will Hear 5 Witnesses in Krupa Charge." "Ehrlich Denies Paying Krupa Valet Bribe."[68]

Then: "S.F. Grand Jury Fails to Indict in Krupa Case." Why? "Insufficient evidence," reported the *Oakland Tribune*.[69] Long before Gene's trial, Ehrlich learned from contacts in Los Angeles that Pateakos was considering filing a claim against Gene for unpaid wages. Ehrlich didn't want any more bad publicity, so he sent his associate, Roy Sharff, to meet Pateakos in Los Angeles and settle the claim. Sharff paid Pateakos $500 and the latter wrote and signed two statements.[70]

The first acknowledged that he had accepted the $500 in "full settlement and payment" for all claims, including "wages unpaid, clothes lost for me, and traveling expenses in accordance with my understanding when joining the Gene Krupa band, and reimbursement for monies laid out." The second, "my free and voluntary statement," said the $500 was paid in settlement of legal claims. "No promises were asked of me before settlement was made, and no requests made of me as to my future actions or conduct."[71]

Ehrlich submitted proof that Pateakos, the allegedly vulnerable minor, had been living in Los Angeles during the time in question with his new wife. Why hadn't Ehrlich notified the prosecution of Pateakos's whereabouts? Because it wasn't his job to prosecute their case for them.[72]

Gene was released from jail in San Francisco on August 9, 1943. He had completed his ninety-day sentence five days earlier, but the authorities were in no hurry to release him since he had been convicted of a felony, despite his pending appeal. Jake Ehrlich went before Judge Foley to seek Gene's release, which the judge granted on $5,000 bail.[73]

Ex-wife Ethel fetched Gene on release day. They went south to Hollywood, where she now lived and had begun working at the Hollywood Palladium.[74] Gene only stayed long enough for the press to report that he could be seen wearing a sports jacket and striped slacks and that he had lost weight.[75]

Gene was a free man, but it was "the end of the world."[76] His career was over. He had been humiliated and feared showing his face in public, let alone dealing with the press and entertainment bigwigs. Arriving in Yonkers at his recently built home he broke out in rashes from the stress of keeping his tortured feelings inside.[77]

In Chicago that month, Gene's brother Julius and his sister-in-law Lillian named their newborn son after Gene; there was now a second Gene Krupa in the world. They wanted brother Gene to know that the whole Krupa family still loved him and were proud of him and his accomplishments despite recent events.[78]

Later, George Wein said, "It was a crime to put Gene in jail for two minutes for smoking marijuana." Wein added that everyone he knew in the old days smoked marijuana.[79]

Dan Morgenstern said, "I'm sure that the reason for that [arrest] was the featuring of Anita and Roy together [in 'Let Me Off Uptown']..."[80]

African-American observers of Gene's travails would have agreed with Morgenstern. "Sorta tough on him," said the *Evansville* (Indiana) *Argus*. "Quite a figure and much on the liberal side—featured pal Roy Eldridge in his band."[81]

Frank Marshall Davis of the Associated Negro Press blamed the prosecution of Krupa on "our potent fascist leaders who resented" Gene's support of Roy Eldridge. "He has consistently gone to the bat for Roy, refusing to play engagements in towns where there would be discrimination against him," and getting arrested telling off a cop who was attempting to force Jim Crow on Roy Eldridge.[82]

Writing for the African-American newspaper *The Pittsburgh Courier*, columnist Billy Rowe suspected that Gene was targeted by authorities as punishment for hiring Roy Eldridge and being vociferously supportive of him, and, by extension, the cause of black people in America. "To our way of thinking, there is a lot of truth to the adage that 'only the good die young'... Only fighters like Gene are given the fascist boot."[83]

There is an interesting postscript to Gene's horrible 1943 and the despicable policies that led to it. Once the grand jury matter concluded, Jake Ehrlich took leave from his law practice to vigorously campaign in the November election for Edmund G. "Pat" Brown, who was running to unseat District Attorney Matthew Brady. Brown won and was thereafter reelected while Brady faded from view. (Later that decade, Ehrlich successfully defended Billie Holiday from charges of opium possession.) Beginning in 1950, Brown was elected twice to the office of Attorney General of California. He ran for governor and won twice, famously defeating in his reelection bid former Vice President Richard M. Nixon. Only Ronald Reagan could stop Brown's bid for a third term. However, Pat Brown's son, Edmund G. "Jerry" Brown, Jr., followed his father into politics and was elected Governor of California on two separate occasions for two terms each.

CHAPTER 17

"I'm Almost Afraid to Look"[1]

Upon emerging from jail, Gene addressed unsettled business with his personal manager, Frank Verniere. The public humiliation attendant the marijuana charges, his jailing, and his conviction on a felony count were extremely hard to bear. He didn't need further humiliation because of the actions of a trusted member of his own organization. In June, when Krupa's New York office was evicted due to nonpayment of rent by the person in charge, Frank Verniere, Gene had had enough. Although the Krupa coffers suffered greatly as the flow of income ebbed, Gene could still maintain his new Yonkers home; eviction from a Manhattan office building shouldn't have come so soon and without warning.

Gene could be too trusting of individuals, especially ones with whom he shared fond memories. Gene's friendship with Verniere dated back to 1928 when Krupa was playing for Thelma Terry and Verniere was the band-boy. In 1937, when Gene re-signed with Benny Goodman, he hired Verniere as his personal manager. *Down Beat* said, "Gene and Frank have been pals for many years and this should make this tie-up a very successful one."[2] Gene set up a publishing company, Variety Music Corp., in concert with Verniere.[3]

At one time, Krupa had trusted Verniere so much that Gene left him in charge of the construction of his Yonkers home while the drummer was on the road, as he usually was. Verniere was simultaneously building his own home on a Linn Avenue property overlooking Gene's. "While Gene was on the road," said neighbor Joe Vetrano, "Frank would have all the high end stuff meant for Gene's house sent to his, and the lower end stuff sent to Gene's."[4]

But mismanagement of Gene's funds was a worse offense. Krupa wasn't home long before he had fired Verniere and hired Johnny Gluskin, already his attorney, as his personal manager.[5]

At home for, as far as he knew, the indefinite future, Gene spent his time commuting to Manhattan to study harmony, arranging, tympani, and piano with Otto Cesana. Otherwise, he tried to mentally center himself and worked on a suntan.[6]

Benny Goodman surprised Gene with a call, inviting him over to jam. After they jammed, Goodman asked Gene to rejoin his band for a domestic tour of military camps sponsored by United Service Organizations Inc., or the USO.[7] The USO objected, but Benny assumed "full responsibility for the move."[8]

The USO engagements were the first test of Gene's public standing. He was anxious about how the troops would receive him but needn't have worried. "The audience reaction to Gene Krupa in all of the camps during the recent Benny Goodman tour . . . exceeded all expectations for sheer, unbounded enthusiasm," reported *Down Beat*.[9] In a gesture of good will, Gene donated his USO salary back to the USO, as well as his compensation for playing with Benny in a Coca-Cola radio broadcast.[10]

Then Benny invited Gene to stay with him for an engagement at the Hotel New Yorker's Terrace Room in Manhattan. Krupa accepted, but the hotel refused to allow him to perform there. A standoff ensued. Benny played the first five days without a drummer! The hotel relented. Krupa occupied his place behind the drums,[11] but his name was kept out of band advertising.

Around this time, Tommy Dorsey attempted to steal Gene for a stint at the Hotel Pennsylvania. But the hotel said *no Gene Krupa, please.*[12]

How would civilians receive Gene? Maybe the servicemen had appreciated him, but they probably loved whatever wartime entertainment they got. Average ballroom patrons might not accept a former jailbird. Yet these engagements proved to be beyond what he could have hoped for.

Of a night at the Terrace Room, *Variety* said, "With Krupa on drums it [the band] serves hair-raising stuff in double doses; when caught the band played 'Stealin' Apples,' an old arrangement, with such drive and fire that the entire population of the room stopped still, including waiters, and cheered lustily when the band finished."[13]

"If there ever was any doubt as to whether or not Gene would be accepted again by his fans after his troubles on the west coast, the doubt can now be banished from all minds," said *Down Beat*. "After each set, Krupa is besieged by hordes of well-wishers and autograph hounds..."[14]

Reviewers who formerly might have yielded to their prejudice against drum solos, only gushed about Gene's playing now. "Without him," said *Billboard*, "the band is great, with him it's magnificent."[15] Writing for *Metronome*, George T. Simon complained a little about Gene's showmanship, but: "Benny's band...was good till Gene came back. Now it's positively stupendous...Gene, too, is great—technically, probably greater than ever before."[16]

Benny's sidemen—many of whom hadn't yet joined when Gene left in March 1938—were thrilled to have Gene now. Goodman bassist Sid Weiss believed, somewhat uncharitably, that the drummer's horrible year had given him a newfound "humility," which caused him to play better. "It was just unbelievable what he did, oh Jesus," said Weiss. "That was one of those times when I couldn't wait to get to work at night. His control, his sensitivity, his ears..."[17]

"You can't begin to realize what Krupa meant to the band unless you were sitting in," a bandmate told *Orchestra World*. "He just pepped up the whole band, kept us on...[our] toes, and I think everybody was happier with Gene in there [than] any other drummer."[18]

Despite more sightings of Gene and Ethel together, he was romantically linked toward year's end with a beautiful singer and actress of stage and screen, Carol Bruce.[19] One columnist joked that if she spent too much time with him she would suffer punctured ear drums.[20] After some months the relationship fizzled, even though Bruce had publicly announced that they would likely wed: "We are very much in love but any marriage plans are indefinite as yet."[21]

Gene decided to stay in New York once Goodman's New Yorker stint had concluded rather than accompany the band to California. Tommy Dorsey grabbed him immediately. Dorsey's usual drummer, Buddy Rich, was in the marines. Here was Tommy's chance to help himself *and* an old friend.

Krupa joined Dorsey for the latter's last night at the Hotel Pennsylvania, but his real Dorsey debut came with an extended engagement at the Paramount Theatre. Gene again worried about his reception. Sure, the troops and the ballroom clientele appreciated him, but what about everyday moviegoers?

For the first series of Paramount performances on December 22, 1943, Gene was unbilled. In a moving scene, "Gene Krupa . . . wept on the stage of the Paramount Theatre yesterday afternoon," said the *New York Daily News*, "as the audience cheered him after he made an unannounced appearance with Tommy Dorsey's orchestra."[22] Thus Gene returned to the paper's front page. The previous May, he had been seen hopping into a patrol wagon on his way to jail. Now he was shown with Tommy Dorsey in a respectable setting in the act of signing a contract.[23]

Daily pandemonium ruled at the Paramount. The atmosphere was emotional every time. "Gene Krupa turned the Paramount Theatre into a madhouse when, in response to the cheers of the kids," reported Ed Sullivan, "he stepped downstage and very eloquently expressed his appreciation for the opportunity Tommy Dorsey had given him. Tore off the roof."[24]

In an era when men weren't supposed to be seen shedding tears, Gene was concerned about appearing unmanly when, a few months later, he looked back on those poignant first days on the Paramount stage. "They say that I cried like a baby," he stated. "Let's say, being a grown man, that I don't cry. Let's say only that, instead of crying, I broke out hot and cold all over."[25]

For the first time since Gene's jailing he was being featured in advertising. In an ad that practically smothered the small mention of the movie playing at the Paramount—*Riding High*, with Dorothy Lamour and Dick Powell—Tommy and Gene exchanged gentlemanly remarks in dialogue balloons. "It's great to have you with us, Gene Krupa!" said Dorsey, trombone in hand. Responded Gene at his drums, "Thanks, Tommy—it's swell to be with you!"[26]

Orchestra World reported that Gene was receiving more publicity now than he had had while a bandleader. National publications "played up the human-interest end of the story—but big!"[27] The magazine later said this state of affairs was "quite a difference from the time when overnight his name was blocked out of all the billboards."[28]

In a surprise incident, some "wise guys" tossed cigarettes at Gene and "heckled" him when he came downstage to make his nightly expression of gratitude at the microphone, prompting an enraged Dorsey to grab the mike and threaten retaliation if he found out who did it.[29] Otherwise, the remaining Dorsey shows were hysterical love fests. Barry Ulanov reported that audiences "yelled and clapped so much [that] the only possible show of enthusiasm left was stunned silence."[30]

Tommy Dorsey had to adjust to Gene's notion of the role of the drummer in a band—not that the drummer should be felt and not heard, or that he should be unobtrusive, but whether he should be allowed to integrate his ideas with those of the other musicians. There was a song, "Hallelujah," which Dorsey had originally recorded in 1940 with Buddy Rich—who, incidentally, sounded profoundly Krupa-influenced on this recording, especially in his use of fills and accents—and Dorsey wanted to play the song live with Gene. There was little time for rehearsal. Tommy said he wanted Gene to play thirty-two bars of drums before the band played the introduction.

"I want to hear the introduction first," said Gene. Tommy said it was "fast, that's all." "No," said Gene. "I want to hear it." Gene later explained that he "wanted what preceded the introduction to say something about the introduction, for you must 'follow' your music—you must get all you can out of it."[31]

Dorsey afforded Krupa the respect he deserved. When the trombonist-leader was sick, he appointed Gene his leader-substitute.[32] Gene was the designated baton-waver during a ballad, "Sleepy Lagoon," while Dorsey soloed.[33] According to gossip columnist Hedda Hopper, Dorsey was paying Gene a little over $500 a week, although other reports apparently said it was $1,000.[34]

There was a heartwarming reunion backstage at the Paramount between Gene and his "little pal," Mel Lewis. The redheaded, freckle-faced boy, about fourteen, was chaperoned by his mother to New York City and the Paramount at Christmastime 1943. Mel left word for Gene that "Red from Buffalo" was there to see him. "Red" was accorded entry immediately.

When Mel entered Gene's dressing room, other men, possibly reporters, were standing around. "Gene looked sharp in his camel hair coat and freshly pressed suit," he remembered later. "You know what I did? I threw my arms around him. I wasn't very big at fourteen; I guess I reached his waist.

"'I don't believe anything they said about you,'" Mel told his mentor. "'That's what I said. And he just held me close. I think I touched him."[35]

Mike Schiffer, for most of his life a jazz pianist and teacher, was thirteen when he heard Gene would be appearing at a Cincinnati store to drum and answer questions. Schiffer had never seen Krupa in the flesh and hoped to interview him for the school paper. The boy took a bus downtown and found the store stuffed with wall-to-wall people and merchandise. It was so crowded he was barely able to squeeze inside the place.

"After he did an energetic solo," said Schiffer, "he wiped his brow, and asked us if we had any questions." One boy queried whether he was chewing gum, and Gene laughed. Perhaps out of nerves, Schiffer couldn't think of any questions and never did write the article for the school paper. But he did have bragging rights with family and friends. "I told my brothers that he played great," he said, "and I told my parents that he was very well-mannered and seemed to be a decent, well-educated gentleman." He spoke a little differently with his friends, telling them that Gene "wasn't some broken-down dope fiend, but was a terrific musician and really nice."[36]

Gene Krupa played live with Dorsey at Carnegie Hall in April 1944 before an invited audience of service men and women broadcast on NBC.[37] He lifted about a dozen songs with his versatile tom-tom work, unpredictable accents, drum roll crescendos, rocking backbeat, shifting ensemble support, and a general mixture of his past and present drumming. "Hawaiian War Chant" was a highlight featuring an extended exchange between Gene and his former sideman, clarinetist Buddy DeFranco, now with Dorsey, much as Gene and Benny went at it on an updated "Sing, Sing, Sing" the previous fall. Songs from this live broadcast were etched on V-Disc.[38]

In February 1944 came welcome legal news. John Pateakos, Gene's former band-boy, now serving in the army in Los Angeles, had signed a letter recanting his 1943 police statement that Krupa had directed him to dispose of the marijuana. Gene's attorney moved to have Pateakos testify to this effect in San Francisco juvenile court, which he did, as a way of ensuring that the recantation would be in the appellate record.[39] Pateakos said he had given the false statement to police because they said "it would go easier with me if I did."[40] The felony charge against Krupa, that he had asked Pateakos to retrieve marijuana cigarettes from his hotel room, made up the entirety of the prosecutor's case against him. Without it, Gene would not have been charged with, let alone convicted of, a felony.

The news got better. On May 29, 1944, the California Court of Appeal reversed Gene's felony conviction on grounds of double jeopardy.[41] The court didn't doubt that the drummer had violated the relevant statute. But this was not as important as the fact that, as the California Attorney General eventually admitted to the court, the misdemeanor to which Gene had pled guilty—contributing to the delinquency of a minor—was a lesser, included offense of the felony for which he was convicted at trial. In other words, both charges arose out of the same set of facts. A criminal defendant could not be prosecuted for or convicted of both, regardless of whether the matter on appeal was the felony or the misdemeanor. Therefore, Gene's felony conviction was reversed.

While he wasn't exonerated of committing the felony (the court didn't mention Pateakos's recantation), he was no longer subject to prosecution for the offense. The court's decision was sufficient for Gene to get on with the rest of his life. As it was, he was a beloved figure eagerly reembraced by music fans upon his return to public view. This was enough for the world of showbiz. In early June 1944, Gene announced the reorganization of his band.

When Krupa left Dorsey, Buddy Rich retook the drummer's seat following six months in the marines. After arriving in Arizona, Tommy's band took a bus to Phoenix for an engagement. Rich noticed placards on all of the telephone poles along the way advertising "Tommy Dorsey and His Orchestra Featuring Gene Krupa." The reason for the outdated notices was that, at booking, Gene was still a Dorsey sideman. But Buddy was livid. At rehearsal time he threatened to quit. "I'm walking out," he said. "I'm not going to sit here and play notes for another drummer." Tommy told Buddy that if he wanted to live he had better stay. Buddy stayed.[42]

CHAPTER 18

"What's This?"

T HE PUBLIC'S RECEPTION OF GENE showed that he hadn't become less popular; he may have become *more* popular, as evidenced in *Down Beat* and *Metronome* poll results. *Down Beat*, still disqualifying bandleaders from the best-on-instruments category, was now un-constrained as to Gene since he had been a sideman during 1943's latter half. He handily won in the drumming category, beating his nearest competitor, Buddy Rich, by a ratio of roughly two to one.[1] Gene won in *Metronome*'s January 1944 poll, having never been dis-qualified due to his earlier bandleader status.[2]

In January 1945, after Gene had resumed his place among the bandleaders, his name was absent from *Down Beat*'s list of the best drummers.[3] But he was again the number one drummer in *Metronome*.[4]

In mid-June, Gene commenced rehearsals in New York with the biggest big band he'd ever had. Its more than thirty musicians and singers would be billed as "The Band That Swings With Strings." They were set for some out-of-town "break-in" dates be-fore their July 20 debut at the Capitol Theatre on Broadway, play-ing in between showings of the David O. Selznick blockbuster, *Since You Went Away*, a World War Two home front drama.

Before and during what would become a record-breaking engage-ment of ten weeks, Gene regularly sat in with his bosom friend Eddie Condon's half-hour Saturday afternoon "Town Hall" con-certs, broadcast over the Blue radio network from Manhattan. Most recently, Eddie and Gene had performed together in a small ensemble supporting Fats Waller at Carnegie Hall in January 1942.

The Town Hall concerts presented a racially integrated ensem-ble with some personnel changing from show to show. Most of the musicians, including Condon, hailed from Nick's Tavern in Green-wich Village. Eddie, in between being repeatedly fired and rehired by Nick, was guitarist-leader of the house band, the tavern's Chief Welcomer and Conversationalist, King of One-Liners, and Cham-pion Imbiber of Liquor. Other Town Hallers came from clubs on Fifty-Second Street or in the Village, or touring bands. Besides Con-don, some participants were of Chicagoan vintage, like early bene-factor Red McKenzie. Among the more notable guests were Miff Mole from the Red Nichols days; influential pianists and com-posers of the 1920s Willie "The Lion" Smith and James P. Johnson; trumpeters Jonah Jones and Hot Lips Page; and bassist Bob Hag-gart, who had risen to prominence with bandleader Bob Crosby.

For Gene, this was a welcome respite from the emotional wringer of the past year and a half, a chance to play with musicians he admired in a relaxed setting, and an excuse to see old pals, espe-cially Eddie, who often beckoned Krupa to the microphone for some chummy banter. "What are you doing here besides playing drums?" Condon asked. "Well, I'm gettin' a lot of laughs, Eddie," replied Krupa, "listening to you talk, old boy." "You're easily amused, I must say that," Eddie suggested.

Despite the genre, Gene's playing contained a combination of whatever he thought was appropriate—the timekeeping press rolls he learned from Baby Dodds, the ride cymbal beat and bass drum bombs he helped pioneer, the as-yet unnamed Bo Diddley beat, some skipping rim shots, and a liberal use of toms. "He might do something that called back to Chicago," said drummer Kevin Dorn, "in the same way that he would sometimes in early recordings play things that would be considered more modern . . ."[5]

Gene made a radical change to his conception of a swing orches-tra when he added strings. His usual guitarist Ray Biondi now oc-cupied one of the violin chairs. Besides violins, there were a cello and two violas. Gene was emulating his most recent employer, Tommy Dorsey, who helped prove that strings weren't antithetical to the objectives of swing, or jazz. Krupa later referred to his "strings" period as "a costly experiment," quipping, "I had an idea that I was some poor man's Kostelanetz."[6]

For the first time, Gene brought in a vocal quartet—the G-Noters, consisting of three men and one woman. Their attractively blended voices made Gene's music seem considerably tamed since 1943. Also, Gene's role in the band became one of not just drummer and bandleader, but conductor. While he had done some conduct-ing with his earlier bands, the string section demanded more. This meant Gene limiting his playing to drum features or songs lending themselves to lengthy solos. Krupa newcomer Joe Dale would play the rest of the time.

The new band had artistic merit, engendered plenty of excite-ment, and broke new jazz ground. As to merit, most of the violin-ists had played with symphony orchestras, including young Paul Nero, who also harbored an affinity for jazz. Nero "felt for the first time . . . [that] strings were being used correctly in a dance band." Rather than being "ornamental" or in the "background," they were treated as a genuine band section with something to say.[7] This was true even during a fairly abstract modern number like "Futurama," which Gene introduced that summer, wherein the strings cried with a rapid, silvery, vibrating voice. Krupa had corralled a stable of new, forward-thinking arrangers—among them, Eddie Finckel and George "The Fox" Williams. Back with the band were Charlie Ventura and trombonist Tommy Pederson. Unfamiliar faces in-cluded pianist Teddy Napoleon, who combined the sounds of Fats Waller and Teddy Wilson and who would figure in Gene's small ensembles for years to come; and seventeen-year-old modern trum-peter Don Fagerquist, to become a years-long Krupa sideman.

Writing for *Billboard* about one of two two-hour Krupa con-certs at Boston's Symphony Hall, Bill Riley praised Gene's "musicianship, the excellence of his band and the fresh, unusual arrangements." Riley added that the strings allowed for a "greatly increased variety of tone color and effect," and that the orchestra was on its way to becoming "one of the country's bands among bands."[8] Barry Ulanov of *Metronome* felt otherwise after seeing Gene's new band perform at the Capitol. The band, he said, was "a lot more commercial and a lot less interesting musically than the old one." Neither did he like the string section, which didn't "play ... too well together, either."[9]

Ulanov and Riley saw differently formatted shows. The one at the Capitol was generally no longer than twenty-five minutes because *Since You Went Away* lasted almost three hours. Shorter movies typically permitted for eight or nine band shows daily. A *Billboard* reviewer saw one of the Capitol performances that Ulanov had attended. "General impression, when informed that a band is only going to do a 25-minute show, his ork won't have a chance to get in its licks," said Paul Secon. "But that assumption was proven wrong."[10]

Krupa had "all eyes on him," Secon said, whether he was behind his drums or up front "clapping his hands" or stamping his feet.[11] Gene used tympani for "Bolero in the Jungle," a new number demanding that the band pound their small tom-toms, as a previous Krupa conglomeration had done for "Blue Rhythm Fantasy." The show concluded with "Drumboogie," lights shining on Gene and casting giant drummer-man shadows above the band.

Teenage friends Ed Shaughnessy and Kenny O'Brien would wake at 4 A.M. to be first in line at the Capitol. They'd bring their lunches in brown paper bags and stay all day. "One of us would go pee while the other watched his seat," said Shaughnessy, who eventually drummed for Doc Severinsen on Johnny Carson's *The Tonight Show*. "All that waiting—we didn't care about the movie—was worthwhile when that band came up in the orchestra pit and the lights went on."[12] (Shaughnessy's friend Kenny O'Brien would play bass with Krupa's Quartet in the early 1960s.)

Just another fellow in the audience whom no one had ever heard of was George Martin, a British naval trainee who spent two weeks in New York before being assigned to, of all places, Trinidad.[13] In the 1960s, he produced records for The Beatles.

With Gene, the Capitol enjoyed its "highest gross" in its first week—$90,000—since "talkie" days.[14] After the ten weeks, the theater presented Krupa with a plaque commemorating the record-breaking engagement, which had attracted 1,113,000 "payees."[15] Gene and *Since You Went Away* were "exceeded in length of run and gross at the Cap only by *Gone With the Wind*, which played at advanced scale [higher ticket prices]."[16] As acknowledged by Capitol management, this success was by no means all movie; *Variety* noted that the "heavy morning business" in particular was likely attributable to Krupa being on the bill.[17]

It was more evident than ever that the crisis of the year before had had no impact on Gene's popularity. His stupendous ten-week run at the Capitol, playing in between showings of a movie with the widest possible audience, meant show business was comfortable with him again. RKO quickly snatched him for a two-picture deal, the first of which would begin filming in early 1945, *George White's Scandals*, a musical.[18] In November, following the end of the record ban, Gene signed a two-year deal with Columbia Records.[19]

In early 1946, Warner Brothers' Looney Tunes incorporated in a short called *Book Revue* caricatures of several of the most popular bandleaders—including Gene—as well as heartthrob Frank Sinatra. The likeness of each star was exaggerated; cartoon Gene, his body accentuated with excessively padded shoulders, tapped away on his drums wearing a somewhat ghoulish red-lipped grin. Later that year, Samuel Goldwyn's *The Best Years of Our Lives* included part of Gene's "Drumboogie" performance from the 1941 movie *Ball of Fire*. Using this clip in what would become a critically praised blockbuster, which, like *Since You Went Away*, was made with the widest possible audience in mind, was another indication of Gene's unmarred popularity.

The next big booking would occur in Chicago with a six-week stint at the Panther Room in the Hotel Sherman followed by a week at the Oriental Theater. But before he and the band arrived, with fewer strings than in New York, they had to survive in America's wilds on a long series of ballroom one-nighters.[20] Unlike the Chicago engagements, these one-night stints were often not so "lucrative"[21] and presented the first indication that Krupa fans generally preferred him behind the drums and not conducting strings. The huge band payroll didn't help.

A NEW TREAT that began at the Capitol in New York was the unveiling of the Gene Krupa Trio, featuring Teddy Napoleon on the piano and Charlie Ventura on the saxophone. There was a marked difference between Gene's new Trio and Benny Goodman's original one. Krupa, Ventura, and Napoleon presented songs familiar and new in which the drums shaped the direction and feel of the entire performance. "Stompin' at the Savoy" was radically reworked, passages ebbing and flowing among cymbals, snare, tom, and bass. "Dark Eyes," the old Russian standard, became a small, moody, quasi-orchestral piece, in which Gene found another place to insert what would become known as the Bo Diddley beat. An original, "10 Ritchie Drive," named for Gene's Yonkers address, was a speedy presentation, conjuring up visions of klutzy comic actors, and, in one version, patternistic cymbal crescendos.

Twenty years hence, John Wilson said on his *The World of Jazz* radio program, "Unlike the Goodman Trio, which played in a pretty straightforward manner, the Krupa Trio built its performances into real musical productions..."[22]

THE CITY FOLLOWING Chicago on the national tour of The Band That Swings With Strings was Detroit. Afterward, it was almost all military bases: the mode of transportation, a B-17 bomber. With no heat and nothing to sit on but your suitcase, the ride wasn't comfortable.[23] But everybody got to wear a dark bomber jacket. This tour would eventually—before year's end—wind up in Los Angeles for a long engagement at the Palladium and the filming of *George White's Scandals of 1945*.

Gene's entourage included not only the musicians, their instruments, singers, band-boys, and managers but also an electrician and the drummer's eldest brother Pete. According to violinist Paul Nero, Pete acted as a "sort of major domo to Gene and kept unwanted people away from him."[24] Gene said his brother was "more or less my manager." "More or less" was probably more accurate than "my manager." Pete was likely there for moral support, particularly in light of Gene's recent West Coast memories.

Getting to Los Angeles was rough going. Problems started in New Mexico. The B-17 got everyone to Roswell, but "bad flying weather" nearly kept them from flying cross-state for a Coca-Cola "Spotlight Band" broadcast in Clovis. After the broadcast, the Army Air Force was to get them safely to Los Angeles for their opening at the Palladium. But the AAF refused. Flying conditions had worsened. The visibility ceiling was at 150 feet and the minimum for the AAF was 500. What could Gene do? He hired a Pullman car for the trip from Clovis to Los Angeles and bought boxes of candy and fruit for his entire entourage. "We had a ball," said trumpeter Bill Conrad.

The train could only go so fast, so they were two days late for Los Angeles. The Palladium management was not amused. They had had to turn away disappointed ticket holders and secured a fill-in band that might have been good (Jan Garber), but it wasn't Gene's. Gene and his group had what should have been an unassailable excuse for their tardiness, but they still lost two days' pay.[25]

AFTER SEVERAL WEEKS at the Palladium, Gene and band, plus an augmented string section, began work on *George White's Scandals*. Two of the movie's stars were true celluloid legends—Jack Haley and Margaret Hamilton, who had, some years earlier, portrayed the Tin Man and the Wicked Witch of the West, respectively, in *The Wizard of Oz*. Underappreciated comedic actress Joan Davis also starred.

In preparation for filming, Gene listened to recordings of the soundtrack made on the RKO lot, memorized his drumming on these pieces, and accurately mimed while filming the relevant scenes. The only number not completed this way was the finale, "Bolero in the Jungle," in which he really was playing his six tympani, flamboyantly and live, during filming.[26] He appeared in five numbers, with some sidemen enjoying actual facetime during "Leave Us Leap," another song on the band's live playlist. In "Leave Us Leap" he engaged in drumstick trickery and spent time away from the drums dancing and adding hand-clap percussion to the grooves of his orchestra. He spoke real lines of dialogue with and without the stars.

MAYBE KRUPA WAS rationalizing lugging around the massive payroll that was The Band That Swings With Strings, and conducting rather than pounding the drums for a significant portion of the show. He said that the public's interest in dancing and melody as opposed to jazz had been increasing. He wanted to meet that interest and believed strings would help. Yet he remained dedicated to jazz and included plenty of it in his records and onstage. His musical objectives, however, were broadening.

The strings' last hurrah would be a series of concert-dance programs beginning with a week at the Orpheum Theater in Los Angeles. From there, Gene's colossal ensemble would play one-nighters in Tulsa, Oklahoma City, Dallas, Fort Worth, Houston, Shreveport, Little Rock, St. Louis, and Chicago.[27]

These shows were especially ambitious undertakings, judging from the program for April 22, 1945, at the Chicago Arena, and perhaps too sophisticated for the average audience. There were twenty-two songs in all, with half devoted to the concert and the other half to dancing. Every section of the band and all vocalists would be featured in both halves, as would Gene's Trio. The concert portion demonstrated Gene's passion for classical music. There were adaptations of Debussy's "Clair de Lune" and Fritz Kreisler's "Caprice Viennois" played alongside Gene's modernist "Futurama" and "Leave Us Leap" and his earliest experimentation with percussion for big band jazz, "Blue Rhythm Fantasy." Some of his star soloists—Charlie Ventura, Tommy Pederson, and Ray Biondi—were spotlighted.[28]

One wishes that at least one of these shows had been recorded for posterity, but Krupa's failed undertaking was destined to fade with the impermanence of sound waves. The show at St. Louis's Kiel Auditorium was a disaster, not so much because of a public skeptical of a different Krupa presentation, but due to stunning national news. It was April 12, 1945, the day that President Roosevelt unexpectedly died of a cerebral hemorrhage after twelve years in office.[29]

Gene's use of a vocal quartet, the G-Noters, who had debuted with the strings in July 1944, while probably not the right fit for a Krupa aggregation, did lead to a musical milestone. This was thanks to Krupa himself and two experimenting G-Noters, Buddy Stewart and Dave Lambert. Whenever possible at nightly band rehearsals during the Capitol Theatre run in the summer of 1944, the singers "noodled around," as Buddy put it, on an unorthodox, nonverbal vocal tune for two. Gene noticed their "pretty progressive ideas" and brought in African-American saxophonist and emerging modernist Budd Johnson to write a band arrangement around what they were doing. On January 22, 1945, the song had its chance. The band was prepared to record only three sides, including "Leave Us Leap." They needed a fourth—fast. Thus, this strange ditty was pulled off the proverbial shelf and given a try. The song was immortalized in one take.[30]

In the finished product, Stewart and Lambert sing soft, nonsensical syllables in legato mode, using their joined voices as one lead band instrument. Their approach was eventually named "vocalese," a kind of bebop scatting. The recording feels airy and sweeping, presaging the lighter big band jazz of the postwar period. "We felt there was a crying need for something new," said Gene, "and didn't know what, so we asked the public in the title, 'What's This?'"[31]

Stewart and Lambert have been called the "first to create a valid, vital music out of the combination of vocals and bop."[32] A review at the time noticed that Anita O'Day's "That's What You Think," in which she smoothly nonsensed her way through what was essentially an instrumental number, could be considered a precursor to

"What's This?"[33] The latter song reportedly sold 50,000 copies upon first release, but, due to a shortage of shellac, 250,000 orders were backlogged.[34] A couple of years later, Nat King Cole answered "What's This?" with "That's What," a stylistic follow-up.

———————

BY MAY, GENE's band was considerably slimmed down, the G-Noters gone with only Buddy Stewart remaining—in time for Frank Dailey's Terrace Room in Newark, New Jersey. It was time for Gene to explain why he had gotten rid of the strings. He told Leonard Feather that they had presented myriad problems: extreme overhead, a lack of consistently good arrangements, inadequate amplification, and the bandleader being obliged to conduct more and play drums less. And, all modesty aside, he preferred his own drumming on ballads.

Gene mentioned the catch-22 he faced if he dialed back the drum solos to accommodate critics' criticisms. "Quite often I've tried to follow the critics' advice by not featuring myself so much, but you know what happens?" Gene said. "People come up to the bandstand and say[,] 'What's the matter, you tired or something?'"[35]

In July big news arrived: Anita O'Day was returning. It happened on the seventh while Gene was playing at the Astor Roof in New York. She had had a big hit with Stan Kenton, "Her Tears Flowed Like Wine" (1944). But she always loved Gene as a musician and a friend. Anita walked in on a Krupa rehearsal in New York on her first day back. "Gene's back was toward me," she remembered, "and when I saw him giving instructions with that familiar hand chop, tears came to my eyes."[36] To ensure that Anita and her husband, Carl, could be together, Gene hired him as another road manager.

The end of World War Two, with Germany surrendering in May 1945 and Japan in September, was a godsend for the countries liberated by the Allies, as well as for the combatants, but not so much for the war industries upon which millions in the United States had relied for their bread and butter. Buffalo, New York, for instance, suffered as plants closed, war workers left the area, and the population's discretionary spending plummeted. While Gene's band was doing well following its downsizing, this wasn't so for his weeklong stint in Buffalo, where, it was reported, the economy caused a "disappointing take."[37] But plant closings weren't limited to Buffalo. Things would change across the board.

Variety called Gene's first week back at the Capitol in New York "big," with a gross of $88,000 as the band shared the stage with the Hedy Lamarr-Robert Walker romantic comedy, *Her Highness and the Bellboy*.[38] Several new Krupa recordings featuring George Williams's advanced arrangements were high on the jukebox charts: two with vocals by Buddy Stewart, "Along the Navajo Trail" and "Just A Little Fond Affection"; a jocular Stewart-O'Day duet, "That Feeling in the Moonlight"; and Anita and Gene's only novelty offering, "Chickery Chick." Gene's and Sammy Kaye's separate renditions of "Chick" reached number one in record sales.[39]

"That Feeling in the Moonlight" was a live favorite. The song's middle required a jitterbug dance routine and Gene obliged, joining the singers out front to the audience's delight.[40]

Anita gave a signature performance on a Krupa-Biondi number titled "Oh, Hot Dawg" for V-Disc. Maybe to appeal to an audience broader than oversexed GIs, for general release the song was renamed "Boogie Blues." It was still sexually suggestive, but mainly because of the lyrics that O'Day contributed: "He's got a face like a fish/Shaped like a frog/But when he loves me/I holler oh, hot dog!" "I don't know where she got those lyrics," said Gene.[41] In fact, they're similar to Jimmy Rushing's words on Count Basie's "Boogie Woogie (I May Be Wrong)" (1937). Regardless, "Boogie Blues" was a powerful mixture of boogie-woogie and blues that remained in the Krupa cache long after Anita had left.

She stayed in the band about six months, unable to make it through their long January-into-February-1946 engagement at Los Angeles's Palladium, walking out minutes before a radio broadcast. "I felt dizzy and frightened that the walls were closing in on me," Anita said. "What I had was a heavy emotional breakdown." She locked herself in the closet at home. Her mental health crisis lasted six weeks; next year saw another crisis when she and Carl were prosecuted for marijuana possession.[42]

Unflappable Gene stayed true to form upon learning of Anita's sudden departure at one of the worst possible moments. "Gee, Anita's the greatest singer around," he told the press. "I can't say anything bad about her." He quickly hired Carolyn Grey as Anita's replacement.[43] Gene and Anita stayed friends for life.

Krupa plucked Anita O'Day from obscurity and made her a star; she became a tremendously influential singer, enjoying a successful solo career. "As a stylist, Anita initiated a whole new trend in band singing," said Dan Morgenstern. "Her throaty voice, slurred delivery, and unique, swinging phrasing had sex, bite and humor... [She] was the best, the most musically complete, of all the talented ladies who sang with the big bands..."[44]

IN FEBRUARY 1946, Gene and Ethel remarried. Since their separation and divorce five years earlier, rumors were constantly circulating about their remarriage. In October 1944, Ethel was "refurbishing" her Hollywood residence as she awaited Gene's California return; in November, she was leaving her job at the Palladium to join Gene in Chicago, where they hoped to "retie the knot"; in January 1945, they went ring-shopping; in February, they "clashed again," their reconciliation off; in March, they were seen eating at Ciro's in Hollywood, their reconciliation on; eleven months on, they were reunited in matrimony and honeymooned in Mexico.[45] Gene and Ethel's relationship was a complicated one.

"He really did love Ethel," commented Gail Krupa, the wife of Gene's only nephew. Among the beautiful things Gene gave Ethel was a Patek Philippe gold watch with her initials inside.[46]

Gene and Ethel had been known for throwing yearly Christmas parties for the band.[47] Yet, according to Bobby Scott, Krupa's pianist for a time in the 1950s and a good friend, Ethel had "antipathy for musicians, seeing them as wayward and malicious little boys." Gene admitted that, as a bandleader, he felt the need to be a "surrogate father" to his sidemen, some of whom were teenagers or barely twenty years old. "The problems never end," Gene said. "Musicians are great human beings, but... we're all kids! And I don't mean

Boy Scouts, either."[48] It may have been a while before Ethel had come to view her husband's charges contemptuously; this could have been another reason for their split.

Bobby Scott also recalled speaking to others close to Gene who thought that the Krupas' remarriage was a "disaster"; their relationship was and would be a rocky one. It took a long time for them to remarry, but it had to happen. Prior to his marijuana ordeal, Gene had been a kind of lapsed Catholic, but that changed afterward. Ultimately, he remarried Ethel because of his renewed faith. To him, it was the right thing to do.[49]

The drummer wasn't going to give Ethel a southern California manse. Instead, she got the beautiful Krupa homestead in Yonkers, with its large L-shaped property and adjacent wooded lot. Gene's Yonkers friends and neighbors became her friends and neighbors. When Gene was home, he and Ethel hosted parties for friends, neighbors, and celebrities alike.

THE KRUPAS' REMARRIAGE was good news in what would become a tough 1946 for the big bands. It's not that, in Gene's case, there weren't successes. An August week's gross at the RKO in Boston led all movie theaters in the city.[50] Later that month, a week at New York's Capitol Theatre brought in $106,000; the three-week gross exceeded all records in the twenty-six years of the Capitol's existence.[51] Despite similar results in various Midwest cities, November brought shocking news. Reported *Billboard*: "Among the first name orksters to take definite action in the tough struggle bands are having today making their nut is Gene Krupa." He closed his New York office and reduced band salaries. Other bands followed suit; some disbanded entirely, like Woody Herman, Les Brown, and Tommy Dorsey. Higher operating costs weren't supported by earnings.[52] These circumstances were driven at least partly by inflation, which skyrocketed after the government lifted wartime price restrictions. The big bands were hurting.

CHAPTER 19

Here We Go Again!

"**G**ENE FEELS VERY STRONGLY THAT he has been taken to the cleaners," wrote George T. Simon in 1948. Past managers had assured Krupa everything was fine when it wasn't. "They took care of it all right," said Simon, "but not for Krupa."

"It's the same way in all entertainment,'" said Gene, who was, according to Simon, "supervising everything connected with his band, from music through business, and from all the latest reports he's doing an amazing job." Gene's day-to-day manager, Ira Mangel, apparently answered to him directly.[1]

The immediate postwar years saw great change. America had survived the traumas of the Great Depression and World War Two. Servicemen came home and either went to college for free under the G.I. Bill or married and started families, or both. They bought mini-homes in the Levittowns springing up in New York, New Jersey, and Pennsylvania, and necessary domestic appliances, which increasingly included television sets. It was a relatively quiet period despite the barely perceptible pall cast by potential nuclear warfare. Minds turned from wartime and prewar entertainment and politics. Anticommunism became the watchword for many a politician. The groundwork was being set, with difficulty, for a long civil rights struggle that took nearly twenty years to yield meaningful change.

The year 1947 saw these things developing, phenomena inconsistent with a craving for the big bands. These large musical conglomerations seemed to have magically sprung forth to assuage the suffering of millions in a time of massive upheaval. Negative economic trends in this new prosaic era continued for the bands that had been the chief generators of excitement in former times. Now, some places where the biggest names in swing, like Gene's, had played and been paid quite handsomely were dropping their "name band" policy altogether due to a downturn in business. New York's Aquarium attempted to drop Gene's four-week engagement starting January 10, but it was forced to agree to a two-week Krupa stint after his agent and the American Federation of Musicians intervened.[2]

Not everything was bad. Gene had transformed his band into a bebop enterprise, meeting with success, commercially and artistically. "I'd been digging Diz and Bird [Charlie Parker] and a few of the guys," Gene said, "and we'd gotten Buddy Wise, Don Fagerquist and Dick Taylor into the band." Left unsaid was how Gene's drumming had been featuring bebop elements before the jazz genre had a name. "What's This?" as we've seen, was dubbed the first bop vocal recording. Gene hired superb modern players besides the aforementioned tenor saxist Wise, trumpeter Fagerquist, and trombonist Taylor. Some rookies were just eighteen years old: the Charlie Parker–influenced, creamy-toned alto saxophonist Charlie Kennedy; Red Rodney of the flexible, soaring trumpet; and a then-unknown alto saxophonist-arranger, Gerry Mulligan. Such Krupa arrangers as Eddie Finckel and George Williams were moving swiftly in a bebop direction.

Krupa was "a modern, progressive-type person," said trumpeter Red Rodney,[3] whose small, skinny frame and schoolboy visage belied his mature talent. Gene's band was "really the first white name bebop band. He tried it, he did it, he let it happen."[4] Gene's "band in the mid and late 1940s was a modern jazz laboratory," jazz writer Burt Korall once observed.[5]

An impressive selection of new bop tunes and bop arrangements of older tunes filled the Krupa band book. Many songs
recorded for commercial sale were rerecorded for the band's Capitol Transcription sessions spanning February 1946 to February 1947.
For radio play only, they may be the most beautifully captured
Krupa band performances before the 1950s. The sound is near
stereo in quality, and every element of every sideman's playing is
heard clearly, including every last Krupa hit on snare, bass drum,
tom-tom, or cymbal.

Whether the recordings are of Gene's innovative drum-centric
trio, with Ventura and Napoleon, in which they turn upside down
"Limehouse Blues" and "Body and Soul"; or of Gene's signature bop
numbers, like "Lover," "Up and Atom," "Calling Dr. Gillespie," "It's
Up to You," and "Bird House"; or the updated "Indiana," "Stardust,"
and "Baby, Won't You Please Come Home," they are a revelation
for anyone doubting the band's superior musicianship and bop inspiration. Buddy Stewart remained the band's male singer and was
still showing his talent for vocalese, as well as singing ballads straight.
"Stewart's musicality was virtually unprecedented in its breadth,"
said John McDonough, "and matched only by his contemporary,
Mel Tormé."[6] Carolyn Grey, Anita O'Day's replacement, possessed
more technique but lacked O'Day's adventurousness.

One song not given the Capitol Transcription treatment was the
sunny earworm, "Disc Jockey Jump," probably the most well-
known of the Mulligan arrangements recorded by Gene's band and
viewed as the "most accomplished." Gene's group was said to have
played the song's "long, linear melodies of a bebop character with
the kind of fluency redolent" of the improvisation of Dizzy Gillespie's sax section. Krupa "effectively underpinned some solos that
[were] also moving in a convincing bebop direction, notably from
altoist Charles Kennedy and trumpeter Don Fagerquist."[7]

Gerry Mulligan, the person and musician, was good and bad for
the band. Gene said that Mulligan was "sort of a temperamental
kid who always wanted to expound on a lot of his ideas."[8]

"We . . . had Gerry playing for a while," Gene said, "but the other
guys on sax said they'd quit if I didn't get him out of there, because

he didn't have command of the instrument then and he was messing up a pretty smooth sax section ... But he was a beautiful arranger."⁹

Mulligan, second alto to Harry Terrill's lead, recalled, "I was always changing notes, and this used to drive Harry crazy." Harry "lunged" at Gerry once after a show. Gene had to separate them. "I was a terrible sideman," Mulligan admitted. The end of his sideman days came when teenager Mulligan yelled at the band, in front of Gene, for playing sloppily. Gene took Mulligan aside and gently rebuked him for his insubordination and the near anarchy he could have caused among the sidemen. Mulligan was out, except for arrangements.¹⁰

Terrill and Mulligan agreed on the high quality of Gene's band. Gerry called it the "most professional band I'd ever written for. They were so professional they sometimes scared the hell out of me. They had no trouble playing anything I wrote."¹¹ Harry said: "It was the happiest, scariest, most lucrative and most musical band I ever played with."¹²

BEBOP WAS SHOWCASED in short films in which Gene and band starred. One was the *Thrills of Music Featuring Gene Krupa and His Orchestra* (1948). Featuring a bright performance of "Disc Jockey Jump," Gene played lightly but found the right spots for some choice rim shots, and the heated but catchy "Bop Boogie," sung by the underappreciated Dolores Hawkins, who, like Gene, could dominate a stage. It's been said that Gene introduced bop to the big screen with *Thrills of Music*.¹³

In 1949, Gene, the band, and Hawkins performed a slightly less heated rendition of "Bop Boogie" in a different short, *Deep Purple*, named for the ballad Gene's male crooner, Bill Black, sang on film. Especially notable in the film was the band's rendition of "Lemon Drop," probably their weirdest song after "What's This?" and maybe "That's What You Think." "Lemon Drop" didn't originate with the Krupa aggregation, but they made it their own, expertly performing a brisk changeable arrangement likely written by George Williams. The performance, bookended by a duet of

African-influenced drums between Gene and an unnamed bongo player, turned to trombonist Frank Rosolino to tantalize with his matter-of-fact, clipped bop vocalese.

Before *Thrills of Music* and *Deep Purple*, Gene and band performed bop in a badly written full-length feature film, *Beat the Band* (1947). Gene costarred with Frances Langford, Ralph Edwards, and Phillip Terry. The bop tune, "Calling Dr. Gillespie," was eclipsed within minutes by a richly toned, ingenious percussion solo Gene took on steam pipes inside what was supposed to have been a "boiler room."

Gene also costarred or appeared in several full-length 1940s features, plus what may be termed a diminutive, rather than full-length, movie. This was *Follow That Music* (1947), the best of the bunch by far and only seventeen minutes long. It was packed with a multifaceted, complete storyline (boy-seeks-fortune-in-the-big-city *and* boy-meets-girl), multitudinous funny lines, good music, a Krupa concerto in percussion for pots and pans, and probably the one instance of Gene comically crossing his eyes in a public presentation. Gene's sidemen play supporting roles. Red Rodney is a kind of band-boy who shows, before it's too late, that he can blow a trumpet. Krupa also introduces his Trio version of "Dark Eyes," albeit while disguised as a Russian chef in a nightclub. Not to worry—it all makes sense in the end. *Follow That Music* was in some places on the same bill with *It's a Wonderful Life*, starring Jimmy Stewart, Donna Reed, and Lionel Barrymore—certainly one of the best film associations one could hope for.

Gene found himself acting again—but also making music—in the Columbia movie *Glamour Girl* (1948). It was such a B-movie that Gene's was the biggest name in it, as reflected in the opening credits. Every other actor or singer lay in smaller typeface below. The film was renamed several times before its release: *Mary Lou*,[14] *Bright Eyes*,[15] and *I Surrender Dear*[16]—which didn't portend well for the finished product. The main reason to see this movie is for the performance of "Melody in F," a song that, alas, they never recorded. It's an unexpectedly dissonant piece handled skillfully by the sidemen as Gene engages in some of his best on-film drumming. His tom-tom tone alone is so real that his playing is almost a tactile experience for audiences.

Two more full-length 1940s features found space for Gene, but not much. Although he received star billing in *Smart Politics* (1948), a Monogram production, he is seen for only part of one song, "Young Man with a Beat," toward the movie's end. His appearance may be summed up as an exciting introductory drum passage that segues into some shouting brass. Marketers viewed the film's—and Gene's—audience as "younger picture-goers."[17] Well over a decade after Gene first achieved fame as the drummer in Benny Goodman's band, he was still thought of as appealing to the youth market.

The last '40s movie in which Gene appeared was *Make-Believe Ballroom* (1949), based on the radio program of the same name hosted by Martin Block and Al Jarvis. "The story is extremely thin and only mildly amusing," read one review, "although it serves well enough as a means to introduce the musical sequences."[18] Besides Krupa's band and the King Cole Trio, other prominent bands included Charlie Barnet's and Jan Garber's; singers to become more familiar in the 1950s also appeared. Krupa's portion was lifted from his *Thrills of Music* short subject of the year before.

One shouldn't conclude, as have many, that these movie roles and appearances made Gene into a matinee idol. That he was in these movies was a measure of his popularity, but most of them were low-budget and burdened by poor acting and awful screenwriting. With the exception of *Follow That Music*, Gene's lines were minimal. He was given little to do other than play music. Yes, he looked great onscreen, but that in itself didn't make him a matinee star.

In 1945, RKO general manager Charles Koerner offered Krupa a long-term movie contract to star in light comedies. His response is instructive in considering to what extent, if any, he had attained the status of a matinee idol. "The loyalty of the band fans who have stuck by me through everything means too much to me to risk losing," he said. "I can't turn my back on them, even for possible stardom in motion pictures."[19]

AFTER A YEAR with Krupa, Red Rodney gave notice that he was moving on. "With Gene Krupa I first got a wide measure of recognition," said Rodney.[20] "But 52nd Street was beckoning . . . It was a difficult thing, because of Gene. I loved him."[21] What Red didn't expect was the gift Gene would give him.

According to Jake Hanna, a Krupa acolyte who achieved success and fame in his own right, every week Gene set aside money for Rodney, unbeknownst to him. "I gave you two hundred [a week]," Gene was to have said. "Did you ever save any?"

"Well, no," said Red. "I spent most of it."

"I knew you'd blow it," said Gene, beckoning him to a room where the pay envelopes were kept. "I put away 50 bucks a week for you," he told Red. "I was paying you two-fifty but I only gave you two hundred. So I wound up with a couple of thousand dollars so you can go out [and do what you want to do]."

"That's the kind of guy Gene Krupa was," said Jake Hanna.[22]

BESIDES BEING A laboratory for modern jazz music, classical pieces were turning up in Gene's live performances—even though he had ditched the strings years earlier.

"The boogie-man who leaves today's younger generation frightened of Toscanini" had added Sibelius's "Valse Triste" to the band book, reported Jay Carmody in a review for the *Evening Star* of a Krupa performance at Washington's Capitol Theatre. The work "clearly was not composed with drums in the creator's mind," said Carmody, "but . . . Krupa brings [it] off with an effect that certainly is arresting." Carmody wondered if it might send youngsters to record stores to learn more about Sibelius.[23]

What happened? Gene, a classical music enthusiast, had asked arranger George Williams to "develop scores" from the material of composers like Sibelius, Rimsky-Korsakov, and Khachaturian, among others. It was not just "Valse Triste" but also "Sabre Dance" and "Scheherazade" to which audiences were introduced.

One of Gene's classical adaptations came earlier on, in summer 1944, when he had just unveiled his new string-laden band. The recording blatantly merged a beautiful old piece with an obscure big band song and stands out among other classical adaptations Gene has done because of its mystery, beauty, and unexpected funkiness. This was "Fish Market," recorded only for a V-Disc but never released to the troops, who were its intended audience. Since then, virtually no one has heard it, other than on a 1999 French import CD.[24]

Notwithstanding the disc's credit to Verdi, it was based on the "sextet" portion of the 1835 opera, *Lucia di Lammermoor*, by Gaetano Donizetti.[25] In this recording, all of Gene's band sections, including the strings, and some of his major soloists, have their turn on the theme. But the extraordinary melding of Donizetti with a mid-tempo, sultry version of 1930s swing tune "Nit Wit Serenade" helps make this record exceptional.

Gene's drumming on the recording provides another example of his versatility. Kevin Dorn said: "It's subtle, but it's also driving ... Sort of like a slow-moving train ... The groove doesn't really change, but he goes from playing on the high-hat—that's giving you one sound. Then he switches to the ride cymbal, which gives it another sound. And then he adds a back-beat to what he's playing on the ride cymbal." These subtle shifts divide the solo into sections of "different textures," but without fills, which would have "disrupted that kind of groove."[26] It's marvelously controlled and one of his most flavorful performances.

Later classical adaptations like "Sabre Dance" worked wonderfully in a live modern jazz context. "*Sabre Dance* and a 10-minute tabloid version of ... *Scheherezade* [sic] (an unusual cleffing in that not just a few but all the themes were treated) were performed, imaginatively written and excitingly played," read a July 1948 *Billboard* review. "Gene cut loose with drumnastics on the latter, not an extraneous show of technique, but a cleverly integrated part of the score."[27]

Gene was proud of these jazz versions of the classics. "They're different from the usual classical adaptations you'll hear," he said. "We don't do it like Freddy Martin does or like Glenn Miller did. We want to give the listener an idea of what a whole composition sounds like and so instead of just taking one theme we take all of the important ones. We break up tempos and make it more or less of a concert affair." Gene said, "We're bringing good music to the dancing public instead of those stinking ballads that the music publishers are forcing down our throats."[28]

Visiting Krupa's household, one might hear not jazz, but classical music, including Leonard Bernstein's, blasting from Gene's speakers.[29] Who was this Gene Krupa? A feral performer of the hottest beats, as his reputation would have it, a devotee of the purest of jazz above all else? Or a genteel seller of soft, semicerebral fare? Was he both?

Gene wasn't afraid of lengthy intellectual discussions in public places about music. The question, "Has Jazz Influenced the Symphony?" began as a conversation between Krupa and classical conductor David Broekman at the 400 Club in New York where the Krupa band was playing. The query eventually made the pages of *Esquire* magazine (February 1947) in an exchange between Krupa and Leonard Bernstein. Just as Gene, though a jazzer, passionately immersed himself in classical music, Bernstein was a jazz enthusiast, enjoying Gene's music, Billie Holliday's, and that of many of Gene's peers. They had crossover musical interests, but their respective outlooks were different. Gene asserted that modern-day classical composers, like Ravel, Prokofiev, and Shostakovich, may have tried to incorporate jazz in their work but failed. He believed it was impossible for trained classical musicians lacking a jazz background to play or write jazz music, while jazz musicians in general couldn't cross the divide into classical.

Jazzers often lacked the opportunity to acquire the "comprehensive musical background" necessary to play classical music. Referring to Louis Armstrong, Earl Hines, Jimmie Noone, and Baby and Johnny Dodds, he said they "came up the hard way. All of them played for dough, played professionally, many while they were still in short pants." They played what they felt, away from the printed page. Jazz should be played by musicians "brought up in its tradition."

Many younger jazz musicians, said Gene, have had the kind of musical training necessary for writing a composite jazz-classical work, which boded well for the future. Gene revealed that he had long had a plan to write a concerto for his band and a seventy-strong symphony orchestra, as a way of merging the two art forms. Even if he failed in the attempt, said Gene, it was the "kind of music I want to hear."

Bernstein sort of agreed with Gene. Twentieth-century composers trying to incorporate jazz in their works unintentionally left out the "unconscious," which Gene might have called the authenticity needed to do it right. Some modern composers, said Bernstein, had found a way to insinuate elements of jazz into their works without creating a true merger of the idioms. Bernstein thought it might only go that far.[30]

IN MID-1948, while playing the reconstituted Glen Island Casino, Gene rehearsed a showmanly band production to engage the audience in a different way. It was a marching rendition of "Four-Leaf Clover" in which they would parade all around the venue. Gene would yell military commands while the band answered in bebop fashion and majorette Dolores Hawkins led the way. It was a hit in ballrooms.[31]

FORTY-ONE-YEAR-OLD drummer Dave Tough died of a fractured skull on December 9, 1948, after a fall likely caused by an alcoholic stupor.[32] His career had been interrupted often by his alcoholism, dating as far back as the early 1930s.[33] Gene was devastated by the news. Dave had been one of his first jazz drumming mentors.

Dave's death put Gene in a depressive funk, worsened by a state of exhaustion after "92 straight one-nighters." He was also "far underweight." Krupa gave more than two weeks' notice to his sidemen that he was taking an overdue month-long break.[34]

The break was interrupted when a sick Benny Goodman took the always reliable Gene away from his homebound vacation on January 9, 1949, to conduct Goodman's band at the Paramount Theatre for shows running through the following Tuesday.[35]

On January 28, Gene was ready to go on the road again. A new-old band member would be joining—Roy Eldridge, who was giving up his own band to play with Gene again.³⁶ Krupa had persuaded Roy to return; maybe he and Dolores Hawkins could create a spark similar to what Roy had had with Anita O'Day.³⁷ The fact that, on January 15, Gene and Roy had shared a stage on the short-lived television program, *The Eddie Condon Floor Show*, may have made the transition a timely one. Roy called his return to the Krupa band "one of the best periods of my life."³⁸

He and Delores generated some O'Day-Eldridge chemistry on "Watch Out!" a George Williams arrangement. She told Roy to "Go, Roy, go!" prompting a highly charged solo, now with a certain amount of bebop audible. À la "Let Me Off Uptown," the band shouted its approval of Roy's playing.

In "Swiss Lullaby," Dolores, Roy, and vocalist Bill Black took turns trying to rid this yodeling waltz of excess corn. Black sang it straight and Hawkins, up-tempo and jazzy. Eldridge yelled at them to "shut up" because he was a "man who needs his sleep." In "if you can't beat 'em, join 'em" mode, he took out his trumpet and blasted it nicely. Maybe it was the variability and humor that the critics liked. The *New York Daily News* saw it as a "winning production number."³⁹ Barry Ulanov called it "one of the handful of genuinely important records of 1949."⁴⁰

"Similau" was another winner. Its Latin-esque melody; drumming exchanges between Gene and Latin percussion specialists; a conventional vocal interpretation by Bill Black; and Frank Rosolino's bebop vocalese interjections make it one of Krupa's more intriguing late-1940s sides. Disc jockeys favored it.⁴¹

Some said Gene's orchestra now emphasized "slow to mid-tempo" fare and a lower decibel level. "Danceability" was the watchword, and public taste was not to be ignored.⁴² *Down Beat* reviewer Ted Hallock all but called Gene's band one of the Mickey Mouse variety, while contradicting himself when he said that "an evening dancing and listening to Krupa is well-spent." Hallock just couldn't handle Krupa's continued popularity, which, as ever, was bad if you wanted respect: "Krupa is drawing ... drawing everywhere he plays ... which is evidently all anyone cares about these days in the music business ... At loot gathering, Gene's gang is making plenty."[43]

—————————

In September 1948, movie star Robert Mitchum and a couple of friends were prosecuted in Hollywood on marijuana charges. Police psychiatrist J. Paul DeRiver asserted that marijuana use was rampant in the film industry, but only Mitchum and Gene Krupa had ever been arrested for it. "It's prevalent among artists for two reasons," said DeRiver. "It peps them up when they're working under strain and it acts as a romantic stimulant."[44]

In February 1949, there was a flurry of internal FBI communications about Gene's 1943 legal nightmare. For two weeks, FBI staff exchanged radiograms to confirm what Gene had been charged with, what he had been convicted of, the holding of the appellate court in reversing the felony conviction, and whether anything further had emerged from the case. They learned that the Supreme Court of California had not accepted the San Francisco District Attorney's appeal and that, locally, the felony matter wasn't dismissed until over a year following reversal.[45]

On July 25 and 26, 1949, three of Gene's twentysomething sidemen—trombonist Herb Randel, trumpeter John Bello, and guitarist Ralph Blaze—were arrested on narcotics charges in Detroit, along with their teenage girlfriends, during a Krupa band engagement at open-air theater Eastwood Gardens. Federal and local authorities seized cocaine in the possession of Randel and Bello and marijuana in Blaze's possession.[46] Gene had earlier warned his sidemen that if they were ever found with narcotics, he would fire them "on the spot." He followed through on the threat.[47] He hoped to prevent anything like what he had gone through in 1943.

The controversy affected the reputations and personal comfort of Gene and the rest of the band, as well as the three new men he had hired at the last minute. Eastwood Gardens attempted to cancel the remainder of the Krupa gig, but the American Federation of Musicians backed Gene. The AFM also advised Gene that he and the band should honor their contract by arriving at the venue on each of the purportedly canceled nights and being ready to play at the prescribed time. This they did. Nevertheless, Eastwood Gardens refused to let them perform. Gene and his sidemen waited for hours on a darkened stage, listening as ticket holders were turned away.[48] Worse, Gene and the band were evicted from their hotel, and another hotel publicly announced that it would refuse their business. Local papers aggressively milked the situation to Gene's and the band's embarrassment.[49]

To Gene's trumpeter Don Fagerquist, the police raids "sounded like a 'plant' or set-up' just to harass Gene again . . . He was just trying to make a clean living, but the police would never leave him alone. If some pusher got arrested three states away, he would say, 'Gene Krupa gave it to me,' and Gene would have to take two or three nights off to answer the charges. It must have been degrading to someone in his position."[50]

For the rest of his life, despite the love he received from his fans, no matter how successful he remained, Gene couldn't free himself from a certain amount of societal disapproval. Long after the 1940s, Gene could tell when law enforcement was around, hoping or expecting him to do something incriminating. "We drew the head of the Nevada State Police narcotics squad," said pianist Bobby Scott about a 1955 engagement he played with Gene in Las Vegas. "He came in night after night to watch for dilated pupils."[51]

Some so-called journalists have been perpetuating the false idea that, like such tragic figures as Charlie Parker, Krupa was a heroin junkie.[52] The scurrilous notion that he lived much of his life as a strung-out drug addict still exists today in some quarters. He was never strung out nor an addict. No evidence exists that he ever used anything harder than marijuana, and that substance was out of his life as of his arrest in January 1943.

A Classical Man

We know that Gene Krupa loved classical music, so much so that he featured adaptations of masterworks covering all of their main themes in his late 1940s shows. Gene had wanted since boyhood to one day play for a symphony orchestra.[53]

Then there was the "jazz concerto grosso" that he had first given thought to in 1936 and that he was actively working on in 1944. The finished product would incorporate "primitive rhythms." Just as he said in his 1947 *Esquire* piece, he intended to unite jazz players with symphony orchestras across the world. Some of his younger fans were alarmed when informed of Gene's plans, although one thirteen-year-old boy wasn't too worried. He figured he'd be "married and a father by that time."[54]

Gene, whose favorite composer was the British-born son of German-Dutch parents, Frederick Delius, shared his passion for classical music with his sidemen. One of Delius's earliest musical influences was African-American, which may be traced to the composer having spent time in Florida as a young man in the late nineteenth century.

Far from finding Gene's enthusiasm a nuisance, his sidemen were inspired to learn more about what he loved. Gerry Mulligan fondly remembered how Gene would travel with a portable phonograph and records. "He used to enjoy having some of the musicians hang out with him in his hotel room, where he'd play stuff for us," said Mulligan. "He'd say, 'Now listen to this, and listen to what the trumpets do here, and listen to the timps here....' The best way to learn about something new is to have somebody who's enthusiastic and who zeroes in on aspects of the music that you might miss if left to your own devices."[55]

Bobby Scott, Gene's pianist in the 1954–1955 Krupa Quartet, said that, one afternoon, with the whole Quartet present in Gene's hotel room, talk turned to classical music. Krupa supplied the band-boy with sufficient cash to buy a new turntable and LPs of Delius's works. They "ordered sandwiches and beer to consume the time," Scott remembered. After the band-boy returned with the goods, the group spent "acres of hours" of enlightening listening. Gene pointed out that Delius had been ahead of his time in using "what can only be termed American materials."[56] Scott did digging of his own in later years to learn more about Delius. Gene, a "record

listener from Bach to Stravinsky, from King Oliver to Dave Brubeck," piqued Scott's "interest in all areas of music."[57]

Gene never realized his dream of playing with a symphony orchestra. "I've either been too busy to make good on an offer," he
said, "or I haven't had an offer when I had the time."[58] The same is
probably true with his ambitious plans for a union of jazz and classical musicians. How he could have finished a major work of the
type he described while he was so busy, year after year, traveling
with a jazz ensemble, boggles the mind.

The Big Bands Shrink

As we've seen, the big bands were hurt by a changing socioeconomic reality as soldiers returned home after World War Two. But
the scaling back and eventual demise of the big bands were rooted
in a time when swing was raging and jitterbugging kids couldn't
get enough.

There was the late 1930s, early 1940s ASCAP[59] and BMI[60] mess.
ASCAP, the first large organization to determine royalty rights and
be governed by its membership, initially represented most musicians who wrote and recorded, and most publishers. The biggest
radio networks and their subsidiaries nationwide tired of negotia-
ting with ASCAP almost yearly. The networks wanted more power
in determining royalties, and founded BMI. BMI gave labels and
artists an ultimatum—if they didn't switch from ASCAP to BMI,
they would no longer be broadcast on radio, nor would networks
play the artists' older ASCAP songs. Contemporary classics affected
included "Stardust," "Dinah," "Stormy Weather," "Avalon," "Strike
Up the Band," and "Who?"[61] A lesser impact in the standoff was
the need for big bands to scrap their ASCAP theme songs and
choose one coming under BMI. Since 1938, Gene's band theme had
been "Apurksody," an ASCAP tune; he now turned to "Drummin'
Man" (later in the 1940s, he adopted his own creation, the more serious—and lovely—"Starburst" as his band's theme).[62]

The ASCAP-BMI controversy eventually settled. Many artists
like Gene returned to ASCAP. A lasting impact of BMI's founding

was bringing national exposure to music for niche audiences. One genre was rhythm and blues, then called "race music." The other was country and western, which rapidly grew in popularity and competed for listeners' dollars with the big bands and solo vocal stars.[63]

———————

THE AUGUST 1942 "recording ban"—really a strike—was approved by the American Federation of Musicians under head Joseph Petrillo to force record labels to negotiate better terms. It wasn't fully resolved until roughly the end of World War Two. During the ban, record labels could release recordings still "in the can" or reissue old ones, but jazz groups and others couldn't provide them with anything new.

The ban led to the start-up of more record labels, benefiting musicians new to recording. It also led to the rise of solo vocalists whom the ban didn't affect. Until the ban, vocalists mostly sang for big bands. Instrumental music dominated band recordings, even those featuring vocalists. But the ban meant singers could record their own sides—generally with choral, but not band backing!—and become bigger stars than they might have otherwise.[64] The incredible success of Frank Sinatra tempted other singers who wanted similar stardom for themselves.

———————

WORLD WAR TWO exacted a toll on the bands. Besides the burdens placed on jazz ensembles, such as traveling restrictions and gas rationing, the draft also wreaked havoc on band viability. The draft left numerous bands leaderless, prompting singers and vocal groups to test the solo waters for themselves.[65] The wartime 1944 "cabaret tax" of thirty percent on people's expenditures in any live music venue predictably drove this business down. Many clubs in the New York City area, as well as in Los Angeles and San Francisco, stopped presenting live jazz altogether. This led to rising unemployment among musicians.[66] Unlike hotels and their ballrooms, which were doing almost unfathomably great business, independent ballrooms were often paying bands at prewar levels despite the fact that the cost of living had increased and bands had expanded in size.[67] Another wartime measure instituted in 1945, the midnight curfew, led to fewer shows and less band income. The big bands and other jazz ensembles relied in part on monies derived from gigs that typically reached into the wee hours of the morning.[68]

Long before war's end, these new burdens affected the success of Gene Krupa's orchestra, especially during the period in 1944–1945 when he was touring with a costly string section.

BEBOP'S RISE ALSO hurt big bands (as did another record ban in 1948!), even those in the bebop avant-garde, as Gene's was, and even though these bands gave the new jazz form much popular exposure. Bebop became primarily the music of small ensembles. They were more economical to run than big bands. That bebop emerged as the dominant jazz form was inevitable. Unfortunately, it developed into a more esoteric, less accessible, less danceable genre, than, say, swing. Many bebop artists performed for themselves rather than the audience. This situation turned off old and young alike, with the latter ripe for something new to dance to. In the 1950s, it was rock and roll.

There would always be big bands. They were just less relevant, less in demand. Gene Krupa was one of the last of the major swing leaders to keep one going.

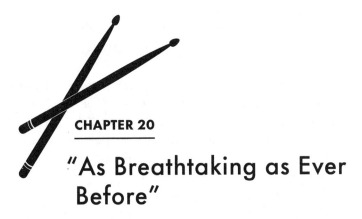

CHAPTER 20

"As Breathtaking as Ever Before"

"I ALWAYS SUPPOSED THAT THE ace drummer man was made of iron," said drummer-educator George Lawrence Stone in October 1949. On a Wednesday night, commented Stone, Gene entered a Boston hospital for a "minor surgical operation." The following morning, "[H]e was running around the hospital visiting the other patients..." (Imagine their surprise!) On Friday night, he was back onstage. Stone quoted him as saying, "I haven't got time to be sick."[1]

An emergency appendectomy came next, two years later. There would be no "running around the hospital" this time. He was stricken on August 18, 1951, after playing at the Surf Club in Virginia Beach, and was transported to a nearby hospital. All engagements for the next month were canceled.[2] While at home, he was hospitalized again for "complications" related to the surgery.[3] Late in October, Gene performed in New York at a Norman Granz "Jazz at the Philharmonic" ("JATP") event, reported *Down Beat*, and "got a huge hand but didn't play his best."[4]

Much had happened in between the two surgeries.

The glamour and profitability of the big bands and swing had ebbed considerably by the early 1950s. Gene was hanging on to his band by the skin of his drums, but making it work somehow. *Metronome* observed that bands in 1950 were engaged in "disband-ing and reorganizing . . . as the leaders tried to cope with the varying changes in public taste and the over-all economic picture." The or-chestras of Tommy Dorsey, Benny Goodman, Charlie Barnet, Woody Herman, Artie Shaw, Count Basie, Buddy Rich, and Ray McKinley—even Duke Ellington—were in trouble, slimmed down to a small ensemble, or disbanded. Gene, *Metronome* said, "made all sorts of changes in personnel, trying to find a group into which he could fit and which could make some money."[5]

He reorganized his orchestra yet again in early 1950. Returning were such stalwarts as trumpeter Don Fagerquist and tenor saxist Buddy Wise, with young Urbie Green added on trombone. One of Gene's first projects involved recording six songs by Fats Waller, who had died far too young, of pneumonia, in 1943. Newly signed by RCA-Victor, Krupa had energetic support from the record company, which placed the Waller collection in its series of similar sets by other bands, titled *Here Come the Dance Bands Again*. The result was a record album: six sides on three records and liner notes housed in a box sporting Gene's inviting visage. The record company aggressively sought disc jockey air-time and seemed to have gotten it.[6]

In Krupa's case, a Waller album was more than something to record for money. As we've seen, Gene's history with Waller went back to 1929 when he recorded with the ad hoc group Fats Waller and His Buddies. Waller's "Honeysuckle Rose" had been an ever-green for many a band, as had "Handful of Keys." The latter was immortalized in a 1937 Goodman Quartet recording; the former the basis for the jam session at the 1938 Benny Goodman Carnegie Hall concert. Gene had recorded it with Goodman in 1934 and again with Red Norvo in 1935. The song popped up when Krupa, Eddie Condon, and other friends accompanied the eccentric piano-playing songwriter at Waller's January 1942 Carnegie Hall concert.

Fully capable of restraining himself when appropriate, Gene did so here, but chose his moments—*fortissimo* snare strikes here; witty, rapid cymbal patterns there; an explosive accented roll elsewhere.

Dan Morgenstern said that the Krupa-Waller album "should be reissued. I think it's one of the best things that Gene did with the big band."[7]

Before the Waller sessions, Gene made changes in "band policy." Young people interested in dancing didn't like bebop. Gene understood and made two relatively contemporaneous switches. The first involved the use of "plain, full band arrangements of standard tunes and pop ballads in good sensible dance tempo." The second was to play the jazz of Gene's youth, popularly referred to as "Dixieland." To perform the latter, he extracted a small group from the band and, in Chicago, found a "novelty hillbilly singer," an Alabaman named Bobby Soots, for the tunes requiring vocals. The Dixieland was, as Gene put it, "murdering the customers every place we play."[8]

For most of these early jazz pieces, Gene went with old-timers, under the moniker Gene Krupa's Chicago Jazz Band. Several sidemen had played or still were with Eddie Condon—trumpeter "Wild Bill" Davison, clarinetist Edmond Hall, baritone saxist Ernie Caceres, and pianist Gene Schroeder. Bobby Soots's entertaining vocal style wasn't just "hillbilly," or he wouldn't have worked so well with the group. His quirky singing was a throwback to the jazz vocals of the 1920s. He also presaged late 1950s rock-era vocalists like the Everly Brothers. Despite the backward-looking nature of the music, the September 1950 recording of "Walking with the Blues," with its strident beat propelled by Gene's crescendoing drums, repeated bass sax line by Ernie Caceres, and baleful vocal by Bobby Soots, danced a nearly parallel line to the recordings of young New Orleans–born rhythm and blues singer and piano player Fats Domino.

Gene Krupa took a nostalgic turn, but it was part of his musical heritage. He embraced it at all stages of his career. He just as happily played 1930s swing when he joined the oft-reunited original Benny Goodman Trio in the 1950s and beyond. Bebop and its offshoots may have been the only modern jazz, adherents looking askance at practitioners of older jazz forms, but it didn't hurt that Gene's change in "band policy" yielded a huge hit with "Bonaparte's Retreat." It merged Gene's military-style snare and more modern ride cymbal timekeeping, and satisfied public taste.

The very last big band track that Gene recorded, not counting later, isolated recording projects or live appearances, was "Off and On," in July 1951. Its riff-filled sound conjured up early 1940s swing as it bade goodbye to the Big Band Era. Months later, his band performed its last one-nighter. Other than a band he assembled for a lucrative extended February 1952 gig at the Paramount Theatre in New York, he was done with touring big bands. Forever.

IN JANUARY 1952, Gene Krupa announced the reformation of his original Trio with Charlie Ventura and Teddy Napoleon. A press release asserted that the Trio's reunion was spurred by the positive reception that their appearance, for "kicks," engendered on Bob Haymes's Dumont television show in December 1951.[9] The three of them hadn't played together as a Trio since 1946. Charlie's emotional sax expressions and Teddy's ornamented stride piano worked wonders with Gene's high-energy conviviality. The reconstituted Trio would unveil itself at Charlie's new place, the Open House Club in Lindenwold, New Jersey, just outside Philadelphia. Then they would announce the tour dates.

Down Beat's Jack Tracy predicted that Gene's renewed Trio would be the "biggest moneymaker jazz has seen in many, many years."[10] Krupa, Ventura, and Napoleon validated Tracey's prescience when their last-minute, little-publicized booking into Chicago's Club Silhouette was jam-packed for every show, and a record breaker.[11]

Of the Open House debut, Billboard exulted, "It's a jazz blend of imagination and improvisation as breathtaking as ever before."[12] Variety declared that the Trio members "literally knock themselves out each set working from 45 minutes to an hour without a letup." Gene himself, being "one of the greatest on the skins ... can put out an infinite variety of stuff."[13]

Gene signed with Norman Granz's Clef Records. The three men recorded a ten-inch record album of six songs, The Gene Krupa

Trio Collates (1952). "Drumboogie," reworked for small group, was as astonishing as ever. Special introductions and endings encased classics like "Star Dust" and "Perdido," the Trio's members drolly playing off each other. "Fine's Idea," a new conception cowritten by Krupa, Ventura, and Napoleon, swept in a thoughtful sophistication overriding the often-blustery vocabulary of the Swing Era. The album's greatest showpiece was "St. Louis Blues," featuring everything one would expect from the Trio—humor (as in Krupa's gentle rim shots, seemingly mimicking the Raven "rapping, rapping" at Poe's "chamber door"), changeable moods, and impeccable musicianship.

"They're doing these cute, funny sorts of things, they're going for different kinds of effects," said Kevin Dorn. "Just the precision of all the things that they're doing. All these figures that they're playing at the same time ... Then they double the tempo, and they double the tempo again, this insane tempo." Dorn compared what they were doing to what Louis Armstrong was known for—playing, with humor, "an incredible variety of different kinds of things, all done at a very high level."[14]

THE TRIO'S REUNION meant get-togethers. During the Open House Club engagement, Gene took Charlie's little daughter Rita to church. After mass, they went to a diner for breakfast. "He was always very attentive and very nice to me," remembered Rita Ventura Lenderman. "I adored him." She added, "We spoke mostly about me. He teased me a lot." He once gave her a large teddy bear that was very special to her.

The Venturas visited the Krupas in Yonkers. Rita recalled loving Ethel's banana bread, which Ethel reliably baked especially for her. "I will always remember Gene," said Rita. "I can see us sitting and talking in that diner clear as day."[15]

The Napoleons also visited the Krupas in Yonkers. Teddy's son Matthew, then a preteen, said, "Where we lived in Queens, we didn't have a back or a front yard or anything. [W]hereas Gene's house was a real house with a yard. In fact, I remember I volunteered to . . . cut the grass. It was an old push mower. And that's just because they had a lawn."

Matthew remembered Ethel being a "darling woman," "almost motherly," quick to present him with baked treats. He played with the Krupas' dogs—Airedale terriers, he said.[16]

Eddie Condon and his extended family also visited. Eddie's daughters Maggie and Liza and their cousin Sue Smith were preteens. Probably remembering an exploration of the Krupas' extra wooded lot, Sue said Gene "taught us how to mark a trail in the woods and find our way back if we ever got lost."[17]

Jack Egan, Gene's neighbor, dear friend, and jazz writer, became his new manager in 1951. "We would look to his holiday cards with great anticipation," said Matthew Napoleon. "Not only were they very hip and funny, but . . . he would insert himself (photographically), way before Photoshop," into the card illustrations.[18]

Egan subjected his chum Krupa to some good-natured ribbing in print—in one case, about Gene's reputation as a loud drummer. "Gene Krupa is said to be working on a pneumatic drill, equipped with cymbals," Egan wrote in 1948, "which will make the rhythm of a drummer more electrifying."[19]

The Trio was served by a roadie named Bud. He "gave up his business, left his family and would, without salary, travel with the Trio, as almost a cult follower with an emphasis on Gene," said Napoleon, "waiting in the wings with a towel after a performance, fetching food and drink, etc. Way beyond what would later be referred to as a groupie." Everyone thought Bud's behavior "odd, but were hard pressed to discourage him."[20]

———————

AFTER TRAVELING WESTWARD and playing in Chicago, Boise, and Los Angeles, next came Honolulu, where they performed two weeks of double gigs—concerts for the U.S. Army during the day and at the Brown Derby club at night. Gene's new agent, Joe Glaser of Associated Booking, was, as Bruce Klauber wrote, "notorious for overworking many of his clients."[21]

Next on the itinerary was an Asian country with which, seven years earlier, America and much of the world had been at war. Before the war, there had been a nascent Japanese interest in jazz. In the 1930s, future Zero pilot Yasuyuki Ishihara loved the Benny Goodman Quartet's twinkling "Moonglow" and other jazz recordings. At age eighteen in 1943, he was drafted and flew missions against the Allies, but listened to the 1930s Goodman small groups before takeoff.[22] Before his draft, jazz might be inadvertently heard—or surreptitiously inserted—in a folk song like "Kusatsu Bushi," which featured "martial vocal choruses" and Krupa-reminiscent drum riffs. Soon Japan banned jazz altogether.[23]

Now in 1952, the Japanese really wanted Western jazzers. The Gene Krupa Trio became the first foreign jazz ensemble to play there since the war. They performed for U.S. troops and the Japanese public. "The Gene Krupa Jazz Trio visited in Japan April 19/May 3 and swept over the country," wrote the President of the Hot Club of Japan, Tay Muraoke, to American jazz writer George Hoefer in May 1952, "playing the leading theaters in Tokyo, Osaka & Yokohama to a full house and was accorded whirling applause."[24]

Muraoke's conservative description barely touched the surface of a volcanic welcome for which the Trio members were unprepared. "Japanese jazz fans . . . couldn't even imagine them coming to Japan," said Krupa fan and rock drummer Akira Suzuki.[25] The welcome they received in each city bordered on the hysterical. There were ticker-tape parades; gifts, bouquets, and Japanese eats galore; thrilled autograph seekers; and every time Gene set up his drum set, someone called the "Gene Krupa of Japan" in assistance. A couple of local drummers were there to "inspect the setup," as Gene put it, "then take out a pad and pencil and sketch the layout for future reference."[26]

An acquaintance who saw the Trio at the Nichigeki Theater told Akira Suzuki that their "sound was very powerful. Only three people created a sound that echoed throughout the hall."[27]

Gene said about the gifts that, besides the prodigious quantities of flowers, "nine times out of ten it was a doll. If I could have carried

them all home, I think I'd have more than there are to be found behind all the game counters on the Coney Island boardwalk."

He was gratified with the passion the Japanese showed for jazz.
There were numerous jazz players and singers, but he noticed they
were imitative of American stars down to the last note sung or
played, and knew no English.[28]

"It was a tremendously successful tour," said Gene. "We came
home with a lot of money. But we worked—good gosh. Instead of
doing one or two shows in one town, we'd play maybe six clubs in
one night... Club to club. Six clubs, six times a night."[29]

Gene said, "If an American jazz musician wants a boost in ego,
and isn't afraid of hard work, let him go to Japan for a few weeks."[30]
Krupa returned to Japan in 1953 with Jazz at the Philharmonic, his
burden much lighter this time, his Trio only one of many groups
on the bill.

Japanese Victor booked Gene's Trio for recording sessions soon
after they arrived in April 1952, where they recorded songs familiar
to American ears—"Drumboogie" and "How High's The Moon"—
and some perhaps only to Japanese ears. "Moon Over the Ruined
Castle" ("Kojo No Tsuki") was a Japanese standard the Trio made
their own, treating it in turns mournfully and cheerfully. "Badger's
Party" ("Shojoji No Tanuki Bayashi") is a brilliant adaptation of
the Japanese children's tune, which starts with a faithful rendering
of the melody and moves ever-so-slowly into experimental territory, allowing the Trio members to challenge themselves while staying true to the original song's aura.[31]

Gene Krupa left a mark on Japan. It's unclear whether the
"Gene Krupa of Japan," whom Gene said had taken care of his drum
set during the Trio's visit, was *the* Gene Krupa of Japan, George Kawasaki. Wrote E. Taylor Atkins, a professor in Japanese and Asian
studies at Northern Illinois University, when young Kawasaki first
sought gigs for himself after the war, the "sounds of Gene Krupa's
solo on 'Sing, Sing, Sing' [were] thundering in his brain."[32] For a
long time, Kawasaki was the most popular Japanese jazz drummer.
He made "Drumboogie" his theme song and excited audiences
with his long solos.

Jazz historian William Minor, the author of *Jazz Journeys to Japan*, believes Krupa's drums on "Sing, Sing, Sing" are reminiscent of Japanese *taiko* drumming.[33] No evidence exists that Gene, always so vocal about his studies and influences, was a 1930s pupil of Japanese percussion. But the very similarity between Gene's performance on the signature Carnegie Hall tune and *taiko* prompted musician Suniko Ichi to use jazz drums as well as *taiko* in his arrangements of Japanese folk tunes.[34]

Later in the year, the Japan-released Krupa Trio record *Drum Boogie* [sic], featuring songs from the Japanese Victor sessions, was announced as the label's top seller.[35]

Gene Krupa in Threes

Gene Krupa could extract the right sound from his drums in seemingly limitless ways. It didn't matter whether the song was slow, fast, midtempo; the mood was sad, celebratory, riotous; he was playing with his big band, someone else's big band, his small group, someone else's small group, an ad hoc small group, or by himself.

One of his trademarks was the triplet, something he used with increasing frequency as his career progressed. "It showed off his technique," said jazz drummer Bruce Klauber. "There was so much he could do while playing the triplets to build excitement, build volume, build drama, etc. It also allowed for various stickings, which addressed the issue of endurance. When played properly and evenly, he could go on forever until the climax of fast sixteenth notes... Finally, soloing with triplets could be done at virtually any tempo."

Jazz drummers Kevin Dorn and John Petters pointed to "Drummin' Man" (1939) as a significant early use of triplets by Krupa in a solo. Said Petters, "The solo builds into a triplet finale and the ride-out on the arrangement is all triplets—all played on the snare drum."

"The wild climax of his solo and final breaks," said Dorn, "are as exciting a use of triplets as I can think of."

Klauber, Dorn, and drumming Krupa neighbor-friend Joe Vetrano cited "Leave Us Leap," especially as performed in the movie *George White's Scandals*, as a superb exemplar of Gene's triplets usage. "Throughout, Gene's time is impeccable," said Vetrano. "Notice how and when he twirls the sticks. That had to take a lot of work with the band to get the timing and mechanics to this level, especially given the pace. His solo is all hand-to-hand single stroke triplets."

Petters saw the "Leave Us Leap" solo as portending Gene's remarkable playing in the 1952 and subsequent live small group versions of "Drumboogie," as well as other lengthy solos.

"Gene would use steady triplets (or even 16th notes or other subdivisions) for long periods of time and he stands out in that regard," said Kevin Dorn. "Whereas most drummers of the time would mix triplets into their phrasing or even play 4 or 8 bars of triplets, Gene would sometimes really milk . . . [it] for everything he could get out of it, which is a great effect and definitely something rock drummers do a lot."

This doesn't mean Gene's use of triplets on something like "Drumboogie" is repetitive or monotonous. We've seen the plethora of drumming ideas Gene utilized in his songs. Dorn cited a live 1952 version of "Drumboogie" to support this notion. "In the triplet section of his solo, Gene plays unbroken triplets for over 80 bars . . . with different accents and moving around the drums . . . I think he was more apt to do that sort of thing than many of his peers."

Petters praised Krupa's liberal use of triplets on all sorts of songs, from a rendition of "China Boy" played with the Condon Mob at a 1944 Town Hall concert to licks he executed after Sid Catlett drummed in *Boy! What a Girl!* Similarly, Dorn mentioned the brilliant, always-evolving Trio versions of "Stompin' at the Savoy" of the '40s and '50s. The pensive "Paradise," from *Gene Krupa: Sextet #2* (1953), has "slow triplet brush breaks," Dorn said. "I remember this blowing me away at 14; he's soloing on a ballad!"[36]

Krupa's use of triplets made him distinctive, kept the fans coming, and contributed to his unique legacy in the drumming world.

CHAPTER 21

"He Was Beautiful"

IT WAS A GOOD IDEA in theory—joining two of the greatest jazz artists ever on a double bill and taking it on tour. Single jazz groups, so said the experts, couldn't attract the crowds or income they used to, so "package" tours were it.[1] In spring 1953, the jazz artists in question were Benny Goodman and Louis Armstrong. Each would assemble a band, with Benny inviting former sidemen, many of whom went back to his earliest days of success. This meant Gene Krupa, pianist Teddy Wilson, trumpeter Ziggy Elman, trombonist Vernon Brown, and vocalist Helen Ward, among others. Lyrical trumpet master Charlie Shavers, writer of "Undecided," one of the most popular tunes for jazzers to play, was also recruited, as was Israel Crosby, the young bassist who had played with Gene on his 1935–1936 classic jazz sides. This would be Benny's first big band in several years.

Gene and Benny hadn't been strangers since Krupa played with Goodman in 1943. Krupa guested with Benny on the radio several times in the late 1940s. On April 1, 1951, the Goodman Trio reunited for a benefit to aid Benny's old arranger, Fletcher Henderson, recovering from two strokes. The place was the WNEW radio studio in New York City, the program a special edition of Martin Block's

Make Believe Ballroom. It was a steaming-hot show, and only got hotter with the incremental additions of several guests, including trumpeter Buck Clayton and trombonist Lou McGarity.

Most recently, on January 25, 1953, the original Goodman Trio reunited on a CBS-TV show, *Omnibus*, with host Alistair Cooke, who reflected nostalgically upon the social and musical impact of the Goodman phenomenon of the late 1930s. The Trio attacked four songs with the same inspiration they had displayed seventeen years earlier; a particular treat afforded viewers were advanced camera shots finally allowing the study of Gene's intricate brushwork, and of his duende in every bodily motion. The *Omnibus* appearance served as a lead-in to news of the Goodman-Armstrong matchup.

Satchmo's musicians, making up a small ensemble, rivaled Benny's in prestige—Gene's friend Cozy Cole on drums, Joe Bushkin (piano), Barney Bigard (clarinet), Trummy Young (trombone), Arvell Shaw (bass), and Armstrong's stalwart, Velma Middleton, on vocals.

The printed souvenir program set forth a schedule of tasty vintage tunes. Benny opened with eight songs ("Don't Be That Way," "Bei Mir Bist du Schön"), Louis followed with ten ("West End Blues," "Big Butter and Egg Man"), Benny with twelve ("King Porter Stomp," "Down South Camp Meetin'"). Following intermission, it was Louis with another seven (like "Muskrat Ramble"). The Goodman Trio closed with two (like "Nice Work If You Can Get It"). "Sing, Sing, Sing," listed as the last of the Trio's numbers and of the concert itself, must have been intended as a full-band performance.[2]

The problem was that no one had consulted Armstrong on who would go on when and for how long! And the program revealed an imbalance in the length of time each band was to play onstage. Louis thought each band should play for an equal amount of time. Given the magnitude of his stardom and that he had virtually invented the jazz they were all playing, rectifying the discrepancy should have been a no-brainer. By just letting it all happen without interference, Joe Glaser, Louis's manager, had made a huge mess of things, which became more apparent with each day.

The personalities of the two principals were polar opposites: Benny's no-nonsense rigidity and his aptitude for offending people versus Louis's relaxed interpersonal style. Louis, his ensemble, and friends arrived while Goodman rehearsed his band. Satchmo's presence naturally created a stir of a long duration. Benny asked him to get rid of the hangers-on so that they all could rehearse. Louis took offense; the hangers-on left, and so did Louis and his musicians.[3]

Leonard Feather later reported that Louis and Benny "talked among friends, but without issuing any official statements, accusing each other of a lack of cooperation."[4] "Considerable friction" existed between the two men about advertising and star billing. All of this was "markedly worrying Benny," reported *Down Beat*.[5]

The tour plans remained in place. The itinerary included thirty-five dates, with stops in places like Detroit, Chicago, Philadelphia, Cincinnati, and Indianapolis. Venues averaged about four thousand seats; some larger arenas were also in view.[6]

The Goodman band performed pre-tour tryouts sans Louis before paying fans in Maine and New Hampshire. These dates yielded $10,000, an impressive sum, according to *Variety* magazine.[7]

For better or worse, countering the accepted wisdom of tepid interest in big bands, Goodman's group joined Satchmo's in New Haven, then Newark. April 15, 1953, was the biggie—two shows at Carnegie Hall. The LPs from the 1938 Carnegie concert had been selling hundreds of thousands of copies since their belated 1950 release. Teenage fans in the late '30s were *in* their thirties now, and ripe for remembering the old days. But, as Howard Taubman wrote for *The New York Times*, "So much more heat and speed were generated that nostalgia for yesterday was turned into today's solid sender."[8] During Trio numbers, said another reviewer, Gene Krupa was "responsible for Goodman's delivering long and deeply felt choruses by both his vocal and percussive persuasions."[9]

Hostilities between Armstrong and Goodman continued. Benny didn't like the "comedy bit" performed by Louis's vocalist, Velma Middleton, and "ordered" it excised from the show. Louis simply told Middleton to "go ahead and do it, honey."[10]

Some critics disagreed with the praise heaped on Goodman by their confrères. Writers pronounced Benny a tired, uninspired forty-three-year-old who couldn't keep up with his own musicians, although the sidemen, including Gene, did attract a healthy dose of derogatory comments. Armstrong's performance and that of his ensemble received virtually universal plaudits. (There is no reason to think that those plaudits were undeserved.)

After arriving in Boston on April 19 for two Goodman-Armstrong concerts at Symphony Hall, Goodman collapsed in his hotel room—twice—and was soon placed in an oxygen tent. He would be unable to perform in Boston. Krupa assumed Goodman's baton, and used it, figuratively speaking, behind his set of drums.[11] Benny never rejoined the tour. Sideman and tenor saxist Georgie Auld took Goodman's parts during band numbers, while another sideman, alto saxist Willie Smith, took Benny's place during Trio performances.[12]

Early on, half-empty houses were reported, and the now-infamous Joe Glaser said he had renegotiated "more favorable deals" for the venues.[13] By tour's end on June 7 in Springfield, Missouri, however, it had drawn an excellent total gross of $340,000. Only three dates were "in the red": Rochester, Cleveland, and Springfield.[14] The Philadelphia engagement on April 30 was so successful that 300 extra *onstage* seats were added. Philadelphia also enjoyed substantial spillover business. The Krupa-Armstrong package played two performances there in one night, reported *Variety*, so "local pubs got the crowds coming and going."[15]

Success was a relief, but suspicions abounded among musicians that Benny had recovered early enough that he could have returned to the tour. To be fair to Benny, he "suffered greatly from lack of rest," reported *Metronome*, due to a back operation, necessitating his sleeping on a "board." He was unable to sleep on the bus at all, which was typically how the tour traveled from gig to gig.[16]

Lest anyone question the quality of the Goodman band without Goodman—but with Krupa leading—recorded highlights from one show in May 1953[17] reveal a sensationally swinging band at least as good as the one in that first flush of 1930s achievement. The band demonstrated unity of feeling and offered rousing trumpet and sax solos. Helen Ward sang with the same beautiful voice and the then-futuristic jazz inflections of yesteryear. Krupa's use of tom-toms was fuller, richer, and more dynamic and intricate than during early iterations of "Sing, Sing, Sing." He dropped more "bombs" than in the 1930s, in just the places to add amusement. In almost every way he pushed himself to exceed prior notions of his abilities.

Trumpeter Al Stewart said, "As soon as Benny was out of the picture, the tension ended." Having Gene as a boss was "a dream. Only once during the time Gene took over . . . did he feel the guys in the band were getting a little lax. But the way he spoke to us about it tells you a lot about what a leader and people-person this guy was. Gene said, 'Guys, let's not forget that this is Benny's band and that we have to give a big performance every time we get up there.' He never had to say another word . . . He was beautiful."[18]

GENE KRUPA AND Cozy Cole performed a "drum battle" during the Goodman (Krupa)—Armstrong tour most every night, resulting in an overpowering display of technique and pizzazz. This happened after Benny's band backed Gene on "Drumboogie," but before both aggregations united for a grand finale of "When the Saints Go Marching In," Louis Armstrong taking the lead, of course.

Gene and Cozy were chatting one day on the plane, traveling between gigs and ruminating about how energy-sapping road life was. Relief from the travel grind would be nice. Both men were indefatigable students of the drums and enthusiastic teachers. Why not open a drumming school?

After the tour, Gene and Cozy contacted their respective lawyers, who gave the idea a thumbs-up. The men invested a "few thousand apiece." School income would be split fifty-fifty. On March 13, 1954, the Gene Krupa and Cozy Cole Drum School, as it was called, situated on 261 West Fifty-Fourth Street in Manhattan in a second-floor "walkup," was open for business.

In a possible first in race relations, a massive ad for the school covering the side of a building showed Gene, a Caucasian, and Cozy Cole, an African-American, grinningly becoming one with drum, cowbell, cymbal, and sticks. Before civil rights, there probably weren't many places in America to see an integrated or mixed-race ad, especially one splashed on the side of a building.

Students of any age, regardless of prior experience, could study various forms of percussion, in private or in groups. Eventually, courses on guitar, piano, music theory, and voice were added. About half a dozen other teachers—boasting classical or jazz backgrounds—eventually gave lessons in their areas of expertise, but the main attraction would always be the two stars. Gene's friend, bassist Milt Hinton, joined the faculty. Krupa and Cole meant to be there for substantial periods. They assumed they would tour less, or one could be there if the other couldn't.

At least at first, Mrs. Cole served as receptionist. A writer from *The New Yorker* was at the school early on to watch the proceedings. The sound of practice pads could be heard. A moment later, the "doors flung open and Krupa came out, shirt collar unbuttoned, hair falling over his forehead, a cigarette in one corner of his mouth." A man in a "dark business suit" followed. Gene asked if he was comfortable with the drag paradiddle. The man answered yes, "looking spent but happy." Cozy explained to *The New Yorker* observer that all drumming students were taught the rudiments—seemingly every variety or combination of ruffs, rolls, ratamacues, and paradiddles—and, once mastering these essentials, they should be able to play with the necessary expression. Mrs. Cole complained about the smoke being generated by Cozy's pipe and Gene's cigarettes.[19]

Gene and Cozy hoped the school would produce "more musicianly drummers." "We want other musicians to respect our instrument more," Gene said.[20] "The gratifying part of it is that each of us has learned a lot from the other, and at the same time, while teaching, each of us has relearned some of the things which we had forgotten about."[21]

At its height, the school taught an average of 135 to 150 on-site students per week. There were also correspondence course students. The latter lessons were drawn from Gene's and Cozy's *Modern and Authentic Drum Rhythms for the Teacher, Student and Professional* (1958). Students practiced diverse rhythms of ethnic groups from across the globe—among others, Polkas, Afro-Cuban, Latin, Irish, Jewish, Calypso, and Italian. They learned time signatures, blues, bop, and popular dance rhythms of earlier decades, like the Cakewalk and the Charleston.[22]

The Krupa-Cole school closed in 1961. Gene said the "school was very successful, financially," but, for him, "teaching all day" and then performing well at night was difficult.[23] Cozy said it eventually became plain that he and Gene were too in demand as performers to teach at the school for any length of time. "It was impossible to run any kind of business with two bosses away, so that's why we closed it."[24]

"When you really find out about a person is when you're up there dealing with him with that money," said Cozy, years later. "Well, any time that you can exchange those thousands together and never squawk, you all right. Well, that's the way it was with Gene Krupa. Never a word said about nothing . . . Never nothing bad said, no arguments, why did you do this, why did you do that? Nothing like that."[25]

CHAPTER 22

"Superficial Glandular Excitement"

Before, after, and around other engagements and commitments, like the Goodman-Armstrong tour and the founding of the Krupa-Cole school, Gene's Trio was winning the public's favor and bringing home a considerable income. "King of drums Krupa came, hit and conquered," a reviewer pronounced in a Swedish newspaper—a fairly representative Swedish press reaction to the Krupa Trio—after Gene's inaugural show. The crowd that first night at Nojesfaltet, an "outdoor amusement field" in Stockholm, attracted a record-breaking attendance of between seven and nine thousand people.[1] The Stockholm jaunt involved seven concerts in four days and, as one American writer put it, the Trio "did enough business to keep Eddie Condon in guitar picks for the next 300 years."[2]

Charlie Ventura had stayed in America to run his Open House club. The new saxist was Flip Phillips, a Jazz at the Philharmonic veteran. Ventura would return to the fold later. Krupa, Napoleon, and Phillips spent a month in Sweden, then elsewhere in Europe.

Gene recorded outside the Trio's confines. The Gene Krupa Sextet's 1953 and 1954 sessions yielded some of the best jazz one could find in three six-track albums. Krupa's drumming alone ranks with some of his best. His fine compatriots initially came out of the then-touring Goodman-Armstrong band—Charlie Shavers, Teddy Wilson, Willie Smith, Steve Jordan, and Israel Crosby. Shavers, who wrote all of the arrangements and most of the songs, stayed for the next two sessions, as did Wilson; the remainder, like Shavers, boasted a JATP pedigree—Bill Harris (trombone), Ben Webster (tenor sax), and Ray Brown (bass). One might choose any song and find a stellar performance. Let's shine a brief spotlight on three tracks of special percussive artistry.

On "Jungle Drums," a mellow piece of African evocation, Gene plays mallets on the tom-toms in a way divorced from the explosive "Sing, Sing, Sing" manner with which he is associated. His tempo is fast but the tone understated, helping it attain a certain symphonic dignity. A change comes: "That one part where it breaks into swing, and then he goes to this just real nasty quarter-note ride cymbal feel," said Kevin Dorn, illustrates "how he can play just quarter notes and have so much emotion and drive. It's very, very cool."

One of the bounciest tunes is "Capital Idea," perfect for dancing. It's especially notable because of a quality not usually recognized in Gene's drumming—subtlety. With the song's opening notes, Gene unleashes tricky stick and rim shots, restrained but celebratory.

"He's doing those stick shots and rim shots near the edge of the drum, close to the tip of the stick," said Kevin Dorn. Other rim shots for which Gene is known are often played with the stick's fatter end for a "fuller, beefy, powerful sound." But here "it's this very delicate kind of sound . . . He could get so many different sounds" by where the stick lands on the snare.

The sprightly beginning ensemble riff Gene answers by a humorous coupling of snare and high-hat (*dupp-dupp-dupp*). "As far as I can tell," said Kevin, "he's doing that with his left hand on the snare drum, so he's playing the high-hat with his right hand, and then he throws in those off-beats with the left hand . . . It's so perfect and such a great response to what the band plays." Without Gene's little fill, it would seem as though something were missing. "That's taste. That's musical sensibility."

Gene's solo on "Overtime" comes after a Teddy Wilson passage during which Gene plays triplets on the closed high-hat. "He goes into that solo coming out of the piano solo, and the transition is very nice," said Kevin. "He's already playing on the closed high-hat behind the piano . . . He could have just gone to the drums as soon as his solo started, but, because [Wilson's solo] was soft . . . he stays on the closed high-hat, and builds" from there, adding surprising snare and splash cymbal accents, all on top of a forceful bass beat. "That choice that he made," said Kevin, "it's just this awareness of 'what's happening right before my solo? What is the shape of this entire piece?'"[3]

In 1954, Charlie Ventura again left Gene to follow his creative muse. Enter Eddie Shu, of diminutive height and pencil-thin mustache, and a saxophonist also versed in trumpet, clarinet, and harmonica. Shu's instrumental versatility effectively enlarged the ensemble. With Shu alternating on clarinet and trumpet, recording a massive-sounding Trio version of "Sing, Sing, Sing" was now possible.

THE TRIO'S DESTINATION in August 1954 was the distant continent of Oceania, more commonly known as Australia. They were scheduled for seven concerts in eleven days,[4] a kinder itinerary than they had faced (without Shu but with Ventura) in Japan two years earlier. Of Oz's seven sprawling states, they missed only the Northern Territory and Tasmania.

"This drumming whirlwind," observed one Australian newspaper, of Gene, "is one of the few men still playing who have experienced jazz close to its birth."[5] The Trio was reportedly paid the highest sum ever earned by a visiting musical act.[6] Gene, Eddie Shu, and Teddy Napoleon left for Sydney, Australia, on August 9, 1954, after playing at the Blue Note in Chicago.[7] They were due in Sydney, in the southeastern corner of Australia, three days later.[8]

"Honestly, they were the most enthusiastic audiences I've played for," said Gene after returning to America. "I think they topped the receptions we used to get here in the States in the old days when swing was the rage."[9]

Every city greeted the Trio with fanfare. In Sydney, they were welcomed at the airport by a "guard of honor" of six of the top dance band drummers plus thirty-one "Krupa fan girls" wearing white sweaters bearing the monogram "GK."[10] One member of the honor guard, Bobby Bell, proclaimed: "There is only one Krupa— and we are his prophets."[11]

When the Trio pulled up in front of King's Cross, their Sydney hotel, Gene "seemed embarrassed" by the media frenzy awaiting them. After he and the others finally squeezed inside, there were forty "radio, magazine and music men packed around" Gene, by then nursing a beer, as he answered questions posed by two daily newspaper reporters.[12] Then there was the "drumming gentleman's gentleman" whose services Gene was offered. Krupa said he "didn't know what he would do with the guy." A Kenyan expatriate gave Gene an "African zebra skin drum."[13]

The Trio found 500 "screaming teenagers" at a Sydney record shop where the men autographed books, scarves, records, and drumsticks. Married women and teenage girls tried to make dates with Krupa. Some cried, "Kiss me, Gene." Others "stroked his hair" and cooed suggestively. One girl said Gene was "dream dust and the light of my life." All Gene could say was, "I can't get tired of my fans."[14]

The Trio's first Australian show, in Sydney, was performed before an audience of eight thousand. One reporter said Gene's drumsticks "flash[ed] off his drums with the symmetry and [at] 10 times the speed of a tap-dancer." At one point, he broke a stick "in a mighty whack at the cymbal. One half spun in the air. Krupa tossed the other end" into the audience.[15]

The next stop was Melbourne, Victoria. When the Trio's plane touched down, "extra police were rushed to the airport as the teenagers broke barriers, climbed fences, and unlocked gates." Thousands of fans blocked the tarmac, keeping the plane from landing for eight minutes.[16] After two wildly enthusiastic receptions at West Melbourne Stadium, two more Melbourne shows were added for the tour's end, which would delay the Trio's departure for home until August 27.[17]

Next was Adelaide, South Australia. Naturally, a "mob" waited outside their hotel.[18] "Astride his stool behind his drums, Krupa was a benevolent monarch of all he surveyed," said a review of the August 19 show in *The Advertiser*, which also commended him for "superb artistry."[19]

Arriving in Brisbane, Queensland, the following day, a thirty-strong corps of drummers greeted Gene with the message, "Welcome, Gene Krupa," tattooed in Morse code![20] Despite suffering food poisoning from tainted spaghetti they had eaten in Adelaide the night before, the Trio seemed fine in Brisbane. The audience was "exhausted," but Gene "skipped offstage fresh as a daisy."[21] Krupa, the sometime surfer, told the press, "Boy, I can't wait to get stuck into your Queensland surf. I heard it even beats Honolulu."[22]

Newcastle, New South Wales, experienced the same pandemonium upon the Trio's arrival seen elsewhere—breathless fan mobbing, seemingly endless autograph signing—plus a reception by the lord mayor.[23] In Perth, Western Australia, the Trio were shown the city sights.[24]

Maybe she liked throwing a wet blanket over the hot thrills of Australian music fans, but Elizabeth Webb, a "distinguished woman columnist" according to her editors at the *News* in Adelaide, seemed trapped inside a twenty-five-year-old time warp. She analyzed the Trio and their Brisbane audience as a judgmental paleontologist might. There was "something unhealthy, something unclean" about the show. Audience members were "rocking their rhythm-drugged bodies as though possessed by a religious ritualistic demon. . . . I am confident," she asserted, "that more than anything else it provides an escape for extrovert and introvert alike, into a world of peculiar excitement and exhilaration in which some of the primitive animal urges, subjugated by convention, may be openly stimulated and enjoyed without censorship." The music itself offered mere "superficial glandular excitement."[25]

Webb would have been horrified to learn that, on the day after the concert, a respectable woman named Mrs. Edna Petersen and drumming instructor Harry Lebler had facilitated the entrance of

Mrs. Petersen's eight-year-old drumming son Colin into the immoral den of that infamous purveyor of "primitive law," Gene Krupa.

Krupa fan Colin Petersen had been taking lessons from fellow Krupa fan Harry Lebler for a year when Lebler suggested Colin participate in the airport festivities upon Gene's Brisbane arrival. Lebler taught Colin a drum solo for the occasion. "This is before the tunnels," said Petersen. "A door opened [on the plane] and you walked down the steps and walked across the tarmac."

There Colin was, set up behind his drum kit, and Gene "comes walking up from the plane . . . And I had never met a man with such charisma before that time." Gene stood next to him as he "played on a bit." Colin dropped a drumstick and Gene retrieved it for him.

That night, Colin and his mother attended the concert, but the real excitement happened the following day. Gene had invited Colin to visit him at Lennon's Hotel, "a sort of top-notch hotel in Brisbane." When the time came for the visit, Mrs. Petersen decided Colin should see Gene privately. It was going to be "a very special moment" for him. "This wouldn't happen today," said Petersen, referring to the year 2023. "You'd never leave a child with a man. It's sad, really."

"We ended up, the pair of us, sitting cross-legged on his king-sized bed, with telephone books [to use as drums] in front of us. Me with my rudiment book, and Gene with a pair of drumsticks overseeing the situation." Gene asked him to do a single-stroke roll, which Colin did. The elder drummer complimented the boy on his technique—Colin was holding his sticks at just the right height for the type of roll he played.

Gene said, "You've gotta strengthen your left hand. I still do it. I've got a rubber ball in my pocket. I just squeeze a rubber ball. I do it all the time." Colin told Gene that Harry Lebler had taught him another way to strengthen the left hand. You take the "broadsheet" of a newspaper, lay it smooth and flat on a surface, and, keeping the palm of your hand in the center of the page without raising it, "gather the rest of the page into your palm into a tight ball." You discard the ball and repeat the process with another page. And another and another.

"So there we are, Gene Krupa and I, with our phone books, with these pages of newspaper, rolling them up into little balls in our left hand and throwing them aside," said Colin. "It's quite a wonderful memory," he said. "What the room would have looked like after my visit!"

Colin had been in the habit of using the adjective "mighty," as in, "I think it's mighty." That Christmas, Colin received a card—"very flashy"—in the mail from Gene. The elder drummer had addressed the card thusly: "To a mighty little man, from Gene Krupa and family."

There is a nice postscript to this story. Colin Petersen became a child star in Australia, playing the lead in two movies, *Smiley* (1956) and *Smiley Gets a Gun* (1958). In the 1960s, three fellows he knew who had been performing around Queensland—Barry, Robin, and Maurice Gibb—asked him to be their drummer. He joined them in early February of 1967 and played on such early Bee Gees hits as "New York Mining Disaster 1941" and "To Love Somebody." Petersen eventually turned to other interests, but now tours in Queensland in *The Best of the Bee Gees*, enjoying himself immensely.

The events of 1954 are permanently etched in Colin's mind. "I remember it all so clearly now," he said of meeting Gene. "He took a genuine interest in what I was doing. He would have seen it in my eyes that this was my world. Wonderful memories."[26]

Still a Drumming Point of Reference

Gene Krupa's name was still synonymous with drums. At a 1950 Horace Heidt talent contest in Washington, DC, an eleven-year-old drummer was dubbed a "little Gene Krupa" by a fellow contestant.[27] A columnist for Washington, DC's *Evening Star* recounted his 1951 visit to the Washington Monument: "When I got to the top my heart was beating faster than Gene Krupa ever did..."[28] The same year, Gene emerged a theoretical tabletop "finger-tapper" in London, Ohio.[29]

There were new Gene Krupas performing across America: the drummer for the Dixieland Quintet, a 1952 ensemble of high school students in Dunn, North Carolina ("First thing you know, we'll have a new Gene Krupa")[30]; a member of a 1952 comedic jazz ensemble, The Goofers[31]; a pharmacist who, in a 1954 Walter Mitty transformation, evoked "Gene Krupa on the drums" in a Lincolnton, North Carolina, ensemble[32]; and four-year-old Jimmy Bradley, a drumming prodigy whom Paramount Television had signed in 1962 for three years. He identified himself as "Gene Krupa" whenever asked his name.[33]

Krupa's fame knew no socioeconomic boundaries. Said one gossip columnist in 1961: "You could dress him [Krupa] in overalls and drop him in an Iowa cornfield and the farmers would know him."[34]

Gene's name came up in retrospectives about others: When the legendary drummer-bandleader Eric Delaney died in 2011, he was described as the "British equivalent of Gene Krupa."[35]

CHAPTER 23

Playing Well With Others

To review Gene Krupa's extensive involvement with Jazz at the Philharmonic ("JATP") in the 1950s, we must first look back to its 1944 inception, when a young Caucasian jazz impresario from southern California named Norman Granz founded it. JATP would be, at all times, a racially integrated group of star musicians whose membership varied from performance to performance.

"Granz's philosophy of jazz rested on his belief in a race-blind democracy of talent as vetted by the jam session," wrote Granz biographer Tad Hershorn. "Granz was one of the few mid-twentieth-century progressives to make capitalism simultaneously serve his adventurous artistic aspirations and a then-radical social agenda of racial and economic justice, integration, and equality."[1]

As passionate as Granz was about presenting a racially integrated lineup of musicians at every show, he was equally passionate about integration offstage. He insisted patrons must sit side by side in the audience regardless of race.

Gene performed at two shows not long after JATP's inception, on February 12 and 18, 1945, when the event was still being held regularly at the Los Angeles Philharmonic Auditorium, from whence came the group's name. Granz had hoped that Gene could make one of the December 1944 events,[2] but, as we've seen, Krupa and band were slowly making their way west at the time; due to weather conditions, they arrived too late even for their earliest Los Angeles Palladium dates at December's end.

The two February 1945 JATP engagements included a variety of white and black jazzers besides Gene: his old piano-playing friend, Joe Sullivan; then-former Krupa-ite Anita O'Day; Billie Holiday; guitarist Slim Gaillard; trumpeters Joe Guy and Howard McGhee; Kid Ory's Creole Band (with Gene's drumming idol, Zutty Singleton); saxists Coleman Hawkins, Charlie Ventura, Willie Smith, and Illinois Jacquet; and bassist Charlie Mingus.[3]

In late 1945, Gene appeared on the first JATP record,[4] drawn from the February 12 concert, but because of his contract with a competing label, he was credited under the fake name the "Chicago Flash."[5] Subsequent editions omitted *any* mention of a drummer having played![6]

Norman Granz' Jazz at the Philharmonic Featuring the Gene Krupa Trio was drawn from two concerts, February 1946 in Los Angeles, and May 1946 at Carnegie Hall. This was released, belatedly, on Granz's label, Clef Records, in late 1951.[7] The timing was interesting; Granz had finally snagged Gene for JATP's most recent touring iteration, after Krupa's emergency appendectomy and big band breakup.[8] ("What are you beating your brains out with this big band for?" Granz had repeatedly asked Gene during the last three years of the band's existence.[9]) The issuance of the album may have been one prompt Gene needed to reform his original Trio with Charlie Ventura and Teddy Napoleon early in 1952.

Initially, having never toured with Gene, Granz was worried he would be egotistical. Krupa was a "top cat to the public," said Granz. "He's like Louis and Benny—tops. So I figured maybe he'd be a great attraction, yes, but you know, a little temperamental?"

To prevent problems from developing, Granz offered Gene a private jet. "What for, Norm?" Gene responded. "I'm no better than anybody else." Indeed, Krupa would have missed the camaraderie of being with other jazzers. Granz recalled how cooperative and easygoing Gene was throughout the first tour. "And the other cats are nuts about him," Granz said.

As for Gene: "No headaches, no ulcers, fine people, just a ball all the time," he said. "I feel like a kid again."[10]

This didn't mean everybody was on board with Gene's particular brand of drumming. Many jazzers still weren't comfortable with the elevated role that Gene had given drumming. Oscar Peterson preferred that Gene keep time on the cymbal instead of in press rolls. Lester Young also preferred cymbals and asked Gene: "Lady Krupa, can I please have my tinky boom?"[11] (Lester called everyone "Lady"—not just Billie Holiday.) As we've seen, however, Gene was highly adaptable to others' sensibilities; he didn't just rely on one form of timekeeping.

Recordings show no absence of musical fellowship between Gene and the others. During the 1953 tour, Gene, with his makeshift trio of Oscar Peterson and Benny Carter, performed "Somebody Loves Me." Listening to the September 19, 1953, performance at Carnegie Hall, one hears that Gene's fills between sections or introductions for soloists were sometimes loud but never interfered with another musician's expressions. One could enjoy Carter's creamy, gently constructed sax solos with no difficulty. Peterson and Krupa engaged in a funny call-and-response for a good portion of the song, either mimicking or replying to each other in rapid-fire fashion; one wouldn't think that the piano and the drums could so perfectly communicate with each other.

When Buddy Rich was there, Peterson, Roy Eldridge, Coleman Hawkins, and others complained that Buddy tried to make them play at a tempo showing "him to best advantage," but to their detriment.[12] There was a drumming philosophy epitomized by Gene, and a drumming ego epitomized by Buddy.

In September 1952, after Gene played with his reformed Trio in Japan and elsewhere, Granz announced a new JATP tour. The lineup was similar to the previous years, with—besides Gene—Roy Eldridge, Charlie Shavers, Ella Fitzgerald, Oscar Peterson, bassist Ray Brown, Flip Phillips, Lester Young, and Benny Carter. The other drummer was Buddy Rich.

Down Beat described the upcoming meeting of the two drummers as the "long-awaited drum battle of the decade."[13] On September 12, 1952, at the Carnegie Hall two-show JATP double-header, *Down Beat* felt differently, calling the drummers' showdown "little more than an audience stimulator." As to the comparative merits of the drummers, the reviewer said that, during "Drumboogie," Gene "surprised with his dexterity and speed . . . He had to follow a Buddy Rich solo [from earlier in the evening] . . . and pretty well succeeded."[14]

February 1953 saw the second-ever European JATP tour, but Gene's first (not counting his non-JATP mostly Swedish jaunt in 1952). It was an especially busy first half of the year for Gene; the Goodman-Armstrong tour was coming up in April. The JATP were to cover a good chunk of western Europe, with a one-day stop in England (March 8) for two performances at the Gaumont State Theatre in London's Kilburn section. JATP, to perform on the same bill with British jazz groups, would be the first American musicians to play in Britain in eighteen years due to a ban on foreign performers. They received special dispensation from the British Musicians' Union and the Ministry of Labor to do it because the shows would benefit the Lord Mayor's National Flood and Tempest Distress Fund.[15]

J. C. Heard, who had played with Cab Calloway, Count Basie, Duke Ellington, and Benny Goodman, among others, was the other drummer on this tour. But the talk was all about Gene. "I sincerely hope that some of our more expert percussionists will have learnt a lesson from Gene Krupa's scintillating display at the State, Kilburn, last Sunday evening," said one *New Musical Express* reviewer. "Never at any time did he drown the soloist. His performance was full of quality, rather than quantity."[16] Gene was approached by Allan Ganley, Tony Crombie, and other "professional drummers who, in unashamed hero-worship, had come to exchange words with Krupa, to shake hands with him if possible," remarked a *Melody Maker* writer. Krupa met one of *his* idols—British drummer and comedic actor Max Bacon.[17]

Gene and his JATP compatriots were celebrated in a ticker-tape parade when they performed in Japan later in 1953. (Gene had

suggested Japan to Granz after his very successful trip a year earlier.) The glamour and star power of jazzers had been transferred
substantially from America to other countries. In the United States,
jazz was increasingly becoming a niche art form.

Buddy Rich returned to JATP in 1955 and 1956 for more Krupa-
Rich duels. Roy Eldridge was almost always there. They were still
like brothers. There was a game they liked to play when traveling
from one gig to the next. "We used to heckle each other when we
were traveling," recounted Roy. "I'd go to sleep and he'd wake me.
I'd wait until he began to snooze and I'd wake him." Things went
differently on a flight to Norman, Oklahoma. Gene and Roy had "declared a truce" because the trip had been rough. But, to Roy's annoy-
ance, when he fell sleep Gene woke him anyway—for good reason.
The plane had caught fire. No one thought they'd get off the plane
alive. "We gathered together," said Roy, "shook hands and said it
had been nice doing the tour and all that." They finally landed—in
Kansas—on just one engine.[18]

Dizzy Gillespie was a frequent JATP star. In 1956, while in Rome
outside of the JATP schedule, he enjoyed an audience with Pope
Pius XII—courtesy of Gene Krupa, whose appointment it actually
was. "I said a prayer for Gene and everyone on the show," Dizzy
wrote to his booking agent, Billy Shaw. "Am very grateful for
Gene's kindness."[19]

Norman Granz's antiracist mission occasionally met resistance.
The landmark U.S. Supreme Court decision on school desegrega-
tion, *Brown v. Board of Education of Topeka*, was barely two
months old, when, in July 1954, Ella Fitzgerald and her associates
were treated abominably because of their race, hurting them and
JATP. The plane was taking them from San Francisco to Sydney,
Australia, and stopped over in Honolulu. Ella, her secretary, and
her pianist left their first-class seats and stretched their legs. But
Pan-American employees refused to let them reboard, causing
them to miss the first scheduled show in Australia. Granz took Pan-
Am to court. Although it's unclear whether the plaintiffs won any
damages, Granz did switch airlines to Scandinavian, which provided a plane specially marked for JATP travel.[20]

BOSTONIAN JAZZ MUSIC impresario George Wein believed, as Norman Granz did, in racial integration. Wein founded the Newport Jazz Festival in July 1954. It featured white and black jazzers performing over several days to white and black attendees who sat where they pleased at this outdoor event. He also fought for the integration of local hotels so that jazz fans of any color could get a room. Newport initially stayed in one place—that is, Newport, Rhode Island, a summer getaway for the wealthiest of the wealthy.[21]

Krupa performed at the first Newport Jazz Festival. George Wein discovered here that Gene had pride, though not of the sort Wein might have expected. On July 17, 1954, Krupa's ensemble were to close the festival. "I was treating Gene as a star," said Wein. "I went into the dressing room and said, 'I need a drummer.' And I pointed at three or four drummers. Jo Jones and a couple of others. And I didn't ask Gene." The excluded drummer approached Wein. "Hey, I don't know if anyone informed you," said Gene, "but I also happen to be a drummer. Why didn't you ask me to play the jam session?" Wein protested that Gene held the prime spot in the festival—last. "I don't care," said Gene. "When you need a drummer, you can ask me."

Pondering this later, Wein remarked, "He really did feel slighted, as if I doubted his qualifications as a capable musician." At future festivals Wein never again neglected to invite Gene to join a jam session. Krupa delightedly accepted every time.[22] He loved jam sessions. They were what made him a true jazz man back in Chicago all those years ago.

Krupa added a bass player toward the end of 1954, transforming the Krupa Trio into the Krupa Quartet. He had long resisted the change because the original Goodman Trio and Quartet had worked just fine without a bassist, and he thought the same went for his Trio. But emphases were shifting. The newer generation of jazz pianists were less interested in the stride piano of an earlier age, nor did they favor the heavier use of the bass end of the piano, both

of which were important parts of Teddy Wilson's and Teddy Napoleon's styles. Young Bobby Scott, who replaced Napoleon and
whom we met earlier, was a modernist. Adding a bassist was a necessity. The debut bassist was John Drew.

GENE'S MARRIAGE TO Ethel was a puzzlement to some of his fellow
jazzers, as we've seen; the couple's incompatibility increased over
time. Relations were volatile. Bobby Scott, Gene's teenage piano
player, witnessed what may well have been a justifiable "verbal assault" on Gene by his wife when the Quartet members brought him
home one night "behind a pint of Black and White Scotch." But
Bobby never heard a bad word about her from Gene's lips.[23]

The Krupas' Yonkers home was the site of frequent gatherings.
Louis Armstrong might be there, or Marlon Brando, whom Gene
publicly commended on his bongo playing.[24] There was no snob-
bery, though, nor did Gene build a figurative wall between his celebrity and neighborhood friends.

Ethel reminisced about Gene's courtship of her with the Bellinos.[25] When Gene toured Australia in August 1954, he told the
press that he would like to bring her to Oz at year's end, although
that didn't happen.[26] The couple also commissioned a painted portrait of themselves sometime in the early 1950s.[27]

It's been said, suggested, or assumed, based on scuttlebutt on and
off the internet, that, during Gene and Ethel's second marriage, he
sought and engaged in relationships with other women. This was a
common circumstance for many a male jazzer out on the road for
extended periods. Ethel had washed her hands of traveling with
Gene a long time before. With her at home, Gene performed hour
after hour and night after night in distant reaches of the United
States and the world before young women who couldn't keep their
eyes off his lean muscularity, handsome features, and masculine mastery of drums. Gene was irresistible. Marie Allison, eventually Buddy
Rich's longtime wife, was the only woman to publicly recount—
mainly in several Rich biographies after Gene's death—an on-again,
off-again relationship with Gene while he was married to Ethel.[28]

Sitting on a plane while touring with Gene during Bobby Scott's time with him in 1954–1955, Bobby noticed that Gene was quite sullen and asked what was wrong. Krupa told Scott that Ethel wasn't well—something to do with her brain—and doctors were brushing off her headaches and balance issues.

Apart from members of his Quartet, Bobby Scott said, Gene socialized little in the year they played together. During an engagement at the New Frontier Hotel-Casino in Las Vegas, Bobby noticed Gene's solitary habits. During the day, Gene ate breakfast in his room and rarely left the hotel. After the Quartet finished performing in the morning's wee hours, he normally played a "few hands" of blackjack and spent some time beating the "dollar one-arm" machine (to collect Vegas coins for Yonkers kids). Then he retired to bed.

A "beautiful" woman in her thirties watched Krupa play night after night, said Scott, and developed a huge crush on Gene. She couldn't understand why he wouldn't as much as acknowledge her socially, let alone romantically, and tearfully confided her feelings to Bobby about it more than once. Finally, he, the young, inexperienced teen, agreed to speak with Gene. Krupa reacted in a "surprisingly sweet manner," telling Bobby that, in effect, he didn't intend to make the woman's dream come true. Ethel had been on his mind. "It'd be wrong, don'cha see?" Gene said. "Certain things you just don't do, Chappie. Certain things you just can't live with, son."[29]

Ethel died on December 8, 1955, of a brain aneurysm.[30] She was in the kitchen when she suffered the aneurysm and was dead before her body hit the floor. Services were held at St. Denis's Roman Catholic Church in Yonkers.[31] Ethel was interred with other Krupa family members at Holy Cross Cemetery in Calumet City, Illinois.[32] Gene joined her there almost eighteen years later.

Gene Records More Records

In Gene's 1950s small group recordings, technology finally caught up to his drumming. His innovations and inspirations are heard in brilliant high fidelity. Every rim and stick shot, high-hat pattern, split double-stroke. Every cymbal crash, however delicate or shimmering. "Sleepy Lagoon," from *The Gene Krupa Quartet* (1955), with its eerie bass-bow introduction and two mood sections. "'S' Wonderful," from *The Jazz Rhythms of Gene Krupa* (1957) with its extended introduction and coda gently segueing from introspective to Latin-derived before the melody's emergence.

"Krupa's Wail," also from *Jazz Rhythms*, is all drums except for some jingle-jangle backing by the Quartet. "He builds the excitement up," remarked Kevin Dorn. "Then he brings it down. Then he builds it up again. And then he brings it down again ... The feel on that is just incredible."[33] "Krupa's Wail" would have worked well in an arena-rock concert two or three decades later.

"Chelsea Bridge," written by Billy Strayhorn, appears in *Hey ... Here's Gene Krupa!* (1959). It's the polar opposite of "Krupa's Wail"—sad, inward-looking, and stunningly beautiful. Gene plays the tom-toms, but "lightly," said Dorn. "The light drum sound makes it especially melancholy." It also shows Gene's versatility, proving that, even on the toms, he was far from just a loud player.[34]

There was one more Krupa Trio studio LP in the 1950s—with Eddie Shu and Teddy Napoleon—called *Sing, Sing, Sing* (1954), and another with the Quartet, *Krupa Rocks* (1958). On the former, the Trio proved that small group versions of songs like "Don't Be That Way" and the title track could be just as hard hitting as the big band interpretations. The latter was filled with beautifully recorded and ingeniously played Krupa accents from all around the drum kit. An especial highlight is "Pick Yourself Up," which has Gene and clarinetist Gail Curtis trading licks.

Gene also recorded two full-length albums with one-off big bands: *Drummer Man* (1956) and *Gene Krupa Plays Gerry Mulligan Arrangements* (1959). The Mulligan arrangements on the latter are fantastic, but Gene mostly takes a back seat, treating the album as more of a Gerry Mulligan project—Mulligan arranges and conducts—than a Krupa offering.

One explanation for Gene's recessed role may be that his late '40s band had played many of Mulligan's arrangements live, but recorded few. Here, by keeping the focus on Mulligan, Gene paid tribute to a significant jazz talent who was once in his employ.

Drummer Man is the better of the two LPs. Roy Eldridge and Anita O'Day reunite with Gene for rerecordings of some of the Krupa band's best, mainly from the 1940s. Among them are "Let Me Off Uptown," "Drumboogie," "Boogie Blues," "Leave Us Leap," and "Wire Brush Stomp." "Fish Fry" is a severe editing of "Fish Market"—Gene's greatest song that nobody knows. Gone is Donizetti; the recording retains "Nit Wit Serenade" for a clever variation. The young phenom Quincy Jones wrote most of the arrangements.

In a Krupa side project with Teddy Wilson and Lionel Hampton (called *Gene Krupa—Lionel Hampton—Teddy Wilson* [1956]), they rerecorded some of the great songs they'd originally waxed with Benny Goodman. Lionel assumes Benny's role as chief soloist. Conceding to modernity, they bring in a bassist—Red Callender. The result is a lively display of talent undimmed by time.

Gene also recorded with Buddy Rich, his friend and friendly competitor. The first LP showcases their inaugural performance together on September 13, 1952, as well as songs by Gene's Trio and others. It was originally called *Norman Granz, Jazz at the Philharmonic, Vol. 15* (1953). Reissued in 1960 to better entice Krupa and Rich fans, it was renamed *The Drum Battle—Gene Krupa and Buddy Rich at JATP*. They play together only on "The Drum Battle" and "Perdido"; the other four songs are by the Krupa Trio. *Krupa and Rich* (1956) is better; each has a feature: "Buddy's Blues" and "Gene's Blues." They play together on "Bernie's Tune."

Finally, there is *Burnin' Beat* (1962), probably the most entertaining of the three. The arrangements are of the 1960s cocktail-party variety. The men trade licks on all eight tracks. The listener is treated to an enlightening comparison of their approaches to the drums.

Gene Knows Diddley

Although the Big Band Era died a premature death, and, as we've seen, the popularity of jazz in general had declined through the 1950s, Gene Krupa could claim a bright spot. He maintained a celebrity exceeding that of most of his contemporaries and was still traveling from coast to coast entertaining people and introducing the unknowing to jazz, if on a smaller scale than before. Although he could claim many a modern jazz drumming influencee, he was no longer at the cutting edge of jazz.

This is where we can see Gene's impact on fledgling rock and roll, through all of its subgenres. Rock might not have existed, or taken all of the twists and turns it did, if it hadn't been for Krupa. This doesn't mean that Gene liked or followed the development of rock. He didn't. But that doesn't matter.

The Bo Diddley beat didn't actually start with Bo Diddley. On the way to full formation, it was heard in the guitar work of "Papa" Charlie Jackson's 1925 record of his own "Shake That Thing." That year, orchestra leader Abe Lyman took the little bit of riff and used it for an interlude in his own rendition of "Shake That Thing." Jazzers in Chicago used it on the cowbell to signal a song's end.

As we've seen, Gene incorporated the riff in his Chicagoan records of April 1928. He did it again in July, during a drum break on the Eddie Condon Quartet recording of "Oh, Baby." A year later, traces of it were heard in Gene's drumming on "Firehouse Blues" with the Mound City Blue Blowers. A notable use of the beat by Gene and others is heard in "Nobody's Sweetheart," from Benny Goodman's 1934 "Bill Dodge" sessions. It snuck into songs by various musicians. Krupa brought it to the fore and developed it into something substantial that could eventually exist independently.

By October 1937, Gene's drumsticks and tom-toms had liberated the riff from its protective cloak, giving it muscle and sinew, on a live Benny Goodman performance of Duke Ellington's "Caravan." This beat opened the gorgeous 1940 Krupa recording of "Tonight," performed in the 1941 movie short, *Gene Krupa and His Orchestra*, in which, as we've seen, he executed the beat using a conga hand drum strapped over his shoulder. "Tonight" was eventually cited as the first recorded use of the Bo Diddley beat (although Gene had been experimenting with it for a while on record, as had others before him) in the 1992 CD compilation *Bo Diddley Beats*, a Rhino release.

From the 1940s through the 1960s, Gene began most of his Trio and Quartet readings of "Dark Eyes" with this beat—in his hands, a fluid, undulating, muscular rhythm. "It's such a classic Gene Krupa rhythm," said Kevin Dorn. "You've gotta listen to him play it to hear the feel that he gets."[35]

Among other songs, this rhythm often turned up in live Trio and Quartet versions of an audience favorite, "Drumboogie." One had to expect this beat to show up somewhere in a Krupa solo, and one's expectations would be met, time and again. Gene Krupa was probably the biggest, most creative, proponent of this beat.

Was it a coincidence that Bo Diddley began using this beat, too? Although Bo claimed credit for it, his drummer, Clifton James, said *he* made it up on the tom-toms. Blues man Willie Dixon confirmed James's claim. James's favorite drummers were Max Roach, Cozy Cole, and Gene Krupa.[36] Blues drummer Fred Below, an alumnus along with Clifton James of seminal blues figures like Howlin' Wolf, said James—and others—*took* the Bo Diddley beat *from him.* Below was a Krupa fan and considered himself of the same drumming ilk as Gene, Art Blakey, and Sonny Payne. As a boy in Chicago, Below went to see the "best of the big black bands," naming Gene's band as one of them![37]

Canadian songwriter-producer-multi-instrumentalist Greg Wells associated the Bo Diddley beat with Krupa's "jungle beats." Wells, rapper Kid Cudi, and producer T-Bone Burnett cowrote a song for the film soundtrack, *The Hunger Games: Songs from District 12 and Beyond* (2012), called "The Ruler and the Killer," which Wells said is a "rockier version" of Gene's Bo Diddley beat.[38]

Tino Gross, founder of the Detroit-area rock group, The Howling Diablos, was inspired to get into drums and music by Gene Krupa's example. He said anyone joining the band had to "understand the Gene Krupa thing," meaning a "tom-tom groove," said Gross. "The closest thing to it that some of these guys would understand is Bo Diddley."[39]

X, a 40-years-running Los Angeles-based punk-rock group, linked the beat ideas of Diddley and Krupa in their song "The Hungry Wolf" (1982). Bassist John Doe said they had "tried to acknowledge" Diddley, while drummer D. J. Bonebrake and lead guitarist Billy Zoom contended they were "thinking of Gene Krupa." At a 2017 Grammy Museum concert, John Doe resolved the difference of opinion. "Are you ready for some Gene Krupa?" he shouted to the crowd.[40]

If one were to list future rock songs based on the Bo Diddley beat, it would read like a history of rock songwriting. These are just the tip of the iceberg: "Not Fade Away," Buddy Holly (1957); "Willie and the Hand Jive," Johnny Otis (1958); "I Want Candy," The Strangeloves (1965); "Magic Carpet Ride," Steppenwolf (1968); "Magic Bus," The Who (1968); "Bad Blood," Neil Sedaka (1975); "Billy Bones and the White Bird," Elton John (1975); "Shame Shame Shame," Shirley and Company (1974); "She's the One," Bruce Springsteen (1975); "New York Groove," Ace Frehley (1978); "Faith," George Michael (1987); and "Desire," U2 (1988).

Gene Krupa in effect had a hand in the writing and recording of these songs. He needn't have been there nor thought of by the artists.

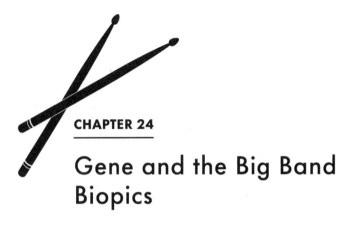

CHAPTER 24

Gene and the Big Band Biopics

FOLLOWING ETHEL'S DEATH, GENE RESUMED dating. "He's human. He's a man," said Marvin Ostroff, Gene's band-boy from 1956 to 1958. "Girls would put a hit on him, you know?"[1] Ostroff was a twentysomething security guard at the Steel Pier in Atlantic City, New Jersey, when he first met Gene and the Quartet. The members then were Eddie Shu, Dave McKenna on piano (or, sometimes, Teddy Napoleon), and John Drew on bass. "We got to a friendly relationship where I would walk him home, home being Haddon Hall [a stately, old hotel]," said Ostroff, who had a drumming background himself.

"We walked to Kornblau's Restaurant at Virginia and Pacific Avenue, a famous restaurant for corned beef specials," said Ostroff. "It was Gene's favorite sandwich in Atlantic City." They went to the beach during the day. "I guess it was like a father-son relationship." Before long, Krupa had offered Ostroff the band-boy job. Marvin's chief duties were driving, unless the distance warranted flying, and setting up and breaking down the instruments.

"I loved my years with him," said Marvin. "It wasn't lord and master . . . Two years of a great time. It didn't cost me anything." Eventually, Ostroff moved on, securing a day job and playing with his own jazz ensemble at night. But he kept in touch with Gene, who, on a Sunday, brought his softball team down to Ventnor, outside Atlantic City, for a game against Marvin's Knights of Pythias team. Afterward, Gene treated everyone to dinner.

Gene's girlfriend, Darlene, was twenty years old. During the wee hours of one Manhattan morning in August 1957, following a Quartet performance, Darlene was riding in the car with Gene and Marvin, Krupa's packed-up drum kit fastened to the roof. They were taking Gene to a church for what was called the "Four O'Clock Actor's Mass." (This mass was intended for Catholics in the performing arts who attended church at off hours.)

At Sixth Avenue and Fourteenth Street, "here comes a car through the red light," said Marvin, "and clobbers me on Gene's side." The car turned over onto Ostroff's side. He believed that the drums tied to the rack prevented the car from rolling over and killing everyone.[2] No one used seatbelts in those days. According to a news report, Darlene sustained "scalp lacerations," Ostroff, "contusions of a toe," and Gene, "contusions of the left shoulder."[3]

———————

BEGINNING IN THE late 1950s, one of Gene's live specialties, which he couldn't have performed without his Quartet, was the late 1930s Bobby Haggart-Ray Bauduc bass-drums duet, "Big Noise From Winnetka." In the original, bassist Haggart whistled a brief refrain leading into the trading of licks between his bass and Bauduc's drums, after which Bauduc, while seated, used his drumsticks for a few measures on the lower end of Haggart's bass as Haggart tackled the higher end. In the late 1950s, Gene turned this into a Krupa tour de force that never failed as a crowd-pleaser. After an inspired drum solo that built up the excitement, he would stand, stroll around his drum kit as he played its different components, and arrive at his bassist's instrument on cue, where he would lean over to perform a substantial sticks-on-bass passage, sometimes punctuating it with a foot stomp or two. Usually, without missing a beat, Gene would conclude with a cymbal crash, the audience delightedly cheering.

———————

WITH THE END of the Swing Era came a collection of 1950s movies about big band figures—*The Glenn Miller Story* (1954), *The Benny Goodman Story* (1956), and *The Gene Krupa Story* (1959). Gene made a cameo in the first, played himself (in a supporting role) in the second, and was the subject of the third.

The best of the three was *The Glenn Miller Story*. It featured Jimmy Stewart in the title role, sufficient drama to keep the viewer engaged, and enough terrific music (plus the Modernaires) to keep Miller fans very happy. Gene, Cozy Cole, and Louis Armstrong found themselves on a little stage together, performing for Stewart-as-Miller in his young musician days. *The Benny Goodman Story*, conversely, was beset with problems: corny dialogue, a poor performance as Goodman by nonactor Steve Allen, and the strangeness of real Goodman alumni in early middle age playing their younger selves.

Gene's substantial musical and acting role in the movie led to six weeks of work from June to August 1955. George Duvivier played bass on the soundtrack and was pleased to work with Gene, a "delightful human being." During the recording of "One O'Clock Jump" for the soundtrack, Benny repeatedly admonished Krupa not to "play so loudly." "Gene was a very easygoing guy," said Duvivier, and simply continued to play. Then Benny firmly "requested" that Krupa play with brushes instead of sticks. Duvivier recalled, "Gene got up, put the sticks down, and said, 'Benny, I suggest you get O'Neil Spencer.' And he walked off the soundstage." (O'Neil Spencer was a *long-dead* jazz drummer!) Universal's musical director, Joe Gershenson, intervened, telling Benny that brushes and "One O'Clock Jump" didn't mesh. Eventually, Gene was persuaded to return and "allowed to play the way he wanted."[4]

The Gene Krupa Story was the least fact-based of the three movies. The moviemakers got right only that Gene was a drummer of Roman Catholic faith raised in Chicago who became a big star with amazing drumming chops and suffered a downfall because of a marijuana charge.

Gene apparently had two goals in mind when selling his life story to Universal. One, he hoped to attract more young people to jazz.[5] By the mid- to late '50s, jazz had long since faded from the attention of America's youth and its overall popularity continued to wane. For someone like Gene, raised on jazz and famous because of it, this was a cultural tragedy. Soon he noticed it was a threat to the livelihood of fellow jazzers, old and young.

Two, as Bobby Scott later put it, Gene wanted the film to "provide for him in his slow autumn walk."[6] At the time, Gene was as internationally famous as ever, never lacking lucrative work. Yet, to drummer Bruce Klauber, the very existence of a Krupa biopic "upped Gene's asking price for the rest of his days."[7]

Twenty-year-old Sal Mineo played Gene from the drummer's teen years into his thirties. Baby-faced Mineo delivered an excellent performance. He had studied the emotional physicality of his subject's drumming and learned the instrument well enough to convincingly mime to brand-new recordings featuring the biographical subject, who himself delivered some of his best playing ever.

"Sal Mineo's miming job," said Klauber, "is the best I've ever seen. Period."[8] Gene, too, was impressed, saying that such an undertaking was "very, very tough" whether miming to your own recordings or not.[9]

But why Sal Mineo? It's true that he was a Krupa fan himself, having attended many a Krupa performance as a child.[10] "They were really trying to hit the teenage market, in a way, with that movie," said Krupa drumming acolyte Tino Gross. "I mean, because Sal Mineo was a teenage heartthrob. That wasn't the average casting. That was like, 'Who's the hottest teenager we got that the kids like?'"[11]

Mineo's presence attracted young people who were thus exposed to jazz, as Krupa had wanted. The movie's ambience anachronistically drifted in and out of 1950s youth culture. James Darren as Gene's best friend "Eddie Sirota" (a character flimsily based on best-friend-forever Eddie Condon) sang in the mode of 1950s male heartthrobs (of whom he was one). Gene's love interest, "Ethel Maguire" (loosely based on his late wife Ethel Fawcett), was the long-suffering girlfriend who took Gene back after his marijuana imbroglio and the fact that he had slept with other women. In a way, *The Gene Krupa Story* was an apology by a truly self-critical Gene for how difficult it was for Ethel to be his spouse.

Gene's own love life could explain the movie's sexually suggestive scenes. The other explanation was the youth market, whose interest in onscreen portrayals of romance was less modest than what their parents had been taught to expect. Regardless, it had to comply with limitations set by the still-extant Hays Office.

Correspondence between Geoffrey M. Shurlock of what was now called the Motion Picture Association of America, Inc. and various Columbia Pictures executives show how hung up the Hays Office still was about sex and drugs. Sal-Gene's affair with a fictional paramour, Gloria, must be "treated with discipline and restraint" and not be shown as the "right" thing to do. The courtship of Ethel mustn't imply that they had ever had premarital sex. To keep viewers from getting too much of the wrong idea, lovers must be left in a standing position. Openmouthed kissing is forbidden. The use of marijuana will not be shown to have any positive effects whatsoever. The "details of drug procurement" between Gene and a "pusher" must be omitted. Finally, no one is allowed to use the word "hell."[12]

Comedian Lenny Bruce was to have joked, "After they cleaned up *The Gene Krupa Story*, Sal Mineo found out he was portraying Lawrence Welk."[13] Still, at least one reviewer criticized the sexual content remaining in the movie. "Just so everyone gets the idea," wrote Jack H. Balten for *The Jazz Review*, "the camera on one drum solo, early on in the story, looks across the heaving bosom of an admirer for almost the entire scene . . . (Did we have to have those nuzzling couples and all that décolletage every time?)"[14]

For fans of jazz drumming, the movie was a godsend. "I've always believed that Gene's playing on the soundtrack was the best of his post-big band career," said Bruce Klauber. "In terms of technique, execution, ideas, 'covering' the various eras of music, etc., Gene Krupa was at the top of his game."[15]

The Gene Krupa Story is notable for its omissions. It lacks any real representation of Gene's best-known recordings. Of the soundtrack's songs, the only one closely connected with his career was "Indiana," which he had recorded multiple times beginning in 1928 when the ensemble's moniker was The Eddie Condon Quartet. There was no "Drumboogie," "Let Me Off Uptown," "Dark Eyes," or "Sing, Sing, Sing!" The film also left out the story of Gene's career: how he got his start in Chicago; who his drumming idols were; the Chicagoans' ups and downs; his commitment to musical education; the bandleaders he played with (aside from Red Nichols, who portrayed himself in the film!); his goals as a bandleader; and the sidemen who were especially important to him, like Roy Eldridge, Charlie Ventura, and Teddy Napoleon. Anita O'Day appeared in the movie as herself, but only in the background, singing "Memories of You." The film didn't even touch upon Gene's early work with African-American musicians and his own efforts on issues of race.

On the plus side, the so-called "Indiana Montage" slyly refers to one of the first songs Gene recorded as a bandleader, "Grandfather's Clock" (1938), with a passage that cleverly uses the tune's varied cymbal work to imitate a clock's mechanism. It less slyly refers to Gene's prodigious stick-on-bass playing on "Big Noise From Winnetka." There is more than a nod to "Blue Rhythm Fantasy, Parts 1 and 2," in the polyrhythms of Gene and the soundtrack's band.

These authentic Krupa sounds aside, it's possible that the only storyline demands Gene made of Columbia were the inclusion of Ethel and Eddie. It appears from a perusal of the movie's papers that Columbia made no effort to contact Gene's scores of friends and colleagues for permission to portray them on film.

Did this really matter?

It mattered to Roy Eldridge, who was hurt, even angry, that he had been left out with nary a mention. Roy was "cool" toward Gene after the movie's release. Nothing that Gene did could make amends—that is, until he sent Roy a brand-new drum set. Roy promptly installed it in his basement and used it for fun, in private recording projects. All was again well between Gene and Roy.[16]

Beyond the movie's numerous faults, Sal Mineo acted and drum-mimed masterfully. The music and its references were great, even if the songs were wrong. Gene's playing was extraordinary. The movie soundtrack was an opportunity for Verve, the Norman

Granz label for which Krupa now recorded, to remarket his back catalogue. Slingerland made use of the movie connection, too. And there were drumming contests again, which drew more attention to the drums as a solo instrument.

Bobby Tribuzio, a drummer playing with a rock group at the Metropole Café in Times Square when Gene was there, met Krupa several times. Bobby mentioned the film to him. "What he said was something that stuck in my mind," said Tribuzio, "was that he liked the music that was in the movie. He said, 'But the movie itself, you know, they prettied it up a little bit. . . .' I took that, not at that moment, but later on, like maybe he liked the movie, but maybe he didn't love it."[17]

The Gene Krupa Story—renamed *Drum Crazy* in Britain and *Jazz Ecstasy* in Germany[18]—became the favorite movie of countless rock-era drummers. It depicted their hero drumming as only he could. It spurred youngsters to become drummers, just as Gene's fame of the '30s and '40s led to countless boys doing the same.

CHAPTER 25

"Being Able to Play a Little Again"

GENE KRUPA WAS IN ATLANTIC City one day when he saw a beautiful woman sunbathing in the sand. Uncle Gene, said nephew Gene H., sat "on her towel at the beach and simply started to talk. Surely he knew all about sex and love; clearly he wasn't afraid to test himself in that genre. He could deal with women and still be Gene Krupa; as I saw it, part of being Gene Krupa was dealing with women." Being shy, nephew Gene H. "wished I could be more like my uncle."[1]

At age fifty, Gene was still a vigorous, athletic man and looked it. One of his favorite physical activities was swimming in icy cold water.[2]

Krupa's new love interest was Patricia Bowler. Then employed as a bookkeeper in Springfield, Massachusetts, she was half his age. Early in 1959, while onstage performing at Chicago's London House, Gene announced their upcoming nuptials.[3] "He just wanted things to be first class for her," said Eddie Wasserman, the Krupa Quartet's late '50s/early '60s reed (and flute) player.[4] In the spring, Gene and Patti married and left New York on the SS *Nieuw Amsterdam*, destination Southampton, England, where they would join JATP for some British dates and also enjoy a honeymoon.[5]

IN 1958, GENE's brother-in-law, husband of his beloved sister Elenor, died of a "lingering illness" at Gene's Yonkers home. Presumably Gene brought him and Elenor eastward so that Michael could be properly cared for in his last days. Like the other Krupas, Michael was buried in Holy Cross Cemetery, South Chicago.[6]

In 1959, around when Gene married Patti, he was starting to notice changes in his physical ability to drum as he used to. His brilliant playing on the *Gene Krupa Story* soundtrack notwithstanding, he believed he couldn't play as fast anymore, and perhaps not so powerfully. "I'd probably liken myself to a pitcher who used to throw very hard, didn't want to get out of the game, and started to pitch with his bean instead of his arm," Gene said.[7] Being a chain smoker for decades hadn't helped.

Drummer Bobby Tribuzio couldn't help noticing Gene's smoking habits. "I never saw him without a cigarette in his hand," said Tribuzio. "He smoked constantly. Constantly. I mean, when I would watch him at the Metropole, when he would come down from the dressing room, he would come down smoking, after smoking his head off upstairs in the room, and walk behind the drums and put the cigarette out . . . I mean, he smoked right up to the last second before he started his next set."[8]

Gene's lessened physical capacity portended a health crisis. It came in November 1960. He suffered a heart attack while in Chicago, which required several weeks of convalescence at Michael Reese Hospital as they waited for a blood clot caused by the heart attack to "dissolve."[9]

Gene's doctors warned him to avoid "talk of future activities." While lying in bed, Gene "wasn't so much concerned about dying as about being able to play a little again," adding that "something hitting you like that can change your whole philosophy." He put aside goals of doing well commercially. He intended to focus on being an artist.[10]

Under doctor's orders to work less, when Gene returned to performing, he committed to drumming just eighteen weeks out of a year. At first, this meant sixteen weeks at the Metropole Café and two weeks in Atlantic City.

Krupa returning to the stage at the Metropole on March 31, 1961, was the "biggest drawing card in the Metropole's . . . history," said columnist Gene Knight. With him for his comeback were saxist-flautist Eddie Wasserman, pianist Dave McKenna, and bassist Kenny O'Brien[11]—the same Kenny O'Brien who, with Ed Shaughnessy, spent all day in 1944 at New York's Capitol Theatre enjoying Gene's band between showings of *Since You Went Away*.

Even working for just eighteen weeks—and not successively—Gene had to be careful. He told columnist Charles McHarry of his hope that continuing to drum wouldn't "further damage his heart if he can control his 'inner excitement.'"[12] This would be a challenge for Gene, a drummer governed by his duende.

Dr. Richard L. Weiss, Director of Echocardiography at Penn Presbyterian Hospital in Philadelphia, stated in 2020 that a heart attack generally causes damage to the heart's left ventricle. This could lead to "shortness of breath and fatigue." Also, due to scar tissue in the heart, Gene would have suffered "lowered cardiac output . . . He is not able to augment the blood flow to his muscles. Therefore, they tire quickly."[13]

THE METROPOLE, GENE's home away from home through much of the '60s, featured jazz and rock. Besides Gene, other jazzers included Lionel Hampton, Woody Herman, and Henry "Red" Allen. "The Metropole was a very hot jazz club," said Tribuzio. "Gene Krupa was definitely a favorite."[14]

Rock acts, with two bands alternating, played the main room during the day, from about 12:45 P.M. to 8:45 P.M. Jazz came on at night, with two jazz groups alternating, and went into the early-morning hours. Rock groups also played on weekend nights upstairs in the "lounge." Bobby Tribuzio wouldn't go home after his band was done but stayed for all of Gene's sets. Outside the club, crowds gathered whenever Gene was performing. "I was a kid, but I remember it was a circus outside, with everyone trying to get a glimpse of what was going on inside," said Bruce Klauber. "There were dozens of people of all ages, races, etc. Street people, parents holding their young drum student children on their shoulders, etc. Man, did I want to go in!"[15] Metropole management made things easier for the gawkers by keeping the front door open so everyone could hear some Krupa licks.

The Metropole was an oddly laid-out club. The main floor was "very narrow." Behind the long bar staffed with eight bartenders was a long "catwalk stage." The second-floor lounge, somewhat smaller than the main floor, was accessed by a long flight of steps commencing to the right of the main entrance. Yet another long flight of stairs led to the dressing rooms. The largest dressing room, offering a couch and a rug, was for the "star." "Gene was starting to feel not too well," said Tribuzio. "He would lay down between each set on that sofa."

When the second-floor lounge was not in use by a band, most of the musicians—whether jazz or rock—would gather there to relax and talk. Gene's Quartet was playing downstairs one evening when Gene himself came up to the lounge to announce that his saxophonist had become ill and he needed a substitute. The rock band with which Bobby's band alternated had a sax player. Gene was "talking to the sax player. We're all young kids. Now this guy is almost shaking. Gene said, 'Listen. I need you to come downstairs and help me out. . . .'

"'Do you know *Tenderly?*'

"The sax player says, 'Yeah.'

"Gene says, 'Just blow it![16] Do you know such-and-such?'

"'Yeah.'

"'Just blow it!'"

Gene "walked him through a few songs" before they went downstairs. "I'll never forget that night," said Tribuzio, "and I'm sure he [the sax player] never forgot that night."

Vibraphonist Terry Gibbs, of jazz's younger generation, found his band alternating with Gene at the Metropole. Gibbs's orchestra had eighteen pieces. The stage was so narrow, said Gibbs, that having his band there "was like a lineup you would see in jail. There was no room." Gene's drums were assembled and occupying space for his next set. "We started to move his drums," said Gibbs. "And the manager of the place came over and said, 'You can't do that. Gene Krupa is the star here.' So Gene was there and heard it and came over and said, 'Wait a minute. Let me tell you something. When I play, I am the star. When Terry Gibbs plays, he is the star. So please move the drums.'" Thereafter, for each of Gibbs's sets, two Metropole employees moved Gene's drums out of the way and moved them back afterward. Gene was "as nice as you can get," said Gibbs.[17]

GENE ENCOURAGED JAZZ drummer Les DeMerle early on at the Metropole and in Atlantic City. "I had a little kid band called the Capitals and Gene was headlining at the end of the Pier where the high-diving horse was," said DeMerle. "That's what Gene had to follow, and all the other bands that played there, too. So the horse would do his high-dive [with a rider] from about 60 feet in the air and jump into this aqua pool. Then Stan Kenton would come on or Basie would come on or Gene Krupa with the Quartet would come on. It was pretty crazy."

At the Pier, Gene would "pass by and pop his head in and make sure I was doing okay," said DeMerle, "and I would go out to hear his shows every night."[18]

DESPITE DOCTOR'S WARNINGS, Gene started expanding his work schedule again. In 1962, besides the Metropole and Atlantic City, he had occasional college dates and other engagements under 300 miles from home. This limited itinerary allowed him to spend more time with Patti and practice for a couple of hours.[19]

Next year, he "regularly" played Philadelphia and Chicago and early in 1963 performed with a big band assembled at Disneyland in Anaheim, California.[20]

Things got busier in 1964, especially during the summertime, when he and his Quartet performed for a couple of weeks at "Jazzland" in the Louisiana Pavilion at the New York World's Fair of 1964–1965.[21] Fortunately, this was close to home. Later in the summer, he joined a jazz tour of Japan organized by George Wein.[22] Mexico City came soon thereafter.[23]

The drummer worked on side projects, too, like the record album *Percussion King* (1961), in which he collaborated with a big band plus several other accomplished drummers and percussionists who happened to be friends and neighbors—Joe Venuto, Doug Allen, and Mousey Alexander, the latter of whom, as Gene put it, "has held my old chair in the Benny Goodman band."[24] The idea was to make the percussionists the "melody men" and the horns the "timekeepers."[25] Aside from the usual components of the drum set, among the other percussion instruments played were vibraphone, castanets, African rope drum, tuned bongos, finger cymbals, Chinese bell tree, maracas, tam-tam, claves, finger cymbals, and glockenspiel.

Gene's unstated goal for the album was to somewhat satisfy his decades-long dream of marrying jazz and classical in more than a casual way. All the pieces were classical, but with jazz arrangements reworked by Gene's old friend George Williams. Some of them Gene's late 1940s band had recorded or played live before—"American Bolero," "Sabre Dance," "Valse Triste."

In 1962, Cozy Cole put out *Drum Beat for Dancing Feet* in which he drum-duetted with Ray McKinley, "Panama" Francis, and Gene. It was similar to Krupa and Rich's *Burnin' Beat* of the same year: each drumming duo trading licks against a band background of familiar tunes and implicitly asking swing fans to return to the fold.

Krupa made a record with protégé Louie Bellson, *The Mighty Two* (1963). Gene hoped to "demonstrate that the basics of drumming, what we call the rudiments, can be used in jazz. The kids are a little bit reluctant to believe that, so we set out to prove something . . ."[26] Like a true mentor, Krupa kvelled over Bellson's accomplishments. "This guy is just amazing," Gene said. "He's become so wonderful on the drums, and he's gone beyond that . . ."[27]

"I wrote all of the 26 rudiments to swing time," Bellson complained about the recording of the album, "and I taught it to Gene up at his house."[28] Bellson couldn't imagine it was just Gene responding as a student of drums, which he so loved being. Fred Thompson, employed by Bellson, actually wrote the songs and the arrangements, except for "The Mighty Two Alone Together" and "Rhythmic Excursion," on which Krupa and Bellson improvised their parts.

There were also reunions. One, with a group of Gene's friends from the old Chicago days, resulted in an NBC-TV special and an LP called *Chicago and All that Jazz!* in 1961. Among the participants besides Krupa were Eddie Condon, Jimmy McPartland, Bud Freeman, Joe Sullivan, and Jack Teagarden (an honorary Chicagoan). Each Chicagoan was individually introduced; each got equal recognition, and this was fine with Gene, who believed he wasn't better than anyone else.

Eddie Condon's fortunes had risen since his tenuous tenure at Nick's in the Village. His lean days were gone by the mid-1940s. Condon had married Phyllis Smith and opened a jazz club of his own, appropriately called Eddie Condon's, which would last for a few decades, though in different Manhattan locations. More than ever, he was a jazz musician, advocate, and personality.

In a different sort of reunion, the original Benny Goodman Quartet recorded *Together Again!* for a 1963 release. The foursome had played at least a couple of gigs together since the halcyon days of the 1930s. On *Together Again*, these fiftysomethings didn't play as fast as they used to, but they blended as well as ever, and took another pleasurable crack at "Runnin' Wild."

Next year saw Gene's last LP on Granz's Verve label: *The Great New Gene Krupa Quartet Featuring Charlie Ventura*. A complete reunion was impossible; Teddy Napoleon was battling lung cancer in 1964, and succumbed at only fifty. Pianist John Bunch took his place. Nabil Totah, a Jordanian immigrant, played bass. Together, they recorded Ellington classics ("Take the A Train," "Sophisticated Lady"), a Hampton standard ("Flying Home"), and more recent fare ("Cry Me a River," "Misty"). "Stomping Waltz" was a reworking of Gene's thrilling, waltz-time extension of "Stompin' at the Savoy," which he had perfected in his original 1940s Trio. "It's a great chance to hear Gene playing in three-four," said Kevin Dorn. "Not a lot of recordings that he did and not a lot of recordings of any of the drummers from that era played in three-four."[29]

———————

DESPITE HIS HEART attack, Gene wasn't giving up his most formidable addiction—smoking—nor was he doing well at reducing his touring schedule. More evidence that his habit was taking a toll surfaced in 1962 when Gene was a guest on *The Tonight Show* with new host Johnny Carson. Gene had just finished performing a particularly satisfying—if taxing—rendition of "Caravan." He couldn't catch his breath.

Carson: "How you feelin'?"

Krupa, gasping: "Pretty winded."

Carson: "Does that wear you out more than it used to, a few years back?"

Krupa, still gasping: "I should say so."[30]

———————

GENE TRYING FOR a normal family life with Catholic Charities' help complicated things. He and his wife adopted two infants: Marygrace, in 1963, and, two years later, Gene Michael, nicknamed "B.G.," or "Baby Gene." Appearing on *The Mike Douglas Show* in March 1966, one could almost feel Gene's heart swelling with fatherly bliss as he revealed the adoptions to a national viewing audience.[31]

As a new father, his Metropole and Atlantic City residencies were one thing, but his burgeoning schedule far from home was another. Krupa Quartet saxophonist Carmen Leggio said Gene's life was "lonely." Leggio said Gene was "bothered" that he couldn't be home as much as he'd have liked, given that he was married with two little children. "Whenever we had a day off," said Leggio, "I don't care where he was, he'd go home." But there was only so much of that he could do. Otherwise, Leggio recalled, Gene "lived like a hermit." He would perform, return to his room to sleep, maybe wake up early for a TV interview, have food sent up. If he wanted a hamburger, he might go out. "Even by then, Gene was still a top attraction wherever we went," said Leggio, "especially when we went to South America. They *really* rolled out the red carpet for him."[32]

The year 1967 was Gene's most hectic year in quite a while. Just some of his appearances included the London House in Chicago,

the Theatrical Restaurant in Cleveland, the Colonial Club in To-
ronto, Baker's Keyboard Lounge in Detroit, the Living Room in
Cincinnati,[33] La Riviera in Tampa, and the Chamberlain High
School in Tampa. He was still trying to promote jazz appreciation.
The kids "are really the ones we're counting on for tomorrow, and
I'm grateful for the chance to play for them," he said. "Some of our
techniques are fundamental to rock."[34]

There were sour notes uttered by self-important jazz critics.
Calling Gene's fans "doughheads" and "peasants," *Toronto Star* reviewer Patrick Scott repeatedly reminded readers of Gene's age—
fifty-eight—while decrying his "limited technical equipment" and
"stunted imagination." "Gene couldn't swing his way out of a revolv-
ing door," Scott sneered.[35]

Scott's hostility would become a moot point. Some jazz clubs
Gene hit at least twice during the year including Cincinnati's Living
Room. And the Living Room was the last place he would ever play
while on tour, because touring was about to come to an end.

Gene Krupa probably performed only one of the scheduled
nights at the Living Room. What people thought was a "mild heart
attack" that sent him home on doctor's orders turned out to be emphysema, another smoker's disease.[36]

CHAPTER 26

"Commence to Rock and Roll"[1]

As GENE'S HEALTH DETERIORATED, IT was more than evident that his drumming had ensnared a huge proportion of young rock drummers, and that the seeds had been planted years earlier. As we've seen, Gene didn't like rock. He disliked the amplification, the electric guitars, and the way that the drummers, to him, played too loud, which he assumed was necessary to overcome electric guitar volume. He thought rock too musically simplistic. This didn't mean that he didn't recognize talent among the rock drummers. He did notice that his drumming "had a continued hold on youngsters," probably "because the percussive thing is so strong in rock."[2] He sensed that a lot of them were in rock because that's where the money was. He met many of them at the Metropole, and he gladly talked shop with them and encouraged their ambitions.

The Gene Krupa Story Story

Gene's rock-era percussive fan base shot up with the release of *The Gene Krupa Story*, or, as it was known in Britain, *Drum Crazy*. Carl Palmer went to see *Drum Crazy* with his father at age eleven. Emerging from the theater, he said, "I knew I had been directed

275

down a path that I would follow for the rest of my life, and that was to be a drummer."[3] He eventually became one-third of the progressive rock group Emerson, Lake & Palmer.

Another such lad lived in London's suburbs. "Perhaps the most singular road-to-Damascus moment," wrote Keith Moon biographer Alan Clayson, happened "when a thirteen-year-old, bolt upright in a cinema seat, watched *Drum Crazy*..."[4] Krupa was now Moon's idol and his most profound influence. In a few years' time, Moon would join Pete Townshend, Roger Daltrey, and John Entwistle to form one of the most innovative rock groups of the 1960s and '70s—The Who. Their distinctive sound had much to do with Moon's powerful freneticism, so similar to Krupa's approach in many ways, as friends and observers noted.

"I was always trying to be the Gene Krupa of rock," said Carmine Appice,[5] who drummed for Vanilla Fudge (best known for their Top 10 cover of the Supremes' "You Keep Me Hangin' On" [1967]) and played with Jeff Beck and Rod Stewart. Appice was inspired by Gene's polyrhythms in *The Gene Krupa Story*.[6] Neil Peart, who gained prominence with Canadian rock band Rush, became a drummer because of the movie. "He was the first rock drummer, in very many ways," said Peart.[7] Hirsh Gardner, drummer-guitarist-vocalist for the band New England and an award-winning Boston-area producer and musician, was "blown away" by Gene's biopic. His parents took him to see Gene's Quartet when he was a boy—it was "much more impressive" to see Gene live than on television. "Nobody played a groove like Gene," said Gardner.[8]

Dallas Taylor, drummer for Crosby, Stills, Nash & Young, knew what he was going to do after seeing Gene's biopic at age ten with his mother.[9] Krupa was the "drummer who influenced me more and most of all," Taylor said.[10] Corky Laing, drummer for the hard-rock group Mountain (best known for the anthem "Mississippi Queen" [1970]), was also inspired by *The Gene Krupa Story*. Krupa was "an amusement park unto himself," Laing said, and his first drumming idol. He loved Gene's "conviction," "passion," and "energy."[11]

Danny Seraphine, drummer for the hit-full jazz-rockers, Chicago, played along with the biopic soundtrack as a boy. Seraphine considered his own playing on the songs "Make Me Smile" and "I'm A Man" as especially Krupa influenced, and still listened to Gene for "inspiration."[12]

Steve Smith, drummer for hit-heavy rockers Journey, "loved" *The Gene Krupa Story*; Krupa was part of his upbringing.[13] A Krupa "fill or solo," Smith said, "jumped out in an exciting and musically appropriate way."[14]

"Sing, Sing, Sing" Swing

Gene's performance of "Sing, Sing, Sing" at the Goodman 1938 Carnegie Hall concert grabbed many future rock drummers. Bobby Tribuzio, longtime drummer for Larry Chance and the Earls (known for "Remember Then" [1962]), first heard the Carnegie recording when his oldest brother brought it home on 78-rpm records. "When I heard 'Sing, Sing, Sing,' that did it for me," he said. "I mean, I'm actually getting goose bumps [talking about it] . . . I really wanted to play drums from that point on."[15] Bill Ward, drummer for Black Sabbath, the group fronted by Ozzy Osbourne, said he tried to play a reasonable facsimile of "Sing, Sing, Sing" while practicing drums as a boy. "Everything I've ever played or sung has trickled down from Gene Krupa," Ward said.[16]

Peter Criss, who gained fame drumming for the becostumed Kiss, said hearing the Carnegie "Sing, Sing, Sing" at age ten "hit me like a lightning bolt from heaven." He called the performance a "master's class in rock and roll drumming before there was rock and roll."[17] Drumming for the Barracudas, a rock group playing the Metropole in the 1960s, he often saw Gene perform and was bold enough to ask for pointers. Gene obliged. "He gave me his time," said Criss, and was "one of the nicest guys on the planet."[18]

Bob Elliot, drummer for hit-heavy British rockers the Hollies, discovered big band music through relatives and neighbors, and practiced as a boy to "Sing, Sing, Sing" on "gravy tins" before he had drums. Elliott turned to rock when he realized playing jazz had become a "minority sport." But Gene gave Elliott a "headstart," with his "phrasing and his fills."[19] The Grateful Dead's Mickey Hart also drummed to "Sing, Sing, Sing" as a boy. "Buddy Rich extended what Krupa had pioneered," said Hart, meaning the "complex interweaving of the percussive possibilities in a drum set."[20]

Tino Gross, founder of the Detroit-area rock group the Howling Diablos, was electrified by "Sing, Sing, Sing" as a boy. He felt alienated from authority figures when young and disliked school. Writing about it later in "Go Gene Go," which would become a Howling Diablos percussive tour de force, he sang: "What will you be when you grow up/I didn't like anything/Until I heard Gene Krupa play 'Sing, Sing, Sing'!" Gross said, "We saw Gene Krupa as one of us," even though Gene was from another era. "He was like a rocker, man!"[21]

From Early Rock On

The *Encyclopedia of Percussion* observed that early and later rock drum features, like Iron Butterfly's "In-A-Gadda-Da-Vida" (1968) and Cream's "Toad" (1966), "used drumming techniques and patterns made popular by Gene Krupa twenty years earlier."[22]

Jerry Allison, drummer for Buddy Holly, was "flipped out" with Krupa, Allison's first influence.[23] Multi-instrumentalist Brian Bennett, longtime drummer for the early British rock group The Shadows, as a boy saw *The Glenn Miller Story*, which featured appearances by Cozy Cole and Krupa, and had a revelation. "That's it," he said. "I want to be Gene Krupa."[24] Billy Gussak, frequently a session drummer for Bill Haley & His Comets and *the* drummer on their iconic hit, "Rock Around the Clock" (1954), "peppered" their songs "with Gene Krupa–style fills."[25]

Sandy Nelson, famous for a slew of drum-oriented rock songs in the late '50s and early '60s, is on everyone's list as one of the most influential rock drummers. His parents took him to see Gene and his band live in the 1940s. This experience motivated his folks to buy him his first drum set.[26] It's no surprise that he cited "Let There Be Drums" (1960), "And Then There Were Drums" (1962), and "Birth of the Beat" (1962) as descendants of "Sing, Sing, Sing."[27]

Kenney Jones's relentless tom-toms at the end of the Faces' "I'm Losing You" (1971) are Krupa-esque. Sure enough, Krupa was a

Jones influence.[28] Doug Clifford, known for drumming with Creedence Clearwater Revival, said that Gene's looks, personality, and rhythm made him decide to play drums. Krupa's playing was about rhythm and the space between notes. He saw Gene as "passing the baton" to him. When young drummers tell Clifford he influenced them, he believes he is "passing the baton" to them.[29]

Tommy Aldridge, drummer for heavy-metal group Whitesnake, called Gene an "innovator, a pioneer." "I still thank him for all he's done for drums and drumming," he said.[30] Topper Headon, drummer for the British punk group The Clash, separately covered "Drummin' Man," and saw himself as a drummer similar to Gene. "I mean, he was a real showman," he said. "The first guy who came along and did some really stylish things—lots of catchy tom-tom fills . . ."[31] Neal Smith, the original drummer for eccentric hard-rocker Alice Cooper, said that Gene was one of his "early influences." Krupa's tom-toms affected his drumming in Cooper's songs "Black Juju" (1971) and "Slick Black Limousine" (1973).[32]

Dino Danelli drummed for the hit-laden rockers the Rascals. While playing in another group appearing at the Metropole, Danelli watched Gene play; Krupa reciprocated the interest. Danelli was such a fan that he used to dress and comb his hair like Gene.[33] Jim Karstein, a drumming purveyor of the "Tulsa Sound," which melded jazz, blues, and folk, was most closely associated with singer-songwriters Leon Russell and J. J. Cale. Karstein said, "Gene was my hero drummer."[34]

Krupa was the favorite of A. J. Pero, drummer for the heavy-metal group Twisted Sister. Pero was inspired by Gene's "rebellious sense of style and the ability to see things differently than most contemporaries."[35] Kenny Aronoff, best known as drummer for John Mellencamp, said, "Gene Krupa not only inspired me because of his technique and musicality, but also for his ability to perform with so much passion and excitement."[36]

An electronic dance band from Liverpool, England, Apollo 440, recorded "Krupa" (1996), which enjoyed worldwide chart success. Founding member Noko said the recording's drumming had an "unmistakable swing" and "needed a catchy title." The name

"Krupa" has an "almost surreal onomatopoeic quality." Apollo 440 emerged from the "UK rave dance scene," said Noko; "it was fitting that we [pay] tribute to an icon of a previous golden age of dance music."[37]

Drummers for Everyone

There are drummers known for playing with everyone, putting their percussive imprint everywhere. Kenny Malone, a Nashville session drummer and member of the Country Music Hall of Fame, played on such humongous hits as Crystal Gayle's "Don't It Make My Brown Eyes Blue" (1977), Doby Gray's "Drift Away" (1973), and Dolly Parton's "Jolene" (1973). Krupa mesmerized Malone when he was young. He tried to "emulate the things that Gene did . . . and how he did them." Malone slowed down Krupa's recordings and "listened to exactly what he played." He said, "Gene understood the basic primal rhythms and he'd keep them simple enough where people could understand them."[38]

Gregg Bissonette drummed on soundtracks—movies (*The Devil Wears Prada* [2006], *Bucket List* [2007]) and television (*Mad About You*, *Friends*)—and for an array of talent, including Bette Midler, David Lee Roth, Maynard Ferguson, Paul Anka, Joe Satriani, and Enrique Iglesias. Bissonette was raised on Gene Krupa, courtesy of his father, who had seen Gene's band as a boy in the 1940s and arranged to have Gregg meet Krupa at a gig in the '60s. "Gene had a lot of chops," said Gregg," but he always went more for laying down the groove."[39]

Storied session musician Steve Gadd saw Gene with his parents in the 1950s in Rochester, where he grew up. "They had matinees on Sunday afternoons," Gadd said, "where they'd play for a couple of hours and sometimes they'd let local musicians sit in. He let me bring my little set of drums, and set them up in front of his. We both played." Then Gene played Steve's little drums and supported the boy's ambitions: "'Keep playing.' You know. [He was] Very encouraging." Later, as a student at the Manhattan School of Music, Gadd found himself outside the Metropole looking in with other Krupa

fans. "Everything about Gene influenced me," said Gadd. "His playing, his charisma—he was special... His groove is in my head."[40]

Gadd has drummed for an array of talent, perhaps most famously on Paul Simon's "50 Ways to Leave Your Lover" (1975) and
Grover Washington, Jr.'s "Just the Two of Us" (1981); other artists
include Steely Dan, Jim Croce, Jackie DeShannon, Chuck Man-
gione, James Taylor, Kate Bush, and Chick Corea. He has also
recorded and toured with his own jazz ensembles.

Rock and Roll Hall of Fame member Hal Blaine may be the most
celebrated session drummer in popular music, playing on a head-
spinning number of hit recordings beginning in the early '60s as a
member of loosely associated studio musicians dubbed "The Wreck-
ing Crew." Blaine drummed on massive hits like The Ronettes' "Be
My Baby" (1963), Herb Alpert's "A Taste of Honey" (1965), The 5th
Dimension's "Up, Up and Away" (1967), the Association's "Windy"
(1967), The Beach Boys' "I Get Around" (1964), Neil Diamond's
"Cracklin' Rosie" (1970), Sonny and Cher's "I Got You Babe" (1965),
The Mamas & the Papas' "Monday, Monday" (1966), Simon and
Garfunkel's "Mrs. Robinson" (1968), and Diana Ross's "Theme from
Mahogany (Do You Know Where You're Going To)" (1976).

Gene Krupa was Blaine's biggest influence. As a boy, he saw
Gene's band at the State Theater in Hartford. "He was the first guy
to somehow shake his head while playing the drums and do crazy
things," said Blaine, "but everything he did was technically perfect."[41]

Music to Surf To

Early rock guitarist Dick Dale is regarded as the founding father of
"surf rock," which he once said could be called "Krupa rock."[42] Dale,
a southern Californian whose pastime was surfing, revealed,
"Where I got my actual feeling and my styles was from listening to
Gene Krupa," adding that "everything I do onstage is with this
drumming rhythm that Gene Krupa put together." He played the
guitar like Gene drummed. When he got his first Fender Strato-
caster, his goal was to get Gene's "tribal thunder sound,"[43] which
led to reverb and expanded amplifier use.[44] Dale's "Miserlou"

(1963) enjoyed a second life when it resurfaced in Quentin Tarantino's *Pulp Fiction* (1994). His guitar sound made an impact on Jimi Hendrix's intense playing, as well as on future heavy-metal stars like Eddie Van Halen.[45]

Before Dale's surf music breached a wall into heavy-metal territory, it led to more surf music. The Beach Boys considered him a major influence on their guitar sound. The group "took Dale's sound and rode it into stardom," said *Billboard*, "which only made his influence ripple to the ends of the earth."[46]

Dale influenced the early '60s group The Surfaris, too. They came up with the famous instrumental, "Wipeout" (1963). Drummer Ron Wilson played a fierce drum pattern to which the others responded on guitar. "Gene Krupa had been doing it for years," said The Surfaris' guitarist Bob Berryhill.[47]

The Surfaris also studied the Ventures, an instrumental group associated with surf music. The Ventures have a Krupa story of their own. Drummer Mel Taylor was an enormous Krupa fan. He heard Gene on the radio as a boy and snapped up his records, finding that Krupa "played with so much emotion and expression." Taylor's son Leon, who took his father's place in the band upon Mel's death in 1996, asked, "How could any drummer not be inspired by Gene?"

The Ventures, who influenced The Surfaris, first gained international fame with their single "Walk, Don't Run" (1960). They covered "Wipeout" (1963) and greatly enhanced it. Mel Taylor absorbed Gene's emotionalism and physicality on record and live. Eventually, the Ventures added Ellington's "Caravan" to their live repertoire; Mel, and later, Leon, used it in tribute to Gene's version of "Big Noise from Winnetka" by using drumsticks to play on the group's bass guitar. Mel "carried on Gene's legacy and I am doing the same by carrying on my Dad's legacy," said Leon. "My Dad learned from Gene. I learned from my Dad."[48]

Punk!

"The next time you listen to your favorite punk albums," said drummer-author S. W. Lauden, "raise a toast to Gene Krupa for inspiring generations of drummers to take new risks while always playing in service of the song—whether or not they're aware of the important influence this jazz drumming great had on their favorite music."[49]

For many rock fans, "classic rock" was the be-all and end-all in the genre. Punk rock, arising during the classic rock era, was more inherently antiestablishment than the rock that shocked the parents of baby boomers, even nihilistic. Punk culture could be in-your-face offensive through imagery and clothing and how they presented themselves to outsiders. Its musical emphasis to the uninitiated was like an unremitting, harsh, aural behemoth. But punk musicians had musical standards, too.

Jerry Nolan, raised in Oklahoma, is best known for drumming with punk groups the New York Dolls (David Johansen fronting), Johnny Thunders and the Heartbreakers, and the Idols. Nolan saw *The Gene Krupa Story* at age twelve and said it "changed my life."[50] He took up drums; he grooved with a friend to "Sing, Sing, Sing."[51] After Nolan moved to New York with his mother, they were among the throngs outside the Metropole trying to catch a glimpse of Krupa, who gave them exciting visuals to remember: the raised arms, the shoulder hunches, the playing "upright," the "rearing back," and the head bobbing. Eventually, Nolan's mother got him inside and they met the man. Jerry found hope for himself because: "Gene was just a normal guy, who dressed and played great, but he could have a conversation with you, making you feel like he was your pal. He was an approachable god."[52]

Nolan's drumming in "Trash" (1973) by the Dolls and in "Baby Talk" (1977) by Johnny Thunders have been cited as homages to Gene. In "Baby Talk," especially, Nolan's "repeated rolls introducing each verse [recall] ... 'Sing, Sing, Sing.'" His Idols bandmate Steve Dior said of Nolan, "If you watched him play drums, you thought you saw Gene Krupa. That tribal rhythm. A lot of floor tom ... He had the style, he had the attitude ..."[53]

Jerry Nolan is generally viewed as the most influential punk drummer. The Sex Pistols, The Clash, the Ramones, and Blondie "played on bills with bands Jerry drummed for," Nolan's biographer,

Curt Weiss, said.[54] Weiss mentioned songs by these groups featuring the Nolan drumming sound.[55] Rat Scabies, the unappealingly self-monikered drummer for the Damned, besides being a Nolan admirer, said Krupa was the biggest influence on punk drumming. Scabies said, with Krupa, it was "all about playing with the band and supporting what's going on around you," until you get to your solo, wherein you could "show off," but then "go back to playing the song. Krupa single-handedly made it seem like the drummer held the whole band together."[56]

John Bonham and Ringo Starr

Along with the previously discussed Keith Moon, John Bonham and Ringo Starr probably make up, to most rock fans' minds, the holy trinity of rock drummers. Moon, Bonham, and Starr cited Gene Krupa as their greatest drum hero.

To John Bonham, the drummer for the iconic Led Zeppelin, "Gene Krupa was a God." Since his boyhood in Britain, Bonham lapped up movies in which Krupa appeared—even *Beat the Band*; John especially enjoyed the "boiler room" scene wherein Krupa played sticks on pipes.[57] Bonham's parents bought Benny Goodman records featuring Gene, including "Sing, Sing, Sing." He "decided that this was the drummer he wanted to emulate and he spent many hours listening to and learning Krupa's technique."[58]

In 1969, Led Zeppelin played Carnegie Hall. *Melody Maker* reported that Bonham "flew around the kit in a blur to the 30 year old tradition of drama laid down by Krupa on the same spot..."[59] In 2022, one writer commented: "It is clear that Gene Krupa was the man who made John Bonham, and for that, we thank him."[60]

It's probably unnecessary to identify Ringo Starr as the drummer for The Beatles. "As he developed his drumming skills he was a great admirer of the American Krupa who he said was 'the best drummer in the world,'" said author-filmmaker Ivor Davis, who covered and traveled with The Beatles for the *London Daily Express* during their first tour of America in 1964.[61] Evident even from a casual listen is the Krupa influence on Ringo's drum solo on "The End" from *Abbey Road* (1969). It's fairly simple, but recalls Krupa's drumming, especially in response to Roy Eldridge, in exciting early 1940s instances of their synergy, such as "Stop! The Red Light's On."

CHAPTER 27

"It Was Just Awful!"

THE 1960S SAW THE DEATHS of two of the four remaining Krupa siblings—widowed Elenor (1964), who had raised Gene, and Peter (1969) both succumbed to heart attacks at ages seventy-one and sixty-eight, respectively. Only Gene's remaining older brother, Julius, still living in Chicago, remained.

"I felt too lousy to play," said Gene, explaining his untimely retirement from live performance following his emphysema diagnosis in late 1967, "and I was sure I sounded lousy. So I decided to go home."[1] He submitted to surgery on his right ear to address hearing loss.

Despite his health decline, Gene accepted an invitation from Benny Goodman to celebrate the thirtieth anniversary of the 1938 Carnegie Hall concert on January 16, 1968, at Goodman's East Sixty-Sixth Street Manhattan penthouse. Gene told people at his table, "I'm falling apart."[2] Many of the old crew were there—Lionel Hampton, Jess Stacy, Helen Ward, Martha Tilton, Chris Griffin, Art Rollini, Ziggy Elman, Carnegie guest musicians "Cootie" Williams, Bobby Hackett, and Buck Clayton, even major music movers and shakers like John Hammond and onetime *Metronome* editor and Krupa friend George T. Simon. Some old hands, besides Benny—

Gene, Hampton, Stacy—jammed until 11:30 P.M. on songs of yester-year like "Someday Sweetheart." According to John McDonough, the unwell Gene played well. "A savage rim shot to the snare," said McDonough, "a throbbing pulse on the bass drum, and the session came alive."

It was inevitable that Gene was, that night, as he was every night, Daddy Krupa. "This man [Benny], apart from being the great genius that he is, musically, had a faculty for picking a tune," said Gene, now joking. "I believe he made a recording of it. 'I Fall Down and Go Boom.'"[3]

———————

IN THE MID-1950S, when Joe Vetrano was just five or six years old, his father took him to a Yonkers softball game. They sat on the third base line.

"Joe, you see that guy running to first base?" said his father, putting his arm around Joe's shoulder and pointing to a short man wearing a gray sweatshirt. "That's Gene Krupa, the world's best drummer." Joe had been playing drums at his uncle's house, but seeing the "world's best drummer" nearby and in the flesh was "'the moment' for me to be a drummer," said Joe.

For years afterward, Joe had been hearing from friends about how nice Gene was and that people could just knock on his door and he would answer it and chat. Finally, on a sweltering July day in 1966, he decided to walk the mile to the Krupa household and hope for the best. His heart thumped as he unlatched and walked through the Krupa gate, made it to the Krupa front door, and rang the Krupa bell. Patti answered; they were getting ready for a funeral, but Gene agreed to come out and say hello. "He was very cordial and not put off at all," said Joe. "I was thrilled and a babbling idiot." Gene asked if he could come back. Joe said yes. Every few months Joe would return and ring the doorbell and Krupa would come out and chat. Joe was hesitant to impose on Gene's family life, so he politely kept the chats short and didn't ask to be invited inside. Things changed a little when, in 1967, Joe's father took him to the Metropole. Gene recognized Joe immediately and sat and talked with the

Vetranos for a half hour before showtime. But it wasn't until mid-1968 that Joe was invited inside the Krupa home. He had the Krupas' divorce to thank for that.[4]

THE BELLINO FAMILY in Yonkers were friends of Gene's going back to the 1940s. They were also friends with Gene's sister, Elenor, whom they called "El," as Elenor and husband Michael had house-sat for Gene during World War Two. Mike Bellino the elder loved Gene like a brother; they met during the war when Mike did Gene's landscaping work. The Bellinos treated Krupa like family. Their "open door" policy had each freely visiting the other as close family members would.

Michael the younger was Gene's godson. He remembered Gene taking him and about half a dozen neighborhood kids to Yankees baseball games in Krupa's 1965 Chrysler station wagon. Gene would buy them whatever they wanted—ice cream and other refreshments. "The whole day was like that," said Michael. "It was just a nice feeling. He was a very gentle person who was, if he could help somebody or do something for somebody, he liked [doing] that."

Young Michael said the Krupa home was a "true step above. It was elegant." It was much bigger and more attractive than the Bellinos' home or the homes of relatives and neighbors. "It was always a treat going out there because it was so nice. His yard was beautiful," said Michael. "There was a patio in the back. A slate patio. He'd like to sit out there. It was nice and sunny in the summertime. We'd sit ... [and] talk."

But Gene was a regular guy. "He didn't have any airs about him," said Michael. "Anybody came to the house, doing work for him, he would talk to them. 'Hi, how are you? How's everything?' He was just a normal person."

I CAN RELEASE her from the daily pain of an unequal marriage, and the struggle to conceal it. She shall be as free as I can render her ... Passion and distrust have left me! ...

and nothing but my grief remains. . . . In an unhappy moment, taken by surprise, and wanting time to think of what she did, she made herself a party to his treachery, by concealing it . . . So let her go! . . . Go, with my blessing for the many happy hours she has given me, and my forgiveness for any pang she has caused me . . . This is the day on which I took her, with so little thought for her enjoyment, from her home . . . She leaves me without blame.
> —John Peerybingle, speaking of wife Dot, thirty
> years his junior, in Charles Dickens's *The
> Cricket on the Hearth* (1845)

In mid-1968, Gene went on an errand. Upon returning home, he found Patti in the arms of his (horse race betting) bookie. The couple divorced after nine years of marriage. Gene was devastated, but blamed himself. "Geezus, Chappie," he told Bobby Scott, "I adopted the kids so they'd . . . have a home and family. Now they're shifted back and forth between us. What the hell did I go and do?" Gene had forgotten that, as he put it, "old men don't marry young women unless they're ready for problems."

"I made the damn mistake and I'll have to live with it, and make the best of a bad situation," said Gene. "There's no one to blame but myself, Chappie."[5]

Fortunately, Patti and Gene's separation was an amicable one. She moved to a nearby apartment. The children were frequently shuttled between the homes, regardless of the more restrictive court-imposed schedule.

When Joe Vetrano rang the doorbell on that fateful day in 1968, instead of Gene answering as usual, it was his manager, Jack Egan. "Hey! You're the kid that's always coming around!" said Egan. "You know what, I think you're just what Gene needs right now. Come on in." Gene was "down," said Egan, because of the divorce. In went Joe, where he found Krupa in the den watching baseball on television. "Hey, kid!" said Gene. "Sit down and watch the game with me." Joe would have preferred talking drums, but he politely joined Gene and watched. A real friendship developed.[6]

Gene got frequent knocks on the door from a variety of admirers. His Yonkers home was a Mecca for drummers and jazz fans, as well as assorted others. Some wanted a picture with him, others drumming tips, and still others to simply tell him, as Joe Vetrano did, how much they admired him. There were plenty of friends and colleagues visiting or phoning. Gene's accessibility was remarkable. Hiding behind an impenetrable gate was not his thing.

He was the benevolent father figure who gave the children in his neighborhood a Christmas present of the LP *A Child's Introduction to the Orchestra* (1954).[7] The kids were introduced to orchestra members like "Muldoon the Bassoon," "Lucy Lynn the Violin," "Poobah the Tuba," "Peter Percussion," and "Crumpet the Trumpet."

Joe Vetrano had a different experience than most. There were drumming tips and sharings of licks. But Gene opened another view to his life to which few were privy. He had kept up with his piano playing, begun in the '30s, and enjoyed learning new classical pieces. Joe wasn't a fan of classical music. Krupa often played a classical piece he had just learned rather than talk about or play drums. Gene would play the piano "all the more when I came over, because he wanted to annoy me!" said Joe. "Now he'd say, 'Sit here and listen to this.' He'd learned a new piece. Then he said, 'Listen to this one!' 'And listen to this one.' So I had to sit through it. But I admired his playing and I admired the fact that he could play as well as he did."[8]

Gene was Joe's surrogate father, teaching him about suits and ties, pressed pants, and dressing impeccably. Krupa would show Joe his closets full of suits, ties, and dress shirts. "I never saw him in shorts," said Joe. "He never wore jeans. On the weekend he would always wear a tailored pair of dress slacks and a shirt, a dress shirt . . . When he went out, it was always a shirt and tie. So he was really a refined . . . gentleman . . . But not overdone . . . I don't think he ever lost touch with his roots."[9]

Joe adopted Gene's habits and tastes in other areas. He liked the fragrance of Gene's aftershave, which was really a cologne called 4711, and bought it for himself. He saw Gene smoke a pipe, so Joe smoked a pipe. "It's very dashing," said Joe, who also bought ties similar to the ones Gene wore.[10] Joe bought wallpaper similar to what Gene used in the stairway leading to the basement. It sported a late '60s, early '70s "paramecium" pattern.

Krupa had a large collection of the ceramic "Toby mugs" made by Royal Doulton. Joe bought a couple for himself. Gene owned a beautiful pocket watch; Joe bought a cheap version. "Gene got a kick out of that," said Joe, who also admired the solid-gold bracelet Gene wore on his left arm; it was probably intended as a weight to keep the left drumming arm balanced with the right. Joe bought something similar to that, too.[11]

Gene Krupa was an avid reader. Joe noticed Gene reading *The Peter Principle* (1972), *The Exorcist* (1971), *The Andromeda Strain* (1969), and *Ball Four* (1970), and read them himself. According to Gene's nephew, Gene H., Uncle Gene was reading A. L. Rowse's *William Shakespeare: A Biography* (1963) during his Yonkers visit in 1970 and "got me talking about the plays."[12] In the 1960s, said Bobby Scott, he would make gifts to Gene of books by Thomas Merton, in whom Gene and Bobby shared an interest.[13] (Merton was a Catholic priest, proponent of social justice, and scholar of Eastern religions.)

Krupa collected beautiful things that were likely too expensive for Joe to purchase himself. "I took my mother over there one day and so he's giving her a tour," he said. "He brought back a lot of things from Europe, like fine china, Lladró ... They're talking about china and crystal and furniture ... like two old ladies ..."

Joe noticed evidence of Gene's religious devotion in the upstairs bedrooms, where a stunning Lladró sculpture of the Madonna, a crucifix, and the Bible were displayed. Gene "was definitely a Catholic but he didn't wear it for everyone to see at home or publicly," Joe said.[14] As fellow Catholics, they would attend Sunday mass at St. Denis's Church. When Saturday night became an option, they would go then instead.[15] Gene didn't separate himself from the other congregants. He was one of them and sat among them.[16]

Fatherhood for Krupa was an unmitigated joy. "He loved both kids like crazy," said Joe. If Gene was sitting in a chair, Marygrace and "B.G." would crawl all over him.[17] Daddy Krupa was always thinking of ways to amuse them. One day he spent a little extra time at a bookstore, Joe recalled, and came out not only with books but an eyeglasses-nose-mustache combination. Gene planned on wearing the disguise at the door to greet the children the next time they visited. He did, and the kids loved it.[18]

B.G. was developmentally disabled, which "broke Gene's heart," said Michael Bellino. But Krupa "played with him. He loved him."[19] In the twenty-first century, B.G. would have been considered a "special needs" child. B.G.'s plight motivated Gene to teach drumming to other developmentally disabled children, which he found rewarding.

Marygrace had behavioral issues; she was known to "act out." Gene told Joe that Marygrace had been acting "fresh." Krupa's idea of correcting bad behavior was to buy her more toys. It didn't help. She was still "fresh." But Gene was a patient man.[20]

JOE RAN ERRANDS for Gene, shuttling Marygrace and B.G. between their parents. Krupa appreciated Joe's trustworthiness so much he let the youngster use his new Ford Mustang Grande (red, with black vinyl top) to go on dates. Gene allowed Joe to take the station wagon for jazz gigs the younger drummer had locally.

Gene was "almost like a Dad, a father, because he wasn't playing as much at the time," said Joe, "and so we spent so much time together he became like a mentor. I learned . . . a lot about life, behavior, and being a gentleman and treating people nicely . . . A lot of little guys would come up to me when I was playing and I gave them a pair of sticks, and encouraged them. I learned that from Gene. You know, if he could do it, so could I."[21]

GENE CONTINUED DRUMMING lessons, years after one would have thought he'd reached a pinnacle impossible to improve upon. Krupa's teachers were Joe Morello, young phenom with the Dave Brubeck Quartet, and drumming educator Jim Chapin, whom Gene had inspired to take up drums back in 1936. "He called me up out of the blue," said Chapin. "He said, 'Jim, I had emphysema, and I wasn't feeling too good. But I'm feeling a little better now.

And I'm getting an itch to play again. Would you come up and teach me?'" Chapin went up to Yonkers Tuesday afternoons at 1:00 P.M. in fall 1968 and spring 1969.[22]

After many months of domesticity, Gene wanted to go out and play again—not necessarily for money, but just to do it. It was the late '60s, but his enthusiasm harkened back to the old Chicago days. He played with whatever group Condon had going at Your Father's Mustache at Seventh Avenue and Tenth Street in Greenwich Village—previously the site of Nick's, where Eddie had once held forth with various Chicagoan groupings. Trombonist Herb Gardner was among the younger members of the Condon contingent. He recalled that, in keeping with Condon's aversion to rehearsals, every performance was a jam session.

This suited Gene just fine. "When you were playing with Gene," said Gardner, "it was never just taking a solo . . . He listened to you. You played something to him and he played something back at you all the time, so that was always fun, because he was truly musical."[23]

Gene could be found in southern New England. Paul Monat, a seventeen-year-old trumpeter, played with Gene at the Stockbridge Inn in Massachusetts, as well as at a club in Wethersfield, Connecticut. An acquaintance had invited Monat to sit in. If Paul was nervous, his anxiety melted away when Gene, with boyish enthusiasm, asked him: "Waddya wanna play, waddya wanna play, waddya wanna play?"[24]

A bigger event in which Krupa participated was the Condon/McPartland Chicagoans engagement on December 5, 1969, at the Holiday Inn in Meriden, Connecticut. The group included a nucleus of the old Chicagoans—Gene, Condon, Jimmy McPartland—plus clarinetist Johnny Mince, a veteran of Bob Crosby and Tommy Dorsey; Welsh pianist Dill Jones, a Krupa Quartet member earlier in the decade; and bassist Bill Pemberton and trombonist Ed Hubble, both of whom had performed with numerous big names in preceding decades. The group merrily played eleven numbers, mainly Chicagoan favorites like "Royal Garden Blues," "Basin Street Blues," "That's a Plenty," and "I've Found a New Baby." Gene, who had taken to wearing a dark green blazer embroidered with his initials, didn't sound like he had been absent from performing at all.

———————

ATONING FOR HIS past marijuana use, and still ashamed of his bout with the law, Gene began speaking to schoolchildren about the perils of smoking cannabis. He held himself out as a prime example of what can go wrong if you do. As a musician, he said, "If you just don't have your full faculties, your technique is not just right … The first thing that marijuana does is distort time and time is the essence to a drummer." He illustrated his remarks by playing on the drums he'd brought along.[25] Gene took his message to kids in courthouses and churches. He said he didn't "dig" jokes about drugs: "They shouldn't have to resort to things like that to get a laugh."[26]

The local Kiwanis club honored him for assisting with their Drug Alert program. He traveled to Albany to perform at a Yonkers Youth on the Move event.[27] Krupa once told Joe Vetrano: "Wherever the kids are, that's where I want to be. I want to do whatever I can to help them."[28]

———————

BY 1970, GENE felt ready to work more regularly. He booked three two-week engagements beginning at May's end. First at the Plaza 9 in Manhattan's Plaza Hotel at Fifth Avenue and Central Park South; the other two at Emerson's in Washington, DC, and the Steel Pier in Atlantic City. "He was so thrilled about how well-received he was," said Joe Vetrano, who drove Gene to his Plaza 9 shows. "He said, 'Look at that. I've still got a name for myself.'"[29]

"Gently dusting his cymbals, grimacing with an upward glance as he throws in a sudden ruffle, his head swinging from side to side," said *New York Times* reviewer John S. Wilson, "he is pacing himself now and even his featured solos involve more crafty showmanship than the wild abandon of his early days."[30]

Joe was puzzled by Gene's encounter with a family that had come to see him at the club. Krupa told Joe he wanted to arrive at the club about an hour early because of an appointment. Accordingly, they arrived early. A club manager knocked on Gene's door. The "people" had arrived. They were husband, wife, and child— Billy. Gene emerged. They chatted and chatted. Joe, as Gene's minder, became concerned it was getting close to showtime, and gently intruded to tell him so. Gene acknowledged the time but asked Joe to retrieve a pair of drumsticks from his "traps" case, which he presented to Billy. The family stayed for all of the performances until about 3:30 A.M.

Afterward, Vetrano and Krupa went to a nearby restaurant. Who should already be seated there but that same family? They walked over to Joe and Gene, again speaking in a friendly and familiar way. Fatherly Gene cautioned Billy about things like going to school and doing homework. Eventually, Krupa and Vetrano parted ways with the family, who seemed like longtime Krupa friends.

Riding home, Joe asked Gene how long he'd known them. Krupa responded that they had just met that night. Joe was incredulous: "Are you shitting me?" Gene explained that the father had called the hotel ahead of time to ask if they could meet before Krupa's performances. Gene being Gene was happy to oblige. "You acted like you know 'em for 50 years!" Joe exclaimed.[31]

———————

GENE KRUPA'S BACK problems began in summer 1970. A freak accident did it, ruining his plans for playing in Washington, DC, and Atlantic City.

Not long after the Plaza 9 engagement, Gene had been pitching for his softball team when he caught his foot on the "rubber" on the pitching mound. As Joe Vetrano put it, Krupa "popped his back out" in excruciating fashion. At first, it seemed Gene's injury had caused a bad case of sciatica, and chiropractic treatment would eventually alleviate the pain. He rested at home, bored but hurting.[32] Then he got a call from Chuck Slate, a drummer, whose small jazz ensemble played weekends at the Chester Inn in Morris County, New Jersey. Slate, a huge Krupa fan, nervously invited Gene to come down and play. Slate and Krupa had a mutual friend in drummer George Wettling, who had died two years earlier.

Gene realized he probably shouldn't accept Slate's offer because of his back pain, but the attraction to play in an informal setting was too great. "I'd love it!" he said. Because of his back, Slate picked him up in Yonkers himself and brought him down to the Slates' home. "Can you imagine?" said Chuck Slate, Jr. "I mean, picking up someone you idolize!"

Gene could have insisted on being put up at a hotel, but relished the notion of spending time with an ordinary family. The only downside was that eight-year-old Chuck, Jr., had to surrender his bedroom that weekend. In the morning, Gene's emphysema acted up. Sitting on the edge of Chuck, Jr.'s bed, he would be "hacking, coughing his brains out," said Slate the younger, "trying to catch his breath." The elder Slate boldly told Gene he needed to stop smoking. "Alright," Gene responded. "I dig it, man. I dig it." But he kept on smoking.

During the day, Chuck, Sr., ran errands. Gene spent most of his time sitting in the kitchen talking to Mrs. Slate as she cooked. Krupa stood out among her husband's musician friends because he didn't only talk about music. It was, said Chuck, Jr., "whatever she wanted to talk about." Gene was thrilled to have a "home-cooked meal" after all the questionable food he had ingested on the road over the years.

The weekend performances attracted overflow crowds. The idea was for Chuck, Sr., to invite Gene up to play on a couple of numbers in each set, which engendered big ovations each time. All was fine until Gene disappeared. They found him in a back room, in horrible agony, "literally collapsed." A family friend found a place for him to get medical attention, which helped. Returning to the Chester Inn, instead of sitting out the remaining sets, he did the opposite. "He got back on the bandstand," said Chuck, Jr. "He was one of those guys who was never gonna let you down." To top it off, Gene made the rounds of the tables at the inn, talking to everybody. "He was such a personable guy," said Chuck, Jr. "He loved people."[33]

This was only the beginning of Gene's long journey to back recovery, but it never really happened. Because chiropractic treatment and other noninvasive measures didn't alleviate Gene's pain, he submitted to a laminectomy in which the "lower fourth and fifth spinal discs" were removed.[34] His postsurgical recovery was a trial. Feeling at his worst, however, he wouldn't turn away people who wanted to meet him—even in his hospital bed! A gay couple in their forties had been sitting a long time in a solarium outside Gene's room. Joe asked them if they were visiting someone. They admitted they were hoping to meet Gene. Joe checked with Gene and told them that he wasn't up to seeing anyone. They said they would just wait. Gene acquiesced. "They're adoring him," said Joe. "They're shaking hands and talking," although maybe only for two or three minutes. "They were so thrilled to see him," Joe said, like "two little kids." Gene finally had to beg off. "You know, guys," he said, "I'm sure you can see that I don't feel well . . . But I'm glad you came by to see me, and I really appreciate it . . ." The two men, having had their dream moment, thanked him for the audience, wished him the best, and left. "There he is, he's in agony, trying to heal from this stupid back operation," said Joe, "and he was still willing to accommodate these two guys who were his fans. That's the way he was!"[35]

More unpleasantness was to come. Gene had become so saturated with painkillers that he needed his stomach pumped. An event was approaching—a combined concert and softball game—on September 26, 1970, to benefit, apparently with son B.G. in mind, "retarded children." It was clear a few days beforehand that Gene wouldn't be able to perform as planned with Anita O'Day and Eddie Shu. The press said Jo Jones was Gene's replacement, but Jones played only on one song. Gene had persuaded Joe Vetrano to take his place for the greater part of the concert. Since people had paid good money to see Gene, and he hated to disappoint, he had himself transported by ambulance to Memorial Field in Mount Vernon, New York, wheeled onstage flanked by a doctor and two nurses, Joe Vetrano standing nervously to Gene's left, and apologized for being unable to perform. The audience, stunned, ultimately "applauded and cheered" for Gene. "He could have done nothing," said Joe. "But he felt the obligation to come out there . . . You make sure you let people know you care."[36]

AT A 1971 Red Balaban and Cats performance in Manhattan, Gene told the audience:

> *The thing we did with Condon [in Meriden, Connect-*
> *icut]—I believe it was a year and a half ago. I enjoyed*
> *it very much that night. I'd been in retirement for per-*
> *haps, oh, two and a half or three years. Well, since that*
> *time, I've had rather a rough time. I had a very serious*
> *operation. This was last summer. On my back. And I*
> *went to a thing given for Louis Armstrong... This was*
> *at the Waldorf... I was very enthused, full of martinis,*
> *and all the bookers were there, and it felt real good to*
> *me, so I said to... [his agent] go ahead and book me on*
> *some gigs. As a result of that, my desk was full of con-*
> *tracts. In sort of a premonition, I thought, well, let me*
> *try it out first, so I got in touch with Red Balaban and*
> *he invited me up to the Red Garter to play. I want to tell*
> *you, before I got up there, I was like a tiger. I was going*
> *to tear these drums to pieces. Well, I couldn't get*
> *through the first set... It was just awful! So for those of*
> *you who heard me that night—forgive me. I'll try to do*
> *better tonight.*[37]

Returning to playing was hard. He kept the engagements to a minimum, meaning no more than a few times a month. "I've never felt more like playing in my entire life," he said. "But I have to cool it and follow a 'reasonable' schedule."[38] He would take his Quartet to mostly local gigs, although they did play in Montreal.[39] Gene might appear, sounding as powerful as ever, as a guest in Detroit with the Six Star International Jazz Band. He performed with Lionel Hampton on Canadian television, resembling a grand-fatherly madman, his white hair flying, his eyes sparkling with the duende he could no longer express physically.

Gene's back pain continued. Although he wouldn't admit it, he was tiring easily, too easily. It was more than just a reduced physical capacity after the heart attack, or the shortness of breath that came with emphysema. He could drum with Balaban and Cats at their usual place, Your Father's Mustache in Manhattan, or in suburban Mount Kisco. Often, he was relieved of his duties by another drummer to ensure he didn't "overextend himself."[40]

On November 26, 1971, Gene and his Quartet joined bandleaders like Woody Herman, Bob Crosby, and Johnny Ray for a "retro" jazz event at the Long Island Arena. Gene "literally stole the show," said Joe Vetrano. "Here was this packed place with all big bands and out comes Gene with his little group. It was obvious the crowd was waiting for him. I remember seeing the crowd stamping their feet and dancing in their chairs. He was magnetic."[41]

In early 1972, Gene still didn't feel that well, but continued to make the rounds at Your Father's Mustache, greeting friends and making new ones. "Krupa is a hard man to pin down," wrote a reporter. "Not because he's unfriendly; truth is, he's too friendly... Try prying him loose for a few minutes and you've got a job on your hands."[42]

On April 3, Gene joined Condon, "Wild Bill" Davison, and a couple of honorary Chicagoans—Kenny Davern (soprano sax) and Gene's onetime pianist, Dick Wellstood—for a performance at the New School for Social Research in Manhattan. Hank O'Neal, since 1972 a photographer, photography historian, and prolific author, was teaching an audio engineering class at the New School. The jazzers' performance was an "an excuse... to have somebody to practice on." His budget was only $400. He easily persuaded them to accept scale ($75 per artist).[43] Hank had just founded the Chiaroscuro record label, which would put the concert out on LP within the year under the title *Jazz at the New School*. The group played early staples like "I Want to be Happy," "Avalon," and two songs—"Sugar" and "China Boy"—which Gene and Eddie remembered well from their maiden December 1927 recording session as part of McKenzie and Condon's Chicagoans.

Raved John McDonough in *Down Beat* about Gene's performance on the LP: "He is inventive, spontaneous, and thunderously exciting. It's not that he does anything that he hasn't done before;

it's just that he does it all so beautifully."[44] Gene's duende was intact, even if it was more difficult to express.

"Someone once said that you whispered with reverence and gave the sign of the cross when you spoke about Gene Krupa," wrote a columnist, somewhat presciently, for *Melody Maker*. This reflection introduced an article about Gene who, despite his infirmities, acted as Slingerland's "genial ambassador" at the March 1972 Frankfurt Trade Fair.[45] Slingerland paid for Gene's service with a case of Scotch, and he was thrilled.

"I was there when he came home," said Joe Vetrano. "He gets out of a taxi cab—an old, dumpy taxi from the airport—and he walks in! I said, 'You took a cab? You...got a cab in front of the airport? That's the way you came home?' I guess he came to terms with his life at that point, and he said, 'I'm just Gene.' He took a lot of delight out of the simple things."[46]

Krupa felt like such a regular guy he had no qualms about playing at nearby Hastings High School wearing household slippers instead of shoes due to an attack of gout that had swollen his feet. He hadn't brought his drums and was obliged to get a set together. "He started inspecting the kids' drums, picking some and rejecting others," said Peter DeLuka, a Krupa friend and the school's music teacher. "When he got up there, with a pieced-together borrowed set of drums, he was great, and the crowd loved him."[47]

OF GENE'S UNHURRIED time in the late '60s and early '70s, Joe Vetrano said, "There are a lot of things that he missed out on in life that when he was retired he was able to do...." A water runoff problem on the side of the house led to planting pachysandra. "He thought that was the greatest thing," said Joe. "So he got into watering. We called it the Gene Krupa Watering Program...And then he got into shrubs...He did little things that any homeowner would do but he finally had a chance."[48]

In September, the original Benny Goodman Quartet appeared together, for the first time in ages, in the *New York Daily News*-sponsored Harvest Moon charity ball at Madison Square Garden.[49]

This was possibly a warm-up for October's Timex All-Star Swing Festival at Lincoln Center, televised later in 1972 and emceed by Doc Severinsen. It featured other legendary jazzers like Ella Fitzgerald, Duke Ellington, and Count Basie. A *Pittsburgh Courier* columnist said, "Age has taken its toll by the looks of the featured artists, but it has not diminished their talent which is still tops." She added that Krupa was "still without peer as a percussionist."[50]

Bassist George Duvivier had been summoned at the last minute to play with the Quartet at that event. He was placed "slightly out of camera range, to be heard and not seen," he said. He wouldn't have been noticed by the audience at all had it not been for Gene. "Gene Krupa, bless his heart," said Duvivier, "made me put the bass down and stand beside him and take a bow."[51]

In December 1972, Gene got a nice surprise. The *Down Beat* readers' poll named him to the *Down Beat* Hall of Fame. He was the first drummer ever selected. The other big honoree, as Jazzman of the Year, was "free jazz" innovator, saxophonist Ornette Coleman. Wrote *Down Beat* editor Dan Morgenstern: "It may seem that Gene Krupa, a symbol of the Swing Era, and the man who put the jazz drum as solo instrument on the map, and Ornette Coleman, not long ago the controversial figurehead of a new phase in jazz, are miles apart—yet our readers have seen fit to honor them both. And that's sort of right, we feel."[52]

Gene still felt unwell. In February 1973, he told Joe, "I've got this sore throat. It won't go away. I think I have the big 'C.'" He meant cancer. The following week Gene saw a doctor and was diagnosed with a form of "benign" leukemia requiring periodic blood transfusions and "medicine to keep the white corpuscles down where they belong."[53] Joe told Gene, "Come on—this'll work, we'll get it fixed."[54]

From the evidence, Krupa may have been suffering from a form of leukemia known as chronic myeloid leukemia (CML). According to Dr. Peter D. Emanuel, hematologist at CHI St. Vincent Hospital in Little Rock, Arkansas, and past editor-in-chief of *The Hematologist*, Gene's symptoms would have included "anemia with fatigue and weakness… [and he would have been] prone to infections." Dr. Emanuel said, "Once you're diagnosed, back then, the

302 ELIZABETH J. ROSENTHAL

average life span would be probably about six months. But he could have had it for a couple of years beforehand, and it just didn't get diagnosed because he didn't have his blood counts checked..."

Gene's heart disease and probable CML made a lethal combination. "The heart's main job is to pump red blood cells around to all parts of the body so they can deliver oxygen," said Dr. Emanuel. "So if you're anemic, you don't have as many red blood cells to carry oxygen around. Your heart then compensates and works hard to get fewer red blood cells around to all parts of the body. The lower the red-count is, the harder the heart's having to work overtime to make up for the anemia."

Dr. Emanuel said an individual's personal habits, such as smoking, would not have been a cause of CML. The cause is a noninherited genetic mutation. If Gene had been diagnosed in the year 2000 instead of 1973, he might have gotten a "targeted, non-chemotherapy agent... [that] revolutionized therapy for CML." Dr. Emanuel said, "Some patients are now being cured and others are on the pill for the rest of their lives and have disease control."[55]

The leukemia diagnosis likely prompted Gene to wax nostalgic and share memories and scrapbooks with Joe. One night at 10 P.M., Joe was about to go home. Gene said, "'Please stay.' So he took out all his pictures, and he took me through a tour of his career. We were there till two in the morning."[56]

THINGS WENT FROM bad to worse for Gene. In April, his den caught fire and was completely destroyed, with everything in it. The home's outside sustained some damage, as did the wall separating the den from the living room. Smoke spread throughout the house. Marygrace had been visiting and already asleep in her room; Gene was in his room working on a puzzle. Then Marygrace appeared. "Dad, I smell smoke." They rushed downstairs in their pajamas and saw the den afire. Gene picked up Marygrace and dashed outside.[57]

The wood paneling in the den was a knotty pine stained dark brown and probably very dry after thirty years. "So it was a tinderbox in that respect," said Joe.[58] Walls were covered in books. "He had his cabinets at the bottom. You know, that was his personal collection." Photos, musical arrangements, memorabilia, transcriptions, were all stored there. The surgical nature of the fire, in obliterating just one room that contained Gene's most meaningful possessions, was bizarre—and especially tragic. The cause may have been a blown television tube, which led to an electrical short. All the clocks in the house had stopped at 9:40 P.M.

The Bellino family and Gene watched as firefighters fought the blaze. Young Michael Bellino saw something else, too—firefighters helping themselves to things of value in Gene's house as they were leaving. "I don't think he was really the same after that fire," said Michael.[59]

Gene, a friend of Tom Carvel's, founder of the ice cream company, stayed at the Carvel Inn nearby while workers cleaned up, repaired, and rebuilt. His ex-wife Patti assisted with home design. Gene dined with the Bellinos on some nights. Tina Bellino, Michael's sister, remembered Gene's dejection as he contemplated the damage to his house and looting by firefighters. "I can still picture that," she said.[60]

Soon appearing in *Down Beat* magazine was an unsigned plea asking its readers to help Gene replace the career items he'd lost. "We think every serious collector who has taken excitement and pleasure from the work of this great man over his long and brilliant career should lend what aid he can in assisting Gene Krupa in rebuilding his library," it read.[61]

GENE PERFORMED AT the New School one more time, days after the house fire. Hank O'Neal, again in charge, didn't know that Gene was as ill as he was, nor about the fire. He just knew he'd been trying unsuccessfully to get Gene on the phone for two weeks. So O'Neal was "terrified." He got to the school early. To his relief, Gene appeared before long, but "seemed in pain and greatly distressed." Only then did Hank learn what was wrong. Gene assured him all would be fine—"he'd taken a handful of painkillers with a glass of scotch ... [and] had his transfusion and was ready to go."[62]

Krupa brought his Quartet—loyal old hands Eddie Shu, Nabil Totah, and John Bunch. "The fact that he showed up," said Hank, "with all of the terrible things happening to him . . . to play a concert for a bunch of kids at the university, and some other people, some grown ups, for 12 cents, really shows you where he was! . . . I mean, Gene didn't have to work. I mean, he had a dollar."

This performance, not commercially released until 2018, is especially wonderful because of new interpretations of old standards, like "Don't Be That Way" and the inexhaustible "Sing, Sing, Sing." The former had elements of jazz-rock fusion. In the latter, Gene's solo relied for minutes on mostly rim shots. They didn't ring, nor were they loud. But Gene turned them into an irresistible flurry of grooving taps building excitement and climaxing as the other Quartet members joined in. Krupa "played his butt off," remarked Hank O'Neal.[63]

CHAPTER 28

"Goodbye, Mr. Drums"

B Y SUMMER 1973, GENE'S FRIENDS were beginning to realize he might not be around much longer. Some of them began taking action to recognize his contributions or arrange special events before it was too late. In early July at a Central Park jazz event, Jo Jones presented Krupa with a "special plaque" signed by, as Jones put it, "practically all the drummers in the world." Gene responded emotionally. "I'll say one thing, ladies and gentlemen. Drummers are the most beautiful people in the world. This is really something... I've gotten so much pleasure doing what I try to do, and I hope that every drummer gets as much enjoyment out of doing what he does as I did, and for them I hope only the best... God bless all the drummers."[1]

The original Benny Goodman Quartet was scheduled in 1973 for June 29 at Carnegie Hall as part of the Newport Jazz Festival, July 14 at Ravinia Park in Chicago, and August 18 at the Saratoga Performing Arts Center in Saratoga Springs, New York. Given Gene's poor health, it's amazing that he did these shows at all. They were highly anticipated performances calculated to bring out the fans. "What did fire him to go on was his instinct for uncompromising dependability," said John McDonough, "which in itself has become something of a minor legend among those who have dealt with him professionally. And perhaps most important, he just wanted to play music…"[2]

Carnegie Hall was a trial for Gene, although his Quartet-mates gave him all the time he needed to rest between numbers. Benny's first vocalist and longtime Krupa friend Helen Ward, in the audience at Carnegie, couldn't stand it after a while. She noticed how Benny, Teddy, Lionel, and guest bassist Slam Stewart took their time between songs fiddling with their seats or checking out mallets or just staring into space, "all just to kill time so that Gene could regain his strength between numbers!"[3] Come the encores, Gene couldn't stand up, so he remained seated as the other musicians left the stage and then returned. "People thought I was nuts!" he said.[4]

David Remnick, editor of *The New Yorker*, attended the concert as a boy with his father. "There was something ominous, even frightening, about the spectacle of this sickly man, now come dangerously alive, at the edge of abandon," Remnick said. He and his father waited at Carnegie's stage door after the concert. Suddenly, an "immense security guard burst" through, "carrying an old man, seemingly unconscious, in his arms. It was Krupa, wrapped in towels." The guard "funnelled" him into a cab's back seat.[5]

Ravinia and Saratoga drew some of the biggest crowds (12,000 and 15,000, respectively) that the Goodman Quartet had ever attracted. Backstage at Ravinia, Gerry Mulligan came by to apologize for his past bad behavior in Gene's late 1940s band,[6] although they had played on the same bills since then and collaborated on one of Gene's 1950s LPs. Mid-concert, Gene was formally presented with his *Down Beat* Hall of Fame award, announced the previous December. Krupa's nephew, Gene H., and new wife, Gail, attended the show and later watched Uncle Gene sign scads of autographs, spending maybe a half hour at it. "The other performers weren't doing this," said Gail. "He alone was doing this." She added, "That was an example of him being quite generous, and treating others with kindness and giving of himself… Especially with him being so sick."[7]

On August 4, 1973, Eddie Condon died at Manhattan's Mt. Sinai Hospital of a bone ailment, a devastating loss for Gene. In his funeral eulogy, Krupa credited Condon for his success. Newport Jazz Festival founder George Wein was struck by what Gene said next. "He made the most beautiful eulogy. But the eulogy was more than just a eulogy about Eddie. It was about himself. I'll never forget it. He says, 'Eddie,' 'cause Gene had cancer, and he said, 'Eddie, get the guys all together'—the guys—that was the key—'get the guys all together, because I'll be joining you soon. And I'll be wanting to play...'"[8]

Later that month, Buddy Rich hosted a party for Gene, inviting drumming influences, friends, and colleagues, as well as Gene's old teacher from Chicago, Roy C. Knapp. Rich brought the original drummer for Blood, Sweat & Tears, Bobby Colomby, as his guest and to represent the younger generation. Colomby described the party as a "thank you and goodbye" event. "We went around the room and did a tribute toast to him," said Colomby. He called the whole thing "amazing" and "meaningful." The proceedings were so emotional, so tearful, that by the end of the evening "everybody looked like shit."[9]

The group presented Gene with a new television to replace the one that had started the house fire, a drumhead signed by everyone at the party, and a sports jacket that Gene wore at home to keep warm.[10]

After that, relatives and friends visited. Gene, bedridden, watched the live broadcasts of the Watergate Hearings.[11] He died on the morning of October 16, 1973, weighing just 112 pounds.

At an October 29, 1973, Manhattan memorial service organized by Frank Ippolito, a drum shop owner and Krupa friend, Joe Vetrano eulogized, "It's enough that someone gets to actually meet their idol. And maybe hear them play once or twice. But imagine what it's like to not just meet your idol but to be able to get to know him as a friend, and love him like a dad. He was my friend, he was my father, he was my uncle, he was my cousin, he was my cohort... What a lucky guy I am."[12]

Press reactions were eloquent and insightful. "Gene Krupa, revolutionary drummer, dies," announced *The New York Times*. "Gene

Krupa ranks with Goodman, with Duke Ellington, and with Louis Armstrong as one of the world's great jazz stars," wrote John Lissner for *The Village Voice*. "His death leaves a giant hole in the music world, one that can never be filled."[13]

Said Bob Mickline of *Newsday*, "His was a natural presence. His theatrical motions grew organically out of his total absorption in playing the drums."

"Krupa was the first drummer to be a solo attraction in his own right and to be recognised as such by the public," wrote John Shaw of the UK's *Jazz Journal and Jazz & Blues*. "His appeal was based on thoroughgoing musicianship, not just brash self-advertisement."[14]

"Gene Krupa began his career in the Twenties as a rebel," said John McDonough in *High Fidelity*. "Then success came, and he became the establishment. Others came along, and he became a tradition. Then a legend. Last October he became a heritage, but the beat goes on."[15]

AFTERWORD

Gene Krupa Remains a Musical and Cultural Force

GENE WAS ONLY SIXTY-FOUR when he died, but his musical and cultural influence is still with us.

A homeless drummer on the streets of New York announces Krupa-style drumming in Martin Scorsese's *Taxi Driver* (1976). The soundtrack to another Scorsese film, *Raging Bull* (1980), features "Drumboogie." In the 1996 "Hurricane Neddy" *Simpsons* episode, Ned Flanders's Beatnik father declines to punish his hyperactive boy because it would be like telling Gene Krupa not to go "BOOM-BOOM-BAH" on the drums. In Episode 7 of *Ken Burns: Jazz* (2001), "Dedicated to Chaos: 1940-45," a homesick sailor serving in World War Two says he'd like nothing better than to go home and hear "Drumboogie" again.

The *Agent Carter* TV series, set in the '40s, used "Drumboogie" in its "Blitzkrieg Button" episode, broadcast in January 2015. A Krupa-Eldridge collaboration recorded by Gene's band, "Full Dress Hop" (1940), was featured in the Marvel movie *Avengers: Age of Ultron* (2015) in a scene involving Captain America and the end of World War Two.

In the Netflix film *The Trial of the Chicago Seven* (2020), Jerry Rubin (Jeremy Strong), declares Gene Krupa the greatest drummer in a dialogue with Abbie Hoffman (Sacha Baron Cohen), who contends that it's Ginger Baker.

The Spielberg-Hanks Apple TV+ series, *Masters of the Air* (2024), tells the stories of American World War Two bomber pilots carrying out raids in Nazi Germany. Gene Krupa gets much more than a name-drop in Episode Six, in which one character, "Rosie" Rosenthal, resents being temporarily sidelined for mental health reasons. He protests to a psychologist that taking a break from flying interferes with his "rhythm." Do you stop Gene Krupa mid-solo "and two weeks later ask him to dip right back in where he left off without missing a beat?" The psychologist replies that Krupa has a responsibility for not only his rhythm, but that of his entire band, or, as the viewer supposes in Rosenthal's case, his flight crew. The episode ends with Krupa-esque toms as Rosenthal, back at the base, tattoos along on the body of the plane.

Gene can impact modern American politics. At a June 24, 2020, U.S. House Judiciary Committee hearing chaired by Jerrold Nadler (D-NY), committee member Louie Gohmert (R-TX) tries to drown out with a constant loud tapping the testimony of former Deputy Attorney General Donald Ayer, who is criticizing the Trump Administration. Despite several attempts, Nadler fails to stop Gohmert. Finally, committee member Hank Johnson (D-GA) says, referring to Gohmert, "Mr. Chairman, can we have Gene Krupa removed?"

Jazz and rock drummers today largely play the drum setup established by Gene, the variety of cymbal sizes and thicknesses he had urged, and the drumming techniques in which he was in the avant-garde eighty to ninety years ago. He was a major inspiration to other drummers from very early in his career, whether the drummers plied their trade in New York, London, or elsewhere in the world. He also played on numerous seminal jazz recordings and was an important part of a jazz movement—the Chicago sound—considered integral to the development of jazz itself. One need only scratch the surface of his drum-shaping of "Sing, Sing, Sing" to feel its worldwide cultural impact. Rock drumming and rock music wouldn't have been what they were without Gene Krupa. He was one of the most important figures in American— and world—music history.

Author Interviews

Albertson, Chris
Apollo 440
Ball, Nicholas
Badanjek, Johnny "Bee"
Bellino, Michael
Bellino, Tina
Berkowitz, Michael
Berroa, Ignacio
Bloch, Ray
Bonoff, Ed
Cangany, Harry, Jr.
Caputo, Randy
Clifford, Doug
Colomby, Bobby
Condon, Maggie
Conigliaro, Brian
Crow, Bill
Dale, Lana
Davis, Ivor
DeMerle, Les
Dorn, Kevin
Edelson, Rachel Goodman
Elliott, Bob
Emanuel, Dr. Peter

Fish, Scott
Gadd, Steve
Gardner, Herb
Gardner, Hirsh
Gibbs, Terry
Gross, Tino
Hancock, Jon
Jackson, Duffy
Kayser, Tormod
Klauber, Bruce
Krupa, Gail and Gene H.
Laing, Corky
Lenderman, Rita Ventura
Little, Steve
Lowell, Lori Sokoloff
Malone, Kenny
Maniatt, Mark
Maurer, Henry
McDonough, John
McEvoy, Michael
Mokry, Geraldine
Monat, Paul
Morgenstern, Dan
Napoleon, Matthew

Ng, Bill
O'Neal, Hank
Ostroff, Marvin
Pacyga, Dominic
Petersen, Colin
Petters, John
Prete, Michael
Rosenthal, Gloria
Rossi, Nick
Schiffer, Mike
Schoenberg, Loren
Seraphine, Danny
Sheppard, Harry

Slate, Chuck, Jr.
Smith, Hal
Smith, Susan
Soph, Edward
Suzuki, Akira
Taddeo, Steve
Taylor, Fiona
Taylor, Leon
Tribuzio, Bobby
Vetrano, Joe
Wein, George
Weiss, Dr. Richard
Zildjian, Craigie

Acknowledgments

My agent, Lee Sobel, deserves the biggest thanks in the world for pairing me with Kensington Books. My editor, James Abbate, has been a dream to work with.

All of my Krupa interviewees gave generously of their time and knowledge and are comprehensively listed elsewhere in this book. A few of them must be singled out for going above and beyond the call of their interviewee duties. They are Kevin Dorn, Bruce Klauber, Gail and Gene H. Krupa, John McDonough, John Petters, and Joe Vetrano, who collectively—and patiently—spent more hours than I can count illuminating Gene Krupa's drumming accomplishments and artistry, affording me access to things I would never have had access to otherwise, and revealing aspects of his life and personality that were crucial to telling his story.

Thanks to Richard Buskin for his invaluable advice, to Hank O'Neal and Loren Schoenberg for suggesting more great people to interview, to Maggie Condon for introducing me to Hank O'Neal, and to Deborah Ross for arranging my interview with the late George Wein, Founder of the Newport Jazz Festival.

Thanks to everyone at the Rutgers Institute of Jazz Studies in Newark, New Jersey—especially Tad Hershorn but also Elizabeth Surles and Vincent Pelote—for their hospitality and congeniality as they helped me sort through their formidable stacks of books of all kinds, archival papers, periodicals, and databases. They took extra time to answer my incessant questions and are to be specially commended for their forbearance.

Thanks to Virginia Frere of Information Diggers, Inc., in Chicago, who rapidly solved mysteries—as if by magic—of Gene Krupa's family background and boyhood. I'm grateful to Stephanie Herz for shedding much-needed light on otherwise incomprehensible Roman Catholic Church birth and death records of nineteenth-century Galicia in Poland. Thanks to Robert White for sharing information about Gene Krupa's maternal ancestors.

Thanks to Kristine Krueger, NFIS Coordinator, Academy of Motion Pictures Arts and Sciences, Margaret Herrick Library, Beverly Hills, for enabling me to peer behind the scenes of Gene Krupa's Hollywood experiences. Ms. Krueger made things pleasant and easy. Assisting were Elizabeth Youle, Research/Special Projects Librarian, and Matt Severson, Oscars.org.

These kind people have also helped me with my research in one way or another: Jeff Apter; Victoria Barnett; Marcia Biederman; Peter Brightman; Sarah Clothier, Manager, American Film Institute Catalog; Chris Dickon; Malte Eiben, Jazz-Museum Bixeiben-Hamburg, Germany; Aidan Gavura, Chicago Public Schools; Jeff Hecht; Joe Jackson; Becky Lowery, the Newberry Library, Chicago; Beth Luey; Lesley Martin, Chicago History Museum Research Center; Dave McMullin, Music Division, New York Public Library for the Performing Arts; Joanne Petersen; Roy Schreiber; Doris Schroeder, Jazzinstitut, Darmstadt, Germany; Catherine Uecker, Head of Research and Instruction, Hanna Holborn Gray Special Collections Research Center, University of Chicago Library; and staff at the Chicago Public Library. Thanks to Henry Maurer for sharing some of his classical music expertise.

Thanks to these individuals for helping me get in touch with more interviewees: Gary Borress, GB Music; John P. DeChristopher, Viper Representation and Consulting; Rob Haywood; Maggi Hickman; Marina Jackson; Gary Krupa; Lynn Rosenthal; Amanda Szabo, American Society of Hematology; and Tuija Takala.

Thanks to the following individuals and organizations for pictures they took or maintained, or both, which they have permitted me to use in this book: Frank Alkyer, Editor and Publisher of *Down Beat*; The Michael Bellino Family; Bill Collins III, Founder, The Sherman Jazz Museum, Sherman, Texas; Maggie Condon; Daniel Esparza, Digital Libraries, University of North Texas; Anahid Avakian Gregg, The Avakian Trust; James J. Kriegsmann, Jr.; Gene H. Krupa; Lori Sokoloff Lowell; Cliff Malloy and Judy Randolph, PoPsiePhotos.com; John McDonough; Kelly McInery, Collections and Print Preservation Associate, LaBudde Special Collections, Miller Nichols Library, University of Missouri–Kansas City; Jane Meditz, Archives Assistant, Irving S. Gilmore Music Library, Yale University; Hank O'Neal; Kathleen Sabogal, Director, Carnegie Hall Rose Archives and Museum; Ronald Seymour, The Maurice Seymour Gallery; Bobby Tribuzio; Joe Vetrano; staff at the New York Public Library for the Performing Arts; and Shutterstock.

Without these repositories of primary sources, I would have been lost: Ancestry.com, Familysearch.org, The Library of Congress's Chronicling America, The Media History Digital Library (Lantern), The National Library of Australia, Newspapers.com, Pressreader.com, RIPM Jazz Periodicals, and The Tom Lord Jazz Discography Online. I'm indebted to Regina Koury, Director, Paul Robeson Library, at Rutgers, The State University of New Jersey, for allowing me access to RIPM during COVID restrictions. Also helpful were Ann Marie Latini, Head of Access Services at the Robeson Library, and Bart H. Everts, Liaison Librarian at the library to the Camden campuses of Rowan University and Camden County College.

I highly recommend these YouTube programs hosted by Loren Schoenberg: *Get Happy: The Benny Goodman Big Band Sessions, 1934-36*; and *Runnin' Wild—The Complete Benny Goodman Victor Small Group Recordings, 1935-39*. Also, be sure to check out Kevin Dorn's YouTube drumming tutorials and John Petters's *Now You Has Jazz Jazz Jazz* radio program on Soundofspitfire.co.uk.

Without my husband, Stan Shur, I wouldn't have been able to start, let alone complete, this book. He bolstered my confidence, pushed me when I needed it, and shared his limitless wisdom with me, as he always does. I love you so much, Stan!

Thanks to my amazing siblings, Maddy and Dan, for helping to care for our mother during her long illness. You made it possible for me to write this book.

Thanks to my high school English teacher, the late Dr. Anthony Demarest, for his encouragement.

I'm immeasurably grateful to Drs. William Holaday, Rachel Levenbach, and Deborah Butzbach for ensuring my health and survival during breast cancer treatment, which happened right smack in the middle of my Krupa research.

Finally—thank you, Gene Krupa, for doing all you did, for being the person you were, for being an inspiration and role model to generations, for giving me countless reasons to tell your life story.

Notes

An Introductory Word: "The Breaking Down of Old Traditions"

1. Cliff Leeman interview by Milt Hinton, the Smithsonian Institution, Reel 3, undated. Accessed at Rutgers Institute for Jazz Studies.

Chapter 1: "Yearning to Breathe Free"

1. Lazarus, Emma. "The New Colossus," 1883; plaque on Statue of Liberty; handwritten manuscript housed at Center for Jewish History, New York; Roberts, Sam. "How a Sonnet Made a Statue the 'Mother of Exiles,'" *New York Times,* 10/26/2011.
2. "These Rare Photographs Show the Last Civil War Veterans, 1890-1950," *Rare Historical Photos*, https://rarehistoricalphotos.com/last-civil-war -veterans-1890-1950/. Accessed 5/6/2023.
3. Thanks to Robert White for the Oslowskis' marriage record.
4. Pacyga, Dominic A. *Polish Immigrants and Industrial Chicago*, University of Chicago Press, Chicago, IL, 1991, pgs. 17–24.
5. *Poland, Select Tarnow Roman Catholic Diocese Church Books, 1612-1900.* Provo, UT, Ancestry.com Operations, Inc., 2014; FamilySearch, 2013.
6. Pacyga, *Polish Immigrants*, pg. 23.
7. *City of Chicago Record and Index of Persons Registered and of Poll Lists of Voters*, Ancestry.com.
8. Sellers, Rod, and Pacyga, Dominic A. *Images of America: Chicago's Southeast Side*, Arcadia Publishing, Charleston, SC, 1998, pg. 27.
9. Ibid., pgs. 62–66.
10. The notorious meatpacking industry dominated an area northwest of the "Steel District." Upton Sinclair shocked Americans with his revelations of the industry's horrific working conditions in his novel *The Jungle* (1906).

11. Interview with Dominic A. Pacyga, 1/21/2022.
12. *Diamond Jubilee: 1882-1957, Immaculate Conception Parish* souvenir book.
13. *City of Chicago Record and Index of Persons Registered and of Poll Lists of Voters.*
14. *Twelfth Census of the United States, Schedule No. 1—Population, Hyde Park Township, State of Illinois, County of Cook,* June 1900.
15. Pacyga, *Polish Immigrants*, pgs. 82–83.
16. Ibid., pgs. 83–91.
17. Ibid., pg. 83.
18. *U.S. Census, Chicago, County of Cook, State of Illinois,* 6/2/1880.
19. *Cook County, Illinois, Marriages Index, 1871-1920.* Provo, UT, Ancestry.com Operations, Inc., 2011.
20. "Notatki Reportera," 12/18/1906, *Dziennik Chicagoski*, pg. 8; "Coroner Sure Krupa Boy was Murdered," 1/25/1907, *The Inter Ocean*, pg. 3.
21. "Lost Boy's Body Found in Swamp," 1/25/1907, *Chicago Tribune*, pg. 6.
22. "Coroner Sure."
23. "Lost Boy's Body."
24. *State of Illinois, State Board of Health, Bureau of Vital Statistics*, Certificate of Death of "Barltomiej [sic] Krupa," 10/19/1916.
25. *State of Illinois, State Board of Health, Bureau of Vital Statistics*, Certificate of Death of "Clem Krupo [sic]," 10/17/1918.
26. "Lost Boy's Body."
27. *U.S. City Directories, 1822-1995*, Record Index. https://www.ancestry.com/imageviewer/collections/2469/images/4724329.
28. Krupa, Gene Harry. *Unfortunate Casting: An Autobiographical Essay.* PhD thesis, Department of English, University of Iowa, July 1975, pg. 6.
29. Interviews with Dominic A. Pacyga, 1/21/2022 and 2/14/2022.
30. Krupa, *Unfortunate Casting*, pgs. 6–7.
31. Author interviews with Gene H. and Gail Krupa, 8/4/2021.
32. *Diamond Jubilee.*
33. Wood, Michele. "The Men Who Made the Music: Gene Krupa," *The Swing Era Into the '50s: How Sex Was Invented.* Time-Life Records, New York, 1971, pg. 38.
34. Krupa, *Unfortunate Casting*, pg. 7.
35. Ibid., pg. 100.
36. Korall, Burt. *Drummin' Men: The Heartbeat of Jazz: The Swing Years*, Schirmer Books, New York, 1990, pg. 45.
37. Interview with Krupas, 8/4/2021.
38. *Fourteenth Census of the United States: 1920-Population,* State of Illinois, County of Cook, Chicago City, 1/11/1920.

Chapter 2: "I Could See This Little Face About Every Night"

1. Krupa, Gene Harry. *Unfortunate Casting: An Autobiographical Essay*. PhD thesis, Department of English, University of Iowa, July 1975, pg. 6.
2. Hecht, Ben. *1001 Afternoons in Chicago*, University of Chicago Press, Chicago, IL, 2009, pg. 275.
3. Savage, Bill. "Introduction." In *1001 Afternoons in Chicago*, University of Chicago Press, Chicago, IL, 2009.
4. Carson, John. "Under Twenty: Interviews," *The Evening Observer* [Dunkirk-Fredonia NY], 9/30/1961.
5. Wood, Michele. "The Men Who Made the Music: Gene Krupa." *The Swing Era Into the '50s: How Sex Was Invented*. Time-Life Records, New York, 1971, pg. 27.
6. Paramount Press Release, "Biography of Gene Krupa," 1/31/1939.
7. Krupa, Gene. "The Voice of Broadway," *Lebanon* [PA] *Daily News*, 9/12/1970, pg. 11.
8. Interview with Ray Bloch, 10/2/2020.
9. Wood, pg. 27.
10. Jeremy, John. "Just One More Time," *Coda*, March 1974.
11. Shaw, Arnold. *Gene Krupa: His Complete Life Story*, Pin-Up Press, New York, 1945, pg. 4; Canadian Broadcasting Corporation Gene Krupa memorial radio broadcast, 10/21/1973 [from 1959 interview].
12. Wood, pg. 27.
13. Ibid.
14. Ibid., pg. 28.
15. "Gene Krupa Memorial Broadcast," Hartford, CT, 11/30/1973 (originally aired in July 1972), https://goldenage-wtic.org/BB-30.html. Accessed in 2019–2020.
16. Krupa, "The Voice of Broadway."
17. "Interview with Zutty Singleton," Smithsonian Institution, Tape 2, Washington, DC, May 1975, pg. 3.
18. Piazza, Tom. "Interview with Milt Hinton," Smithsonian Institution, Tape One, Washington, DC, January 1977, pgs. 6–7.
19. Ibid., pg. 38; Taylor, Billy, "Interview with Milt Hinton," Smithsonian Institution Jazz Oral History Project, 1992.
20. Piazza, pg. 114.
21. Korall, Burt. "Gene Krupa," *International Musician*, September 1972.
22. "Here Comes the Fitch Bandwagon!" Radio host Tobe Reed interviews Gene Krupa, early 1940s.
23. "Gene Krupa Memorial Broadcast."
24. Blesh, Rudi. *Eight Lives in Jazz: Combo USA*, Hayden Book Company, Inc., New York, 1971, pg. 135.
25. Wood, pg. 28.
26. Author interview with Joe Vetrano, 7/14/2019.
27. Blesh, pg. 135.

28. "Arizona Deaths, 1870-1951," database with images, *Family Search* (https://familysearch.org/ark:/61903/1:1:FLVK-7VS:6, April 2020), Mary Krupa, 1923; citing Phoenix, Maricopa, Arizona, reference, Department of Library and Archives, Phoenix, Arizona, FHL microfilm 2,114,519.

29. *Thirty-Fourth Annual Catalog of St. Joseph's College, Rensselaer (Collegeville P.O.) Indiana: Year Book 1924-25, Announcements 1925-26*, pgs. 3, 5, 10–13.

30. Ibid., pgs. 13–17, 21, 26.

31. Ibid., pgs. 62–63.

32. "The Drift," *Stuff* [St. Joseph's College student newspaper], 10/16/1940, pg. 2.

33. "Following the Flickers," *Stuff*, 5/26/1939, pg. 2.

34. Fischer, Ed. "Downbeat King Holds Warm Spot for St. Joe," *Stuff*, 10/8/1938, pgs. 1, 4.

35. Blesh, pg. 136.

36. Fischer, pg. 1; "The Drift," pg. 2.

Chapter 3: "There's a Maniac Who Wants to See You"

1. Lishon, Maurie. *Franks for the Memories*, A Rebeats Publication, Cook's Music, Alma, MI, 1993, pg. 101.

2. Blesh, Rudi. *Eight Lives in Jazz: Combo USA*, Hayden Book Company, Inc., New York, 1971, pg. 137.

3. Mezzrow, Mezz, and Wolfe, Bernard. *Really the Blues*. New York Review Books, New York, 2016, pg. 113.

4. Wood, Michele. "The Men Who Made the Music: Gene Krupa," *The Swing Era Into the '50s: How Sex Was Invented*. Time-Life Records, New York, 1971, pg. 28.

5. Condon, Eddie. *We Called it Music: A Generation of Jazz*, Da Capo Press, New York, 1992, pg. 146.

6. Blesh, pg. 137.

7. Wood, pg. 28.

8. Brown, Theodore Dennis. *A History and Analysis of Jazz Drumming to 1942, Volume I*, PhD dissertation in Music Education, University of Michigan, 1976, pgs. 132, 136, and 140.

9. Dodds, Baby, and Gara, Larry. *The Baby Dodds Story*, Contemporary Press, Los Angeles, 1959, pgs. 20, 26, 39, 41, and 55.

10. Korall, Burt. "Gene Krupa." *International Musician*, September 1972.

11. McClellan, John. "Gene Krupa Studied Techniques of Many Other Drummers," *Boston Traveler*, pg. 21. Caps in original.

12. Blesh, pg. 139.

13. Krupa, Gene. "My Twelve Favorite Drummers," *Music and Rhythm*, November 1941.

14. Krupa, Gene. "Gene Krupa on Drummers," *Metronome*, October 1943.

15. Blesh, pg. 139.

16. Krupa, Gene. "Gene Krupa on Drummers."
17. Ibid.
18. Chamberlain, Dorothy, and Wilson, Robert, eds. *The Otis Ferguson Reader*, December Press, Highland Park, IL, 1982, pg. 18.
19. Blesh, pg. 137.
20. Ibid.
21. Hodes, Art. "Writings: Notes and Manuscripts 1944," *Hodes Papers*, Box 10, Folder 11, Rutgers Institute of Jazz Studies, Newark, NJ.
22. Blesh, pg. 137.
23. Mezzrow and Wolfe, pg. 153.
24. Ibid., pgs. 153–157.
25. Dexter, Dave, Jr. "Young Boyce Brown—A Tragedy of Jazz?" *Down Beat*, October 1939.
26. Hodes, Art, and Hansen, Chadwick. *Hot Man: The Life of Art Hodes*, University of Illinois Press, Chicago, 1992, pg. 29.
27. Hodes, Art. "Playing for Kicks," *The Jazz Record*, 7/1/1943.
28. Miller, Paul Eduard, and Hoefer, George. "Chicago Jazz History," *Esquire's 1946 Jazz Book*, Da Capo Press, New York, 1979, pg. 15.
29. Blesh, pg. 137.
30. Goodman, Benny, and Kolodin, Irving. *The Kingdom of Swing*, Stackpole Sons, New York, 1939, pg. 74.
31. Condon, pg. 150.
32. Blesh, pg. 138.
33. Goodman and Kolodin, pg. 74.
34. Ibid., pgs. 73–74.
35. Fischer, Ed. "Downbeat King Holds Warm Spot for St. Joe," *Stuff*, 10/8/1938, pgs. 1, 4.
36. Shaw, Artie. "The Trouble with Cinderella," *Down Beat*, 6/3/1953, pg. 26.
37. Panassié, Hugues. *Hot Jazz*, translated from the French [*Le Jazz Hot*] by Lyle and Eleanor Dowling. M. Witmark & Sons, New York, 1936, pg. 140.
38. Kenney, William Howland. *Chicago Jazz: A Cultural History: 1904-1930*, Oxford University Press, New York, 1993, pg. 88.
39. Sudhalter, Richard M. *Lost Chords: White Musicians and Their Contributions to Jazz, 1915-1945*, Oxford University Press, New York, 1999, pg. 199.
40. Avakian, George. LP liner notes, *The Golden Era Series Presents Chicago Style Jazz: The Original 1927-1935 Classics*, Columbia Records, Cat. No. CL-632, 1955.
41. Condon, pg. 151.
42. Ibid., pgs. 152–154.
43. Condon, pg. 154.
44. Mezzrow and Wolfe, pg. 163.
45. Jones, Max. *Talking Jazz*, Papermac, London, 1990, pg. 39.

46. Voice of America Interview with Gene Krupa, Part One, 1969. https://www.youtube.com/watch?v=CmwUKPg5n8g. Accessed 5/18/2023.
47. Hadlock, Richard. *Jazz Masters of the 20s*, Da Capo Press, New York, 1988, pg. 124.
48. Author interview with Nick Ball, 8/11/2019.
49. Tilles, Robert. "Percussion Discussion: Innovation," *Music Journal*, 5/1/1967, pg. 42.
50. Schuller, Gunther. *The Swing Era*, Oxford University Press, New York, 1989, pg. 724.

Chapter 4: "I'll Be a Friend with Pleasure"

1. Gene Krupa recorded this side with Bix Beiderbecke on 9/8/1930, with vocals by Wes Vaughan.
2. Jacobson, Kay. "The Golden Pumpkin," *Jazz Quarterly*, vol. 2, no. 3 (1944).
3. Mezzrow, Mezz, and Wolfe, Bernard. *Really the Blues*. New York Review Books, New York, 2016, pg. 170.
4. Ibid., pgs. 173–175.
5. Robins, Anthony W. *New York Art Deco: A Guide to Gotham's Jazz Age Architecture*, Excelsior Editions, New York, 2017, pgs. 81–83.
6. Ibid., pgs. 90–91.
7. Blesh, Rudi. *Eight Lives in Jazz: Combo USA*, Hayden Book Company, Inc., New York, 1971, pg. 140.
8. Condon, Eddie. *We Called it Music: A Generation of Jazz*, Da Capo Press, New York, 1992, pgs. 170–171.
9. Ibid., pgs. 171–172.
10. Blesh, pgs. 140–141.
11. Condon, pg. 172.
12. Ibid., pgs. 172–173.
13. Snyder, Robert W. "Early Twentieth Century New York and Denys Wortman." Sturm, James and Elston, Brandon, eds. *Denys Wortman's New York: Portrait of the City in the 1930s and 1940s*, Drawn & Quarterly, Montreal, Quebec, Canada, 2010, pg. 17.
14. Blesh, pgs. 140–141. Caps in original.
15. Condon, pg. 174.
16. Undated newspaper clipping, Condon archives, New York Public Library.
17. Condon, pgs. 178–179.
18. Blesh, pg. 141.
19. Waller, Maurice, and Calabrese, Anthony. *Fats Waller*, Schirmer Books, New York, 1977, pg. 90.
20. Stroff, Stephen M. *Red Head: A Chronological Survey of "Red" Nichols and His Five Pennies*, The Scarecrow Press, Inc., Lanham, MD, 1996, pg. 97.
21. Shipton, Alyn. *A New History of Jazz*, Continuum, New York, 2007, pg. 106.

22. *Drummin' Man.* BBC Radio Two, Part One, 1/9/2009.

23. Brown, Theodore Dennis. *A History and Analysis of Jazz Drumming to 1942, Volume I*, PhD dissertation in Music Education, University of Michigan, 1976, pg. 337.

24. Ibid., pg. 341.

25. "Swinging Through the Years with Joe Sullivan," *Tempo*, June 1936.

26. Francis, Harry, "Gene Krupa," *Crescendo*, November 1973, pg. 2; Francis, Harry, "As I Heard It," *Crescendo*, March 1981, pg. 16.

27. Ibid.

28. Mezzrow and Wolfe, pg. 254.

29. Kaminsky, Max, and Hughes, V. E. *Jazz Band: My Life in Jazz*, Da Capo, New York, 1963, pg. 22.

30. Voice of America interview with Gene Krupa, Part One, 1969.

31. Peyser, Joan. *The Memory of All That: The Life of George Gershwin*, Billboard Books, New York, 1998, pgs. 171–172.

32. Korall, Burt. *Drummin' Men: The Heartbeat of Jazz: The Swing Years*, Schirmer Books, New York, 1990, pg. 55.

33. Wood, Michele. "The Men Who Made the Music: Gene Krupa," *The Swing Era Into the '50s: How Sex Was Invented*, Time-Life Records, New York, 1971, pg. 30.

34. Pollack, Howard. *George Gershwin: His Life and Work*, University of California Press, Berkeley, CA, 2006, pg. 471.

35. See, e.g., Green, Stanley. *Ring Bells! Sing Songs! Broadway Musicals of the 1930s*, Galahad Books, New York, 1971.

36. Jablonski, Edward. *Gershwin: A Biography*, Doubleday, New York, 1987, pgs. 197–198, 381.

37. Peyser, pg. 73.

38. Kaminsky and Hughes, pg. 47.

39. Wood, pg. 30.

40. Kaminsky and Hughes, pg. 47.

41. Korall, pg. 59.

42. Krupa, *Metronome*, October 1943.

43. Wood, pg. 30.

44. *Drummin' Man.*

45. "Happy Birthday, Louis, From . . . ," *Down Beat*, 7/14/1950.

46. Korall, pg. 56.

47. Department of Commerce and Labor—Bureau of the Census, *Thirteenth Census of the United States: 1910*-Population, City of New York; Department of Commerce—Bureau of the Census, *Fifteenth Census of the United States*: 1930 Population Schedule, New York City.

48. "Hotel History—Hotel Dixie/Carter," *HNR Hotel News*, 9/5/2014. https://www.hotelnewsresource.com/article79667.html. Accessed 4/1/2022.

49. Author interview with Michael Bellino, 5/5/2019.

50. Shaw, Arnold. *Gene Krupa: Complete Life Story*, Pin-Up Press, New York, 1945, pg. 9.
51. Alden, Ken. "Gene Krupa Tells 'Why I Left Benny Goodman,'" *Radio Mirror,* July 1938.
52. Author interview with Michael Bellino, 5/5/2019.
53. Shaw, pg. 9.
54. Korall, Burt. *Drummin' Men: The Heartbeat of Jazz: The Swing Years*, Schirmer Books, New York, 1990, pg. 64.
55. Erwin, Pee Wee, and Vaché, Warren W. *This Horn for Hire*, The Scarecrow Press and the Institute of Jazz Studies, Rutgers University, Metuchen, NJ, 1987, pg. 89.

Chapter 5: "Ask Any of the Boys Around New York"

1. Alden, "'Why I Left Benny Goodman.'"
2. "Gene Krupa Memorial Broadcast," Hartford, CT, 11/30/1973 (originally aired in July 1972), https://goldenage-wtic.org/BB-30.html. Accessed in 2019–2020.
3. Author interview with Tormod Kayser, 11/18/2021.
4. Moeller, Sanford Augustus. *The Moeller Book*, Ludwig Masters Publications, Boca Raton, FL, 1956, pg. 2.
5. Korall, Burt. "A Day with Gene Krupa," *Down Beat*, 3/29/1962, pg. 17.
6. Erwin and Vaché, pg. 89.
7. Balliett, Whitney. *Collected Works: A Journal of Jazz 1954-2000*, St. Martin's Press, New York, 2000, pg. 217.
8. Snyder, Robert W. "Early Twentieth Century New York and Denys Wortman." Sturm, James and Elston, Brandon, eds. *Denys Wortman's New York: Portrait of the City in the 1930s and 1940s*, Drawn & Quarterly, Montreal, Quebec, Canada, 2010, pg. 16.
9. Allen, Frederick Lewis. *Since Yesterday: 1929-1939*, Harper & Row, New York, 1968, pgs. 47, 50.
10. Korall, *Drummin' Men*, pgs. 59–60.
11. Miano, Lou. *Russ Columbo: The Amazing Life and Mysterious Death of a Hollywood Singing Legend*, Silver Tone Publications, Forest Hills, NY, 2001, pg. 79.
12. Goodman, Benny, and Kolodin, Irving. *The Kingdom of Swing*, Stackpole Sons, New York, 1939, pg. 120.
13. Miano, pg. 79.
14. Voice of America interview with Gene Krupa, Part One, 1969.
15. Miano, pg. 82.
16. Ibid., pg. 89.
17. Ibid., pg. 82.
18. Ibid., pgs. 91–95.

19. Krupa, "Broadway," *Lebanon Daily News and Daily Times*, 9/12/1970, pg. 11.
20. Miano, pg. 93.
21. Ibid., pg. 96.
22. Ibid., pg. 109.
23. Korall, *Drummin' Men*, pg. 60.
24. Condon, Eddie. *We Called it Music: A Generation of Jazz*, Da Capo Press, New York, 1992, pg. 231.
25. Morgenstern, Dan. "Fond Reminiscence with Eddie Condon," *Down Beat*, 2/11/1965, pg. 26.
26. Korall, *Drummin' Men*, pgs. 60–61.
27. "The Man Behind the Band: Spud Murphy," *Tempo*, August 1934.
28. Interview with Toots Mondello by Loren Schoenberg, 8/3/1992 and 8/4/1992. https://www.youtube.com/watch?v=VV_v3jfgsVk. Accessed 6/8/2021.
29. Frazier, George. "Bang the Drum Slowly," *Boston Globe*, 10/18/1973.
30. Interview with Cliff Leeman by Milt Hinton, The Smithsonian Institution Jazz Oral History Project, Reel 1, undated, pg. 63.
31. Conniff, Frank. "An Unsung Hero in Rights Fight," Hearst Headline Service, undated (1960s).
32. Interview of Gene Krupa by William B. Williams for WNEW-NY, 1964.
33. The New Deal's National Recovery Administration.
34. Erwin and Vaché, pg. 88.
35. Wood, Michele. "The Men Who Made the Music: Gene Krupa," *The Swing Era Into the '50s: How Sex Was Invented*. Time-Life Records, New York, 1971, pg. 32.
36. Ibid., pg. 30.
37. Ferguson, Otis. "John Hammond," *H.R.S. Society Rag*, September 1938, pgs. 1–7.
38. Hammond, John, and Townsend, Irving. *John Hammond on the Record: An Autobiography*, Summit Books, New York, 1977, pgs. 108–112.
39. Rust, Brian. CD liner notes, *Benny Goodman and His Orchestra: Like a Bolt From the Blue the 1934 Sessions*, Halcyon Records, 2017.
40. See, e.g., Special Correspondent, "Fantastic Band Offered Hylton," 7/7/1934, *Melody Maker*, pg. 1; "Black and White Fantasy: Hylton Undecided," *Melody Maker*, 7/14/1934, pg. 1; "Benny Goodman Black and White Band Offered Contract," *Melody Maker*, 7/21/1934, pg. 1; Our Own Correspondent, "Goodman Fantasy Band Nearer England," *Melody Maker*, 8/4/1934, pg. 1; Hammond, John, "The Black-and-White Band and Its Latest Developments, *Melody Maker*, 8/25/1934, pg. 4; "Trip to England for Black and White Orch. Is Off," *Down Beat*, October 1934, pg. 8; "Black and White Band Blocked by English Booker," *Down Beat*, May 1935, pg. 1; "Hammond Rubs Salt in Yankee Sores," *Melody Maker*, 5/18/1935.
41. Connor, D. Russell. *Benny Goodman: Listen to His Legacy*, The Scarecrow Press and the Institute of Jazz Studies, Metuchen, NJ, 1988, pg. 44.

42. Hammond, John. "Counterpoint," *Melody News*, 11/1/1934.
43. Interview with Jo Jones by Milt Hinton, National Endowment of the Arts Oral History Project, undated, pg. 133.
44. "Buddy Rogers Bids Chicago Friends Farewell," *Down Beat*, October 1934, pg. 8.
45. "Buddy Rogers Band Well Liked at College Inn," *Down Beat*, August 1934, pg. 8.
46. Carroll, Sidney. "Inside New York," *Ken*, 7/28/1938, pg. 84.
47. Author interview with Kenny Malone, 9/21/2019.
48. Schoenberg, Loren. *Get Happy: Benny Goodman the Complete Big Band Recordings* (YouTube series), posted 10/8/2020/. https://www .youtube.com/watch?v=vYX5nrj6AV8. Accessed 7/29/2021.
49. Schuller, Gunther. *The Swing Era: The Development of Jazz 1930-1945*, Oxford University Press, New York, 1989, pg. 28.
50. Jazz round table moderated by Marshall Stearns, 8/23/1955, Marshall Stearns Papers at Rutgers Institute of Jazz Studies, Tape 19 (converted to CD).
51. Author interview with Dan Morgenstern, 1/31/2019.
52. Frazier.
53. Davidow, Thomas D. "What Is Duende?" *Thomas D. Davidow & Associates*, 3/13/2015. http://tdavidow.com/pages/what-is-duende.html. Accessed 6/21/2023.
54. Lorca, Federico Garcia. "Theory and Play of the Duende." Translated from Spanish by A. S. Kline, 2007. https://www.poetryintranslation .com/PITBR/Spanish/LorcaDuende.php. Accessed 6/21/2023.
55. Author interview with Gloria Rosenthal, July 2018.

Chapter 6: "In the Palm of His Hand"

1. "Prospects for Orchestras Brighter," *Melody News*, October 1, 1934, pgs. 1, 6.
2. Goodman, Benny, and Kolodin, Irving. *The Kingdom of Swing*, Stackpole Sons, New York, 1939, pg. 163.
3. Ibid.
4. Hammond, John, and Townsend, Irving. *John Hammond on the Record: An Autobiography*, Summit Books, New York, 1977, pg. 143.
5. Maher, James T. LP liner notes for *The Essential Gene Krupa*, Verve Records, V6-8571, 1963.
6. Ibid.
7. Goodman and Kolodin, pg. 164.
8. Author interview with Loren Schoenberg, 2/20/2019.
9. Connor, pg. 46.
10. Author interview with John Petters, 11/20/2018.
11. Ward, Helen. CD liner notes, *Benny Goodman and His Orchestra From the Famous "Let's Dance" Broadcasts*, Circle Records, New Orleans, LA, 1998.

12. "Gene Krupa Memorial Broadcast," Hartford, CT, 11/30/1973 (originally aired in July 1972), https://goldenage-wtic.org/BB-30.html. Accessed in 2019–2020.

13. Eisenberg, Emanuel. "Up Beat on Broadway," *New York World-Telegram, Metropolitan Week-End Magazine Section*, 4/3/1937. Goodman Yale Archives, Goodman Scrapbook.

14. Ward.

15. Chaban, Matt A. V. "At 90, Still a Haven for Broadway Performers," *New York Times*, 12/29/2014. https://www.nytimes.com/2014/12/30/nyregion/for -90-years-the-whitby-has-been-a-bastion-for-broadway-performers.html. Accessed 4/1/2022.

16. Erwin and Vaché, pgs. 147–148.

17. Connor, *Listen to His Legacy*, pg. 51.

18. Allen, Walter C. *Hendersonia: The Music of Fletcher Henderson and His Musicians, a Bio-Discography*. Published by Walter C. Allen, Highland Park, NJ, 1973, pg. 320.

19. Connor, *Listen to His Legacy*, pg. 53.

20. Ibid., pgs. 51–52.

21. Hammond, John. "N.Y. as Backward as Chicago," *Down Beat*, June 1935.

22. Oakley, H. M. "Goodman's Playing Defies Adequate Description," *Down Beat*, August 1935.

23. Brown, Theodore Dennis. *A History and Analysis of Jazz Drumming to 1942, Volume I*, PhD dissertation in Music Education, University of Michigan, 1976, pg. 354.

24. Author interview with Loren Schoenberg, 8/15/2019.

25. Schoenberg, Loren. *Get Happy: The Complete Big Band Sessions, 1934-36*, "Episode 16." Posted 12/1/2020. https://www.youtube.com/watch?v=ZpVmZF LwWOg. Accessed 8/25/2021.

26. "The Metronome Nominates for Musicians Hall of Fame Gene Krupa," *Metronome*, May 1935.

27. Goodman and Kolodin, pgs. 185–186.

28. Brown, pg. 361.

29. Smith, Hal. *Get Happy: The Complete Big Band Sessions, 1934-36*, Episode 28. Posted on YouTube 3/11/2021. https://www.youtube.com/watch?v= J22WVXTRuTg. Accessed 11/8/2021.

30. Smith, Hal. *Get Happy: The Complete Big Band Sessions, 1934-36*, Episode 30. Posted on YouTube 3/19/2021. https://www.youtube.com/watch?v= lbFr6DURfEM. Accessed 11/11/2021.

31. Gene Krupa interview on *Vibrations* US-TV show, broadcast on 3/5/1972.

32. Peplowski, Ken. *Runnin' Wild—The Complete Benny Goodman Victor Small Group Recordings, 1935-39*, Episode One. Posted on YouTube 12/4/2021. https://www.youtube.com/watch?v=ZpPt9hVvorM. Accessed 12/10/2021.

33. Ibid.
34. "The Secret of the Goodman Quartet," *Down Beat*, October 1938.
35. McDonough, John. *Down Beat*, 3/7/1968, pg. 22. Obtained at Rutgers Institute of Jazz Studies.
36. *The Palomar Summer Suggestions*, Summer 1935, Benny Goodman Yale Archive.
37. Norris, Frank. "The Killer-Diller: The Life and Four-Four Time of Benny Goodman," *Saturday Evening Post*, late 1937, Benny Goodman Yale Archives, Goodman scrapbook.
38. Goodman and Kolodin, pgs. 193–196.
39. Dupuis, Robert. *Bunny Berigan: Elusive Legend of Jazz*, Louisiana State University Press, Baton Rouge, LA, 1993, pg. 112.
40. "Who Can Explain It?" 1956 newspaper clipping, Institute of Jazz Studies.
41. Goodman and Kolodin, pgs. 198–199.
42. Nye, Carroll. "Dis and Data," *Los Angeles Times*, 8/24/1935.
43. Goodman and Kolodin, pg. 199.
44. Dupuis, *Bunny Berigan*, pgs. 114–115.
45. Lockie Music Exchange ad in *Tempo*, September 1935, pg. 2.

Chapter 7: "When Mr. Krupa Beats Those Riffs, He Don't Let You Down"

1. From "Vibraphone Blues," written and sung by Lionel Hampton and recorded by the original Benny Goodman Quartet on 8/26/1936.
2. Kolodin, Irving, "Chapter 7: Swing Is Here" [italics in original]; Goodman, Benny, and Kolodin, Irving, *The Kingdom of Swing*, Stackpole Sons, New York, 1939, pgs. 172–174.
3. Goodman and Kolodin, pgs. 201–202; Rollini, Arthur. *Thirty Years with the Big Bands*, University of Illinois Press, Urbana, IL, 1987, pg. 45.
4. Goodman and Kolodin, pg. 204; Dmytryk, Jean Porter, *Chicago Jazz and Then Some*, BearManor Media, Albany, GA, 2010, pg. 81.
5. "Goodman's Music Is a Classic in Modern Idiom," *Down Beat*, November 1935.
6. Slingerland ad, "Says Gene Krupa, 'The King of Swing,'" *Down Beat*, November 1935.
7. Goodman and Kolodin, pg. 209.
8. Cone, Carl. "Society and Musicians Sit Spellbound by Brilliance of Goodman Band," *Down Beat*, December 1935–January 1936.
9. "Benny Goes to Town!" *Orchestra World*, January 1936.
10. Ward, Geoffrey C., and Burns, Ken. *Jazz: A History of America's Music*, Alfred A. Knopf, 2000, pg. 234.
11. Sales, Grover. *Jazz: America's Classical Music*, Da Capo Press, 1992, pg. 109.

12. "Too Advanced Jazz for U.S., Clicks Big in France, and England," *Variety*, 12/4/1935.
13. Schoenberg, Loren. *Get Happy: Benny Goodman: The Complete Big Band Sessions, 1935-1936*, Episode 23, posted on YouTube 2/7/2021. https://www.youtube.com/watch?v=VZEwyCpZOmo. Accessed 10/1/2021.
14. P.E.M., "Kickin' the Discs Around," *Music and Rhythm*, August 1941, pg. 28.
15. Avakian, George M. "Collector's Corner," *Tempo*, 3/18/1940.
16. Chilton, John. *Roy Eldridge: Little Jazz Giant*, Continuum, London and New York, 2002, pg. 129.
17. Meehan, Reg. "Why Roy Eldridge Gave up His Band to Join Gene Krupa," *Music and Rhythm*, June 1941, pg. 11.
18. "WB Angle in Chi," *Variety*, 4/15/1936, pg. 46.
19. Schenker, Anatol. CD liner notes, *Gene Krupa and His Orchestra 1935-1938*, Classics 754, 1994.
20. *Music and Rhythm*, May 1941.
21. Wilson, Teddy, Ligthart, Arie, and van Loo, Humphrey. *Teddy Wilson Talks Jazz*, Cassell, New York, 1996, pg. 40.
22. Martin, Henry, and Waters, Keith. *Jazz: The First 100 Years*, Enhanced Third Edition, Cengage Learning, 2016, pg. 150.
23. Morgan, Alun. "The Great Big Small Bands," *Swing: A 'Jazz and Blues' Quarterly Retrospect*, pg. 15, Rutgers Institute of Jazz Studies.
24. Hampton, Lionel, and Haskins, James. *Hamp: An Autobiography*. Warner Books, New York, 1989, pg. 53.
25. Krupa, Gene. "Gene Krupa on Drummers," *Metronome*, October 1943.
26. Krupa, Gene. "My Twelve Favorite Drummers," *Music and Rhythm*, November 1941.
27. Hampton and Haskins, pgs. 26–33.
28. Ward and Burns, pg. 236.
29. Goode, Mort. LP box set liner notes, "Volume 3: The Second Half of 1936," *Benny Goodman: The RCA Victor Years 1935–39*, RCA/Ariola International, Cat No. 5704-1-RB.
30. Connor, D. Russell. "Program Notes: Introduction," LP liner notes, *Benny Goodman Treasure Chest*, BOMR, 716502, a Division of Book-of-the-Month-Club, Inc., 1981.
31. Abel. "Hotel Pennsylvania (New York)," *Variety*, 10/13/1937.
32. Vaché, Warren W. *Sittin' in With Chris Griffin*, Studies in Jazz No. 46, The Scarecrow Press and the Institute of Jazz Studies, Lanham, MD, 2005, pg. 48.
33. Rollini, pgs. 44, 52, 58, 120.
34. Collier, James Lincoln. *Benny Goodman and the Swing Era*, Oxford University Press, New York, 1989, pgs. 91, 156.
35. See, e.g., Goodman, Benny, and Kolodin, Irving. *The Kingdom of Swing*, Stackpole Sons, New York, 1939, pgs. 163–164.

36. Erwin, Pee Wee, and Vaché, Warren W. *This Horn for Hire*, The Scarecrow Press and the Institute of Jazz Studies, Rutgers University, Metuchen, NJ, 1987, pgs. 137–139.
37. Cook, Rob. *The Slingerland Book*, Second Edition, Rebeats, Alma, MI, 2004, pg. 27.
38. Ibid., pg. 35.
39. Ibid., pg. 36.
40. Tegler, Brooks. *GK: The Tools That Built the GENE KRUPA Legend*, Rebeats, 2021, pg. 22.
41. Cook, pg. 37.
42. The Howard Miller Show CBS radio interview with Gene Krupa, apparently broadcast in Chicago around 1956-1957. Taken from the *Classic Archives Old-Time Radio Channel*, https://www.youtube.com/watch?v=f6jA L4vvJuE. Accessed 4/29/2020.
43. Connor, D. Russell. *Benny Goodman: Listen to His Legacy*, The Scarecrow Press, Inc. and the Institute of Jazz Studies, Metuchen, NJ, 1988, pg. 46.
44. Author interview with Craigie Zildjian, 2/7/2019.
45. Cohan, Jon. *Star Sets: Drum Kits of the Great Drummers*, Hal Leonard, Milwaukee, WI, 1995, pgs. 5, 20, 34, 35, 63, 67, 68, 71, 73, 77, 89, 91, 93, photo section [pg. 7].
46. Ludwig, William F. II. *The Making of a Drum Company: The Autobiography of William F. Ludwig II*, Rebeats, Alma, MI, 2001, pgs. 21, 28, 29.

Chapter 8: "A Guy Named Krupa Plays the Drums Like Thunder"

1. From "I Like to Recognize the Tune" by Rodgers and Hart, featured in the 1939 Broadway musical, *Too Many Girls*; recorded by Gene Krupa and His Orchestra on 9/20/1939, with vocal by Irene Daye.
2. Rowland, Sam. "Gene Krupa Tells His Idea of Drumming," *Down Beat*, July 1936.
3. Frazier, George, "Satchelmo's Band Is Worlds Worst; Norvo Excels," *Down Beat* June 1936; Simon, George T., "What's What," *Rhythm*, September 1936.
4. Rowland, ibid., *Down Beat*, July 1936.
5. Krupa, Gene. "Drummers' Dope," *Metronome*, March 1937.
6. Ibid.
7. Krupa, Gene. "Drummers' Dope," *Metronome*, April 1937.
8. Krupa, Gene. "Krupa Urges Study of Drum Rudiments," *Metronome*, January 1938.
9. Wright, Gordon. "Best Record Sides of 1936," *Metronome*, January 1937.
10. Schoenberg, Loren. "The Sessions," CD liner notes, *Benny Goodman: The Birth of Swing (1935-1936)*, BMG Music-Bluebird, 1991, Cat. No. 61038-2.

11. Smith, Hal. *Get Happy: The Complete Benny Goodman Big Band Sessions, 1934-36, Episode 30*, posted 3/19/2021, https://www.youtube.com/watch?v=lbFr6DURfEM. Accessed 11/11/2021.
12. His son was singer-songwriter Harry Chapin.
13. Jim Chapin interview with Arthor von Blomberg, 1994, *Gene Krupa Show*, posted 5/30/2012, https://www.facebook.com/watch/?v=4091837299470. Accessed 2/16/2022; *Jim Chapin: The Charismatic Krupa 1995*, posted 9/9/2018, https://www.youtube.com/watch?v=GALfY3X3KFQ. Accessed 5/1/2020.
14. Tracy, Sheila. *Bands, Booze and Broads*, Mainstream Publishing, Edinburgh and London, 1995, pg. 115.
15. Hammond, John. "Hot Club Used as Pawn—Says J.H.—Mills May Start Record War," *Down Beat*, April 1937, pg. 16.
16. Silver, Nathan. *Lost New York*, American Legacy Press, New York, 1967, pg. 82.
17. Connor, *Listen to His Legacy*, pg. 66.
18. "Swing Master at the Met," *Boston Post*, May 21, 1937.
19. Rollini, pg. 56.
20. Wilson, Teddy, Ligthart, Arie, and van Loo, Humphrey. *Teddy Wilson Talks Jazz*, Cassell, New York, 1996, pg. 34.
21. *Caesar's Hour*, 11/1/1954, https://www.youtube.com/watch?v=OsJVNSOk7Q4&t=35s. Accessed circa 2022.
22. Ferguson, Harry, Jr. "Benny and His Boys on a One Nighter," *Metronome*, November 1937.
23. Jazz round table moderated by Marshall Stearns, 8/23/1955, Marshall Stearns Papers at Rutgers Institute of Jazz Studies, Tape 19 (converted to CD).
24. Ad, "Lots of Fun to Play Drums," *New York Daily News*, 6/7/1939, pg. 28.
25. Dmytryk, Jean Porter. *Chicago Jazz and Then Some*, BearManor Media, Albany, GA, 2010, pg. 130.
26. Collier, *Swing Era*, pg. 220.
27. "Krupa Signs New Contract With Goodman," *Down Beat*, May 1937.
28. "8 Whites & 6 Negroes Win Places in All Time Swing Band," *Down Beat*, July 1936, pg. 1; "All-American Band Voting Reveals Taste in Music World," *Down Beat*, December 1937, pg. 22; "Krupa, Wilson Winners," *Metronome*, January 1937.
29. "Goodman, Krupa, Dawn Win O.W. Awards," *Orchestra World*, February 1938, pg. 11.
30. "Life on the American Newsfront: Worst Air Crash in U.S. History Takes 19 Lives," *Life*, 11/1/1937, pgs. 38–39.
31. "Science & Industry: Hayden Planetarium Shows Four Ways in Which the World May End," *Life*, 11/1/1937, pgs. 54–58.
32. "Showing Itself in Spain Italy Offers to Withdraw," *Life*, 11/1/1937, pgs. 64–66.

33. "Art: Negro Who Turned Sculptor at God's Command Gets Manhattan Exhibition," *Life*, 11/1/1937, pg. 79.
34. "The Camera Overseas: The Yellow Race Looks at Its Dead in War," *Life*, 11/1/1937, pg. 100.
35. "The Lunts, World's Greatest Acting Team, Again Make Fun of Married Love," *Life*, 11/1/1937, pgs. 106–109.
36. "Life Goes to a Party To Listen to Benny Goodman and His Swing Band," *Life*, 11/1/1937, pgs. 120–124.
37. "Memphis Censors Cut Race Stars from Film," *Pittsburgh Courier*, 2/5/1938, pg. 6.
38. O'Kane, Bernice. "It's a Fact!" *Tribune* (Watertown, MA), 5/7/1937.
39. Goodman, Benny, and Kolodin, Irving. *The Kingdom of Swing*, Stackpole Sons, New York, 1939, pg. 206.
40. Hammond, John. "Hysterical Public Split Goodman and Krupa," *Down Beat*, April 1938, pg. 6.
41. Hammond, John. "Goodman 'Killer' Arrangements Detracts from Band's Musicianship," *Down Beat*, February 1937, pg. 7.
42. "Musicians," *Down Beat*, 12/6/1973, pg. 35.
43. Alden, Ken. "Gene Krupa Tells 'Why I Left Benny Goodman,'" *Radio Mirror*, July 1938.
44. Krupa, Gene. "Gene Krupa on Drummers," *Metronome*, October 1943.
45. Crease, Stephanie Stein. *Rhythm Man, Chick Webb and the Beat That Changed America*, Oxford University Press, New York, 2023, pgs. 20–21.
46. Ibid., pgs. 8–16.
47. Ibid., pgs. 20–21.
48. Ellington, Duke. "Jazz as I Have Seen It," *Swing: The Guide to Modern Music*, July 1940, pg. 10.
49. Crease, pg. 56.
50. Hammond, John, "The Critical Viewpoint: John Hammond Says," *Tempo*, June 1937, pg. 2; Oakley, Helen, "Call Out Riot Squad To Handle Mob at Goodman-Webb Battle," *Down Beat*, June 1937, pg. 1.
51. See, e.g., Bradshaw, Tiny. "Swingland," *Philadelphia Independent* [African-American newspaper], 5/23/1937; "Chick Webb Defeats Ben Goodman," *Metronome*, June 1937; Hammond, pg. 2.
52. Krupa, Gene. "'Chick Cut Me to Ribbons!'—Gene," *Down Beat*, August 1939, pg. 8.
53. Krupa, Gene. "My Twelve Favorite Drummers," *Music and Rhythm*, November 1941.
54. Lucas, John. "Beating It Out With the Tubmen," *Down Beat*, 6/1/1943, pg. 14.
55. Krupa, Gene. "Gene Krupa on Drummers," *Metronome*, October 1943.
56. Bushell, Garvin, and Tucker, Mark. *Jazz From the Beginning*, The University of Michigan Press, Ann Arbor, MI, 1990, pg. 104.

57. "Chick Webb's Song Hits Are His Final Dirge," *The Dayton Forum* [Ohio, an African-American newspaper], 6/30/1939.

58. "Overtones," *Tempo*, August 1939, pg. 2.

59. Collier, *Swing Era*, pgs. 255–256.

60. Schoenberg, Loren. *Runnin' Wild—The Complete Benny Goodman Victor Small Groups, 1935-39, Episode 2*, posted on 12/11/2021, https://youtube.com/watch?v=n3FfdOq-t7c. Accessed 12/22/2021.

61. Feather, Leonard, *The Book of Jazz*, Horizon Press, New York, 1957, pg. 166; Giddins, Gary, and DeVeaux, Scott, *Jazz*, W. W. Norton & Company, New York, 2009, pgs. 183–184.

62. Green, Abel. "Disk Reviews," *Variety*, 9/4/1935.

63. Scholl, Warren. "Release New Records on Mezz Mezzrow and All-Star White & Black Band," *Down Beat*, December-January 1935-1936.

64. Ferguson, Otis. *The Otis Ferguson Reader*. December Press, Highland Park, IL, 1982, pg. 71.

65. *Ken Burns: The Roosevelts: An Intimate History*. "Part Five: The Rising Road (1933-1939)." Broadcast on 9/18/2014.

66. *Ken Burns: The Roosevelts: An Intimate History*. "Part Seven: A Strong and Active Faith (1944-1962)." Broadcast on 9/20/2014.

67. *Jazz Night in America*, "The Legacy of the Benny Goodman Quartet," NPR, from WBGO and Jazz at Lincoln Center, posted on 4/21/2016, https://www.npr.org/2016/04/21/475146316/the-legacy-of-the-benny-goodman-quartet. Accessed 6/15/2021.

68. Keller, Keith. *Oh, Jess! A Jazz Life*, The Mayan Music Corporation, New York, 1989, pg. 86.

69. Author interview with John Petters, 6/9/2019.

70. Smith, Hal. *Get Happy: Benny Goodman: The Complete Big Band Sessions, 1934-36, Episode 19*, posted on 1/1/2021, https://www.youtube.com/watch?v=b_RR8DWmW-8. Accessed 8/31/2021.

71. Connor, pg. 71.

72. Schoenberg, Loren. *Get Happy: Benny Goodman: The Complete Big Band Sessions, 1935-1936, Episode 29*, hosted by Loren Schoenberg, posted on YouTube 3/13/2021, https://www.youtube.com/watch?v=x8iziJ42DXY. Accessed 11/10/2021.

73. Schoenberg, Loren. *Runnin' Wild—The Complete Benny Goodman Victor Small Groups, 1935-39, Episode 8*, https://www.youtube.com/watch?v=gaJoyh5_Ezw. Accessed 2021.

74. Schoenberg, Loren. *Get Happy: Benny Goodman: The Complete Big Band Sessions, 1935-1936, Episode 31*, posted 3/25/2021, https://www.youtube.com/watch?v=IfM-_1G8clM. Accessed 11/12/2021.

75. Morgenstern, Dan. *Drummin' Man Part Two*, broadcast on BBC Radio Two, 1/16/2009.

76. Brucato, Richard. "Krupa Band Loud, Brassy, Does O.K. on First Big Job," *Orchestra World*, June 1938, pg. 10.
77. Hammond, John, "Benny Goodman's Carnegie Hall Concert," *Tempo*, February 1938, pg. 8; Hammond, John, "Krupa Beat Weak & Lips Page Band Just Bad," *Down Beat*, September 1938, pg. 2; Feather, Leonard. "Band Reviews: Gene Krupa B+," *Metronome*, May 1943.
78. Erwin, Pee Wee, and Vaché, Warren W. *This Horn for Hire*, The Scarecrow Press and the Institute of Jazz Studies, Rutgers University, Metuchen, NJ, 1987, pgs. 89–90.
79. Firestone, Ross. *Swing, Swing, Swing: The Life and Times of Benny Goodman*, W. W. Norton & Co., New York, 1993, pg. 206.
80. Schuller, Gunther. *The Swing Era: The Development of Jazz 1930-1945*, Oxford University Press, New York, 1989, pg. 29.
81. Wilson, Teddy, Ligthart, Arie, and van Loo, Humphrey. *Teddy Wilson Talks Jazz*, Cassell, New York, 1996, pg. 40.
82. Author interview with Kevin Dorn 8/16/2021.
83. Brown, Theodore Dennis. *A History and Analysis of Jazz Drumming to 1942, Volume I*, PhD dissertation in Music Education, University of Michigan, 1976, pgs. 372, 379.

Chapter 9: "Hey!"

1. Hancock, Jon. *Benny Goodman: The Famous 1938 Carnegie Hall Jazz Concert*, Prancing Fish Publishing, UK, 2008, pg. 47.
2. McDonough, John. "The Class of '38 Swings Into '78," *Chicago Tribune*, 1/15/1978, Arts and Fun, Section 6, pg. 3.
3. Author interview with John Petters, 11/20/2018.
4. The New York Preservation Archive Project. https://www.nypap.org/preservation-history/carnegie-hall/#:~:text=The%20fa%C3%A7ade%20of%20Carnegie%20Hall%20exhibits%20a%20prominent,process%2C%20with%20extremely%20thick%20concrete%20and%20masonry%20walls. Accessed 8/4/2023; Backes, Aaron D. "History of New York's Carnegie Hall," ClassicNewYorkHistory.com, posted circa 2020, https://classicnewyorkhistory.com/history-of-new-yorks-carnegie-hall/. Accessed 8/4/2023.
5. "Dixie Senators Leave Senate Floor as 'Torture Lynchings' Are Described," *Pittsburgh Courier*, 2/5/1938, pg. 6.
6. Ewing, Annemarie. "Carnegie Hall Gets First Taste of Swing," *Down Beat*, February 1938, pg. 5.
7. Hancock, pg. 82.
8. Ewing, pg. 5.
9. Ibid., pg. 7.
10. "A 'Swing Concert,'" 1/17/1938, clipping from Benny Goodman scrapbook, Goodman Papers, Yale University.

11. Davis, Hal. "Radio Spotlight: Radio Ed Hears Special Goodman Concert Piping," *Orchestra World*, February 1938.
12. R.C.B. "Program of Swing in Carnegie Hall," *New York World-Telegram*, 1/17/1938.
13. Simon, George T. "Benny and Cats Make Carnegie Debut Real Howling Success," *Metronome*, February 1938, pg. 44.
14. Hancock, pg. 105.
15. Morrison, Hobe. "Goodman's Vipers Slay the Cats," *Variety*, 1/19/1938, pg. 46.
16. Mantle, Burns. "Goodman Jam Session Jams Carnegie Hall," *New York Daily News*, 1/18/1938, pg. 43.
17. Simon, "Benny and Cats Make Carnegie Debut Real Howling Success."
18. R.C.B. "Program of Swing."
19. Perkins, Francis. "Benny Goodman 'Swings It Out' in Carnegie Hall, *New York Herald-Tribune*, 1/17/1938.
20. H.E.P. "Goodman Came, Saw, and Laid a Golden Egg!" *Down Beat*, February 1938, pg. 6.
21. Hammond, John. "Benny Goodman's Carnegie Hall Concert," *Tempo*, February 1938, pgs. 8, 12.
22. Author interview with Kevin Dorn, 2/19/2022.
23. Tackley, Catherine. *Benny Goodman's Famous 1938 Carnegie Hall Jazz Concert*, Oxford University Press, New York, 2012, pgs. 119–124.
24. Hancock, pg. 114.
25. Ibid.
26. Tackley, pg. 91.
27. Firestone, pg. 161.
28. Associated Press. "Beatle Bumbling Rouses Longing for Benny Goodman," *Boston Record-American*, 5/1/1964.
29. Tilles, Robert. "Percussion Discussion: Innovation," *Music Journal*, 5/1/1967, pg. 43.
30. Rubens, William Roger. "Radiohound," *Orchestra World*. September 1936.
31. Erwin, Pee Wee, and Vaché, Warren W., *This Horn for Hire*, The Scarecrow Press and the Institute of Jazz Studies, Rutgers University, Metuchen, NJ, 1987, pg. 131; Vaché, Warren W., *Sittin' in With Chris Griffin*, Studies in Jazz No. 46, The Scarecrow Press and the Institute of Jazz Studies, Lanham, MD, 2005, pg. 45.
32. Fields, Howard. "Woodshed Transcription: Gene Krupa's Drum Solo on 'Sing, Sing, Sing,'" *Down Beat*, May 1995, pg. 66.
33. Author interview with Kevin Dorn, 2/19/2022.
34. Sykes, Guy. "Benny Goodman's Carnegie Hall Concert," *Tempo*, February 1938, pg. 9.
35. Author interview with Kevin Dorn, 9/13/2022.
36. Hanscom, Joe. "Pickets, Cameras Attend Concert," *Metronome*, February 1938, pg. 40.

37. Ewing, pg. 5.
38. Shaw, pg. 20; Hancock, pgs. 118–119.
39. Ewing, pg. 7.
40. Krupa, Gene. "Krupa Gets His Kicks," *Metronome*, February 1938.
41. Author interviews with Ed Bonoff, 2/25/2019 and 3/6/2019.
42. "'Sing, Sing, Sing,' Is Musicians' Favorite Arrangement," *Down Beat*, December 1937, pg. 23.
43. G. W. "Best Records of 1937," *Metronome*, January 1938, pg. 21.
44. Gardner, Elysa. "Back in the Swing of Things," *Los Angeles Times*, 8/2/1998.
45. Zirpolo, Mike. "'Sing, Sing, Sing' (1937) Benny Goodman," *Swing & Beyond: Where Swing Is King*, posted 7/9/2017. https://swingandbeyond.com/2017/07/09/sing-sing-sing-1937-benny-goodman/. Accessed 7/18/2019.
46. Decker, Todd. *Music Makes Me: Fred Astaire and Jazz*, University of California Press, Los Angeles, 2011, pg. 223.
47. Stearns, M. W. "Victor's Symposium of Swing," *Tempo*, October 1937, pg. 20.
48. Deffaa, Chip. *Swing Legacy*, The Scarecrow Press and the Institute of Jazz Studies, Rutgers University, 1989, pg. 76.
49. Brown, Theodore Dennis. *A History and Analysis of Jazz Drumming to 1942, Volume I*, PhD dissertation in Music Education, University of Michigan, 1976, pg. 438.
50. Cliff Leeman, interviewed by Milt Hinton, Smithsonian Institution, Reel One, undated.
51. See, e.g., Stearns, M. W. "New Records: Briefs on the Best Releases of the Month," *Tempo*, June 1938, pg. 9.
52. Sinclair, Amy. "EMI Catalogue Partnership and EMI Robbins Catalog, Inc. v. Hill, Holliday, Connors, Cosmopulous, Inc. and Spalding Sports Worldwide," 2000 U.S. App. LEXIS 30761. 11 DePaul J. Art, Tech., & Intell. Prop. L. 319 (2001).
53. Horton, Cole. "From World War to Star Wars: The Cantina," *Starwars.com*, posted 8/19/2014, https://www.starwars.com/news/from-world-war-to-star-wars-the-cantina.
54. Author interview with Mike McEvoy, 2/18/2022.
55. Brown, pg. 419.
56. Interview by Milt Hinton of Quentin Jackson, Smithsonian Institution, Reel Four of Seven, June 1976, pg. 29.

Chapter 10: "I'm Givin' You Air"

1. From "Like the Fella Once Said," recorded by Gene Krupa and His Orchestra on 9/30/1940, with vocal by Irene Daye.
2. Shaw, Arnold. *Gene Krupa: His Complete Life Story*, Pin-Up Press, New York, 1945, pg. 9.

3. Holly, Hal. *Tempo*, October 1937, pg. 18.
4. Cerulli, Dom. "Gene Krupa," *International Musician*, April 1960, pg. 11.
5. Alden, Ken. "Gene Krupa Tells 'Why I Left Benny Goodman,'" *Radio Mirror*, July 1938, pg. 40.
6. Firestone, pg. 222.
7. Hampton, Lionel, and Haskins, James. *Hamp: An Autobiography*. Warner Books, New York, 1989, pg. 70.
8. Hammond, John. "Hysterical Public Split Goodman & Krupa...," *Down Beat*, April 1938, pgs. 6, 8.
9. Rollini, Arthur. *Thirty Years with the Big Bands,* University of Illinois Press, Urbana, IL, 1987, pg. 64.
10. "Krupa Leaves B. G. to Start His Own Ork, MCA Handling," *Billboard*, 3/12/1938, pg. 11.
11. Connor, D. Russell. *Benny Goodman: Listen to His Legacy*, The Scarecrow Press, Inc. and the Institute of Jazz Studies, Metuchen, NJ, 1988, pg. 83.
12. Hampton and Haskins, pg. 70.
13. Rollini, pg. 64.
14. Alden, pg. 40.
15. Hammond, pgs. 6, 8.
16. Kolodin, Irving. "Benny Goodman Isn't Hungry Anymore," *Music and Rhythm*, July 1942, pg. 36.
17. "Benny and Gene Kiss and Make Up," *Metronome*, June 1938, pgs. 7, 30.
18. Krupa, Gene. "When's a Musician Ready to Lead His Own Band?" *Variety*, 1/3/1940.
19. Schuller, Gunther. *The Swing Era: The Development of Jazz 1930-1945*, Oxford University Press, New York, 1989, pg. 724.
20. Klauber, Bruce. From *Gene Krupa: Ace Drummer Boy* Facebook group, April 2020.
21. Author interview with Les DeMerle, 2/10/2019.
22. Korall, Burt. *Drummin' Men: The Heartbeat of Jazz: The Swing Years*, Schirmer Books, New York, 1990, pg. 55.
23. Ibid, pgs. 71–72.
24. Wriggle, John. *Blue Rhythm Fantasy: Big Band Jazz Arranging in the Swing Era*, University of Illinois Press, Urbana, IL, 2016, pgs. 106–107.
25. Ibid., pgs. 30–42.
26. "Chappie Willet May Arrange for Krupa's New Band," *Pittsburgh Courier*, 4/2/1938, pg. 21.
27. Simon, George T. "Krupa's Band Kills Cats at Atlantic City Opening," *Metronome*, May 1938, pgs. 9, 10.
28. "New Krupa Band Draws Over 5000 in Opening Date at Steel Pier," *Tempo*, May 1938, pg. 1.
29. Ward, Helen. CD liner notes, *Benny Goodman and His Orchestra From the Famous "Let's Dance" Broadcasts*, Circle Records, New Orleans, LA, 1998.

30. Krupa, Gene. "Gene Talks About Music," liner notes, *Drummin' Man: Gene Krupa*, LP box set, Columbia Records, C2L-29, 1963.

31. Author interview with Dan Morgenstern, 1/31/2019.

32. Krupa, Gene. LP notes, *Gene Krupa's Sidekicks*, Columbia Records, CL 641, 1955.

33. Shipton, Alyn. *A New History of Jazz*, Continuum, New York, 2007, pg. 425.

34. Feather, Leonard. *The Jazz Years: Earwitness to an Era*, Da Capo Press, Cambridge, MA, 1987, pg. 96.

35. Krupa, "Gene Talks About Music."

36. Wriggle, pgs. 108–119.

37. "Gene Krupa Celebrates First Year as Leader: Film Boosts Band," *Orchestra World*, June 1939.

38. Since the 1960s, the Democratic Republic of the Congo.

39. Wriggle, pg. 150.

40. Author interview with Kevin Dorn, 2/19/2022.

41. "Inside Stuff—Music," *Variety*, 5/25/1938.

42. "Krupa Gets $5,000 for Theater Tour," *Billboard*, 5/28/1938, pg. 11.

43. Brucato, Richard, "Krupa Band Loud, Brassy; Does O. K. on First Big Job," *Orchestra World*, June 1938, pg. 10; "Gene Krupa, New Swing King, Says It's Only the Beginning," *Indianapolis News*, 9/29/1938, pg. 25.

44. "Dorsey, Krupa, Berigan Booked With Refund-If-Not-Satisfied Proviso," *Variety*, 4/13/1938, pg. 40.

45. Dupuis, Robert. *Bunny Berigan: Elusive Legend of Jazz*, Louisiana State University Press, Baton Rouge, LA, pgs. 180–181.

46. "Swing Bands Put 23,400 in Frenzy," *New York Times*, 05/30/1938, pg. 13; "All Day Swing Carnival Draws 25,000," *Metronome*, July 1938.

47. Breck, Park. "Neighbors Call Constables to Calm Cats," *Down Beat*, July 1938.

48. Cohen. "Stanley, Pitt," *Variety*, 7/6/1938.

49. Pete. "Fox, Detroit," *Variety*, 7/13/1938.

50. Kiley. "Lyric, Indpls.," *Variety*, 9/28/1938.

51. Hammond, John. "Krupa Beat Weak & Lips Page Band Just Bad," *Down Beat*, September 1938.

52. "Reviews of Records," *Billboard*, 7/23/1938, pg. 75.

53. Wright, Gordon. "DISCussions," *Metronome*, December 1938.

54. MacArthur, Harry. "'Crime School' Enlivened by the 'Dead End' Boys," *Evening Star* [Washington, DC], 6/18/1938, pg. 34.

55. Monahan, Kaspar. "Gene Krupa's Band Is Whoopin' 'Er Up," *The Pittsburgh Press*, 7/2/1938, pg. 10.

56. See, e.g., Cohen, "Pitt," *Variety*, 9/28/1938; "Four-Star J. Dorsey's Platters," *Orchestra World*, October 1938; "Swing Band Thrills Crowd," *The Courier-Journal* (Louisville, KY), 10/7/1938, pg. 1; Gillette, Mickey, "Sax-O-Fax," *Tempo*, December 1938.

57. Stengel, John B., "Gene Krupa Wants a New-Style Swing," *The Courier-Journal* (Louisville, KY), 10/1/1938, pg. 45; Kiley, "Indpls.," *Variety*, 9/28/1938.
58. Sher, Jack. "Mamma, Buy Me a Drum! Gene Krupa's Story," *South Bend Tribune*, 9/11/1938, pg. 3.
59. Krupa, Gene. "Introduction," *Gene Krupa Drum Method*, Robbins Music Corporation, New York, 1938.
60. Famularo, Don, and Glass, Daniel. *Around the Kit: Tribute to the Late Great Gene Krupa*, hosted by Joe Gansas and Daniel Glass, posted on YouTube 12/5/2016, https://www.blogtalkradio.com/aroundthekit/2019/08/19/gene-krupa-tribute-rebroadcast. Accessed May 2020.
61. Krupa, *Gene Krupa Drum Method*, pgs. 56–58.
62. Brown, Theodore Dennis. *A History and Analysis of Jazz Drumming to 1942, Volume I*, PhD dissertation in Music Education, University of Michigan, 1976, pg. 374.
63. Author interview with Kevin Dorn, 12/17/2022.
64. Author interview with John Petters, 6/9/2019.
65. Smith, Hal. *Get Happy: Benny Goodman: The Complete Big Band Recordings, 1934-36*, Episode Six, posted on YouTube 9/28/2020, https://www.youtube.com/watch?v=YVUyoMnhMrc&t=135s. Accessed 7/23/2021.
66. Krupa, *Drum Method*, pg. 70.
67. Balliett, Whitney. *Collected Works: A Journal of Jazz 1954-2000*, St. Martin's Press, New York, 2000, pg. 217.
68. Interview with Jo Jones by Milt Hinton, NEA Jazz Oral History Project.
69. Kaminsky, Max, and Hughes, V. E. *Jazz Band: My Life in Jazz*, Da Capo, New York, 1963, pg. 47.
70. Deffaa, Chip. *Swing Legacy*, The Scarecrow Press and the Institute of Jazz Studies, Rutgers University, 1989, pg. 215.
71. "Musicians," *Down Beat*, 12/6/1973, pg. 17.
72. Ibid.
73. Scott, Bobby. "Gene Krupa: '. . . I'll Miss You, Old Man,'" *Down Beat*, 12/6/1973, pg. 16.
74. Interview with Mel Lewis by Loren Schoenberg, 1989, posted on YouTube 7/13/2018, https://www.youtube.com/watch?v=knwz5LnI3KU&t=27s. Accessed 5/19/2020.
75. Author interview with Les DeMerle, 1/10/2019.
76. "Musicians," 12/6/1973, pgs. 17, 35.
77. "Gene Krupa Memorial Broadcast," Hartford, CT, 11/30/1973 (originally aired in July 1972), https://goldenage-wtic.org/BB-30.html. Author accessed in 2019–2020.
78. Lees, Gene. *Cats of Any Color*, Oxford University Press, New York, 1995, pg. 100.
79. Author interview with Dan Morgenstern, 1/31/2019.

Chapter 11: "Some Like It Hot"

1. Information is based on Paramount production documents provided to the author by the Academy of Motion Pictures Arts & Sciences.
2. Our Own Correspondent, "Krupa Is Still Not Satisfied," *Band Wagon*, 12/30/1939, pg. 4.
3. "Exclusive Candids of Gene Krupa's Paramount Film," *Orchestra World*, March 1939, pg. 13.
4. Edwards. Paramount press release, 3/6/1939. Provided to the author by the AMPAS.
5. Krupa, Gene. "'One-Nighters Are My Worst Gripe!' . . . Gene Krupa," *Music and Rhythm*, November 1940, pgs. 21–22.
6. Gross, Ben. "Listening In," *New York Daily News*, 3/30/1939; "Radio Personals," *Motion Picture Daily*, 3/30/1939.
7. "On the Upbeat," *Variety*, 10/4/1939.
8. "The Gallup Poll," *Swing*, May 1940.
9. "Chicago Joints Jump; Swing Bands Are Back," *Down Beat*, April 1939, pg. 2; "Chicago Stuff," *Tempo*, May 1939, pg. 6; Reynolds, Ed, "Chicago." *Swing*, April 1939, pg. 34; "Swing Blows Windy City Into New Wild Heat Wave," *The Bandstand*, April 1939, pg. 2; Blade, Jim, "Ropes Up as Krupa Opens Panther Room; Hold Moran; Pryor Splits," *Orchestra World*, April 1939, pg. 9; Reynolds, Ed, "Chicago," *Swing*, May 1939; White, Hal, "Teagarden for Crosby; Zurke Set with Morris," *Orchestra World*, May 1939, pg. 10.
10. Slow, Jerome. "Krupa's Cagers on Hand to Give Gene's Ork Big Chicago Welcome," *Down Beat*, April 1939.
11. "Paramount Sets Record," *New York Times*, 4/25/1940.
12. Gertie and Rose. "Bandy-ing Around," *Swing*, June 1940.
13. Higgins, Joe. "And *Still* They Come!" [italics in original headline], *Orchestra World*, June 1940, pg. 5.
14. Tracy, Sheila. *Bands, Booze, and Broads*, Mainstream Publishing, London, 1996, pg. 199.
15. Ibid., pg. 197.
16. Borst, Tracy. "On the Road," *Modern Drummer*, Oct-Nov, 1979, pg. 23.
17. Ibid.
18. Krupa, Gene. Interviewed by Tobe Reed. *Fitch Bandwagon radio show*, circa 1941.
19. Wood. "Paramount, N.Y.," *Variety*, 5/1/1940, pg. 46.
20. Borst, pg. 23.
21. Colin, Charles. "The Reviewing Stand," *Orchestra World*, June 1940, pg. 8.
22. Silver, Nathan, *Lost New York*, American Legacy Press, New York, 1967, pgs. 192–196; *The WPA Guide to New York City: The Federal Writers Project Guide to 1930s New York*, The New Press, New York, 1992, pgs. 627–648 [reprint of 1939 New York City Guide by the Guilds Committee for

Federal Writers' Publications, Inc., New York. Book was part of the American guide series].

23. "Krupa at Fair," *New York Daily News*, 9/12/1939; "Ugh! Heap Tough," *Down Beat*, 10/15/1939.
24. Fields, John. "Krupa Goes Native," *Swing*, February 1940.
25. Green, Abel. "War, Rain Hurt, But New York Fair Indicates How Showmanship Pays," *Variety*, 7/16/1940.
26. "3 Art Exhibits Opened," *New York Times*, 7/10/1940; "Krupa's Expo Hypo," *Variety*, 9/25/1940.
27. P.E.M. "Critics in the Doghouse: Gene Krupa's Band," *Down Beat*, May 1939.
28. Barrelhouse Dan. "Ozzie Nelson Moves Out of Schmalz Rut," *Down Beat*, 8/15/1940, pg. 14.
29. "Gene Krupa Orchestra," *Swing*, October 1940, pg. 17.
30. Kibort, S. B. "Too Many Drummers Are Showmen," *Down Beat*, February 1939, pg. 14.
31. Land, Dick C. "Drums Should Be Felt—Not Heard," *Down Beat*, 11/1/1939.
32. Simon, George T. "Artie Shaw Kicks With 'Seabiscuit Gusto!'" *Metronome*, February 1939, pg. 12.
33. Hershe, Mrs. Harriet. "Don't Talk About Collectors—I Married One with a Wax Head," *Music and Rhythm*, November 1940, pg. 34.
34. Author interview with John Petters, 11/20/2018.
35. Eck. "State, Hartford," *Variety*, 9/13/1939.
36. Burton. "Shea's Buffalo," *Variety*, 12/6/1939.
37. Krupa, Gene. "Krupa Rakes Sideline Jivesters," *Down Beat*, 2/1/1940, as reprinted in July 1994 issue of *Down Beat*.
38. "14,000 Musicians Name Top Bands: Tom Dorsey, Goodman Win High Honors," *Down Beat*, 1/1/1940; A Staff Writer, "11 Leaders on Down Beat's All-American 1939 Band," *Down Beat*, 1/1/1940, pg. 12.
39. Kaitz, Madeleine. Letter to the Editor, "Chords and Discords: Down Beat Is Unfair in Its Poll," *Down Beat*, 12/1/1940, pg. 10.
40. "James Leads All-Star Band," *Metronome*, January 1940, pgs. 7, 12–14.
41. "Barnet, Elman, Christian, Beneke, Crash All-Stars," *Metronome*, January 1941, pgs. 7, 10, 14, 28–29.
42. "Greatest Band of All Time Records for Musicians' Charity," *Metronome*, February 1939; "All Stars Wax Great Record!" *Metronome*, March 1940, pgs. 7, 10, 31; "All-Stars Spotted Goodman, Dorsey Men," *Metronome*, February 1941.
43. Miller, Paul Eduard. Down Beat's Yearbook of Swing, Down Beat Publishing Company, Chicago, 1939, pgs. 88–124.
44. Author interview with John Petters, 11/20/2018.
45. Rhythm, Polly. "New Records," *Glamour of Hollywood*, April 1941.
46. Jax. "Diggin' the Discs with Jax," *Down Beat*, 7/1/1943.

47. Smith, Charles Edward. "Collecting Hot," *Esquire's Jazz Book, Vol. 1*, 1944 [reprinted from original publication in February 1934 *Esquire*].
48. Ibid.
49. Edwards. Press Release, Paramount Pictures, March 1939.
50. "Gutbucket Drippings," *Down Beat*, January 1939.
51. "Gene Krupa Socko on Boston Date," *Metronome*, January 1940.
52. "Gutbucket Drippings," pg. 15.
53. "Gene Gifford," *Tempo*, August 1935.
54. Abel. "Strand, N.Y.," *Variety*, 8/31/1938.
55. "Just a Gene Krupa at Heart," *Evening Star* [Washington, DC], 9/13/1939, pg. C-12.
56. Dumont, Cedric. "Dumont on 'Army Leave' Joins Jam Band," *Orchestra World*, May 1940, pg. 4.
57. Eck. "New Acts," *Variety*, 12/21/1938, pg. 41.
58. "Are Girl Musicians Superior?" *Up Beat*, January 1939.
59. Ad, "Slingerlands Are Played the World Over," *Down Beat*, 6/15/1940.
60. "Polish 'Krupa' A War Refugee," *Orchestra World*, September 1940.
61. "Cozy Corner Hails New Orchestra for Holiday Celebrants," *The Detroit Tribune*, 12/21/1940, pg. 8.
62. Wern. "Golden Gate, S. F.," *Variety*, 12/24/1941.
63. Rosie, John. "Victor Feldman: 1934-87," National Jazz Archive (UK), https://nationaljazzarchive.org.uk/explore/interviews/1634260-victor-feldman-interview-1. Accessed 12/8/2023.
64. Turner, Shirley E. "Beating Drums Roosevelt Boy's Favorite Hobby," *Evening Star* [DC], 7/26/1942, pg. E-7.
65. "'G. I. Variety Revue' At Bayview Park Tomorrow Evening," *The Key West Citizen*, 7/25/1945, pg. 4.
66. "New Team Opens at Kentucky Lounge," *Suburbanite Economist* [Chicago, IL], 11/11/1942, pg. 6.
67. MacArthur, Harry. "Tyrone Power Gets Rough in New Film at Capitol," *Evening Star* [DC], 4/27/1940, pg. B-16.
68. Brown, Betty. "Interviewing Charlie Spivak," *The New Baton*, September 1945.
69. Watson, Athelene. "Are Birds 'People'? All You Have to Do Is Watch Them at Work or at Play; Then You'll Be Convinced Some of Them Are," *The Frontier* [O'Neill City, Holt County, Nebraska], 5/9/1940.

Chapter 12: Enter "Little Jazz"

1. "Gene Krupa (OK 6009)," *H.R.S. Society Rag*, February 1941, pg. 27.
2. Dexter, Dave, Jr. "8 New Basie Sides; Tesch Album Issued; Duke Tunes by Steele," *Down Beat*, 3/15/1941.

3. Korall, Burt. *Drummin' Men: The Heartbeat of Jazz: The Swing Years*, Schirmer Books, New York, 1990, pg. 67.

4. Mel Lewis interview by Loren Schoenberg (1989), posted on YouTube 7/13/2018, https://www.youtube.com/watch?v=knwz5LnI3KU&t=27s. Accessed 5/19/2020.

5. "Reflections," *Down Beat*, Oct-Nov, 1979, pg. 22.

6. O'Day, Anita, and Eells, George. *High Times, Hard Times*, Limelight Editions, New York, 1997, pgs. 40–43.

7. Crockett, Davy. "The Walkathon of the 1930s," posted 11/3/2018, *Ultra Running History*, https://ultrarunninghistory.com/the-walkathon-walk -till-you-drop/. Accessed 9/6/2023.

8. O'Day and Eells, pgs. 76–77.

9. Ibid., pg. 96.

10. Ibid., pgs. 101–102.

11. Krupa, Gene. LP notes, *Gene Krupa's Sidekicks*, Columbia Records, CL 641, 1955.

12. Meehan, Reg. "Why Roy Eldridge Gave up His Band to Join Gene Krupa," *Music and Rhythm*, June 1941, pg. 11.

13. Ibid.

14. "On the Upbeat," *Variety*, 10/30/1940.

15. Chilton, John. *Roy Eldridge: Little Jazz Giant*, Continuum, London and New York, 2002, pgs. 108–109.

16. Author interview with Dan Morgenstern, 1/31/2019.

17. Interview with Cootie Williams by Stanley Dance, The Smithsonian Institution, Washington, DC, May 1976, pg. 217.

18. Author interview with George Wein, 1/18/2019.

19. Meehan, pg. 11.

20. Author interview with Dan Morgenstern, 1/31/2019.

21. "Glenn Miller's 'Choo Choo' Hits 1,000,000 Mark in Disc Output and May Become All-Time High," *Variety*, 1/14/1942.

22. "The Box Office Slant," *Showman's Trade Review*, 12/6/1941.

23. Author interview with Dan Morgenstern, 12/2/2019.

24. Goldwyn papers, Academy of Motion Picture Arts and Sciences Margaret Herrick Library, memoranda dated 11/11/41 and 11/25/1941.

25. Vergun, David. "First Peacetime Draft Enacted Just Before World War II," U.S. Department of Defense, 4/7/2020, https://www.defense.gov/News/ Feature-Stories/story/Article/2140942/first-peacetime-draft-enacted-just -before-world-war-ii//. Accessed 9/7/2023.

26. Orodenker, M. H. "Selling the Band," *Billboard*, 2/7/1942, pg. 23.

27. Ad, "Keep 'Em Flying," *Billboard*, 1/17/1942, pg. 61.

28. Gene Krupa interview, CBC Krupa Memorial Broadcast, 10/21/1973.

29. Klauber, Bruce H. *The World of Gene Krupa: The Legendary Drummin' Man*, Pathfinder Publishing of California, 1990, pgs. 161–162.

30. Author interview with Rita Ventura Lenderman, on or about 7/12/2019.
31. Zammarchi, Fabrice, and Mas, Sylvie. *A Life in the Golden Age of Jazz: A Biography of Buddy DeFranco*, Parkside Publications, Seattle, WA, 2002.
32. Kuehn, John, and Astrup, Arne. *Buddy DeFranco: A Biographical Portrait and Discography*, Scarecrow Press and the Institute of Jazz Studies, Rutgers—The State University of New Jersey, Metuchen, NJ, 1993, pgs. 14–15.
33. "All Musical Equipment Scarce," *Variety*, 3/4/1942.
34. Davis, Hal. "Shellac Ban Blasts Disc Output," *Orchestra World*, May 1942.
35. "End of One-Nighters in Sight," *Down Beat*, 5/15/1942.
36. Ibid.
37. "New Gas Ban Ruins 1-Niters: Summer Band Spots Hard Hit," *Variety*, 5/26/1943.
38. "More Grief Promised Bands," *Variety*, 5/27/1942.
39. Gayer, Dixon. "Two Blows to Band Travel: Railroads Frozen and Gas Doled," *Down Beat*, 10/15/1942, pgs. 1, 13.
40. Ibid.
41. "OPA May Ease Eastern Gas Ban: Ace Spots Close: Relief May Come by Spring," *Orchestra World*, February 1943, pg. 5.
42. O'Day and Eells, pgs. 113–114; Chilton, John. *Roy Eldridge: Little Jazz Giant*, Continuum, London and New York, 2002, pgs. 126–128.
43. Chilton, pg. 128.
44. "Anita O'Day Cuts Out from Gene," *Down Beat*, 1/15/1943; Lee, Dottie, "Sharps and Flats," *Orchestra World*, February 1943.
45. O'Day and Eells, pgs. 120–121.
46. "Anita O'Day Cuts Out."
47. "Anita O'Day Back with Krupa," *Orchestra World*, February 1943; "Anita O'Day Back with Gene Krupa," *Down Beat*, 2/1/1943.
48. O'Day and Eells, pg. 122.
49. Erwin, Pee Wee, and Vaché, Warren W. *This Horn for Hire*, The Scarecrow Press and the Institute of Jazz Studies, Rutgers University, Metuchen, NJ, 1987, pgs. 131–132.
50. Shaw, Arnold. *Gene Krupa: His Complete Life Story*, Pin-Up Press, New York, 1945.
51. Provines, June. "Front Views and Profiles," *Chicago Tribune*, 10/18/1939.
52. Egan, Jack. "Park Hill Building Bug Is Nipping at the Musicians," *Down Beat*, 5/1/1941.
53. "Gene Krupa Shows How to Play Drum in These Fantastic Sound Pictures," *Life*, 6/9/1941.
54. Connor, D. Russell. *Benny Goodman: Listen to His Legacy*, The Scarecrow Press, Inc. and the Institute of Jazz Studies, Metuchen, NJ, 1988, pg. 145.
55. Cooper, Loma. "Who's Suspicious?" *Swing*, November 1940, pg. 36.
56. The Thin Man, "Inside Stuff," *Music and Rhythm*, January 1942; Inglis, Andy, "Sharps and Flats," *Orchestra World*, February 1942.

57. Harris, Leslie. "Miami," *Variety*, 4/29/1942; Florida State Divorce Records, Florida Department of Health, https://www.archives.com. Accessed 10/4/2019.
58. "Rag Time Marches On . . . : Lost Harmony," *Down Beat*, 6/1/1942.
59. "Krupa Reads Paper, Learns About Divorce," *The Minneapolis Star*, 4/10/1942, pg. 24.
60. "Inside Stuff," *Music and Rhythm*, January 1942; Rowe, Billy, "Billy Rowe's Notebook," *Pittsburgh Courier*, 2/28/1942.
61. O'Day and Eells, pg. 101.
62. Ibid., pg. 100.
63. Holly, Hal. "Los Angeles Band Briefs," *Down Beat*, 12/15/1942.
64. Inglis, "Sharps and Flats."
65. Schuller, Gunther. *The Swing Era: The Development of Jazz 1930-1945*, Oxford University Press, New York, 1989, pg. 727.
66. Dorn, Kevin. "Gene Krupa's Wild 1941 'Drumboogie' Beat," posted on YouTube 11/15/2020, https://www.youtube.com/watch?v=Qsc6X9aWX7l. Accessed 6/30/2021.
67. Griffith, Mark. "Gene Krupa," *Modern Drummer*, January 2009, pgs. 75–76.
68. Author interview with Kevin Dorn, 2/19/2022.

Chapter 13: "I Would Spend $10 Anytime to Come to a Negro's Defense"

1. Jenkins, Willard. "Fab 5 Freddy: The Max Roach Influence," *Jazz Times*, posted on 5/26/2011, https://jazztimes.com/features/interviews/fab-5-freddy-the-max-roach-influence. Accessed 8/18/2019.
2. "Musicians," *Down Beat*, 12/6/1973.
3. "Melody Maker Is Loud in Praise of Jimmie's Style," *Pittsburgh Courier*, 1/16/1937, pg. 19.
4. Morris, Earl J. "Swing Band Plays Funeral Dirge as Musician Is Buried," *Pittsburgh Courier*, 2/25/1939, pg. 20.
5. "Dempsey Presents Lambda MU award," *Phoenix Index*, 8/10/1940, pg. 5.
6. Your Optic. "Derbyville," *The Evansville* [Indiana] *Argus*, 12/27/1940, pg. 6. Caps in original.
7. Merguson, W. R. "Questions and Answers," *Pittsburgh Courier*, 12/24/1938, pg. 14.
8. Reller, Walt. "Stan Dougherty Draws for the USO," *Down Beat*, 11/15/1941.
9. Boykin, Ulysses. "The Jumpin' Jive," *Detroit Tribune*, 6/6/1942, pg. 13.
10. "Group to Select Jordan Winners," *Indianapolis Recorder*, 10/25/1947, pg. 5; "Baltimore Housewife Wins Jordan Contest," *Indianapolis Recorder*, 12/6/1947, pg. 3; "All-Out Fight May Foil Memphis Anti-Negro Censors," *Pittsburgh Courier*, 10/25/1947, pg. 18.
11. Ad, Harlem Records Supply Company, *Pittsburgh Courier*, 12/20/1947, pg. 17.

12. "Canada Lee on Wallace Program Tonight," *Ohio Daily-Express*, 11/14/1947, pg. 1.
13. "Robinson Ball," *New York Daily News*, 10/1/1949, pg. 63.
14. "New Stage Show," *Pittsburgh Courier*, 9/22/1956, pg. 20.
15. "Krupa-Gluskin Go Movie," *Billboard*, 9/14/1946, pg. 35.
16. "Screen Guild to Release Herald's Six Negro Pix," *Film Daily*, 8/12/1947, pg. 2; Kubit, Adrian, "Eastern Production Looks Up," *Film Daily*, 9/10/1947, pg. 149.
17. "Gotham Scene of Many Flickers with Sepia Stars," *Pittsburgh Courier*, 4/12/1947, pg. 17.
18. "Releases Negro Features," *Boxoffice*, 12/25/1948, pg. 21.
19. "And Now It's Soundies," *The Band Leaders*, September 1944, pg. 54.
20. Cantor, Mark. "Gene Krupa 'the Ace Drummer Man' and His Orchestra: Three Panoram Soundies," *IAJRC Journal*, March 2010, pgs. 37–39.
21. "Soundies," *Home Movies*, February 1943.
22. Advertisement, "Pep Up Your Programs!" *Business Screen Magazine*, No. 3, Vol. 6, 1945.
23. "Official Catalog," *Movie Makers*, April 1946.
24. "KTTV on Coast Will Use Platter Pusher to 'Spin' 1,000 'Soundies,'" *Variety*, 5/10/1950.
25. Teddy Wilson interviewed by Milt Hinton for the Smithsonian Institution Jazz Oral History Project, 9/2/1979.
26. "Negro Members Bar White Units From the South," *Variety*, 12/3/1941.
27. McDonough, John. "Face Yonkers, Drummers! Gene Krupa Lived There." *High Fidelity*, March 1974.
28. "Arrest of Krupa, Eldridge Arouses York, PA: Bury Restaurant Refuses Service to Negro Patrons," *Pittsburgh Courier*, 12/13/1941, pg. 20.
29. Rowe, Billy. "Band Contest Takes on True American Aspect: Gene Krupa Leads Contest After His Stand Against Racial Hypocrisy in U.S.," *Pittsburgh Courier*, 12/20/1948, pg. 21; "Basie Wins Again," *Pittsburgh Courier*, 1/2/1942, pg. 20.
30. Rowe, Billy. "Krupa to Get 'Chu' Berry Memorial Award: Pabst Beer Awards Designed for All as Kansas City and St. Louis Dances Take Shape," *Pittsburgh Courier*, 2/7/1942, pg. 19; "'Chu' Berry Award to be Presented," *Pittsburgh Courier*, 2/28/1942, pg. 21.
31. Bolden, Frank E. "Orchestra Whirl," *Pittsburgh Courier*, 2/14/1942, pg. 19.

Chapter 14: Giving Careers a Lift

1. "Backstage with Tex Beneke," interview with Leisure World Historical Society, Seal Beach, CA, 7/25/1998, https://www.youtube.com/watch?v=g5CAWvbAldg&t=80s. Accessed 2/16/2022.

2. "On the Upbeat," *Variety*, 7/10/1940; Photo caption, *Metronome*, August 1940; and Flynn, Ed, *Down Beat*, 8/1/1940, pg. 3.

3. Emery, Fred. "On and Off the Air," *The Forum* [Dayton, OH], 11/8/1940, pg. 3.

4. Ad, *Metronome*, October 1941; ad, *Down Beat*, 10/1/1941; ad, *Down Beat*, 11/15/1941.

5. Bracken, Jimmy. "The Diary of Our Own Jimmy Bracken," *Metronome*, February 1942, pg. 24.

6. Lishon, Maurie. *Franks for the Memories*, A Rebeats Publication, Cook's Music, Alma, MI, 1993, pg. 122.

7. Interview with Louie Bellson by Anthony Brown, conducted 10/20/2005, Smithsonian Jazz Oral History Program, pgs. 2–4; *The All Music Guide to Jazz*, Third Edition, Miller Freeman Books, San Francisco, CA, 1998, pg. 81.

8. "Dave Black," *The Telegraph* [UK], 12/13/2006, https://www.telegraph.co.uk/news/obituaries/1536733/Dave-Black.html. Accessed 12/4/2018.

9. Sonny Igoe Interview by Monk Rowe, Emerson, NJ, 7/31/2003, https://www.youtube.com/watch?v=NYJZgtIXfWk. Accessed 4/29/2020.

10. Feather, Leonard. *The Encyclopedia of Jazz*, Bonanza Books, New York, 1964, pg. 263.

11. Dial, Patterson. "Wild Boy," *Evening Star* [Washington, DC], 3/7/1937, pgs. 9–16.

12. "Swing Champions," *Motion Picture Daily*, 10/28/1938.

13. "Name Leaders Head UHCA's National Advisory Board," *Tempo*, November 1938.

14. "Crackpot College," cartoon, *Sunday Star* [Washington, DC], 1/8/1939, pg. 3.

15. Wolfert, Ira. "Does Jitterbugging Mean We're All Going Mad?" *Evening Star* [Washington, DC], 7/14/1940, pg. F-3.

16. Allen, Frederick Lewis. *Since Yesterday: 1929-1939*, Harper & Row, New York, 1968, pgs. 213–215.

17. Feder, Sid. "Little Alsab Needs a Ration Card—Or maybe Just Less Work by Rider," *The Wilmington* [NC] *Morning Star*, 6/8/1942, pg. 5.

18. See, e.g., "Night Club Reviews: Minnesota Terrace, Mpls.," *Variety*, 1/27/1943.

19. Henry, Bill. "By the Way," *Los Angeles Times*, 2/19/1944, pg. 9.

20. Carmody, Jay. "Jungle Night Club's Business Is Howling, Ex-Scribe Finds," *Evening Star* [Washington, DC], 3/6/1944, pg. B-16.

21. "Freeman, Back from London, Says U.S. Boys Yen Boxing, Dancing, Shows," *Variety*, 4/14/1943, pg. 18.

22. Sawyers, June Skinner. *Chicago Portraits*, Loyola University Press, Chicago, 1991, pgs. xiii, 148–149.

23. Flora, Joseph M., and MacKethan, Lucinda H., eds. *The Companion to Southern Literature*, Louisiana State University Press, Baton Rouge, 2002, pg. 383.

24. Cushman, Karen. *The Loud Silence of Francine Green*, Laurel-Leaf Books, New York, 2006, pg. 100.

25. Conlon, Christopher. "Welcome Jean Krupa, World's Greatest Girl Drummer!" *The Oblivion Room: Stories of Violation*, Evil Jester Press, New York, 2013, pgs. 133–142.
26. Algren, Nelson. *The Man With the Golden Arm*, Doubleday, New York, 1949.

Chapter 15: Famous Fans and Drumming Descendants

1. Southpaugh, Edgar. "Skippy Grows Up," *Hollywood*, March 1938, pgs. 32, 46.
2. Cooper, Jackie, and Kleiner, Dick. *Please Don't Shoot My Dog: The Autobiography of Jackie Cooper*, William Morrow and Company, Inc., New York, 1981, pg. 117.
3. Hartley, Katherine. "Play Truth and Consequences with Fred Astaire," *Photoplay*, May 1939.
4. Astaire, Fred. "Hollywood," *New York Daily News*, 2/27/1939, pg. 28.
5. Ford, Carol M., Groundwater, Linda J., and Young, Dee. "Who Was Bob Crane?" *Bob Crane: Life and Legacy*, https://www.vote4bobcrane.org/about. Accessed 9/21/2023.
6. *The Bob Crane Show*, KNX-CBS Radio, circa 1960, https://www.youtube.com/watch?v=GJcKsZMoLxk. Accessed 9/21/2023.
7. Sikov, Ed. *Mr. Strangelove: A Biography of Peter Sellers*, Hyperion, New York, 2002, pgs. 38–39.
8. Atkins, Al. "Sharps and Flats," cartoon, *Orchestra World*, October 1937.
9. Author interview with Duffy Jackson, 1/4/2019.
10. Author interview with Dan Morgenstern, ibid., 1/31/2019.
11. Lucas, John. "The Great White Way," *Just Jazz No. 4*, edited by Sinclair Traill and The Hon. Gerald Lascelles, Souvenir Press Ltd., London, 1960, pg. 95.
12. Burns, Le Roy. "Drums: Jim Chapin—Introducing a Bright Student," *Metronome*, December 1955.
13. Hadlock, Richard. *Jazz Masters of the 20s*, Da Capo Press, New York, 1988, pg. 140.
14. "Sneaking Into Theater to Hear Gene Krupa's Big Band," Interview with Frankie Dunlop, 10/16/1984, with Scott K. Fish, posted circa 2019, https://www.youtube.com/watch?v=8f9ZNyAy5_A. Accessed 9/22/2023.
15. Fish, Scott K. "Frankie Dunlop: Gene Krupa's Kindness to an Upcoming Drummer," *Life Beyond the Cymbals*, posted on 5/16/2015, https://scottkfish.com/2015/05/16/frankie-dunlop-gene-krupas-kindness-to-an-upcoming-drummer/. Accessed 9/22/2023.
16. Powell, Josephine. *Tito Puente: When the Drums Are Dreaming*, Authorhouse, Bloomington, IN, 2007, pgs. 45–48.
17. Author interview with Lori Sokoloff Lowell, 9/8/2023.
18. Thress, Dan, "African Drummers in Paris: Tony Allen, Brice Wassy, and Mokhtar Samba Invest Rich African Rhythms Into the Music of France,"

Drum! May-June 2001; "Tony Allen: July 30, 1940-April 30, 2020," *Drummerworld*, drummerworld.com/drummers/Tony_Allen.html. Accessed 12/10/20.

19. Author interviews with Steve Little, 5/21/2019 and 6/20/2021.
20. Williams, Martin. "Krupa Collected." *The Saturday Review*, 1/11/1964, pg. 70.
21. Author interview with Ignacio Berroa, 4/2/2019.
22. Author interview with Bruce Klauber, 1/11/2019.
23. Author interview with Bruce Klauber, 7/12/2019.
24. Korall, Burt. *Drummin' Men: The Heartbeat of Jazz: The Swing Years*, Schirmer Books, New York, 1990, pgs. 145–146.
25. Klauber, Bruce H. *Gene Krupa: The Pictorial Life of a Jazz Legend*, Alfred Publishing Co., Inc, Los Angeles, 2005, pg. 15.
26. *Charlie Parker Rare Recording Practicing With Benny Goodman (China Boy-Avalon)*, February 1943, posted on YouTube 6/1/2017, https://www.youtube.com/watch?v=jjUC5nkz8Vg. Accessed 9/23/2023.
27. Peplowski, Ken. *Runnin' Wild—The Complete Benny Goodman Victor Small Groups, 1935-39, Episode 2*, posted on YouTube 12/11/2021, https://www.youtube.com/watch?v=n3FfdOq-t7c. Accessed 12/22/2021.
28. Dodds, Baby, and Gara, Larry. *The Baby Dodds Story*, Contemporary Press, Los Angeles, 1959, pgs. 83–84, 87.
29. Balliett, Whitney, "Musical Events: Jazz Records," *New Yorker*, 1964; Rutgers Institute of Jazz Studies, Papers of John S. Wilson.
30. Kettle, Rupert. "G. Krupa: A Musical Perspective," *Modern Drummer*, Oct.-Nov. 1979, pg. 25.
31. DeMicheal, Don. "Drums in Perspective: The Styles, and How They Developed," *Down Beat*, 3/3/1960.
32. Brown, Bernie. "Krupa on Drumming Today and Yesterday," *Down Beat*, 12/2/1965.
33. Tomkins, Les. "Chico Hamilton: Interview 2," *National Jazz Archive Presents the Story of British Jazz*, 1972, https://nationaljazzarchive.co.uk/stories?id=289. Accessed 11/13/2018.
34. Author interview with Ed Soph, 6/5/2020.
35. "Names in the Swing News," *Swing*, May 1940.
36. Simon, George T. "Simon Says..." *Metronome*, November 1943.
37. DeMicheal, Don. "Evolution of the Drum Solo," *Down Beat*, 3/30/1961, pg. 24.
38. Herb. "Paramount, N.Y.," *Variety*, 4/8/1942.
39. Tormé, Mel. *Traps the Drum Wonder: The Life of Buddy Rich*, Oxford University Press, New York, 1991, pgs. 114–115.
40. Klauber, Bruce. *Gene Krupa America's Ace Drummer Man* Facebook group, circa February 2020, in discussion thread concerning the Krupa LP, *Krupa Rocks*.
41. Author interview with Terry Gibbs, 1/10/2019.

42. Author interview with Joe Vetrano, 1/2/2020.

43. Korall, pg. 258.

44. "Gene Krupa and Buddy Rich: Interviewed by Voice of America's Willis Conover," *Metronome*, April 1956, pg. 28.

45. "Gene Krupa: Rhythm Is His Business," *Tempo*, August 1937, pg. 2.

46. Fields, John. "Krupa Goes Native," *Swing*, February 1940.

47. Edwards. No title, Paramount Pictures press release, 2/28/1939.

48. Edwards. No title, Paramount Pictures press release, undated (probably spring 1939).

49. Walker, Danton. "Broadway," *New York Daily News*, 5/18/1939, pg. 48.

50. "Drummer in a Museum," *Time*, 4/28/1941.

51. Krupa, Gene. "The Beat of the Drum," *The Band Leaders*, July 1945, pgs. 12, 13, 58, 59.

52. Krupa, Gene. "It's the Rhythm That Stays With 'Em," *Music Journal*, October 1960, pgs. 12, 72–73.

53. "Krupa Kills Kats at Met Museum," *Down Beat*, 8/1/1942.

54. "Gene Krupa Gives Swing 'Low Down,'" *New York Times*, 7/12/1942.

55. "Krupa Kills Kats at Met Museum."

56. "Off the Stand," *Swing*, October 1940, pg. 24.

57. Hancock, Jon. *Benny Goodman: The Famous 1938 Carnegie Hall Jazz Concert*, Prancing Fish Publishing, Shrewsbury, Shropshire, UK, 2008, pg. 47, citing *Collier's*, February 1939.

58. "Gene Krupa, New Swing King, Says It's Only the Beginning," *The Indianapolis News*, 9/29/1938, pg. 28.

59. Edwards. Paramount Pictures press release, 4/5/1939.

60. Aubrecht, Michael. "Sweat Gene Sweat," *Off Beat With Michael Aubrecht*, posted on 9/14/2015, https://maubrecht.wordpress.com/2015/09/14/sweat-gene-sweat/. Accessed 11/2/2018.

61. "Gene Krupa: Rhythm Is His Business," *Tempo*, August 1937; Lieber, Perry, "Gene Krupa," RKO Radio Studios; "Krupa Authority on Baseball," *Sporting Globe* [Melbourne, Australia], 7/21/1954, pg. 16; North, Art. "He Beats All," *New York Daily News*, 5/8/1960, pg. 4.

62. "Food-Poisoned Krupa Yearns for Surf," *Maryborough Chronicle* [Queensland, Australia], 8/21/1954, pg. 5.

63. Carson, John. "Under Twenty: Interviews," *The Evening Observer* [Dunkirk-Fredonia, NY], 9/30/1961.

64. Ibid.

65. Krupa, Gene Harry. *Unfortunate Casting: An Autobiographical Essay*. PhD thesis, Department of English, University of Iowa, July 1975, pg. 88.

66. Author interview with Bill Crow, 4/28/2019; see, e.g., "Krupa Jumps at Sherman," *Down Beat*, 11/1/1944.

67. The Square. "Strictly Ad Lib," *Down Beat*, 9/14/1944.

68. Author interview with Bill Crow.

69. North, Arthur. "Krupa: King of the Beat," *New York Daily News*, 5/13/1962.

70. Author interview with Duffy Jackson, 1/4/2019.

71. Feather, Leonard. "Feather's Nest," *Down Beat*, 5/1/1958.

72. Krupa, Gene. "'Make Your Drum Breaks Mean Something'—Krupa," *Metronome*, November 1939, pg. 47.

73. Krupa, Gene. "Drummers' Dope," *Metronome*, January 1937.

74. Krupa, Gene. "Drummers' Dope," *Metronome*, June 1938.

75. Lee, Amy. "McKinley Didn't Lead Band for Bradley Was a Natural," *Metronome*, circa April 1940.

76. "'Drummers Sure Do Make Good Band Leaders!'" *Metronome*, May 1940.

77. McKinley, Ray. "Introducing Ray McKinley in 'How to Beat a Drum,'" August 1940.

78. Krupa, Gene. "Krupa Gets His Kicks," *Metronome*, February 1938.

79. Krupa, Gene. "My Twelve Favorite Drummers," *Music and Rhythm*, November 1941, pg. 44.

80. See Graham, Charles. *The Great Jazz Day*, Da Capo Press, 2000.

81. Jones, Jo. *The Drums* (1973), https://www.youtube.com/watch?v=SizJQ5 T045w&t=1531s. Accessed 2/9/2024.

82. Mattingly, Rick. *The Drummer's Time*, Modern Drummer Publications, Inc., Cedar Grove, NJ, 1998, pg. 59.

83. Brown, Anthony. "Louie Bellson: NEA Jazz Master (1994)," Smithsonian Jazz Oral History Program, Oct. 20–21, 2005, pgs. 24–25.

84. Ibid., pgs. 10–11.

85. Tormé, Mel. *Traps the Drum Wonder: The Life of Buddy Rich*, Oxford University Press, New York, 1991, pgs. 96–97.

86. Author interview with Les DeMerle, 1/10/2019.

Chapter 16: "I'm Out Here All Alone on a Shelf"

1. Line from "Boogie Blues," song Gene Krupa and His Orchestra recorded with Anita O'Day, first on V-Disc in July 1945, then for public sale on 8/21/1945. Krupa rerecorded it at a Capitol transcription session on 2/20/1946 with new vocalist Carolyn Grey.

2. Blesh, Rudi. *Eight Lives in Jazz: Combo USA*, Hayden Book Company, Inc., New York, 1971, pg. 156.

3. Adams, Cydney. "The Man Behind the Marijuana Ban for All the Wrong Reasons," *CBS News*, 11/17/016, https://www.cbsnews.com/news/harry -anslinger-the-man-behind-the-marijuana-ban/. Accessed 8/27/2022.

4. Anslinger, H. J., and Cooper, Courtney Riley. "Marijuana—Assassin of Youth," *Reader's Digest*, February 1938, reprinted and condensed from original printing in *The American Magazine*, July 1937, https://www.dru-glibrary.org/schaffer/history/e1930/mjassassinrd.htm. Accessed 9/6/2022.

5. Solomon, David. "Introduction" to "The Marihuana Tax Act of 1937." *Schaffer Library of Drug Policy*, https://www.druglibrary.net/schaffer/hemp/taxact/mjtaxact.htm. Accessed 8/24/2022.

6. "'Weed' Takes Two More Lives," *Orchestra World*, October 1941.

7. Ad, "The Best Bands in the Land in Big M-G-M Shows!" *Motion Picture Herald*, 10/3/1942; "Bands Becoming More Active These Days," [Washington, DC] *Evening Star*, 11/27/1942.

8. Wallace, Kevin. "Krupa's Band Hits Deck at the Golden Gate," *San Francisco Examiner*, 1/14/1943.

9. "Krupa Pleads Not Guilty in S.F. 'Dope' Case," *Oakland Tribune*, 1/20/1943.

10. Ibid.; "Krupa's Orchestra to Visit Sweet's," *Oakland Tribune*, 1/17/1943; "Krupa, Master of Drums, Due Here," *Oakland Tribune*, 1/18/1943.

11. Ehrlich, J. W., *A Life in My Hands: An Autobiography*, G.P. Putnam's Sons, New York, 1965, pgs. 131–132; Averbuch, Bernard, and Noble, John Wesley, *Never Plead Guilty: The Story of Jake Ehrlich*, Farrar, Straus and Cudahy, New York, 1955, pgs. 144–145.

12. "Gene Krupa Is Arrested," *New York Times*, 1/21/1943; "Krupa Bailed on Reefer Charge," *New York Daily News*, 1/21/1943; "Krupa on Tour Pending Hearing," *Oakland Tribune*, 1/21/1943; "Hearing Today for Gene Krupa," *San Francisco Examiner*, 1/26/1943.

13. "Gene Krupa Linked to Dope Case: 'Swing' Drummer Seized by U.S. Agents," *San Francisco Examiner*, 1/20/1943.

14. Averbuch and Noble, pg. 145.

15. Ehrlich, pg. 132.

16. "Krupa on Tour Pending Hearing"; "Krupa Bailed on Reefer Charge."

17. Morgenstern, Dan. Transcript of Interview with Roy Eldridge, Institute of Jazz Studies at Rutgers University—Newark, 6/15/1982 and 6/22/1983, pg. 137.

18. "Krupa, Free on 2G Bail, Continues Tour Pending Trial on Reefer Rap," *Variety*, 1/27/1943.

19. Averbuch and Noble, ibid., pg. 146.

20. "Krupa on Tour Pending Hearing."

21. Ibid.

22. "Gene Krupa Ordered to Trial in Dope Case," *San Francisco Examiner*, 1/21/1943.

23. "Krupa Must Face Charges," *Oakland Tribune*, 1/27/1943.

24. Walker, Danton. "Danton Walker: New York Letter," *Philadelphia Inquirer*, 2/1/1943.

25. Walker, Danton. "Broadway," *New York Daily News*, 2/9/1943.

26. "Krupa Big in Omaha," *Variety*, 2/3/1943.

27. Canfield, Ford. "Krupa Biz Booms at Sherman," *Orchestra World*, March 1943.

28. "Krupa Loses Shoes in Blaze," *San Francisco Examiner*, 2/14/1943; "Chicago Band Briefs," *Down Beat*, 3/1/1943.

29. "Krupa Still King Despite Gov't Jam," *Billboard*, 3/27/1943.
30. Shal. "Earle, Philly," *Variety*, 4/7/1943.
31. The Tiger. "Gene Krupa Sends 3,500 at Madison," *Down Beat*, 3/1/1943.
32. "Inside Stuff—Orchestras," *Variety*, 3/10/1943.
33. "Krupa Enters Guilty Plea," *San Francisco Examiner*, 4/20/1943; "Krupa Admits Guilt," *Motion Picture Daily*, 4/20/1943; "Krupa Guilty; Had Boy Valet Tote Reefers," *New York Daily News*, 4/20/1943; "Krupa Pleads Guilty," *Variety*, 4/21/1943.
34. "Report of 'Guilty' Plea Jams Krupa on Several Dates; N.Y. Par Looks for Out," *Variety*, 4/28/1943.
35. "Krupa Defers Par, N.Y., Date Pending Outcome of Frisco Morals Charge," *Variety*, 5/5/1943.
36. "Bottle and Nipple is Latest Fashion in Opium Layouts," *New York Daily News*, 3/7/1943.
37. Averbuch and Noble, pg. 178; Ehrlich, pg. 136.
38. Ehrlich, pg. 137.
39. Averbuch and Noble, pg. 151.
40. "'Hot' Drummer," *New York Daily News*, 5/19/1943.
41. Winchell, Walter. "Up and Down Broadway with Walter Winchell," *San Francisco Examiner*, 5/16/1943.
42. Winchell, Walter. "Walter Winchell: On Broadway," *The North Adams* [Mass.] *Transcript*, 5/29/1943.
43. "Eldridge Fronts Krupa Band; Trial June 8," *Orchestra World*, June 1943.
44. Krupa, Gene Harry. *Unfortunate Casting: An Autobiographical Essay*. PhD thesis, Department of English, University of Iowa, July 1975, pg. 83.
45. "News of the Month: Benny Offers Gene His Old Job," *Metronome*, August 1943.
46. O'Day, Anita, and Eells, George. *High Times, Hard Times*, Limelight Editions, New York, 1997, pgs. 123–124.
47. "Krupa Felony Trial Delayed by S. F. Court," *San Francisco Examiner*, 6/9/1943.
48. Averbuch and Noble, pgs. 151–152.
49. Ibid.
50. Ibid., pgs. 152–153.
51. "Foley Rejects Plea to Locate Krupa Witnesses," *San Francisco Examiner*, 6/30/1943.
52. "Krupa Gets 1 to Six Years in Dope Case," *New York Daily News*, 7/3/1943.
53. Averbuch and Noble, pgs. 153–154.
54. Ibid., pg. 154.
55. Ibid., pgs. 153–157.
56. "Foley Turns on Prosecutor in Krupa's Trial," *San Francisco Examiner*, 6/30/1943; "Krupa Convicted in Marihuana [sic] Case; 1 to 6 Year Term Faced," *San Francisco Examiner*, 7/1/1943.

57. "Gene Krupa Is Sentenced," *Oakland Tribune*, 7/2/1943.

58. "Krupa Gets 1 to 6 Year Sentence," *San Francisco Examiner*, 7/3/1943.

59. Ibid.; "Krupa Convicted," *San Francisco Examiner*, 7/1/1943.

60. "Krupa's Term Set Today," *San Francisco Examiner*, 7/2/1943.

61. "Krupa Freed on Bail in Dope Case," *San Francisco Examiner*, 8/10/1943.

62. "Krupa Ork Folds [,] Gates Scatter," *Down Beat*, 7/1/1943.

63. "Inside Stuff-Orchestras-Music," *Variety*, 8/4/1943.

64. "Report of 'Guilty' Plea Jams Krupa on Several Dates."

65. Mahlock, Cato. Letter to the Editor, "Downbeat on Krupa Bit but USO Show Plenty OK," *Variety*, 7/21/1943.

66. "Krupa Gets a 'Bum Rap,' S.F. Insiders Say; Appealing 1-6 Year Sentence," *Variety*, 7/7/1943.

67. Averbuch and Noble, ibid., pg. 176.

68. "Ehrlich Denies Paying Krupa Valet Bribe," *San Francisco Examiner*, 7/23/1943.

69. "S.F. Grand Jury Fails to Indict in Krupa Case," *Oakland Tribune*, 7/24/1943.

70. Averbuch and Noble, pg. 181.

71. Ibid., pgs. 181–182.

72. Ibid., pgs. 176–184; Ehrlich, pgs. 139–141.

73. "Krupa Freed on Bail in Dope Case," *San Francisco Examiner*, 8/10/1943.

74. "Surface Noise," *Capitol: The News From Hollywood*, 4/201943; Sullivan, Ed, "Little Old New York," *New York Daily News*, 8/16/1943.

75. "Krupa in H'wood Awaiting Appeal," *Billboard*, 8/21/1943.

76. Balch, Jack. "Krupa Discovers He Still Has a Future," *St. Louis Post-Dispatch*, 6/1/1944.

77. O'Day and Eells, pg. 124.

78. Author interviews with Gail Krupa and Gene H. Krupa, 7/28/2021, 7/31/2021, and 8/4/2021.

79. Author interview with George Wein, 1/18/2019.

80. Author internew with Dan Morgenstern, 1/31/2019.

81. "Derbyville," *Evansville Argus*, 7/23/1943.

82. Davis, Frank Marshall. "Passing Parade: Fascism Reaches Down to Swing," *Jackson* [Mississippi] *Advocate*, 8/7/1943.

83. Rowe, Billy. "Billy Rowe's Notebook," *Pittsburgh Courier*, 7/24/1943.

Chapter 17: "I'm Almost Afraid to Look"

1. From "All My Life," recorded on 4/24/1936 by the Benny Goodman Trio, with vocal by Helen Ward.

2. "Krupa Signs New Contract with Goodman," *Down Beat*, May 1937.

3. Horvath, G. B. S. "Leaders Are Becoming Song Publishers!" *Music and Rhythm*, April 1941; "Appeal of ASCAP to Dismiss Action by BMI Refused," *Broadcasting*, 3/2/1942.

4. Author interview with Joe Vetrano, 8/18/2021.
5. "Krupa Switches Mgrs.: Gluskin Vice Vernier[e]," *Variety*, 8/25/1943.
6. "News of the Month: Gene in NY," *Metronome*, September 1943.
7. "Krupa to Benny," *Metronome*, October 1943.
8. "Krupa Clicks on USO Tour with Goodman; May Stick with Band," *Variety*, 9/29/1943.
9. The Square. "Strictly Ad Lib," *Down Beat*, 10/15/1943.
10. "Krupa Nixes Hub Date Not to Embarrass B.G.," *Variety*, 10/6/1943.
11. Firestone, Ross. *Swing, Swing, Swing: The Life and Times of Benny Goodman*, W. W. Norton & Co., New York, 1993, pg. 321; "Bargain Basement," *Billboard*, 10/23/1943, pg. 13.
12. "Bargain Basement."
13. Wood. "Night Club Reviews: Terrace Room, N.Y.," *Variety*, 10/20/1943.
14. "Benny Mulls Concert Tour, No Dates Set," *Down Beat*, 11/15/1943.
15. Grennard, Elliott. "On the Stand: Benny Goodman," *Billboard*, 10/23/1943, pg. 15.
16. Simon, George T. "Benny, Barnet A, 1, Say Band Reviews," *Metronome*, November 1943.
17. Collier, James Lincoln. *Benny Goodman and the Swing Era*, Oxford University Press, 1989, pg. 309.
18. "Krupa Steps Out," *Orchestra World*, December 1943, pg. 7.
19. Sullivan, Ed. "Little Old New York," *New York Daily News*, 12/11/1943, pg. 7.
20. Manners, Dian. "Men, Maids, and Manners," *Down Beat*, 2/1/1944.
21. Schallert, Elza. *Los Angeles Times*, 5/10/1944, pg. 12.
22. "Krupa Weeps as Fans Cheer Him," *New York Daily News*, 12/23/1943, pg. 31.
23. "New Job," *New York Daily News*, 12/23/1943, pg. 1.
24. Sullivan, Ed. *New York Daily News*, 12/29/1943, pg. 18.
25. Balch, Jack. "Krupa Discovers He Still Has a Future," *St. Louis Post-Dispatch*, 6/1/1944, pg. 27.
26. Ad, "Holiday High-Jinks at the Paramount!" *New York Daily News*, 12/27/1943, pg. 28.
27. "Don't Say We Didn't Tell You!" *Orchestra World*, February 1944.
28. Edwardson, Audrey, "The Ork Whirl," *Orchestra World*, May 1944.
29. "Finks' Greeting," *Down Beat*, 2/1/1944.
30. Ulanov, Barry. "Tommy Dorsey: For Krupa, Stupor," *Metronome*, February 1944.
31. Tilles, Robert. "Percussion Discussion: Innovation," *Music Journal*, 5/1/1967.
32. "Tommy Dorsey's 12 ½ G Plus % In 2 Theatre Dates," *Variety*, 1/12/1944.
33. Cohen. "Stanley, Pitt," *Variety*, 2/2/1944.
34. Hopper, Hedda. "Looking at Hollywood," *Los Angeles Times*, 1/31/1944, pg. 11.
35. Korall, pg. 78.
36. Author interview with Mike Schiffer, 2/27, 2/28, 3/26, and 3/30/2019.

37. Robertson, Alastair. CD Liner notes, *Tommy Dorsey and His Orchestra: The Carnegie Hall V-Disc Session April 1944*, Hep Records, CD40, England, 1990.
38. Records not for public sale and sent only to troops.
39. "Ex-Krupa Valet Repudiates Testimony in Narcotics Case," *San Francisco Examiner*, 2/16/1944, pg. 26.
40. Noble and Averbuch, pg. 187.
41. *People v. Krupa*, 64 Cal. App. 2d 594 (1944).
42. Levinson, Peter J. *Tommy Dorsey: Livin' in a Great Big Way: A Biography*, Da Capo Press, 2005, pg. 197.

Chapter 18: "What's This?"

1. "BG Crowned King Fifth Time: Tommy Dorsey Sweet Winner, Krupa on Tubs," *Down Beat*, 1/1/1944, pgs. 1, 13.
2. "Benny, Tommy, Gene, Lionel, Carney Swamp Contest; Bing Tops Sinatra," *Metronome*, January 1944.
3. "Spivak Gets Crown from TD, Duke Wins, Bing Is New Voice," *Down Beat*, 1/1/1945.
4. "News of the Month: Duke, Cole Win Band Contests; Seven New All-Stars Elected," *Metronome*, January 1945, pgs. 9, 28.
5. Author interview with Kevin Dorn, 2/19/2022.
6. Krupa, Gene. Howard Miller Show, CBS radio, circa 1956, *The Classic Archives Old-Time Radio Channel*, https://www.youtube.com/watch?v=f6jAL4vvJuE&fbclid=IwAR2HvowhXKyVt7QZt89Ak1acACHQlbXuqm-Riw9mVpqxdnfRbwiTSckw_ZTQ&app=desktop. Accessed 4/29/2020.
7. Ehrlich, Evelyn. "Strings Are Thing, Krupa Fiddler Says," *Down Beat*, 2/1/1945.
8. Riley, Bill. "On the Stand: Gene Krupa," *Billboard*, 10/21/1944, pg. 16.
9. Ulanov, Barry. "Stage Show Reviews: Gene Krupa: Not a Killer, Just a Filler," *Metronome*, September 1944.
10. Secon, Paul. "Vaudeville Reviews: Capitol, New York," *Billboard*, 7/29/1944, pg. 26.
11. Ibid.
12. Shaughnessy, Ed, and Flans, Robin. *Lucky Drummer: From NYC Jazz to Johnny Carson*, Rebeats Publications, Alma, MI, 2012, pgs. 2–3.
13. Womack, Kenneth. *Maximum Volume: The Life of Beatles Producer George Martin: The Early Years, 1926-1966*, Chicago Review Press, Chicago, 2017, pg. 12.
14. "'Dragon Seed' Soars to $125,000 to Pace N. Y., 'Since'-Krupa Wow 90G, Others Helped by Overflow," *Variety*, 7/26/1944.
15. "Music Grapevine," *Billboard*, 10/7/1944, pg. 20.
16. "B'way Total High; 'Creek' Record 73G, 'Impatient' Forte 30G, 'Angels'-Vaude Tall 31G, 'Casanova' Wow 120G in 2d," *Variety*, 9/27/1944.
17. Wood. "Capitol, N. Y.," *Variety*, 7/26/1944.

18. "Krupa Signs With RKO for Two Pics," *Variety*, 7/26/1944.

19. "Report Jimmy Dorsey Offered 25G for Decca Release; Krupa to Col.," *Variety*, 11/22/1944.

20. "Krupa Mulls Longest Wartime 1-Nite Tour," *Variety*, 9/13/1944.

21. "Shaw Finds Ops No Like 3G Against 50%," *Billboard*, 12/9/1944.

22. Wilson, John. Program #673, Gene Krupa, *The World of Jazz*, broadcast on 4/13/1968.

23. Ashby, Neal. "Drummer Man Gene Krupa Swings In, Out on Bomber," *The Des Moines Register*, 12/23/1944, pg. 6.

24. Crosbie, Ian. "Let Me Off Uptown," *Coda*, March 1974, pgs. 5–14.

25. "Failure of Krupa Ork to Show May Cause Tighter Contracts," *Billboard*, 1/6/1945, pg. 15; "Krupa Misses Opening Nite," *Down Beat*, 1/15/1945; Crosbie, pgs. 5–14.

26. Emge, Charles. On the Beat in Hollywood, *Down Beat*, 3/1/1945; "White Wants Krupa," *Down Beat*, 4/1/1945.

27. Brady, Dr. William. "Hotcha! That Drummer Man Is Here," *St. Louis Star and Times*, 4/12/45, pg. 16.

28. Allied Arts Corporation, Edgar L. Goldsmith, Warren E. Thompson Present Gene Krupa and His Orchestra in a Concert and Dance, Sunday Evening, April 22nd, at 7:30 P.M., Chicago Arena.

29. "Krupa Lonesome with 2G," *Billboard*, 4/21/1945, pg. 28.

30. Krupa, Gene, LP liner notes, *Gene Krupa's Sidekicks*, CL 641, Columbia Records, 1955; "Laughing Boy," *Metronome*, May 1949, pg. 24.

31. *Gene Krupa's Sidekicks*.

32. Friedwald, Will. *Jazz Singing: America's Great Voices From Bessie Smith to Bebop and Beyond*, Charles Scribner's Sons, New York, 1990, pg. 226.

33. "Gene Krupa," *Metronome*, July 1945.

34. Ulanov, Barry. "Dave Lambert," July 1947, pg. 12.

35. Feather, Leonard. "Genial Gene Talks Back," *Metronome*, September 1945.

36. O'Day, Anita, and Eells, George. *High Times, Hard Times*, Limelight Editions, New York, 1997, pg. 143.

37. "Buffalo Gives Poor B. O. to Gene Krupa; Layoffs the Reason," *Billboard*, 9/29/45, pg. 39.

38. "B'way Up; '92d St.'-Copa Big 114G, 'Highness'-Krupa Bouncy 88g, 'Pierce' Plus Morgan-Stooges Wham at 70G," *Variety*, 10/3/1945.

39. Tunnis, Jack "One Spot." "The Cash Box Disc-Hits Box Score," *Cash Box*, 12/31/1945.

40. Sippel, Johnny. "Night Club Reviews: College Inn, Hotel Sherman, Chicago," *Billboard*, 12/1/1945, pg. 36.

41. Krupa, Gene. "Gene Talks About the Music," LP liner notes, *Drummin' Man: Gene Krupa*, Columbia Records, C2L-29.

42. O'Day and Eells, pgs. 146–147.

43. "I'm Not Mad—Krupa," unknown publication, April 1946, Rutgers Institute of Jazz Studies.
44. Morgenstern, Dan. "Gene Krupa/Anita O'Day," *Down Beat*, 4/11/1974.
45. "Ethel and Gene Krupa to Wed?" *Capitol: The News from Hollywood*, September 1944; Walker, Danton, "Broadway Beat," *Philadelphia Inquirer*, 10/11/1944, pg. 27; Carroll, Harrison, *The Morning Herald* [Uniontown, PA], 11/3/1944, pg. 18; Manners, Dian, "Men Maids & Manners," *Down Beat*, 11/15/1944; Manners, Dorothy, "'Bloomer Girl' Due to Go On Sale in Hollywood," *San Francisco Examiner*, 11/23/1944, pg. 9; Carroll, Harrison, "Behind the Scenes: Hollywood," *The Press Democrat* [Santa Rosa, CA], 1/9/1945, pg. 12; Kilgallen, Dorothy, "On Broadway," *Pittsburgh Post-Gazette*, 2/19/1945, pg. 20; Hopper, Hedda, "Hedda Says—Here and There in Hollywood," *The Pittsburgh Press*, 3/2/1945, pg. 21; Walker, Danton; "Broadway," *New York Daily News*, 2/1/1946.
46. Author interview with Gail Krupa, 7/28/2021.
47. Grace, Frank. "Gene Krupa Is Tops Among Drummers," *Ocala* [Florida] *StarBanner*, 5/25/2006, https://www.ocala.com/news/20060525/gene-krupa-is-tops-among-drummers. Accessed 10/7/2018.
48. Scott, Bobby. "Gene Krupa: The World Is Not Enough," *Gene Lees Jazzletter*, January 1984, pgs. 1–8.
49. Ibid.
50. "'Smoky'-Krupa Fancy 39G Tops Hub; 'Wed' 41G in 2, 'Music' 25G, Both 2d," *Variety*, 8/14/1946.
51. "B'way Booms; 'Notorious' Huge 150G, 'Claudia'-Blaine-Colonna Sock 132G 'Mexico'-Krupa-Green Great 106G," *Variety*, 8/21/1946; "Broadway Newsreel," *Film Bulletin*, 9/16/1946.
52. "Krupa Economy Moves Seen as a Cue to Similar Action by Other Name Bandsmen," *Billboard*, 11/9/1946, pg. 17; "Sidemen Co-op on Band Slices," *Variety*, 12/4/1946; "Woody Herman to Break Up Band," *Variety*, 12/11/1946.

Chapter 19: Here We Go Again!

1. Simon, George T. "No Noisemaker, Krupa," *Metronome*, September 1948, pg. 14.
2. "Aquarium, N.Y., Joins with 400 Club in Exiting From Name Band Field," *Variety*, 1/15/1947.
3. Gitler, Ira. *From Swing to Bop*, Oxford University Press, 1985, pg. 215.
4. Lees, Gene. *Cats of Any Color*, Oxford University Press, New York, 1995, pg. 100.
5. Korall, Burt. *JazzTimes*, November 1992, pg. 40.
6. McDonough, John. CD box set liner notes, *The Complete Capitol Recordings of Gene Krupa and Harry James*, Mosaic Records, Stamford, CT, 1999, MD7-192, pg. 5.

7. Shipton, Alyn. *A New History of Jazz*, Continuum, New York, 2007, pg. 387.
8. Simon, George T. *The Big Bands*, Schirmer Books, New York, 1971, pg. 310.
9. Crosbie, Ian. "Let Me Off Uptown," *Coda*, March 1974, pg. 13.
10. Josephson, Sanford. *Jeru's Journey: The Life and Music of Gerry Mulligan*, Hal Leonard Books, Milwaukee, WI, 2015.
11. Crosbie, pg. 13.
12. Ibid., pg. 14.
13. Fuller, Walter. *Pittsburgh Courier*, 3/26/1949, pg. 22.
14. "Krupa in Col. Pix," *Variety*, 7/9/1947.
15. Wilk, Ralph. "Hollywood Vine-Yard," *Film Daily*, 7/18/1947.
16. Wilk, Ralph. "Hollywood Vine-Yard," *Film Daily*, 9/5/1947.
17. "'Smart Politics' with Freddie Stewart and June Preisser," *Harrison's Reports*, 1/10/1948.
18. "'Make Believe Ballroom' with Ruth Warrick, Virginia Welles and Jerome Courtland," *Harrison's Reports*, 4/23/1949, pg. 66.
19. Heffernan, Harold. "Home-Coming Is Different," *The Evening Star* [Washington, DC], 4/10/1945, pg. A-14.
20. Gardner, Mark. "Red Rodney Talks," *Jazz Monthly*, April 1970, pg. 2.
21. Lees, pg. 100.
22. "Jazz Drummer Jake Hanna Talks About Gene Krupa," Monk Rowe Interview of Jake Hanna, 10/11/1997, https://www.youtube.com/watch?v=WiPAbgu8zYM. Posted 4/30/2018. Accessed 2/16/2022.
23. Carmody, Jay. "Krupa, Sibelius and Maisie Blended in Capitol's Bill," *Evening Star* [Washington, DC], 10/17/1947, pg. A-24.
24. *Gene Krupa and His Orchestra 1942-1945* [CD], Classic Records, Cat. No. CLASSICS1096.
25. Thanks to Henry Maurer for identifying the piece.
26. Author interview with Kevin Dorn, 2/19/2022.
27. Wexler, Jerry. *Billboard*, 7/24/1948, pg. 18.
28. Simon, "No Noisemaker, Krupa."
29. Krupa, Gene, and Bernstein, Leonard. "Jazz Forum: Has Jazz Influenced the Symphony?" *Esquire*, February 1947, pgs. 46.
30. Ibid., pgs. 46, 47, 118, and 152.
31. "Krupa All Eyes for Video," *Down Beat*, 7/14/1948; jeg, "Capsule Comments," *Down Beat*, 10/6/1948, pg. 23.
32. "Dave Tough, 41, of Austin High Gang, Dies After Fall," [probably] *Down Beat*, 12/29/1948.
33. Feather, Leonard. "Feather's Nest: The Dave Tough Story," *Down Beat*, 7/1/1953, pg. 21.
34. "Krupa Tees Off Again Jan. 18 at U. of Detroit," *Variety*, 1/12/1949.
35. "Benny Goodman Does Quick Fade at N.Y. Par," *Variety*, 1/12/1949.
36. "Roy Eldridge," *Variety*, 1/26/1949.
37. Crosbie, pg. 13.

38. Chilton, John. *Roy Eldridge: Little Jazz Giant*, Continuum, London and New York, 2002, pg. 162.
39. Watt, Douglas. "Record Review," *New York Daily News*, 7/24/1949.
40. Ulanov, Barry. "Roy," *Metronome*, December 1949, pg. 13.
41. "Records Most Played by Disk Jockeys," *Billboard*, 4/23/1949, pg. 144.
42. Zhito, Lee. "On the Stand: Gene Krupa," *Billboard*, 4/30/1949, pg. 42.
43. Hallock, Ted. "Krupa Band Not Drawing Raves, But Pulling Crowds," *Down Beat*, July 1949.
44. "Guilds Defend Show Colony as Movie Star Faces 'Dope' Charges," *Pittsburgh Courier*, 9/11/1948, pg. 22.
45. FBI Radiograms dated 2/12/1949 through 2/28/1949. Obtained from Federal Drug Enforcement Administration (OPRA request).
46. Associated Press. "3 Krupa Bandsmen Held in Narcotics Case," *Evening Star* [Washington, DC], 7/26/1949, pg. A-3; "3d Krupa Player in Dope Cell," unknown newspaper, August 1949 (accessed at Rutgers Institute of Jazz Studies).
47. Simon, George T. "The Editors Speak," *Metronome*, September 1949, pg. 42.
48. "Krupa Fights Ban in Dope Arrests," unknown newspaper, August 1949 (accessed at Rutgers Institute of Jazz Studies).
49. Simon, "The Editors Speak."
50. Crosbie, pg. 13.
51. Scott, Bobby. "Gene Krupa: The World Is Not Enough," *Gene Lees Jazzletter*, January 1984, pg. 5.
52. See, e.g., Cohen, Martin. "I See You With My Heart," *TV Radio Mirror*, February 1962.
53. Brown, Bernie. "Krupa on Drumming Today and Yesterday," *Down Beat*, 12/2/1965.
54. Torre, Marie. "Krupa's Going Long Hair, But Hepcats Won't Fret," unidentified publication, 1944.
55. Josephson. *Jeru's Journey.*
56. Scott, "Gene Krupa: The World Is Not Enough," pg. 3.
57. Scott, Bobby. "On the Record: 'The Old Man' Gene Krupa," *TV-Radio Mirror*, September 1962, pg. 17.
58. Brown, "Krupa on Drumming."
59. The American Society of Composers, Authors and Publishers.
60. Broadcast Music, Inc.
61. See, e.g., Clevenger, Russell, "BMI—Offers New Music Source," and Paine, John G., "ASCAP: Leaders Face 'Frozen' Books," *Orchestra World*, September 1940, pg. 7; "Bandleaders Will Need New Themes if ASCAP Tunes Are Barred," *Orchestra World*, October 1940, pg. 6; "ASCAP-BMI Battlefront," *Orchestra World*, December 1940, pg. 17; Bodec, Ben, "ASCAP-RADIO: BLOW BY BLOW," *Variety*, 1/8/1941, pg. 131; "ASCAP ON THE

DOWNBEAT," *Billboard*, 11/8/1941, pg. 9; "ASCAP AND RADIO—WHO WON?," *Orchestra World*, December 1941, pg. 6.

62. Webb, Gene. "Gene Krupa: The Last Interview," *Down Beat*, 3/14/1974.

63. Schneider, John. "This Boycott Changed American Music," *Radioworld*, 5/4/2015 and 8/27/2020. https://radioworld.com/columns-and-views/this-boycott-changed-American-music. Accessed 11/16/2023.

64. See, e.g., Levin, Mike, "Showdown Looms on Discs: Petrillo Resolved to Halt Recordings," *Down Beat*, 7/1/1942, pg. 1; Levin, Mike, "All Recording Stops Today," *Down Beat*, 8/1/1942, pg. 1; "AFM Hurts Public Morale, Senate Witnesses Charge," *Orchestra World*, October 1942; "Petrillo Issues New Disc Edict," *Down Beat*, 1/1/1943, pg. 3; "Settlement Near on Record Ban; Proposal Offered," *Orchestra World*, March 1943; "Petrillo Begins Negotiations to Lift Record Ban," *Down Beat*, 3/1/1943, pg. 15; "Industry Lawyers Hold Little Hope That WLB Will Even Try to Solve Complicated AFM-Disk Co. Issue" and "Petrillo's Disk Crackdown Only Pertains to E.T.s," *Variety*, 7/7/1943, pgs. 41, 43; "Inside Stuff—Orchestras," *Variety*, 11/17/1943; DeVeaux, Scott, "Bebop and the Recording Industry: The 1942 AFM Recording Ban Reconsidered," *Journal of the American Musicological Society*, Spring 1988, pg. 126.

65. Sekro, Art. "They're on Their Own!" *Orchestra World*, December 1943, pg. 9.

66. "30% Tax May Affect 15,000 Jobs," *Orchestra World*, May 1944.

67. "All Work and No Pay Makes Any Maestro Hit the Blue Notes," *Orchestra World*, October 1944.

68. "Musicians Hit by Curfew Rule, Pacts in Doubt," *Down Beat*, 3/1/1945.

Chapter 20: "As Breathtaking as Ever Before"

1. Stone, George Lawrence. "Technique of Percussion," *International Musician*, October 1949.

2. "Gene Krupa Operated On," *New York Times*, 8/19/1951; "Gene Krupa Undergoes Operation in Virginia," *Sunday Star* [Washington, DC], 8/19/1951, pg. A-32; "On the Upbeat: New York," *Variety*, 8/22/1951.

3. Sullivan, Ed. "Little Old New York," *The Daily Record* [Dunn, NC], 9/4/1951, pg. 4.

4. "Ella, Oscar Peterson Star as 'JATP' Tour Begins," *Down Beat*, 10/19/1951.

5. "History of the Year," *Metronome Yearbook*, early 1951.

6. "Carle, Krupa Assigned to 'Dance Band' Album Series; Big Station Play," *Variety*, 3/1/1950.

7. Author interview with Dan Morgenstern, 1/31/2019.

8. "Band Business Is on Way Up Again, Says Krupa," *Down Beat*, 8/25/1950, pg. 3.

9. Egan, Jack. "The Gene Krupa Trio Story," press release, undated. Posted on Facebook by Joe Plumeri, son of Don Palmer (Dom Plumeri), on Facebook's *Gene Krupa That Ace Drummer Man* Facebook Group.

10. Tracy, Jack. "Krupa 3 Will Be Biggest Jazz Attraction in Years," *Down Beat*, 5/7/1952, pg. 2.

11. "Trek to Japan for Krupa Trio," *Billboard*, 4/12/1952, pg. 17.

12. Orodenker, Maurie H. "On the Stand: Gene Krupa Jazz Trio," *Billboard*, 2/16/1952, pg. 46.

13. Gagh. "New Acts: Gene Krupa Trio," *Variety*, 2/20/1952.

14. Author interview with Kevin Dorn, 2/19/2022.

15. Author interview with Rita Ventura Lenderman, circa 7/12/2019.

16. Author interview with Matthew Napoleon, 9/10/2020.

17. Author interview with Susan Smith, 4/13/2019.

18. Author interview with Matthew Napoleon, 10/1/2020.

19. Egan, Jack. "Those Spare Time Blues . . ." *In the Groove*, March 1948, pg. 5.

20. Author interview with Matthew Napoleon, 10/1/2020.

21. Klauber, Bruce. "Toward the Rising Sun," *JazzTimes*, November 2021, pg. 45.

22. Minor, William. *Jazz Journeys to Japan: The Heart Within*, University of Michigan Press, Ann Arbor, MI, 2004, pg. 104.

23. Ibid., pg. 8.

24. Muraoka, Tay, President, Hot Club of Japan, letter to George Hoefer, dated 5/14/1952, Rutgers Institute of Jazz Studies.

25. Author interview with Akira Suzuki, 3/13/2021 and 3/28/2021.

26. Tracy, Jack, "'Greatest Welcome Since Goodman Era' for Gene Krupa Trio Japanese Tour," *Down Beat*, 6/18/1952; Krupa, Gene, "Gene Krupa on Japan," *Metronome,* August 1952, pgs. 13, 31.

27. Author interview with Akira Suzuki, 3/13/2021 and 3/28/2021.

28. "Gene Krupa on Japan."

29. Gene Krupa interview, *CBC Krupa Memorial Broadcast*, 10/21/1973.

30. "Gene Krupa on Japan."

31. Recordings from author's private collection.

32. Atkins, E. Taylor. *Blue Nippon: Authenticating Jazz in Japan*, Duke University Press, Durham, NC, 2001.

33. Minor, pg. 12.

34. Ibid.

35. "Col, Victor in Nippon Ride '52 Biz Upbeat, LP Disks Going Over Big," *Variety*, 12/24/1952.

36. Author interviews with Kevin Dorn on 10/14/2023 and 11/6/2023, John Petters on 11/16/2023, Bruce Klauber on 10/14/2023, and Joe Vetrano on 10/13/2023 and 11/8/2023.

Chapter 21: "He Was Beautiful"

1. Anderson, Ernie. "This Jazz Was Dazzling—Even For Armstrong!" *Melody Maker*, 5/9/1953, pg. 3.
2. *Benny Goodman Louis Armstrong 1953 Jazz Concert Programme*, Tad Hershorn—Norman Granz Papers, Folder "1-53-7-53," at Rutgers Institute of Jazz Studies.
3. Hammond, John, and Townsend, Irving. *John Hammond on the Record: An Autobiography*, Summit Books, New York, 1977, pgs. 314–315.
4. Feather, Leonard. "BG-Louis Tour Is Cited as Bitterest Jazz Hassel Ever," *Down Beat*, 6/3/1953.
5. "Concerts Go on Without Benny," *Down Beat*, 5/20/1953.
6. "Goodman's New Ork: All-Star Unit to Join Armstrong on Tour," *Billboard*, 2/7/1953.
7. "B. G. Orch Pulls 10G in 2 Dates," *Variety*, 4/15/1953.
8. Taubman, Howard. "Atom Bomb on Carnegie Hall? No, Man! Goodman and Satchmo Armstrong's All Stars Beat It Out," *New York Times*, 4/18/1953, pg. 16.
9. Congdon, Richard H. "Benny's Bash Boffo!" *Record Changer*, 5/5/1953, pg. 6.
10. Guttridge, Len. "What Happened When BG Left," *Melody Maker*, 5/23/1953, pg. 4.
11. "Goodman Collapses, Put in Oxygen Tent," *New York Times*, 4/20/1953.
12. Schoenfeld, Herm. "Goodman-Armstrong 'Flashback' to '38 Jazz Idiom Dimmed by Time," *Variety*, 4/22/1953.
13. "Goodman-Satchmo P'kge Hit by Internal Beefs; B. G. May Not Come Back," *Variety*, 4/29/1953.
14. "BG (Krupa)-Satchmo Troupe Mops Up Sock 340G Gross; Only 3 Dates in Red," *Variety*, 6/10/1953.
15. "BG's Bow-Out From Jazz P'kge Dents B.O. Slightly; Granz Switches Billing," *Variety*, 5/6/1953.
16. "Big Rift," *Metronome*, July 1953.
17. Recording from author's private collection.
18. Myers, Marc. "Interview: Al Stewart (Part 3)," *JazzWax*, September 2009. Posted on 9/30/2009. https://www.jazzwax.com/2009/09/index.html. Accessed 3/24/2019.
19. "O.K. on the Paradiddles," *New Yorker*, 4/24/1954, pg. 24.
20. Krupa, Gene. "The Basis of Jazz," *Metronome*, July 1954.
21. Krupa, Gene. "Jazz Old: Krupa Says Study Is Investment," *Jazz Today*, October 1957, pg. 15.
22. Krupa, Gene, and Cole, Cozy. *Gene Krupa—Cozy Cole Correspondence Course*, circa 1958.
23. Webb, Gene. "The Last Interview," *Down Beat*, 3/14/1974.

24. Interview with Cozy Cole, Jazz Oral History Project, Rutgers University Institute of Jazz Studies, conducted by Bill Kirchner, April 1980, Cassette #5, pgs. 5–10.
25. Interview with Cozy Cole, pgs. 5–11.

Chapter 22: "Superficial Glandular Excitement"

1. Winquist, Sven G., "9,000 Cheer as Krupa Opens in Sweden," *Melody Maker*, 7/12/1952, pg. 12; "Krupa Trio Draws 7,000 in 1st Sweden Concert," *Variety*, 7/16/1952.
2. Condon, Bob. "Swedes Sweet on Ray, Krupa, Sinatra, 3-D," *Variety*, 3/4/1953.
3. Author interview with Kevin Dorn, 12/17/2022.
4. "Krupa's Quickie Aussie Concerts; 7 in 11 Days," *Variety*, 7/14/1954.
5. Armstrong, John. "Leader of Jazz for Newcastle," *Newcastle Morning Herald and Miners' Advocate* [Australia], 7/3/1954, pg. 5.
6. "Krupa Will Earn Fortune in a Week," *Newcastle Sun* [Australia], 6/10/1954, pg. 27.
7. "Sign Krupa Trio for Australia . . ." *Billboard*, 7/10/1954, pg. 27.
8. "Krupa Due on August 12," *Newcastle Morning Herald and Miners' Advocate*, 8/5/1954, pg. 11.
9. Egan, Jack. "Krupa Lauds Australian Taste in Jazz," *Down Beat*, 11/3/1954.
10. "Guard of Honor for Gene Krupa," *Newcastle Sun*, 8/12/1954, pg. 26.
11. "You Can Mark Off 'K' for Krupa Day," *Mirror* [Perth, Australia], 8/14/1954, pg. 12.
12. "Mr. Gene Krupa Gives Us the Drum on It," *Daily Telegraph* [Sydney], 8/13/1954, pg. 9.
13. Ibid.; "Yank Drummer Goes British in Australia," *Variety*, 8/25/1954.
14. "Gene's Busy Day," *The Sun* [Sydney], 8/14/1954, pg. 1; "Teenagers Mob Krupa," *Daily Telegraph*, 8/15/1954, pg. 9.
15. "Krupa's Solo Sends Crowd," *Daily Telegraph*, 8/14/1954, pg. 7.
16. "Fans Mob Krupa," *The Argus* [Melbourne], 8/16/1954, pg. 5; "Crazed Crowd Cries for Krupa," *Daily Telegraph*, 8/16/1954, pg. 12.
17. "Krupa Beats Drums in Stadium Clash," *The Age* [Melbourne], 8/18/1954, pg. 3; "Gene Krupa for Further Concert," *The Age*, 8/19/1954, pg. 4.
18. "Krupa Mobbed," *The News* [Adelaide, South Australia], 8/19/1954, pg. 14.
19. "A Benevolent Monarch," *The Advertiser* [Adelaide], 8/20/1954, pg. 3.
20. "Welcome Tattoo: Dots, Dashes for Krupa," *Courier-Mail* [Brisbane, Queensland], 8/20/1954, pg. 1.
21. "Teen-Agers Shrieked as Krupa Beat Daylight Out of Drums!" *Truth* [Brisbane], 8/22/1954, pg. 47.
22. "Food-Poisoned Krupa Yearns for Surf," *Maryborough Chronicle* [Queensland], 8/21/1954, pg. 5.

23. "Gene Krupa Arrives: Hundreds Seek His Autograph," *Newcastle Sun*, 8/23/1954, pg. 13.
24. "You Can Mark Off 'K' for Krupa Day."
25. Webb, Elizabeth. "What I Saw at the Krupa Show Frightened," *The News* [Adelaide], 9/9/1954, pg. 24.
26. Author interview with Colin Petersen, 4/21/2023.
27. Sigwald, Ralph. "I Can't Believe It Myself!" [probably] *TV-Radio Mirror*, December 1950.
28. McLemore, Henry. "Disguised as a Reporter, He Calls Mr. Truman 'Harry,'" *Evening Star* [Washington, DC], 2/8/1951, pg. 19.
29. "Our Town," *Madison County Democrat* [London, OH], 4/27/1951.
30. Aycock, Linda. "Teen Tattle Tales," *The Daily Record* [Dunn, NC], 5/2/1952.
31. Herm., "New Acts: The Goofers," *Variety*, 12/24/1952.
32. "What the Dum-Goo? Whassa Matter With That Leg? Next Weekly Dance Set Saturday," *The Lincoln Times* [Lincolnton, NC], 11/15/1954.
33. "4 Yr. Old Is Star Drummer," *Arizona Tribune* [Phoenix], 8/31/1962.
34. McHarry, Charles. "On the Town," *New York Daily News*, 4/26/1961.
35. Chamberlain, Rich. "Chris Wright Pays Tribute to Eric Delaney," *MusicRadar*, 8/23/2011. https://musicradar.com/rhythm/chris-wright-pays-tribute-to-eric-delaney-490005. Accessed 12/4/2023.

Chapter 23: Playing Well With Others

1. Hershorn, Tad. *Norman Granz: The Man Who Used Jazz for Justice*, University of California Press, Berkeley, CA, 2011, pg. 4.
2. "Granz Lines Up Next Bash Fest," *Down Beat*, 12/15/1944.
3. Dexter, "6th Philly Jazz Concert Way Off Beam," *Capitol: The News from Hollywood*, March 1945; "Philharmonic Jazz Concert," *The Jazz Record*, April 1945, pg. 16.
4. Known now as *Jazz at the Philharmonic Volume I*.
5. "Granz Sells But Holds," *Down Beat*, 2/2/1961, pg. 11.
6. "Best Albums: Jazz at the Philharmonic," *Modern Screen*, February 1946, pg. 12.
7. "Names Take Jazz Concert," *Pittsburgh Courier*, 2/9/1946; Feather, Leonard, "Concerts: Jazz at the Philharmonic," *Metronome*, July 1946; Granz, Norman, Liner Notes, *Norman Granz' Jazz at the Philharmonic Featuring the Gene Krupa Trio*, Clef Records, Cat. No. MG C-600, 1951.
8. "Granz Sets 48 Dates for Big Jazz Safari," *Billboard*, 9/15/1951, pg. 16.
9. "Gene Krupa Memorial Broadcast," Hartford, CT, 11/30/1973 (originally aired in July 1972), https://goldenage-wtic.org/BB-30.html. Accessed in 2019–2020.
10. Freeman, Don. "Krupa Scores Personally, Too, with 'JATP' Troupe," *Down Beat*, 1/25/1952.

11. McDonough, John. Box set liner notes, *Classic Jazz at the Philharmonic Jam Sessions (1950-1957)*, Mosaic Records, Cat. No. MD10-275, Stamford, CT, 2022, pg. 20.
12. Chilton, John. *Roy Eldridge: Little Jazz Giant*, Continuum, London and New York, 2002, pg. 195.
13. "Krupa-Rich, Shavers-Eldridge Will Battle in New JATP Tour," *Down Beat*, 9/24/1952.
14. Webman, Hal. "Granz Mints Money and Music With 12th JATP," *Down Beat*, 10/22/1952, pg. 21.
15. "Jazz at the Phil. to Play London!" *Melody Maker*, 2/28/1953, pg. 1; "Granz Unit to Play for British Flood Fund, Cracks Ban on AFMers," *Variety*, 3/4/1953.
16. The Slider, "Ad Lib," *The New Musical Express*, 3/13/1953, pg. 3.
17. Brown, Tony. "This Day Made History," *Melody Maker*, 3/14/1953, pg. 2.
18. Chilton, pg. 192.
19. Gillespie, Dizzy. "Chords and Discords," *Down Beat*, 5/16/1956, pg. 4.
20. "Fitzgerald, Granz Gain in Bias Case," *Pittsburgh Courier*, 2/11/1956, pg. 32.
21. "Jazz on the Plush," *Mademoiselle*, July 1955; "Newport Jazz Festival," *Our World*, November 1954, pg. 35. Tad Hershorn papers at Institute of Jazz Studies, folder titled, "Clippings 1/55-12/55 Chrono."
22. Wein, George, and Chinen, Nate, *Myself Among Others: A Life in Music*, Da Capo Press, 2004, pg. 142; Author interview with George Wein, 1/18/2019.
23. Scott, Bobby. "Gene Krupa: The World Is Not Enough," *Gene Lees Jazz-letter*, January 1984, pg. 6.
24. The Square, "Strictly Ad Lib," *Down Beat*, 11/15/1951, pg. 5; author interview with Michael Bellino, 6/17/2019.
25. Author interview with Michael Bellino, 5/5/2019.
26. "Fans Mob Krupa," *The Argus*, 8/16/1954, pg. 5.
27. "In the Galleries: Exhibition by M. Svet Shows Taste for Delicate Firmness," *Los Angeles Times*, 2/21/1954, pg. 95.
28. See, e.g., Tormé, Mel, *Traps: The Drum Wonder*, Oxford University Press, New York, 1991, pgs. 107–110; Minahan, John, *The Torment of Buddy Rich: A Biography*, Writer's Showcase Presented by *Writer's Digest*, an imprint of iUniverse.com, Lincoln, NE, 2000, pgs. 128–136; Berglund, Pelle, *Buddy Rich: One of a Kind*, Hudson Music/Hal Leonard, Milwaukee, WI, 2019, pgs. 185–188.
29. Scott, "The World Is Not Enough," pgs. 2–3.
30. Author interview with Michael Bellino, 5/5/2019.
31. "Mrs. Ethel Krupa," *New York Daily News*, 12/10/1955.
32. "Krupa," *Chicago Tribune*, 12/12/1955.
33. Author interview with Kevin Dorn, 2/19/2022.
34. Ibid.

35. Kevin Dorn YouTube post: "A Classic Gene Krupa/Jo Jones Drum Pattern (with some variations and some exercises." Posted 4/18/2021. https://www.youtube.com/watch?v=v8h8QGOt4No. Accessed 7/7/2021.

36. Fish, Scott K. Scottkfish.com, "Clifton James: I Wanted My Own Style of Playing," posted 12/9/2015. https://scottkfish.com/2015/12/09/clifton-james-i-wanted-my-own-style-of-playing. Accessed 1/14/2019.

37. Fish, Scott K., Scottkfish.com. "Fred Below: The Beatles Wouldn't Have Been the Beatles," posted 3/9/2016. https://scottkfish.com/2016/03/09/fred-below-the-beatles-wouldnt-have-been-the-beatles/. Accessed 1/15/2019.; Fish, Scott K., Scottkfish.com. "Fred Below—Magic Maker," posted 1/10/2018. https://moderndrummer.com/article/september-1983-fred-magic-maker/. Accessed 4/25/2019.

38. Jusino, Teresa. "Producer Greg Wells Brings Music to the Hunger Games," *PopMatters*, posted 4/24/2012. Accessed 1/17/2019.

39. Author interview with Tino Gross, 1/5/2019.

40. Willman, Chris. "X Recalls Rise and Fall of L.A. Punk Scene in 40-Year Celebration at Grammy Museum," *Variety*. Posted on 10/15/2017, https://variety.com/2017/music/news/x-band-grammy-museum-1202590223/. Accessed 12/15/2023.

Chapter 24: Gene and the Big Band Biopics

1. Author interview with Marvin Ostroff, 1/30/2019.

2. Author interviews with Ostroff on 11/16/2018 and 1/30/2019.

3. "Krupa Injures Shoulder; 3 Others Hurt in Crash," *New York Post*, 8/5/1957.

4. Berger, Edward. *Bassically Speaking: An Oral History of George Duvivier*, The Scarecrow Press, Metuchen, NJ, 1993, pgs. 165–166.

5. McNamara, Helen. "Krupa Opens Here," *The Telegram* [Toronto, ON], 3/18/1958.

6. Scott, Bobby. "Gene Krupa: The World Is Not Enough," *Gene Lees Jazzletter*, January 1984.

7. Author interview with Bruce Klauber, 12/23/2023.

8. Ibid.

9. Webb, Gene. "The Last Interview," *Down Beat*, 3/14/1974.

10. George. "The Monthly Record," *Photoplay*, March 1960.

11. Author interview with Tino Gross, 1/5/2019.

12. National Academy of Motion Picture Arts and Sciences archives, *The Gene Krupa Story*, correspondence dated 7/25/1958, 4/30/1959, 6/5/1959, 7/2/1959.

13. "Hollywood," *Photoplay*, April 1960.

14. Balten, Jack H. "Movie Review: The Gene Krupa Story," *The Jazz Review*, May 1960, pg. 37.

15. Author interview with Bruce Klauber, 12/23/2023.
16. Chilton, John. *Roy Eldridge: Little Jazz Giant*, Continuum, London and New York, 2002, pg. 226.
17. Author interview with Bobby Tribuzio, 9/23/2019.
18. "Munich Newsnotes," *Billboard*, 5/23/1960, pg. 43.

Chapter 25: "Being Able to Play a Little Again"

1. Krupa, Gene Harry. *Unfortunate Casting: An Autobiographical Essay.* PhD thesis, Department of English, University of Iowa, July 1975, pg. 33.
2. North, Art. "He Beats All," *New York Daily News*, 5/8/60, pg. 34.
3. "U.S.A. Midwest: The Drummer Takes a Wife," *Down Beat*, 2/5/1959, pg. 10.
4. Klauber, Bruce H. *The World of Gene Krupa: The Legendary Drummin' Man*, Pathfinder Publishing of California, 1990, pg. 169.
5. "Granz Getz Stitt for JATP!" *Melody Maker*, 4/25/1959.
6. "M. J. Bloch, Broker, Dies," *Daily Calumet*, 4/19/1958, pg. 1.
7. Klauber, pg. 134, citing *Down Beat*, 3/5/1959.
8. Author interview with Bobby Tribuzio, 9/23/19.
9. "Chicago," *Down Beat*, 1/19/1961, pg. 51.
10. Simon, George T. "The Jazz Beat: With Time on His Hands," *New York Herald Tribune*, 9/3/1961.
11. Knight, Gene. "The Knight Watch: Quick Quartet to Back Krupa," *New York Journal American*, 3/30/1961.
12. McHarry, Charles. "On the Town," *New York Daily News*, 4/26/1961.
13. Author interview with Dr. Richard L. Weiss, July 6 and 18, 2020.
14. Author interview with Bobby Tribuzio, 9/23/2019.
15. Author interview with Bruce Klauber, 3/27/2020.
16. "Blowing" is jazz lingo for playing, regardless of instrument.
17. Author interview with Terry Gibbs, 1/10/2019; Gibbs, Terry, and Ginell, Cary, *Good Vibes: A Life in Jazz*, Lanham, MD, 2003, pg. 228.
18. Author interview with Les DeMerle, 2/10/2019; see, e.g., Hubbell, Diana, "Remembering When Horse Diving Was an Actual Thing," posted 5/9/2023. https://www.atlasobscura.com/articles/horse-diving-atlantic-city-steel-pier. Accessed 12/29/2023; Levin, Kris, "High Diving Horses of the Atlantic City Boardwalk," *Ripley's*, posted 2/11/2020. https://www.rip-leys.com/weird-news/high-diving-horses/. Accessed 12/29/2023.
19. North, Arthur. "Krupa: King of the Beat," *New York Daily News*, 5/13/1962.
20. Wilson, John S., Article draft, 1963, John S. Wilson Papers at the Rutgers Institute of Jazz Studies; McNamara, Helen, "Showman Krupa Swings Into Town," *Toronto Telegraph*, 10/22/1963.
21. "Top Jazzists to Perform at World's Fair Jazzland," *Cash Box*, 3/21/1964, pg. 40.

22. Selchow, Manfred. *Profoundly Blue: A Bio-Discographical Scrapbook on Edmond Hall*, Uhle & Kleimann, Germany, 1988, pgs. 510–511.

23. "Mexico," *Cash Box*, 8/22/1964, pg. 49.

24. Krupa, Gene. Liner notes, *Percussion King*, Verve Records, 1961, Cat. No. V-8414.

25. Simon, "Time on His Hands."

26. Interview with Gene Krupa on WNEW-radio by William B. Williams, promoting *Together Again* (circa 1964).

27. Ibid.

28. Brown, Anthony. "Louie Bellson: NEA Jazz Master (1994)," Smithsonian Jazz Oral History Program, Oct. 20-21, 2005, pg. 83.

29. Author interview with Kevin Dorn, 12/17/2022.

30. Recording from author's private collection.

31. Gene Krupa interviewed on *The Mike Douglas Show*, 3/9/1966. https://www.youtube.com/watch?v=3aeXVvvcl-U. Accessed 12/30/2023.

32. Klauber, pg. 172 (emphasis in original).

33. Roginski, Jerianne, "Chicago," and Gross, Mike, "New York," *Billboard*, 1/28/1967; McNamara, Helen, "Contrasts in Jazz," *Toronto Telegraph*, 3/7/1967; Gross, Mike, "New York," *Billboard*, 4/1/1967.

34. Parker, John. "Legendary Jazzman Gene Krupa Gives Kids Taste of the '30s," *Tampa Tribune*, 4/23/1967.

35. Scott, Patrick. "Krupa: Sedate Relic of Swing," *Toronto Star*, 9/19/1967.

36. "Gene Krupa Suffers Mild Heart Attack," *The Daily Times* [New Philadelphia, OH], 10/31/1967, pg. 9.

Chapter 26: "Commence to Rock and Roll"

1. From "Get Rhythm in Your Feet," recorded by Benny Goodman and His Orchestra on 6/25/1935, Helen Ward on vocals.

2. Lissner, John. "Goodbye, Mr. Drums," *Village Voice*, 10/25/1973.

3. Klauber, Bruce H. *Gene Krupa: The Pictorial Life of a Jazz Legend*, Alfred Publishing Co., Inc, Los Angeles, 2005, pg. 15.

4. Clayson, Alan. *Keith Moon: Instant Party*, Chromebooks, Surrey, UK, 2005, pg. 72.

5. Cianci, Bob. *Great Rock Drummers of the Sixties*, Hal Leonard, Milwaukee, WI, 1989, pg. 20.

6. Klauber, pg. 16.

7. Polcaro, Rafael. "The 10 Drummers That Rush's Neil Peart Listed as Influences," *Rock and Roll Garage*. Posted 3/20/2022. http://rockandrollgarage.com/the-10-drummers-that-rush-neil-peart-listed-as-influences/. Accessed 4/11/2023.

8. Author interview with Hirsh Gardner, 3/25/2019.

9. Chawkins, Steve. "Dallas Taylor Dies at 66; Drummer for Crosby, Stills, Nash & Young," *Baltimore Sun*, posted 1/19/2015. Accessed 5/8/2023.

10. von Bernewitz, Robert. "Dallas Taylor—An Interview with the Drummer for Crosby, Stills, Nash, & Young," *Musicguy247 Blog*, https://music guy247.typepad.com/my-blog/2015/02/dallas-taylor.html. Posted on 2/9/2015. Accessed 6/6/2019.

11. Author interview with Corky Laing, 8/26/2019.

12. Author interview with Danny Seraphine, 2/4/2019.

13. Brown, Jake. *Beyond the Beats: Rock & Roll's Greatest Drummers Speak!* Music Square Media, Ashland, OH, 2018, pg. 188.

14. Klauber, pg. 13.

15. Author interview with Bobby Tribuzio, 9/23/2019.

16. Shteamer, Hank. "Bill Ward," *Heavy Metal Bebop*, 11/20/2019. https://heavymetalbebop.podbean.com/e/bill-ward/. Accessed 6/14/2021.

17. Criss, Peter, and Sloman, Larry "Ratso." *Makeup to Breakup: My Life in and Out of Kiss*, Scribner, New York, 2012.

18. Leaf, David, and Sharp, Ken. *Kiss: Behind the Mask*, Warner Books, New York, 2003, pg. 130.

19. Author interview with Bob Elliott, 7/20/2019.

20. Hart, Mickey. *Drumming at the Edge of Magic*, HarperSanFrancisco, 1990, pg. 61.

21. Author interview with Tino Gross, 1/5/2019.

22. Beck, John H., ed. *Encyclopedia of Percussion*, Garland Publishing, New York, 1995, pgs. 181–182.

23. Fish, Scott K. "Jerry Allison: Keep Everything Relatively Simple," posted 12/29/2015, https://scottkfish.com/2015/12/29/jerry-allison-keep-everything -relatively-simple/. Accessed 7/3/2019.

24. Glass, Daniel, and Smith, Steve, eds. *The Roots of Rock Drumming*, Hudson Music, 2013, pg. 129.

25. Glass, Daniel. *The Ultimate History of Rock 'n' Roll Drumming: 1948-2000*, www.danielglass.com, 2005, pg. 8.

26. Glass and Smith, pg. 104.

27. Griffith, Mark. "Gene Krupa," *Modern Drummer*, January 2009, pg. 74; Cianci, pg. 129; Glass and Smith.

28. Cianci, pgs. 95, 103.

29. Author interview with Doug Clifford, 1/14/2019; Wilkening, Matthew, "Creedence Clearwater Revival's Doug Clifford Discusses His Influences, Punk Rock and Revisited's Future," *Ultimate Classic Rock*, posted 10/13/2011, http://ultimateclassicrock.com/creedence-clearwater-revival-doug-clifford-interview/. Accessed 10/24/2018.

30. Klauber, pg. 14.

31. "A New Headonism," *Rhythm*, May 1986, pg. 52.

32. "Neal Smith," *SickThingsUK*, undated, https://www.sickthingsuk.co.uk/08-musicians/m-ns.php. Accessed 7/9/2019.

33. Cianci, pgs. 52–53.

34. Wooley, John. "Last Man in the Band," *Oklahoma Magazine*, 2/23/2017, https://okmag.com/blog/last-man-in-the-band/. Accessed 7/9/2019.

35. Pfeiffer, John. "A. J. Pero: 1959-2015," *The Aquarium*, 4/8/2015, https://www.theaquarian.com/2015/04/08/shoreworld-asbury-park-music-in-film-festival-aj-pero-1959-2015/. Accessed 12/8/2018.

36. Klauber, pg. 15.

37. Author interview with Noko [member of Apollo 440], 2/21/2019.

38. Author interview with Kenny Malone, 9/21/2019.

39. "Tribute to the Late Great Gene Krupa," *Around the Kit*, hosted by Joe Gansas and Daniel Glass, 12/5/2016, https://www.blogtalkradio.com/aroundthekit/2016/12/05/tribute-to-the-late-great-gene-krupa-tonight. Accessed 5/5/2020.

40. Author interview with Steve Gadd, 4/3/2019.

41. O'Hare, Kevin. "Drummer Hal Blaine Has Provided Beat Behind Some of Music's Greatest Hits," *The Republican*, posted 10/9/2011, http://blog.masslive.com/playback/2011/10/hal_blaine_has_provided_beat_b.html. Accessed 12/23/2018.

42. Crisafulli, Chuck. "Riding a '60s Splashback," *Los Angeles Times*, 8/18/1996, https://www.latimes.com/archives/la-xpm-1996-08-18-ca-35223-story.html. Accessed 7/5/2019.

43. "Rock and Roll; In the Groove; Interview with Dick Dale [Part 1 of 2]," broadcast 9/1995, *WGBH Media Library & Archives*. http://openvault.wgbh.org/catalog/V_9449F909C2F849C89824FB4EBD2DE5C6. Accessed 5/20/20.

44. Hart, Otis, and Tsioulcas, Anastasia. "Dick Dale, Surf Guitar Legend, Dead At 81," *NPR*, 3/18/2019, https://www.npr.org/2019/03/18/704329806/dick-dale-surf-guitar-legend-dead-at-81. Accessed 4/8/2019.

45. Rueb, Emily S., and Pareles, Jon. "Dick Dale, 81, King of the Surf Guitar, Dies," *New York Times*, 3/17/2019.

46. Enos, Morgan. "The Beach Boys Remember Dick Dale: 'He Was Part of a Whole Other Category," *Billboard*, 3/19/2019, https://www.billboard.com/music/rock/dick-dale-dead-the-beach-boys-remembered-8503160/. Accessed 1/8/2024.

47. James, Gary. "Gary James' Interview with Bob Berryhill of The Surfaris," *classicbands.com*, undated, http://www.classicbands.com/SurfarisInterview.html. Accessed 7/5/2019.

48. Author interview with Leon Taylor, 8/30/2019.

49. Lauden, S. W. "Gene Krupa: The Original Punk Drummer," *Legsville*, 6/7/2022, http://legsville.com/gene-krupa-the-original-punk-drummer/. Accessed 3/4/2023.

50. Antonia, Nina. Author blog, "Sticks and Style: The Art of Jerry Nolan," August 1991, https://ninaantoniaauthor.com/archives/sticks-style-the-art-of-jerry-nolan/. Accessed 9/25/2018.

51. Weiss, Curt. *Stranded in the Jungle: Jerry Nolan's Wild Ride*, Backbeat Books, Milwaukee, WI, 2017, pgs. 11, 13.

52. Ibid., pg. 20.

53. Ibid., pgs. 129, 171; Lauden, S. W., ed., *Forbidden Beat: Perspectives on Punk Drumming*, Rare Bird, Los Angeles, 2022, pg. 30.

54. Lauden, "The Original Punk Drummer."

55. Ibid.

56. Lauden, *Forbidden Beat*, pg. 213.

57. Welch, Chris, and Nicholls, Geoff. *John Bonham: A Thunder of Drums*, Backbeat Books, 2001, pg. 17.

58. Bonham, Mick. *John Bonham: The Powerhouse Behind Led Zeppelin*, Southbank Publishing, London, 2005, pg. 21.

59. Welch, Chris. "Led Zeppelin at Carnegie Hall," *Melody Maker*, 10/25/1969, pg. 20.

60. McStarkey, Mick. "The Drummer Led Zeppelin's John Bonham Called a 'God,'" *Far Out,* posted 5/31/2022. http://faroutmagazine.co.uk/drummer-john-bonham-called-a-god/. Accessed 6/1/2022.

61. Author interview with Ivor Davis, 9/3/2020.

Chapter 27: "It Was Just Awful!"

1. Wilson, John S. "Krupa, Back on Drums at 61, Leads Quartet at Plaza," *New York Times*, 6/1/1970.

2. McDonough, John. CD liner notes, *Gene Krupa Live at the New School*, Chiaroscuro Records, CR(D) 207, 2018.

3. Gene Krupa interview by William B. Williams from WNEW in New York, 1/16/1968; McDonough, John, unknown title, *Down Beat*, 3/7/1968, pg. 20.

4. Author interview with Joe Vetrano, late 2018.

5. Scott, Bobby. "Gene Krupa: The World Is Not Enough," *Gene Lees Jazz-letter*, January 1984, pgs. 7–8.

6. Author interview with Joe Vetrano, late 2018.

7. "Round the Wax Circle," *Cash Box*, 1/5/1957, pg. 12.

8. Author interview with Joe Vetrano, 10/2/2018.

9. Ibid.

10. Author interview with Joe Vetrano, 8/18/2019.

11. Author interview with Joe Vetrano, 7/14/2019.

12. Krupa, Gene Harry. *Unfortunate Casting: An Autobiographical Essay.* PhD thesis, Department of English, University of Iowa, July 1975, pg. 95.

13. Scott, Bobby. "Gene Krupa: '. . . I'll Miss You, Old Man,'" *Down Beat* 12/6/1973, pg. 16.

14. Author interview with Joe Vetrano, 1/11/2021.
15. Author interview with Joe Vetrano, 10/2/2018.
16. Author interview with Joe Vetrano, 1/11/2021.
17. Author interview with Joe Vetrano, 7/14/2019.
18. Author interview with Joe Vetrano, 10/31/2018.
19. Author interview with Michael Bellino, 6/17/2019.
20. Author interview with Joe Vetrano, 10/31/2018.
21. Author interview with Joe Vetrano, 10/2/2018.
22. Jim Chapin interview, *Gene Krupa Story 2021-2022*, from 1994 Frankfort Messe in Germany, posted 5/30/2012, https://www.facebook.com/watch/?v=4091837299470&_rdr. Accessed 2/16/2022.
23. Author interview with Herb Gardner, 10/4/2018.
24. Author interview with Paul Monat, 10/30/2018.
25. Silver, Roy R. "Gene Krupa Tells L.I. Teen-Agers About Drugs," *New York Times*, 11/22/1969.
26. Marchionni, Carmel. "Gene Krupa, Percussionist," newspaper unknown, spring-summer 1970. Institute of Jazz Studies.
27. "A Different Drummer," *The Herald Statesman* [Yonkers, NY], 10/17/1973, pg. 18.
28. Author interview with Joe Vetrano, 10/2/2018.
29. Author interview with Joe Vetrano, 7/14/2019.
30. Wilson, John S. "Krupa, Back on Drums at 61, Leads Quartet at Plaza," *New York Times*, 6/1/1970.
31. Author interview with Joe Vetrano, 10/2/2018.
32. Ibid.
33. Author interview with Chuck Slate, Jr., on 6/20/2021.
34. O'Haire, Patricia. "Night Owl Reporter: Play Play Play," *New York Daily News*, 1/19/1972.
35. Author interview with Joe Vetrano, 10/2/2018.
36. Author interview with Joe Vetrano, 10/31/2018.
37. Recording from author's private collection.
38. Korall, Burt. "Gene Krupa," *International Musician*, September 1972.
39. "Lack of Locations in Montreal Rock Scene," *Billboard*, 12/25/1971, pg. 44.
40. Klauber, Bruce H. *Gene Krupa: The Pictorial Life of a Jazz Legend*, Alfred Publishing Co., Inc, Los Angeles, 2005, pg. 150.
41. Author interview with Joe Vetrano, late 2018.
42. O'Haire, "Night Owl Reporter."
43. Author interview with Hank O'Neal, 12/21/2018.
44. McDonough, John. "Various Artists: Jazz at the New School," *Down Beat*, 6/7/1973, pg. 29.
45. Hayes, Chris. "Jazz Scene: Krupa: Drum Crazy," *Melody Maker*, 3/25/1972, pg. 32.
46. Author interview with Joe Vetrano, 10/2/2018.

47. Kates, Brian. "Musicians Remember a Colleague," *The Herald Statesman*, 10/17/1973, pg. 4.
48. Author interview with Joe Vetrano, 10/2/2018.
49. Smith, Jack. "Goodman, Hampton and Krupa Will Have the Ball Swinging," *New York Daily News*, 9/20/1972.
50. Garland, Hazel. "Video Vignettes," *Pittsburgh Courier*, 12/16/1972, pg. 14.
51. Berger, Edward. *Bassically Speaking: An Oral History of George Duvivier*, The Scarecrow Press, Metuchen, NJ, 1993, pg. 166.
52. Morgenstern, Dan. "37th Down Beat Readers Poll," *Down Beat*, 12/21/1972, pg. 14.
53. Choice, Harriet. "... But Krupa Remembers It Well," *Chicago Tribune*, 7/8/1973.
54. Author interview with Joe Vetrano, 8/18/2019.
55. Author interview with Dr. Peter D. Emanuel, 5/20/2019.
56. Author interview with Joe Vetrano, 10/31/2018.
57. Conversation among Gene Krupa, Buddy Rich, John McDonough, Frank Bellino, and others on 7/14/1973, backstage at Mister Kelly's in Chicago. Tape recording made by John McDonough.
58. Ibid.
59. Author interview with Michael Bellino, 5/5/2019.
60. Author interviews with Tina Bellino, 6/2/2019 and 1/12/2024.
61. "To All Jazz Collectors," *Down Beat*, 9/13/1973.
62. O'Neal, Hank. CD liner notes, *Gene Krupa: Live at the New School*, Chiaroscuro Records, CR(D) 207, 2018.
63. Author interview with Hank O'Neal, 12/21/2018.

Chapter 28: "Goodbye, Mr. Drums"

1. Jo Jones and Gene Krupa, Central Park, award presentation, July 1973, https://www.youtube.com/watch?v=rVy5mg0zrLs. Accessed 1/19/2024.
2. McDonough, John. "Face Yonkers, Drummers! Gene Krupa Lived There," *High Fidelity*, March 1974.
3. Ward, Helen. CD liner notes, *Benny Goodman and His Orchestra 1935 From the Famous "Let's Dance" Broadcast First Release*, Circle Records, CCD-50, 1998.
4. Conversation among Gene Krupa, Buddy Rich, John McDonough, Frank Bellino, and others on 7/14/1973, backstage at Mister Kelly's in Chicago. Tape recording made by John McDonough.
5. Remnick, David. "Paul McCartney Doesn't Really Want to Stop the Show," *New Yorker*, 10/18/2021.
6. McDonough, "Face Yonkers, Drummers!"
7. Author interview with Gail Krupa and Gene H. Krupa, 8/4/2021.
8. Author interview with George Wein, 1/18/2019.

9. Author interview with Bobby Colomby, 4/2/2019.
10. Author interview with Joe Vetrano, 9/20/2019.
11. Author interview with Joe Vetrano, 10/31/2018.
12. Author interview with Joe Vetrano, 10/2/2018.
13. Lissner, John. "Goodbye, Mr. Drums," *Village Voice,* 10/25/1973.
14. Shaw, John. "Gene Krupa," *Jazz Journal and Jazz & Blues,* January 1974, pg. 3.
15. McDonough, "Face Yonkers, Drummers!"

Index